REINTERPRETING
CHRISTINE DE PIZAN

REINTERPRETING

Christine de Pizan

EDITED BY EARL JEFFREY RICHARDS

with Joan Williamson, Nadia Margolis,
and Christine Reno

The University of Georgia Press
Athens and London

© 1992 by the University of Georgia Press   Athens, Georgia 30602

"The Preface to the *Avision-Christine* in ex-Phillipps 128" © 1990 by
Christine Reno
Designed by Erin Kirk
Set in Garamond #3 by Tseng Information Systems, Inc.
Printed and bound by Braun-Brumfield
The paper in this book meets the guidelines for
permanence and durability of the Committee on
Production Guidelines for Book Longevity of the
Council on Library Resources.

Printed in the United States of America

96   95   94   93   92   C   5   4   3   2   1

Library of Congress Cataloging in Publication Data

Reinterpreting Christine de Pizan / edited by Earl Jeffrey Richards,
    with Joan Williamson, Nadia Margolis, and Christine Reno.
        p.   cm.
    Includes bibliographical references and index.
    ISBN 0-8203-1307-6 (alk. paper)
    1. Christine, de Pisan, ca. 1364–ca. 1431—Criticism and
interpretation.   I. Richards, Earl Jeffrey.
PQ1575.Z5R45 1992
841'.2—dc20   90-45959
                                                              CIP

British Library Cataloging in Publication Data available

To Charity Cannon Willard,
who, like Christine de Pizan, has led with
the *pioche d'inquisicion,* "the spade of inquiry"

Contents

Preface

It is a happy honor to dedicate this volume of essays on Christine de Pizan to Charity Cannon Willard. The essays here serve a double purpose: to continue the effort of reinterpreting Christine that Charity Cannon Willard's works have initiated and encouraged, and to honor the patient and careful scholar herself.

Charity Cannon Willard was born on August 9, 1914, in Eureka, Illinois. She studied at Eureka College and Hiram College (where both her parents taught) and then completed a master's degree at Smith College in 1936 with a thesis entitled "Jeanne d'Arc comme source d'inspiration littéraire au XVe siecle." From Smith she went to Radcliffe, where in 1940 she received the Ph.D. in Romance philology with an edition of Christine's *Livre de la Paix* (revised and published in 1958). It was in J. D. M. Ford's medieval French seminar at Harvard that she met her future husband, Sumner Willard; both wanted to do their seminar papers on Marie de France. Married in May 1944, they have been an example of what both colleagues and friends would call a *mout bele conjointure*, a "most fair joining" of two remarkable individuals.

When her husband became a professor of foreign languages at the United States Military Academy at West Point, Charity Cannon Willard found that wives were permitted to teach only on a temporary basis. During the early years of their marriage, she filled in for professors on leave of absence and spent summers in Europe, searching out the existing manuscripts of Christine de Pizan's works. From 1961 until her retirement eighteen years later, she taught French and Spanish at Ladycliff College in Highland Falls, New York. With this full-time appointment, she became the first West Point colonel's wife to pursue a professional career. She was created a Chevalier de l'Ordre des Palmes Académiques by the French government in 1983 and in 1988 was honored by Hiram College with its Distinguished Alumni Award.

Since her retirement from teaching, she has concentrated on the scholarly monographs that she had been preparing for decades. The fruits of these efforts include her biography of Christine (1984), the critical edition (with Eric Hicks) of the *Livre des Trois Vertus* (1989), and her English translation of the same work (1989). In press is a collection of translations from various works by Christine which she has edited.

Charity Cannon Willard has encouraged and inspired many scholars. She has quietly and consistently let her scholarship speak for itself, just as Christine's writings, in their championing of universal human ideals, quietly but forcefully propound their principles.

For many years Joan Williamson had planned a collection of essays for Charity Cannon Willard, and her important efforts toward the realization of this volume are gratefully acknowledged. Thanks are also due to Christine Reno and Nadia Margolis for their own contributions and their respective translations of the essays by Liliane Dulac and Gianni Mombello. I am grateful to Brigadier General (retired) Sumner Willard for his constant readiness to lend a hand. I wish to thank Elizabeth Makowski and Nancy Grayson Holmes of the University of Georgia Press for their friendly support and encouragement throughout the stages of planning and preparing this volume. It is also a pleasure to thank the many colleagues who have contributed to this collection in its joint purpose of honoring Charity Cannon Willard and of proposing a new basis for interpreting Christine de Pizan's work, and to thank Douglas Kelly and Katharina Wilson for their comments on the manuscript. Finally, I would like to thank Maureen Curnow for suggesting the volume's dedication.

Introduction

EARL JEFFREY RICHARDS

The growing interest in Christine de Pizan, overwhelmingly indebted to the pioneering research of Charity Cannon Willard during the last fifty years, has focused on several fundamental questions of literary critical evaluation. What happens when a woman writer enters a previously male-dominated literary culture? Does the nature of literature itself change? Christine as an Italian and as a woman was doubly an outsider to the French letters of her day. What happens when a foreigner attempts to work within an "alien" literary culture? Moreover, her choice of the vernacular over Latin, the dominant literary language of the Middle Ages, compounded her distance from the mainstream.

This seeming threefold marginality, however, only defines Christine's initial position within the literary culture of her time, for her entire career was devoted to redefining the universal appeal of letters. This triple marginality also defines the three overlapping areas into which the essays here have been organized: Christine and the beginnings of feminist thought; Christine and medieval French literature; and Christine between the Church Fathers and humanists.

I

Ever since Gustave Lanson dismissed Christine de Pizan in his *Histoire de la littérature française* (1894), students of the Franco-Italian writer have been on the defensive. Christine was, among other things, Lanson claimed, "a good daughter, a good wife, a good mother, but otherwise one of the most authentic blue-stockings ever to appear in [French] literature, the first of that insupportable line of women authors." [1] As early as 1902, no less a scholar than Gustav Gröber, one of the pioneers of Romance philology, was the first to focus, more or less positively, on Christine's feminism. [2] Since that time, Christine's feminism has been at the center of controversy, either because the very application of a modern political term to a medieval figure is adjudged hopelessly anachronistic or because Christine's feminism seems not to go far enough in attacking patriarchal domination.

While not providing definitive answers to all the issues, the essays here help establish a historically more accurate picture of Christine's feminism.

Liliane Dulac's "The Representation and Functions of Feminine Speech in Christine de Pizan's *Livre des Trois Vertus*," translated by Christine Reno, helps situate Christine's works, and most directly the *Livre des Trois Vertus*, both within a larger literary context of female speech and within a specific social one. Ever since Ovid in the *Metamorphoses* relegated Echo to the passive position of repeating male discourse, the question of feminine speech in literary texts has been a problematic one. With careful documentation, Dulac shows the social importance and multiple resources of feminine speech in Christine's work.

Thelma Fenster's "Did Christine Have a Sense of Humor? The Evidence of the *Epistre au dieu d'Amours*," adroitly addresses some of the most important questions raised in recent scholarly discussions of Christine's writings and should banish, once and for all, the lingering prejudice against Christine the humorless drudge and blue-stocking. One of the resources of feminine speech that Christine ably deployed was humor, an indirect but no less potent rhetorical strategy against her adversaries in the Quarrel over the *Roman de la Rose*. Fenster conveys an acute sense of Christine's intelligence in her critical reception of the *Rose* and proves that Christine probably had the last laugh.

Glenda McLeod's "Poetics and Antimisogynist Polemics in Christine de Pizan's *Le Livre de la Cité des Dames*" gives a clear exposition of the moral and ethical context in which Christine's work arose historically. She reveals both the generic and allegorical sophistication of the *Cité des Dames* and facilitates new comparisons both to Dante's allegorical procedures and to those of the *Rose*. This contribution, taken together with Christine Reno's commentary on the Preface to *L'Avision-Christine*, will provoke a reconsideration of Christine's position in the Quarrel of the *Rose*. She sheds new light on the central role of morality in Christine's works and establishes what the context for this moral commitment was. When one considers the vast proverbial literature with misogynist content circulating during the Middle Ages found in Hans Walther's collection *Proverbia Sententiaeque Latinitatis Medii Aevi, Lateinische Sprichwörter und Sentenzen des Mittelalters* (Göttingen: Vandenhoeck und Ruprecht, 1963–65), one can see how deeply entrenched literary misogyny was when Christine began to write. McLeod's contribution should also be read in tandem with Fenster's: the moral seriousness of Christine's writings is all the more striking when considered together with their frequent humor.

"Christine de Pizan's *Le Livre de la Cité des Dames*: The Reconstruction of Myth," by Eleni Stecopoulos, with Karl Uitti, considers Christine's treatment of myth and history. Stecopoulos and Uitti demonstrate convincingly how Christine consistently recast mythological materials, largely taken from Boccaccio, as history, quite a stark contrast to the contemporary tendency to mythologize history or to see, as Joseph Campbell did, mythic structures beneath historical events.

Lori Walters's "Fathers and Daughters: Christine de Pizan as Reader of the Male Tradition of *Clergie* in the *Dit de la Rose*," breaks new ground in elucidating Christine's relationship to Eustache Deschamps. Christine in a letter to Deschamps had called him her master (surely a Dantean ploy), and, as Walters demonstrates, went on in her subsequent career to beat Deschamps at his perhaps anxiety-ridden game of certifying his poetic legitimacy. Here Walters shows that Christine—perhaps inspired by Dante's relationship to Vergil—transcended the anxiety of influence characteristic of Deschamps's relationship to Machaut.

Eric Hicks's "A Mirror for Misogynists: John of Salisbury's *Policraticus* (8.11) in the Translation of Denis Foulechat (1372)," ties the specific context for literary misogyny in Christine's writings to the influence of John of Salisbury who, as Kate Forhan's research is beginning to demonstrate, was a seminal thinker for Christine's politics. Christine's implicit answer to John of Salisbury is reminiscent of the treatment that she affords another of her major sources, Boccaccio. These male "authorities" provided a sanction for misogyny which Christine attempted to show was fundamentally inconsistent with the tradition to which they belonged. Most significantly, this passage from John of Salisbury stresses the unanimity of the classical authorities in denouncing female weakness, a point of departure for Christine's meditations on the fitness of women for learning at the beginning of the *Book of the City of Ladies*. Christine faced the double task of proving her mastery of a literary culture marred by misogyny and of demonstrating that literary culture must necessarily be universal if it is not to become an instrument of oppression.

II

The essays discussed above all hint at Christine's integral position in medieval French letters. Hers was not a marginal role, even if earlier historians of French literature like Gustave Lanson begrudged her even the smallest part. The criticisms which Christine leveled at the most popular medieval French work, the *Roman de la Rose*—that it insulted women and Reason—have worked to her disadvantage in the minds of many modern scholars who identify perhaps too easily with the *Roman de la Rose* itself, an easy temptation to be sure given the *Rose*'s erudition and irony. For critics like D. W. Robertson, Jr., and John Fleming, Christine missed the *Rose*'s "Christian" irony, and for Sheila Delany, Christine missed the *Rose*'s exploration of sensuality. Despite all of the *Rose*'s positive features, Christine's criticisms of it are probably right, and she probably shared Dante's reservations about the poem. Where Jean de Meun speaks openly of *coilles*—testicles—Dante defers to silence, "è più bello/tacer che dire" (Pg. 25.43–4). The *Rose* perpetuates misogynist stereotypes, and in its artfulness it cultivates an endless *mise en abysme* of rational discourse. All the same, it was the most popular work of medieval French literature, and by choosing French as her language Christine could not avoid using or confronting many of the literary and linguistic innovations of the *Rose* so favored by her immediate predecessors in the vernacular.

More important for Dante and Christine, though, was the issue of cultural legitimacy at the heart of the *Rose*, the question of the transferral of literary culture from Greece to Rome to France, the *translatio studii*. Jean de Meun proclaimed himself the successor of the great love poets of antiquity—Ovid, Catullus, Tibullus—whereas Dante saw himself in the line of Homer, Vergil, Horace, Ovid, and Lucan. Christine, who took the title of her own poetic autobiography, *Le Chemin de long estude*, from Dante's exclamation to Vergil that long study had made the Latin poet Dante's author, pointedly volunteered her services to her opponents in the Quarrel of the *Rose* in demonstrating the differences between Dante and Jean de Meun. Underlying the great dispute over the *Rose* was the fundamental question of the nature of literary art itself. Christine's relationship to the *Rose* and to medieval French literature can be viewed more productively from this perspective.

With deft philological precision and incisiveness, Nadia Margolis, in her "Elegant Closures: The Use of the Diminutive in Christine de Pizan and Jean de Meun," demonstrates that the *Rose* was frequently in Christine's mind when she wrote, but hardly in a way that would indicate that Christine was in the least troubled by the potential anxiety of the *Rose*'s influence. Quite the contrary was the case, with telling implications for influence studies. Christine had never been blind to the poetic merits of the *Rose*, but she was independent enough to turn the tables rhetorically on Jean de Meun. When seen against the larger context of female speech as elucidated here by Liliane Dulac, Christine's use of diminutives, as Margolis shows, turns into a powerful weapon for her feminist concerns.

In "Stylistic Conventions in *Le Livre de la mutacion de Fortune*," Jeanette Beer examines Christine's application of the medieval rhetorical devices of *dilatatio, amplificatio,* and *abbreviatio* as a basis for reconstructing Christine's relationship with her audience, what is now called, following Wolfgang Iser, the "inscribed reader." The *Roman de la Rose*, of course, supplied numerous examples of *amplificatio,* but Christine specifically dissociated herself from both the *Rose* and Machaut's *Livre du Voir-Dit*. The *Livre de la muta-cion de Fortune* is a work of literary apprenticeship which reveals a number of flaws, particularly Christine's inability to integrate the difficult question of Jewish history into the historical vision underlying the work. Nadia Margolis's Stanford dissertation from 1977 remains probably the most balanced treatment of this thorny issue.

Barbara Altmann in her essay "Reopening the Case: Machaut's *Jugement* Poems as a Source in Christine de Pizan," addresses Christine's relationship to Machaut's poetry. She demonstrates in detail how indebted Christine's work was to earlier medieval French lyrical composition, and in so doing helps to reconstruct the vernacular context of Christine's works and to determine their relation to the *Roman de la Rose* and medieval French lyric. Her relationship to Machaut is important, but given the importance of the *Rose* for Machaut, Christine's response to Machaut must necessarily have been a highly critical, if indeed not skeptical, one. Altmann shows how critical and provocative Christine's reception of this literary tradition was, as, for example, Christine's depiction of male beauty in the *Dit de Poissy*, in which courtly conventions regarding female beauty are ironically, ingeniously, and innovatively reworked. Since Christine's irony has largely been overlooked by critics, this essay is especially important.

Maureen Curnow's "'La Pioche d'Inquisicion': Legal-Judicial Content and Style in Christine de Pizan's *Livre de la Cité des Dames*," explores an important stylistic feature of Christine's work which is difficult to render in modern English. By contemporary standards, legal language is counted more as a stylistic weakness than as a strength. Legal training in the Middle Ages was, it must be recalled, closely tied to the survival of ancient rhetoric, and when Boncampagno da Signo, an early thirteenth-century jurist in Bologna, claimed, for example, never to have read (that is, lectured on) Cicero ("non legi Ciceronem"), a controversial avowal positing a separation between legal and rhetorical education, he met with great resistance. Christine's knowledge and application of legal terminology and style reflects the assumptions linking law and rhetoric which are central to Christine's work.

In "Christine de Pizan and Antoine de la Sale: The Dangers of Love in Theory and Fiction," Allison Kelly brings to light important new evidence regarding the reception of Christine's writings among later medieval French poets. Although Antoine de la Sale never cited Christine, as Kelly shows, her influence on him is pervasive and parallels between both *Livre de la Cité des Dames* and the *Livre des Trois Vertus*, in particular, and his *Petit Jehan de Saintré* are striking, especially between the figure of Dido in the *Cité des Dames* and Belles Cousines in *Saintré*. Antoine de la Sale, with his complex irony (some writers actively seek refuge in ambiguity and, in Antoine de la

Sale's case, this tact allows him, as Kelly notes, both to affirm Christine's point of view and to express misogynist opinions as well), apparently failed to perceive any humor in Christine's writings, and his *Saintré*, as such, is perhaps the first in a long and cherished tradition of male misreadings.

Gianni Mombello's piece on "Christine de Pizan and the House of Savoy," here ably translated and edited by Nadia Margolis, is a further illustration of the proverb, *habent sua fata libelli*. Mombello provides a sobering reminder of the concrete facts of literary reception and of obstacles impeding the survival of literary monuments. His work here also draws our attention to the important historical discontinuities in the transmission of any writer's work, even of an author like Christine whom one would like to think of as a classic. We all too often forget that an author's fortunes are tied to unusual combinations of material circumstances.

III

The question of Christine's relation to vernacular writers begs the larger question of her connection to the various forms of the Latin literary culture of the Middle Ages, ranging from Patristic lore to later Latin commentaries on the Scripture and to the new forms of humanist writings, particularly as illustrated in the works of Boccaccio and Petrarch.

Christine Reno has furnished an important key to understanding Christine's use of allegory in her edition, translation, and commentary on the hitherto unpublished preface to *L'Avision-Christine*. She illustrates Christine's ties to the allegorical exegetical tradition and to Boccaccio's poetics and shows again that Christine was the child of two worlds, two traditions, Italian humanism and French medieval literature. Reno expands our appreciation of the importance of Boccaccio's exegetical works for understanding Christine's writings and demonstrates convincingly that Christine must have read the *Genealogiae deorum gentium libri XIII* in the original Latin. At the same time, this preface helps reconstruct the reader's expectations within Christine's text.

Joël Blanchard's contribution, "Compilation and Legitimation in the Fifteenth Century: *Le Livre de la Cité des Dames*," originally published in French and translated by this volume's editor, shows in detail the complicated and delicate rhetorical processes entailed in Christine's adaptation of earlier sources in the *Cité des Dames*, which need to be seen as growing out of her earlier experience in the *Mutacion de Fortune*. In Blanchard's work compilation emerges as a central principle of aesthetic organization and affords an important basis for an aesthetic evaluation of Christine's work rather than a content-oriented analysis. On this last point, Blanchard discounts the feminist content of the *Cité des Dames*, and while this part of his analysis may not find the assent of all readers—for some it is not feminist at all, for others it is not feminist enough—he raises in fundamental terms the question of the specific historical referentiality of Christine's work. Blanchard's work is reminiscent of the Ernst Robert Curtius chapter in *European Literature and the Latin Middle Ages* (1948) on the book as a symbol in the Middle Ages, which in Christine's case may have had Dantean inspiration. In the final vision of the Celestial Rose in *Paradiso* 33.85ff., Dante claimed that he saw the loose pages of the universe bound together in a single volume:

> Nel suo profondo vidi che s'interna,
>   legato con amore in un volume,
>   ciò che per l'universo si squaderna.

Earl Jeffrey Richards's "Christine de Pizan, The Conventions of Courtly Diction, and Italian Humanism" reviews her relationship to medieval French and Italian letters and shows how Christine radically transformed inherited forms under the impact of humanist literary culture. Uppermost in Christine's mind was the competition between different paradigms of vernacular eloquence as embodied quite differently by the *Roman de la Rose* and the works of Dante, Boccaccio, and Petrarch. Christine's repudiation of the *Rose* needs to be seen as part of her overall preference for and cultivation of Dantean and Petrarchan models. Before Christine, only Petrarch had openly rejected the *Rose*, and in light of the overall pattern of Christine's reception of Petrarch, it may be that Christine's critique of the *Rose* can ultimately be traced back to Petrarch. As Barbara Altmann's essay here shows, Christine's equally critical relationship to Machaut, who had so interiorized the narcissistic values of the *Rose*, is completely consistent with her attitude toward the centerpiece of medieval French literature. Moreover, while Machaut's works, by cultivating the delicate but petrified conventions of courtly lyric, served as a mirror for the ruling feudal classes and implicitly favored class divisions, Christine's writings pioneer a unifying nationalist ideology, transcending such separatism. This nationalism displaces rather than resolves class divisions, and Christine's only solution to the contradiction entailed by the displacement was to appeal to a notion of Christendom united under the French leadership of Joan of Arc ready to reconquer the Holy Land. Thus for Christine, religious alterity (including her attacks on the Jews in the *Mutacion de Fortune*) proves to be more deeply rooted than gender differences.

In her highly evocative essay "Orleans, the Epic Tradition, and the Sacred Texts of Christine de Pizan," Patricia Stäblein-Harris shows the sensitive connection between the ambiguity or multireferentiality of sacred language and exegesis—what medieval Christian commentators often called the *polysemous* quality of sacred texts—and Christine's own application of the sacred in her works. In a manner wholly consistent with Christian rhetorical prac tice inspired by the union of divine and human in the Incarnation, Christine forged a link between the historical and the sacred. The abuse of sacred language in the *Roman de la Rose* had been an important issue during the Quarrel.[3] Stäblein-Harris also establishes a provocative analogy between Christine's understanding of the sacred in literary texts and contemporary critical applications of sacred exegesis, as, for example, Harold Bloom's use of Midrash—the interpretation of Scripture in the synagogue, a practice known in the Middle Ages to Hugh of Saint Victor and other Church authorities, in which a tension was present between oral exegesis and written text.[4] It might also be remembered that the opening of the Gospel of Saint John, "In the beginning was the Word," points to the ontological primacy of the Word in the Christian tradition, and the attempt of sacred language (sometimes resorting quite openly to mystification) to regain this status for language. Above all, Stäblein-Harris shows that Christine's attempts to embue her text with sacral qualities answer the *Rose*'s flirtation with obscenity.

Angus J. Kennedy's bibliography of Christine de Pizan scholarship for the years 1980–87 concludes this volume and documents the explosion of Christine studies in recent years. He shows how rapidly in the last few years gaps in basic scholarship are being closed, so that one must inevitably think of Maurice Roy's wish, expressed over a century ago, to see all of Christine's work available in critical editions. It is perhaps significant that a number of contributors to this volume have produced scholarly editions of several of Christine's works. Charity Cannon Willard's influence on the current generation of Christine scholarship is also unmistakably apparent in this bibliography.

When taken together, the contributions here afford a new basis for interpreting Christine's works. They strengthen the growing sense of Christine's importance and uncover an extraordinary degree of intellectual complexity and sophistication in her works. Christine's works have been faulted on political grounds because they lack a certain militancy. In her not always successful striving to incorporate universal categories borrowed from the Church Fathers and humanists, Christine avoided the kind of dialectical confrontations so central to misogyny. Long before Adorno and Horkheimer investigated the contradictions apparent in the dialectical principle of the Enlightenment, Christine attempted in her own way to transcend the limitations of dialectic—itself so central in medieval philosophy.[5] Like later Enlightenment thinkers, she also attempted, albeit in the name of medieval Christian universalism, to demythologize history. The growing universalism of Christine's work, despite the faulty historical vision of the *Livre de la mutacion de Fortune*, in which Christine failed to integrate Jewish history into universal history, must be seen as the central organizing characteristic of her work. From this universal vision stems the feminist and emancipatory project of Christine's writings.

A new picture of Christine begins to emerge with far-reaching implications for current literary critical thinking. It is not that the nature of "literature" itself must inevitably change with the entry of new authors or of new publics, but that new authors and new publics force the question of the presumptive universal appeal of literary culture. To be sure, Christine constructed a separate refuge for worthy women, a City of Ladies, but her aim was to demonstrate that women were the equals of men in all realms of human activity. Male accomplishments are thus shown to be first and foremost human accomplishments, and not gender-specific. Christine thus shares the belief of Erasmus that all initiates of the Muses were her compatriots, that literary culture abhors national, linguistic, and gender divisions. Christine was above all a forerunner to that realm of universal literary culture which Erasmus again, a century later, termed the republic of letters.

Notes

Please note that for technical reasons all citations from the *Livre des Trois Vertus* could not be keyed to the new critical edition by Willard M. Hicks.

1. "Let us not tarry with the excellent Christine de Pizan, good daughter, good wife, good mother, and for the rest one of the most authentic blue-stockings ever to appear in our literature, the first of that insupportable line of women authors . . . who have no better business during the lifetime which God has granted them than to multiply the proofs of their indefatigable facility, equal to their universal mediocrity." ("Ne nous arrêtons pas à l'excellente Christine de Pisan, bonne fille, bonne épouse, bonne mère, du reste un des plus authentiques bas-bleus qu'il y ait dans notre littérature, la première de cette insupportable lignée de femmes auteurs . . . qui pendant toute la vie que Dieu leur prête, n'ont affaire que de multiplier les preuves de leur infatigable facilité, égale à leur universelle médiocrité," in *Histoire de la littérature française* [1894], 12th ed. [Paris: Hachette, 1912], 166–67.)

2. Gustav Gröber, "Die Frauen im Mittelalter und die erste Frauenrechtlerin," *Deutsche Revue* 4 (1902): 343–51.

3. During the Quarrel, Christine's ally, Jean Gerson, noted: "When he [Jean de Meun] speaks of holy and divine matters, he sometimes mixes in extremely dissolute and filthy words; but filth will never enter into paradise as he describes it." ("Quant il parle des choses saintes et divines et espirituelles, il mesle tantost paroles tres dissolues et esmouvans à toute ordure; et toutevois ordure ja n'entrera en paradis tel comme il descript," in Eric Hicks, ed., *Le Débat sur le "Roman de la Rose"* [Paris: Champion, 1977], 62.)

4. Harold Bloom, *A Map of Misreading* (New York: Oxford University Press, 1975), 42.

5. Theodor W. Adorno and Max Horkheimer, *Dialektik der Aufklärung: Philosophische Fragmente* (Amsterdam: Querido, 1947; reprint, Frankfurt: Fischer, 1988).

PART ONE

 hristine

AND THE BEGINNINGS
OF FEMINIST THOUGHT

The Representation and Functions of Feminine Speech in Christine de Pizan's *Livre des Trois Vertus*

LILIANE DULAC

TRANSLATED BY CHRISTINE RENO

The *Livre des Trois Vertus*, a didactic work addressed to women of every station, assigns to women's speech an important and multifaceted social role that it alone can fulfil.[1] However, the initial image in which the author announces her project is not devoid of ambiguity (ff. 3v–4r, 1.1). The three allegorical Virtues hold up to Christine the model of the skillful bird-catcher, and recommend that she "capture" and "train" her pupils effectively. This image translates the author's conviction with regard to her own discourse, a woman's discourse directed exclusively toward women. While the animal image might appear somewhat condescending to women, if not downright scornful, nothing could be further from the case.

The author must, of course, make use of subterfuges; she must fashion traps to catch "those women who are reticent and difficult to control" (f. 3v, 1.1) and bring them into the glorious City of Ladies[2] which is the abode of exemplary women. Entrance into this "cage" involves a moral elevation. The distance between the "bird-catcher" and her pupils will grow progressively smaller until it eventually disappears, since the message which is destined to capture her audience is also meant to instruct them. The cage serves as a place where women learn about speech and its powers. Thus, they will be, as it were, briefed on how to handle any situation that might arise. The models that they will learn are, for the most part, models of discourse. Whether it is a question of Christine's own discourse or of modes of speech she will teach her emulators—and these two mirror each other in many subtle ways—the dignity of women's speech occupies the center stage of this work. Christine presents a broad range of wise words, suitable for all conditions, ages, and circumstances, but especially for the group to whom most of her attention is directed—princesses. The study will limit itself to the first part of the work addressed to "princesses and noble ladies."

We must begin by examining the formal status of women's speech in the text. With regard to speech that is actualized—so-called direct discourse—four different levels can be discerned.

On the first of these, the author addresses in a brief preface the young princess for whom the work was written, Margaret of Burgundy: "Je, Christienne, vostre humble servante, desireuse de faire chose qui plaise vous peust, se tant valoie que faire la sceusse, ay fait et compillé au nom de vous et pour vous singulierement cestui present livre.[3] ("I, Christine, your humble servant, desirous of doing something to please you—if indeed I could be capable of such an accomplishment—have written this present work in your name and especially for you.") The work closes on a fervent declaration which is also written in the first person: "Et je, Christine, demouray auques lassee pour la longue escripture, mais tres resjoye." (f. 97v, Conclusion; "And I, Christine, felt somewhat weary after my long effort, but nonetheless very happy.").

This conclusion, in which the author pictures the fortune of her work, is as little developed as the brief preface, which, moreover, is lacking in the principal manuscripts.[4] Thus, at the outset of her work, the author very quickly turns the floor over to the three Virtues, Reason, Rectitude, and Justice, and even, on many an occasion, to a companion of theirs, Worldly Prudence.

The allegorical figures of whom the author portrays herself as the faithful secretary come into play on the second level. Christine claims to write under their dictation: "Comment fille d'estude, as tu ja remis et fichié en mue l'outil de ton entendement et delaissié en secheresse encre, plume et le labour de ta main dextre ou quel tant seulx delicter? . . . Or sus, sus, baille ça ta main. Drece toy, plus ne soies accropie en la pouldriere de recreandise. Entens noz sermons et tu feras bonne oeuvre." (f. 3r–v; 1.1; "Come, daughter of learning, have you allowed the tool of your understanding to lie idle and left to run dry your ink and pen, and wither away the work of your right hand in which you used to take such delight? . . . Rise quickly, and give us your hand. You must not wallow in the dust of idleness. Heed our sermons, and you will do good work.")

The allegorical figure is, of course, a transparent mask for the author and lacks any real solidity. This aspect becomes obvious when the admonishment from the *Livre du duc des Vrais Amans*[5] is brought into the text. This virtuoso piece is a prime example of an authorial intervention, since it refers to one of Christine's works. Formally, it is Prudence who is speaking, and not the author.

Nonetheless, the choice of this particular form of allegorical enunciation is not without significance. The Virtues' discourse is true, in an absolute sense, above and beyond the truth to which a mere author could aspire. The

Virtues are daughters of God, and their speech continues and amplifies the Gospel. The noble lady being instructed "voldra estre bien infourmee de tout ce qui touche nostre foy, des articles, et des commandemens et de tout ce qui affiert a sauvement (f. 20r, 1.11; "is eager to be informed of everything concerning our religion: the articles of faith, the commandments, and everything related to salvation").

At the receiving end of the communication are women, to whom the allegorical discourse is targeted. This character of the work successfully avoids a potential objection: Can the Virtues' advice apply to men as well as women? The three Virtues' mission does not involve the reformation and instruction of men, however rough and cruel they might be toward their wives: "Si respondons a ycelles que nostre dottrine en ceste presente oeuvre ne s'adrece pas aux hommes quoy que il fust besoing a tout plein que bien fussent endottrinez." (f. 23v, 1.13; "And thus we reply that our doctrine in this present work is not addressed to men, even though they are very much in need of teaching.")

On this level the lesson often consists of models of indirect discourse. The allegorical figure indicates the "manner" of the discourse by giving the substance of the words that the wise princess must speak.

On a third level, the Virtues quote directly certain figures to whom they refer in their teaching, as for example the monologue of the wise princess meditating on the perils to which her erroneous ways have exposed her: "O miserable chetive et aveuglee creature, comment puet en toy avoir tant de force cel oultrageulx orgueil que il te fait oublier les tres grans punicions de Dieu, non obstant que il te sueffre si longuement demouree plungee en tant de deffaulx sans te payer de tes dessertes?" (f. 8v, 1.4; "Oh miserable, abject, blind creature! How can your outrageous pride lead you to forget God's severe punishments, even if He has suffered you to remain steeped in your errors for so long without sending you the punishment you deserve?")

This particular moral deliberation is, however, less lengthy than are the interventions of a key figure, the governess to the young married princess.

This "wise lady" is especially noteworthy for her skillful use of language at every turn. Whether she is speaking to her mistress or to a gallant who wants to strike up a relationship with the young lady, she knows how to speak, and better yet how to write, in a particularly effective manner. We will come back to a letter from her pen which is surely one of the most interesting pages in the entire work.

Finally, on the fourth level, the characters to whom the allegorical figures yield the floor in turn quote others who express their reservations or objections. Thus, for example, the wise lady's letter includes the reflection of the young princess who is tempted by courtly love; the monologue in which she formulates her reasons for taking a lover is reproduced in direct style: "C'est que joennesce aise et oyseuse lui fait penser: 'Tu es joenne. Il ne te fault que plaisance. Tu puez bien amer sans villennie. Ce n'est point de mal puisqu'il n'y a pechié. Tu feras un vaillant homme. On n'en sara riens. Tu en vivras plus joyeusement et auras acquis un vray serviteur et loyal ami.' Et ainsi toutes telz choses." (f. 49r, 1.27; "For it is the ease and leisure of youth which makes her think: 'You are young, and need to enjoy yourself. You can love without doing any wrong; there is no harm in it, for there is no sin. You will inspire a man to valor. You will not be found out. Your life will be made more joyful, and you will have gained a true servant and loyal friend.' And thus and so forth.")

Thus the book consists of different levels of discourse put together in rather complex fashion. The first effect achieved by this manner of construction is an unmistakable variety which breaks the monotony of third-person didactic discourse: "The wise princess will do, will realize, will say."

Use of these multiple levels permits a dramatization of speech, which is sometimes organized into little comic scenes; as for example the dialogue upon the return from a ball (ff. 41v–42r, 1.25) or a secret conversation between the princess and her companions, who criticize the unwelcome advice of the governess with a particularly difficult temperament: " 'Feu d'enfer l'arde! Ja n'en serons delivres.' Et l'autre respondra: 'M'aist Dieux, Madame, il fault semer des pois sur les degrez, si se rompra le col.' " (f. 45r, 1.26; " 'May she burn in hell-fire! Will we never be free of her?' And the other will reply: 'So help me God, Madam, you should scatter peas on the stairs, so that she'll break her neck.' ")

We should note that this edifice of discourse creates the image of a society where speech plays a central role. Nothing is more necessary to women of rank than great skill in speaking.

How can this emphasis on the spoken word be explained? In the perspective of what content, which functions? Without analyzing what real society can say to us on the subject, I shall limit myself to a few aspects of the fictive society that the text depicts amidst this proliferation of feminine discourses. The essential message of the book, as we have seen, is immediately apparent: women must know how to speak effectively and first of all in their private lives. Effective speech is an essential part of women's education. In ordinary social intercourse, their speech will always follow upon reflection and deliberation: "Prudence et sobrece apprendront a la dame a avoir parler ordonné et sage eloquence, non pas mignote, mais rassise, coye, et assez basse et a beaulz traiz, sans faire mouvemens des mains, du corps, ne grimaces du visage, la gardera de trop rire." (f. 19v, 1.11; "Prudence and sobriety will teach the lady to have well-ordered speech and wise eloquence; she will not try to be coy, but rather poised, calm, her words beautifully phrased and spoken in a measured voice, without movements of the hand or body, facial grimaces, or excessive laughter.")

The discourse will of course be appropriate to the situation. The young princess who is widowed, for example, must "moult faire la sage" (f. 38r, 1.23), which is to say give every indication of great prudence. This careful behavior is largely the result of her manner of speaking.

Speech is meant to create a positive self-image in society; such speech will not be so much the reflection of a certain quality of soul as the instrument of one's reputation. To this end, the princess will know how to make acquaintances and speak with people of all estates: lords, bourgeois, priests, scholars, simple folk, "si que leurs voix et leurs paroles lui puissent estre, se mestier est, escu et deffense contre les murmures et rapors de ses envieux mesdisans et les puissent estaindre" (f. 28v, 1.17; "so that their voice and their words can serve, if need be, as shield and defense against the murmurs and reports of her envious detractors, and thus silence them").

Words circulate, producing glory or shame, whence the necessity of making sure that the favorable remarks are spread and achieve dominance. It is less important to be virtuous and charitable than to be recognized as such. The princess will give gifts but will be especially vigilant that they are recognized. This Pharisaism is an act of "just hypocrisy," according to Christine, for if it defies the teaching of the Gospel,[6] it is nonetheless considered indispensable to the upper class: "Si disons de rechief que ceste maniere de juste ypocrisie est comme neccesaire a princes et princepes qui ont a dominer aultruy | a qui plus reverence affiert que autre gent." (ff. 29r–v, 1.17; "Let us say once again that this manner of just hypocrisy is necessary to princes and princesses who rule over others, and to whom more reverence is due than to other people.") Such a usage of speech in a wide circle of relations supposes considerable freedom of action. Unfortunately, women whose husbands "keep them in such tight rein that they scarcely dare to speak, even to their servants or immediate entourage" (f. 34v, 1.21) are not readily able to put such ideas into practice. The teaching of the Virtues is directed exclusively to those women who are not held in a state of servitude; one of the principal liberties of the married princess is the possibility of speaking with whom she chooses. To those deprived of such freedom, the author holds out the hope that they might one day touch the hearts of their domestic tyrants through prudent and attentive behavior: in their case, speech is yet to be won.

Beyond the sphere of private life, speech becomes a principal factor in political conduct: the lady of high rank who knows how to speak can be of service in official matters. She will, of course, be competent in military, judicial, and financial affairs; but competence in language is indispensable.

Thus, in the event of difficulties that tax her wisdom, her circumspection, and above all her knowledge of discourse, she will be able to play the intervening role of mediatrix. She will remain acutely alert to the people's grievances and to threats of rebellion, responding by words of peace, but she will also find the words necessary to arouse her husband's interest in the complaints of his subjects: "Si sera ceste dame . . . advocate et moyenne entre le prince son mary ou son en/fant se elle est veusve, et son peuple." (ff. 13v–14r, 1.8; "Thus the lady will be . . . an advocate and intermediary between her husband or her child if she is a widow, and her people.")

In addition, the princess must know how to intervene in conflicts arising between her husband and important vassals. She will use her speech to maintain peace and insure acceptance of his power (ff. 36v–37r, 1.22).

This political role of speech is referred to several times in the book as a factor indispensable to stability and security; and speech of a pacificatory nature is eminently feminine, "for men are by nature bolder and more hot-blooded," that is, more tempestuous and more likely to rely upon force: "Mais nature de femme est plus paoureuse et aussi de plus doulce condicion. Et pour ce se elle veult et elle est saige estre puet le meilleur moyen a pacifier l'homme qui soit." (f. 15v, 1.9; "But it is the nature of a woman to be more timid and also sweeter. And for this reason, if she wishes, and is wise, it can be the best possible way to pacify men.")

A woman, thus, can play a particular role in strengthening the loyalty and confidence of her husband's subjects, which constitutes, in Christine's eyes, a surer rampart than a fortress: "Car il ne pourroit avoit cité ne fortresse d'aussi grant deffense, force et poissance comme lui puet estre l'amour et benivolence de vrais subgiez." (f. 31r, 1.17; "For no fortress can offer defense, strength, and power equal to the love and goodwill of true subjects.")

This speech, which elicits esteem and respect, is totally devoid of naïveté; it is of necessity premeditated and cunning. In speaking to undeclared enemies who hide their intentions, the wise lady "will use this discreet dissimulation and prudent craftiness" (f. 28r, 1.16). Such dissimulation will keep the rebels from finding out that their designs have been discovered.

However well-defined the place of feminine speech in the political realm, it must be said that the *Livre des Trois Vertus* places a much heavier emphasis on the role of feminine speech in the private sphere. This function is best illustrated in the person of the governess, the only character in the work to be individualized, albeit indirectly, by a name. This wise and grave lady, named Sebille de la Tour in the letter taken from the *Livre du Duc des Vrais Amans* (f. 46v, 1.26), is charged with overseeing the princess's conduct. Her speech thus assumes a didactic role. Beyond delivering a moral lesson, the lady knows how to use her speech to influence actions, modify certain situations, and, in general, direct the life of the young princess. Her speech thus both guides and constrains. Dame Sebille is of necessity somewhat wily; she traps her mistress, as does the birdman his prey, so as to train and instruct her more effectively. By her regular manner of speaking, she will attempt to create an affective bond that is strong enough to put her in a position of power over her pupil. She will attempt to please her, telling her stories and amusing her, in order to be able, if necessary, to correct her more effectively. Christine writes at length about the manner in which the governess must know how to speak in various circumstances, especially those involving affairs of the heart. She will strengthen the young princess's affection for her husband. A go-between in legitimate relationships, she will transmit to each of the spouses affectionate greetings from the other, as well as tender words, love letters, and little gifts. At certain moments, she will turn the conversation to the husband's advantage, for example, when the princess, returning from a ball, seems to be attracted by the charms of some young nobleman: "Mais je n'en voy nul qui me semble tant plaisant, ne tant bel, ne gracieux que fait monseigneur et m'en suis bien prise garde." (f. 41v, 1.25; "But I didn't notice anyone who seemed as pleasing, or handsome, or as charming as milord, and I was looking very carefully.")

Is the husband old and ugly? No matter, she will praise him for the imposing figure he cuts, and especially for his eloquence: "Car il m'estoit avis qu'entre les autres il sembloit si bien seigneur et prince. Et comment le fait il bon oir/parler, que parle il sagement." (ff. 41v–42r, 1.25; "It seemed to me that compared to the others, he stood out as the most lordly and princely. And how good it is to hear him speak, for he speaks so wisely.")

It is the wise lady's difficult task to keep young gallants away from her mistress by setting traps for them. She wins their confidence with her pleasant manner so that they declare their desire to use her services. Thus she will be in a better position to discourage them, keep them away, and prevent any amorous interchange (ff. 46v–51v, 1.27).

What if the princess who is the object of such solicitude becomes rebellious and wants to yield to illicit love? In that situation the governess must refrain from speaking and step back. Her final intervention takes the form of written discourse: the above-mentioned letter. Here the didactic treatise fuses with the realm of poetry and the novel. The letter is very elaborately composed. One of its most remarkable sections is the refutation of the arguments that the prudent counselor advances in favor of courtly love. Her strategy is to anticipate the reasons the princess might give for yielding to the temptation of an adventure. Her anticipation involves four principal arguments that are refuted in the course of an imaginary debate.

—Does the princess imagine that love brings pleasure? In fact, it leads only to sorrow.

—Is she convinced that love is not sinful? The sort of love that is conceived outside the marriage bond does indeed lead to sin.

—It is said that the love of a woman inspires valor and prowess among men. But must a woman come to ruin to make a man valorous? A woman derives no benefit from the services she renders a young knight. If he performs an exploit, he is serving his own interests and not those of the lady.[7]

—Does the princess believe that love permits her to acquire a true friend who will be in her service? In reality, this type of love leads to constant dissimulation, to the point where a lover cannot serve his lady at all; here we recognize the situation and lesson of the *Cent ballades d'Amant et de Dame*.[8] At any rate, men are more often liars and deceivers.

This letter does more than employ dialectical argumentation; it also plays upon feelings. The Lady's tone reveals respect, or love, or pity. In this way, the Lady establishes the equation between love and unhappiness in her young pupil's mind all the more effectively. The sorrow resulting from courtly love is itself a phenomenon made up largely of words: an adventure will provoke an outflow of slanderous talk that will spread dangerously, and the moral and social position of the princess might be compromised to the point where she will be unable to play the role to which her rank calls her, that of moderator and peacemaker. The letter is thus a model of didactic discourse, speech that is all the more effective and powerful because it is written. Christine stresses this point: "Pour ce que ce qui est escript en lettres est aucunes foiz mieulx retenue et plus perce le cuer que ce qui est dit de bouche . . ." (f. 47r, 1.27; "since what is written down is sometimes retained better, and touches the heart more effectively, than that which is merely spoken . . .").

In fact, the governess's function is a sort of mirror of the mission that Christine takes on in her work. The wise lady has the charge of instructing the princess, notably in a large number of particularly delicate and perilous situations. And that is precisely what the author claims to be doing herself in her treatise: reviewing precise and well-defined situations as a kind of moral handbook for noblewomen.

The governess's most efficient tool is the written letter. Thus Sebille de la Tour can be seen as a kind of writer on a small scale. She knows how to use all of language's resources, from dialectical argumentation to speech that is both expansive and moving.

I should like to explore a bit further the way in which Sebille de la Tour's letter constitutes a *mise en abysme* of both the work and Christine. The letter appears representative of a more general phenomenon: the book's apology and justification of itself.

At the end of the *Livre des Trois Vertus*, Christine takes the floor in order to praise her own work and express the wish that it be widely diffused, whatever the cost.[9] This appeal, however, is simply the culmination of a theme that runs the length of the work and whose contours I have attempted to define: the social importance and multiple resources of feminine speech. The treatise demonstrates that women must know how to speak adequately and dare to do so, when their own good is at stake as well as that of their husbands and all those who live under their authority. Each woman, in her rank and place, is invited to use wisely speech that she will have learned like an art, and this is especially true for women at the top of the social order.

But who possesses the art of persuasive language to the highest degree; who can use discourse containing all discourses, better than the "daughter of study," the author of the book—Christine herself? One might well wonder about the motives for this self-justification. The answer no doubt lies in the various sorts of resistance to which the book alludes. The role with which it aims to endow women is often refused them in reality. How many of them are held in servitude? How many can practice the virtue to which the author exhorts them? Without liberty and without virtue, women, the theoretical object of Christine's lessons, will not be able to apply them. Whence perhaps an unceasing effort to impose the image of an exemplary, utopian society where feminine speech, and thus the book itself, would exercise all its power and all its efficacy.

Notes

1. Quotations from *Le Livre des Trois Vertus, ou Trésor de la Cité des Dames* are taken from Boston Public Library MS 1528, containing 98 ff.; references in parentheses are to this codex. Critical editions based on this manuscript include L. L. Debower, "*Le Livre des Trois Vertus* of Christine de Pisan" (Ph.D. dissertation, University of Massachusetts, 1979); and the recent edition *Le Livre des Trois Vertus*, ed. Charity Cannon Willard with Eric Hicks (Paris: Champion, 1989). Translations include D. Carstens-Grokenberger, ed., *Christine de Pisan: Buch von den drei Tugenden in portugiesischer Uebersetzung* (Münster: Aschendorff, 1961); *The Treasure of the City of Ladies; or, The Book of the Three Virtues*, trans. Sarah Lawson (Harmondsworth, U.K.: Penguin Books, 1985); *A Medieval Woman's Mirror of Honor: The Treasury of the City of Ladies*, trans. Charity Cannon Willard, ed. Madeleine Pelner Cosman (New York: Persea Books, 1989). A few critical studies that should be mentioned are Liliane Dulac, "Inspiration mystique et savoir politique: Les Conseils aux veuves chez Francesco da Barberino et chez Christine de Pizan," in *Mélanges à la mémoire de Franco Simone: France et Italie dans la culture européenne*, vol. 1, *Moyen âge et renaissance* (Geneva: Slatkine, 1980), 113–41; H. R. Finkel, "The Portrait of the Woman in the Works of Christine de Pisan" (Ph.D. dissertation, Rice University, 1972); M. Laigle, "*Le Livre des Trois Vertus*" *de Christine de Pisan et son milieu historique et littéraire*, Bibliothèque du XVe siècle, no. 16 (Paris: Champion, 1912); Charity Cannon Willard, "A Fifteenth-Century View of Women's Role in Medieval Society: Christine de Pizan's *Livre des Trois Vertus*," in *The Role of Woman in the Middle*

Ages, ed. R. T. Morewedge (Albany: SUNY Press, 1975), 90–120; Charity Cannon Willard, "The Three Virtues of Christine de Pisan," *Boston Public Library Quarterly* 2 (1950): 291–305; and Charity Cannon Willard, "The Manuscript Tradition of the *Livre des Trois Vertus* and Christine de Pizan's Audience," *Journal of the History of Ideas* 27 (1966): 433–44.

2. "Si que nulle | ou pou qui s'i embate ne puisse eschapper, et que toutes ou la plus grant partie d'elles soyent fichees en la cage de nostre glorieuse cité, ou le doulz chant apprengnent de celles qui desja y sont hebergees comme souveraines et qui sans cesse deschantent alliluya avec la teneur des beneurez angelz. ("So that none| or few who are caught there can escape, and so that all, or the majority of them, may be placed in the cage of our glorious city, where they may learn the sweet song of those who are already sheltered there as sovereign ladies, and who unceasingly sing songs of praise in chorus with the blessed angels," ff. 3v–4r, 1:1.)

3. Raymond Thomassy, *Essai sur les écrits politiques de Christine de Pisan, suivi d'une notice littéraire et de pièces inédites* (Paris: Debécourt, 1838), 186.

4. Ibid., 182–96. This preface is found, for example, in Paris, B.N. fr. 1177, ff. 114r–v.

5. Paris, B.N. fr. 1177, ff. 46v–51v, 1:27. *Oeuvres poétiques de Christine de Pisan*, ed. Maurice Roy, 3 vols. (Paris: Firmin Didot, 1886–96), 3:160–71. Cf. Liliane Dulac, "Christine de Pisan et le malheur des *Vrais Amans*," in *Mélanges de langue et de littérature offerts à Pierre Le Gentil* (Paris: SEDES, 1973), 223–33; Charity Cannon Willard, "Lovers' Dialogues in Christine de Pizan's Lyric Poetry from the *Cent ballades* to the *Cent ballades d'Amant et de Dame*," *Fifteenth-Century Studies* 4 (1981): 167–80; and Charity Cannon Willard, "Christine de Pizan's *Cent ballades d'Amant et de Dame*: Criticism of Courtly Love," in *Court and Poet: Selected Proceedings of the Third Congress of the International Courtly Literature Society (Liverpool, 1980)*, ed. Glyn S. Burgess (Liverpool: Francis Cairns, 1981), 357–64.

6. "When you give alms, for example, do not blow a horn before you in synagogues and streets like hypocrites looking for applause. You can be sure of this much, they are already repaid. In giving alms you are not to let your left hand know what your right hand is doing. Keep your deeds of mercy secret, and your Father who sees in secret will repay you" (Matthew 6:2–4).

7. Jean-Charles Huchet, *L'Amour discourtois: La "Fin amors" chez les premiers troubadours* (Toulouse: Privat, 1987). Henri Rey-Flaud, *La Névrose Courtoise* (Paris: Navarin, 1983).

8. Christine de Pizan, *Cent ballades d'Amant et de Dame*, ed. Jacqueline Cerquiglini (Paris: Union général d'éditions, 1982).

9. "Me pensay que ceste noble oeuvre multiplieroye par le monde en pluseurs copies quel qu'en fust le coust, seroit presentee en divers lieux a roynes, princepces, et haultes dames | afin que plus fust honnouree et exaucee si que elle en est digne, et que par elles peust estre semmee entre les autres femmes." ("I thought to myself that, whatever the cost, I would circulate this noble work throughout the world in numerous copies to queens, princesses and noble ladies| so that it would receive the honor and praise it deserves, and through them, become known to even more women," ff. 97v–98r.)

Did Christine Have a Sense of Humor?
The Evidence of the *Epistre au dieu*
d'Amours

THELMA FENSTER

A few years ago, at a conference session devoted to the work of Christine de Pizan, someone asked, "Yes, but *did* she have a sense of humor?" The question seems but one more in a number of tentative and circumspect approaches that have sometimes been made to Christine's writings. It has been argued, for example, that she was an unoriginal literary camp follower; she was an overreacting, silly *woman;* she was a prude who failed to understand the *Roman de la Rose* as well as we do; she was wanting in her Marxism; and, she certainly was no feminist. Or, she was a feminist. In that vein, calling Christine a feminist has had its own peculiar consequences, for the fifteenth-century writer has occasionally been confused point-for-point with modern feminists who, as everybody knows, have no sense of humor. And so, the question persists: Did Christine have a sense of humor? [1]

Christine was capable of and enjoyed using wordplay, sarcasm, satire, irony, and the like, but of course, none of these rhetorical strategies is necessarily funny; and certainly, deciding whether something is humorous can be a highly individual matter. Then, too, whether a reader grants the existence of some kinds of humor, perhaps especially of ironic humor, can depend upon expectations: a learned male writer—Jean de Meun, for example—could be expected to possess the subtlety necessary to write with both wit and irony, but a woman, without a university education, might not. It is often said, therefore, that Christine is quite in earnest when at the beginning of the *Cité des Dames*, having just read Matheolus's deeply antifeminist *Lamentations*, she deplores the fact that she was born a woman. But Christine Reno has pointed out the staginess, the profound irony, that are surely present in that sigh: "This long opening lamentation is, of course, nothing but a set-up." Reno further describes the entire first chapter of the *Cité* as "a marvelous display of sustained irony." [2] It is hard to imagine that Christine's regret at having been born female could be otherwise, coming as it does from a woman who wrote with conviction and eloquence about what she saw as women's natural exemplary qualities.

The use of wit certainly had its advocates among Latin authors admired by Christine's contemporaries. In his *De oratore* Cicero claimed:

> Vel quod ipsa hilaritas benevolentiam conciliat ei, per quem excitata est; vel quod admirantur omnes acumen uno saepe in verbo positum maxime respondentis, nonnunquam etiam lacessentis; vel quod frangit adversarium, quod impedit, quod elevat, quod deterret, quod refu-tat: vel quod ipsum oratorem politum esse hominem significat, quod eruditum, quod urbanum, maximeque quod tristitiam ac severitatem mitigat et relaxat, odiosasque res saepe, quas argumentis dilui non facile est, ioco risuque dissolvit.

> (Merriment naturally wins goodwill for its author; and everyone ad-mires acuteness, which is often concentrated in a single word, uttered generally in repelling, though sometimes in delivering an attack; and it shatters or obstructs or makes light of an opponent, or alarms or repulses him; and it shows the orator himself to be a man of finish, accomplishment and taste; and, best of all, it relieves dullness and tones down austerity, and, by a jest or laugh, often dispels distasteful suggestions not easily weakened by reasonings.)[3]

It is worth noting that of all the oratorical skills, however, Cicero thought that wit was the least susceptible of being acquired, the one most likely to be a gift. Finally, Quintilian in his discussion of humor said: "Ex omni-bus argumentorum locis eadem occasio est" ("All forms of argument afford equal opportunity for jests").[4]

It has been said that Christine's wit was perhaps at its keenest in the let-ters she wrote during the debate over Jean de Meun's *Roman de la Rose*, no doubt one of those times when she most needed a sense of humor. Reno comments that "the smug condescension of her adversaries [Jean de Mon-treuil, provost of Lille, and Gontier and Pierre Col, the latter canon of Notre Dame and of Tournai, and all of them royal secretaries] probably goaded Christine into sharpening the most effective weapon she had avail-able, her wit. And before the quarrel was over, she was to use it to full force."[5] Of the *littérateurs* who were Christine's opponents, probably Pierre Col wrote with the greatest verve; but the "wit" of all three often turned into facile high-handedness. They themselves could take matters quite seri-ously, determined as they were to brook no opposition whatever to the writ-ing of that *auctor,* Jean de Meun, whose *auctoritas* they sternly upheld. Re-markably enough, though, their lack of a sense of humor in that regard has not yet earned modern critical condemnation.

Christine's wit had its particular style and purpose. As a skillful interlocutor, she knew that humor allowed one to utter truths that might not be said otherwise. Quite to the contrary of the sober, self-righteous portrait of her that has occasionally been painted, it was she who often used humor to mock excessive seriousness when she found it in others—that is, their way of attributing too much importance to themselves or to their own interests. Christine herself commented on her approach in the form of a particular metaphor, that of the puncturing instrument:[6] responding early in the debate to Gontier Col, who called Christine a "femme passionnee," an "emotional woman," she writes: "Veulles toy reduire a memoire que une petite pointe de ganivet ou cotelet puet percier un grant sac plain et enflé de materielles choses" ("Please remember that the small point of a knife can pierce a bulging, swollen sack") and follows that up with: "et ne sces tu que une petite moustelle assault un grant lyon et a la foiz le desconfist?" ("and don't you know that a small fly can attack a great lion and quickly put him to flight?").[7] When Pierre Col's entry into the debate forced Christine, or perhaps gave her the opportunity, to take up once more arguments she had made in her earlier correspondence, she again had recourse to that image, replying to Col that: "souvent avient que par une petite pointelette est curey une grant enflure" ("it often turns out that by a small lancet a great boil can be cured").[8] Inevitably, of course, the small knife and the lancet—perhaps even the fly—conjure images of other pointed objects, such as swords and lances, and writing implements. In fact, the metaphor shows Christine consciously defining the role she saw for herself: someone who, through her writing, could undermine pretense and pomposity—as something of an *eiron* calling the bluff of the arrogant *alazon*.

In a similar vein, Sylvia Huot has argued recently that in Christine's opinion the *Roman de la Rose* erred in trying to present an impenetrable face: Christine said it was like an alchemical treatise, "opaque, deceptive, a self-contained system that leads to no higher knowledge of the self or the world."[9] (In the *Mutacion de Fortune*, in fact, Christine accuses Jean de Meun of acting like his own character, Faux Semblant or "False Seeming.") Citing the *Avision*, where Fraud makes "sure that none of the light from Truth's mirror penetrates the wall" and where, therefore, "Fraud is the principle of opacity," Huot arrives at Christine's criticism of the *Rose* as an "impenetrable and *deshonneste*" work.[10] Thus "Christine situates herself along with Dante as an inspired poet, able to discern fraudulent surface and hidden truth."[11] There can be no doubt that falseness was a serious matter to Christine, and so she wrote about it with passion. It is true as well, however, that her desire to expose fraudulence inspired some of her funniest passages, those in which, in one way or another, she lays bare what she sees as flatulent posturing.

The metaphor of the pointed object could be said to describe a debating technique—the deflating of an opponent's argument by calling attention to its flaws in logic—that Christine employed particularly well in that early literary quarrel. Reno gives two examples: in the first, Christine replies to Pierre Col's defense of Jean de Meun's use of direct language in naming the genitalia, saying: "Mais tu, qui tant te debas et par tant de repliques que plainnement se doivent nonmer par nom et que bien dist la Raison Jehan de Meung, je te prie chierement—tu qui yés son tres especial desciple, comme tu dis—pour quoy ne les nonmes plainnement en ton escripture sans aler entour le pot?" ("But you, who argue in so many ways that they should be named by their name and that Jean de Meun's Reason spoke truly, I ask you sincerely—you who are his special disciple, as you say—why don't you name them openly in your writing without tiptoeing around the matter?")[12] Answering a letter from Jean de Montreuil in which he had accused Christine of daring to overstep the boundaries appropriate to the female sex, she says: "Et ne me soit imputé a follie, arrogance ou presompcion d'oser, moy femme, reprendre et redarguer aucteur tant subtil et son euvre admenuisier de louenge, quant lui, seul homme, osa entreprendre a difamer et blasmer sans excepcion tout un sexe." ("And may foolishness, arrogance, or presumption not be imputed to me, a woman, for reproaching and upbraiding such a learnèd author, or for stealing some of his praise, when he, one man, dared to undertake the defamation and blame of an entire sex, without a single exception.") As Cicero had already said, acuteness in itself is a quality that gives pleasure.

But less often written about is Christine's success as a wry and amusing *critique des moeurs,* another characteristic way in which she sought to wield her pointed implement. Although there are some quite funny moments in the collection of *Cent ballades,* the lyric poems Christine wrote at the start of her career, it is in the *Epistre au dieu d'Amours* of 1399 (which indeed sometimes repeats material from the lyric poetry) that Christine created for the first time a sustained series of humorous sketches that satirize or otherwise make fun of certain types of behavior. The *Epistre* is a mock royal letter whose author, Cupid, the King of Love, speaks with Christine's voice. Many of the poem's arguments would have been familiar to a medieval audience; in fact, Christine is often able to display her learning by advancing some established views, including theological ones. The work's freshness, therefore, comes not always from the substance of its defensive points but rather from the way in which they are cast: in the fiction of Cupid's letter, for example. Another example lies in the deft humor of Christine's mocking portraits, which provide a demonstration in themselves that humor is to the purpose, a central element of the rhetorical strategy. Cupid/Christine condemns false swains, the slandering of women, and base conduct among nobles, whose comportment ought to be exemplary. Insincere suitors, with their lovesick poses, on the one hand, and the crowing they do about their alleged successes with the ladies on the other, are Christine's first target (lines 32–66, 105–58); she moves on to the pettiness of learned but misogynous clerical schoolmasters (259–80, 291–308, 323–40), and that leads up to her mockery of Ovid and Jean de Meun (281–88, 321–22, and especially 365–406). Christine's criticism of false suitors emphasizes the staged quality of their courting, so much a matter of public display. The only sincere thing about them is their doggedness. The passage in question is rather lengthy to quote entirely (lines 36–66); this is a portion of it:

> Vont disant que griefment les atise
> L'amour d'elles, qui leurs cuers tient en serre,
> Dont l'un se plaint, a l'autre le cuer serre,
> L'autre pleure par semblant et souspire,
> Et l'autre faint que trop griefment empire;
> Par trop amer tout soit descouloure
> Et presque mort et tout alengouré.   (Lines 38–44)

> (Go declaring that a woman's love
> Inflames them sorely, keeps their hearts locked up;
> The first laments, the second's heart is wrenched,
> The next pretends to fill with tears, and sighs;
> Another claims to sicken horribly:
> Because of love's travail he's grown quite pale,
> Now perishing, now very nearly dead.)

Christine satirizes the busy industry of these would-be swains as they scurry about making a spectacle of their amorous endeavors:

> D'aler souvent et de venir se peinent,
> Par ces moustiers ça et la se pormeinent
> En regardant, s'apuyent sur autelz
> Par faulx semblans; mains en y a de telz.
> Par mi rues leurs chevaulx esperonnent,
> Gays et mignos a cliquettes qui sonnent.
> Moult font semblant d'en estre embesongnez,
> Mulles, chevaulx n'y sont pas espargnez.
> Diligens sont de bailler leurs requestes;
> Moult enquierent ou sont nopces et festes,
> La vont plusieurs mignos, jolis et cointes.
> Si font semblant de sentir de noz pointes
> Si qu'a peines les peuent endurer!   (Lines 47–59)

> (Sparing themselves no pain to come and go,
> They promenade in church and peer about,
> Bending their knees upon the altar steps

In fake devotion: many are like that!
They spur their horses up and down the streets
Jaunty and handsome, jingling as they go.
They make a show of great activity,
And spare no horse or mule. Then ever so
Attentively they tender their requests,
Asking about the weddings and the feasts,
At which those polished, ardent, gallant swains
Display how much they feel our arrows' cut,
So much that they can barely stand the pain!)

As a group Christine's false lovers—foppish and long-languishing
Romeos, diligently and arduously working at appearing sick with love for
their ladies and claiming to perish from the pains of their ardor—are not
unworthy of Molière's comic stereotypes.

In another portrait Christine unmasks those knights, arrogant poseurs,
who would (and should) present themselves as chivalrous, risk-taking, and
brave. In contrast, she shows them seated in warm, beefy comfort, engaging in the sort of facile banter which need only deal in the language of sexual
adventure to be thought amusing:

Plusieurs y a qui deussent leur paroles
En bons contes drecier sans bourderie
A raconter pris de chevalerie;
Mais aux grans feus a ces soirs, ou sur couches
La rigolent l'un l'autre, et par reprouches
S'entredient: "Je sçay bien de tes fais:
Tele t'aimë, et tu le jolis fais
Pour seue amour, mais plusieurs y ont part;
Tu es receu quant un autre s'en part!   (Lines 122–30)

(Many of them should turn their talk instead
Toward telling fitting tales without bold lies,
Stories that show the worth of chivalry.
But lolling at those toasty evening fires,
They rib each other, and by means of taunts
Exchanged, they say: "I know what you're about:
Your sweetheart's such a one, you play the beau
To have her love; but many get their part,
For you are greeted as another parts.)

The homonymic rhyme on *fais* is prelude to the one on *part* (where the expression *avoir part a* means "to have sexual relations with"), as the pair *part/
part* brings the conversation to its climax. Christine says that the envious go
on to calumniate the lady, although they know no ill of her; and:

Et lors cellui qui en est rigollé
Monstre semblant qu'il en soit adolé;
Mais moult lui plaist de ce qu'on l'en rigolle,
Et de son beq mainte parole volle
Qui blasme vault, combien qu'il s'en excuse;
En excusant celle nomme et accuse,
Et fait semblant de celer et couvrir
Ce qu'il lui plaist a dire et descouvrir.   (Lines 133–40)

(And then the object of their taunting glee
Pretends that he is pained by what they say;
And yet, their teasing pleases him quite well.
Many a guilty word comes flying from
His chirping throat, although he makes excuse;
As he's excused, it's she who's named, accused,
And he pretends to hide and cover up
The very thing he gladly bares to all.)

To be sure, that bit of moralizing is serious; at the same time, though, it is amusing as a piece of fine psychology joined to the depiction of the lover as a boastful bird, not unlike the foolish bird of lore whose vanity cost him his dinner. It gains in both depth and delivery when we realize that Christine is playing wittily on a proverb, "Qui s'excuse s'accuse" ("He who makes excuses for himself accuses himself"), as she alters it to say that, on the contrary, the devious self-accuser ends up accusing not himself but the lady. Introducing that vignette a few lines earlier, Christine had said that such men were terrible gossips; they talked everywhere about their exploits, whether true or not, and even nobles, the particular object of her lesson, did the same:

Et les nobles font leurs parts et leur cernes
En ces grans cours de noz seigneurs les ducs,
Ou cheus le roy, ou ailleurs espandus.
Et la tiennent de tieulx plais leur escoles!   (Lines 118–21)

(And nobles share the news in huddled groups
In courts belonging to the dukes, our lords,
Or yet before the king, or elsewhere spread.
Of stuff like that their learned discourse comes!)

The sarcasm of the final quip, involving the expression *tenir escoles,* emphasizes the great chasm between the base subject of the nobles' conversations and the high, model tone Christine thinks ought to be theirs.

As prologue to her comments on Ovid, Christine depicts amusingly the travail of a false lover bent on seduction, for whom

> . . . il n'est peine qui ne lui soit legiere
> A endurer ne faissel a porter.
> A autre riens ne se veult deporter
> Fors a pener a elles decevoir,
> Pour y mettre cuer et corps et avoir.
> Et par lonc temps dure la triolaine,
> Souventes fois avient, et celle peine,
> Nonobstant ce que moult souvent ilz faillent
> A leurs esmes ja soit ce qu'ilz travaillent.   (Lines 356–64)

> (. . . all exertion seems quite small
> To him, and every burden light to bear.
> No other recreation does he seek
> Except his striving toward beguiling her,
> Employing all his body, heart, and wealth.
> This torment, with its toil and moil, goes on
> For very long, repeated many times,
> Despite the fact that men may often fail
> At their pursuits, however much they strive.)

Then, in her criticism of Ovid, Christine once more exercises a bit of sarcasm:

> Et de ceulx parle Ovide en son traictié
> De l'Art d'Amours, car pour la grant pitié
> Qu'il ot de ceulx compila il un livre
> Ou leur escript et enseigne a delivre
> Comment pourront les femmes decevoir
> Par faintises et leur amour avoir.   (Lines 365–70)

> (Now Ovid talks of men like that within
> *The Art of Love*; the pity that he felt
> For them encouraged him to write a book
> In which he teaches them and openly
> Elucidates the way to trick women
> By means of subterfuge, and have their love.)

She goes on to suggest that Ovid's book really ought to be named the *Livre de grant decevance et de faulce apparence*.

Taking on clerkly schoolmasters, Christine deplores their niggling preoccupation with petty matters. They buzz about at every moment, every which way, creating meaningless drivel equally "en françois" and "en latin"; what they write passes for learning, which they teach to young and impressionable boys. She says:

> Si se plaignent les dessusdites dames
> De plusieurs clercs qui leur surmettent blasmes.

Dictiez en font, rimes, proses et vers,
En diffamant leurs meurs par moz divers.
Si les baillent en matiere aux premiers,
A leurs nouveaulx et jeunes escoliers,
En maniere d'exemple et de doctrine
Pour retenir en aage tel doctrine.
En vers dient, Adam, David, Sanson,
Et Salomon, et autres a foison,
Furent deceu par femme main et tart:
Et qui sera dont li homs qui s'en gard?
Li autre dit que moult sont decevables,
Cautilleuses, faulces et pou valables.
Autres dient que trop sont mençongieres,
Variables, inconstans et legieres.
D'autres plusieurs grans vices les accusent
Et blasment moult, sans qu'en riens les excusent.
Et ainsi font clercs et soir et matin,
Puis en françois leurs vers, puis en latin,
Et se fondent dessus ne sçay quieulx livres,
Qui plus dient de mençonge q'uns yvres.   (Lines 259–80)

(The ladies mentioned here above complain
Of many clerks who lay much blame on them,
Composing tales in rhyme, in prose, in verse,
In which they scorn their ways with words diverse.
They give these texts out to their youngest lads,
To schoolboys who are young and new in class,
Examples given to indoctrinate
So they'll retain the doctrine when they're grown.
Thus, "Adam, David, Samson, Solomon,"
They say in verse, "a score of other men,
Were all deceived by women morn and night;
So who will be the man who can escape?"
"They're treacherous," another clerk opines,
"And false and cunning; they're no good at all."
"They're dreadful liars," other men pronounce,
"They're faithless and fickle, they're low and loose."
Of many other wrongs they stand accused
And blamed, in nothing can they be excused.
And that's what clerks are up to noon and night,
With verses now in Latin, now in French,
They base their words on I know not what books
Which tell more lies than any drunkard does.)

In addition to the sprightly interest brought to the passage by its rhymes (especially, perhaps, by the contrasting pair *accusent*/*excusent* and by *matin*/

latin) and by certain syntactic elements (*Puis . . . puis*), there seems surely to be an oblique reference to Jean de Meun's *Roman de la Rose* in the "livres, / Qui plus dient de mençonge q'uns yvres." In the *Rose*, in a disclaimer that Christine would not have failed to notice,[13] Jean's Poet says that *he* is not responsible for what is said there about women, for he is merely repeating what he found in the ancient books, and they were written by men who were neither foolish nor *drunk*. Here Christine pretends not to know "quieulx livres" the schoolmasters consult as she reasserts that *veritas* resides neither *in vino* nor in the books to which Jean so readily deferred—nor, for that matter, in the *Rose* itself.

In pointing up hypocrisy and falseness, the preceding passages ridicule the exaggerated self-absorption of their masculine targets, implying a certain trusting unselfconsciousness on the part of the women such men deceive or calumniate. Those contrasting traits are most clearly drawn when Christine finally arrives at her explicit mockery of Jean de Meun's *Roman de la Rose*. It comes at the midpoint of the *Epistre*, around line 400; indeed, the *Rose* criticism brings the entire series to a crescendo, for in the remainder of the poem Christine enters primarily into a debate mode, taking up one by one the antifeminist arguments of invisible opponents. About Jean de Meun she says:

> Et Jehan de Meun ou *Rommant de la Rose*:
> Quel lonc procés! Quel difficile chose!
> Et scïences et cleres et obscures
> Y mist il la, et de grans aventures!
> Et que de gent supploiez et rouvez,
> Et de peines et de baras trouvez
> Pour decevoir sans plus une pucelle—
> S'en est la fin, par fraude et par cautelle!
> A foible lieu fault il dont grant assault?
> Comment peut on de pres faire grant sault?
> Je ne sçay pas ne vëoir ne comprendre
> Que grant peine faille a foible lieu prendre,
> Në art, n'engin, ne grant soubtiveté.   (Lines 389–401)

> (And Jean de Meun, his *Romance of the Rose*—
> Oh what a long affair! How difficult!
> The erudition clear and murky both
> That he put there, with those great escapades!
> So many people called upon, implored,
> So many efforts made and ruses found
> To trick a virgin—that, and nothing more!
> And that's the aim of it, through fraud and schemes!
> A great assault for such a feeble place?

How can one leap so far so near the mark?
I can't imagine or make sense of it,
Such force applied against so frail a place,
Such slyness, cleverness, and subtlety.)

She finishes off that observation by finding, as she liked to do, an error in the logic of those who criticize women. She says that since so much plotting and scheming are necessary to deceive both noblewoman and peasant, then women must not be the easy marks that some men claim they are (402–6). An excellent illustration of Quintilian's recommendation against long-windedness in wit ("Sed acutior est illa atque velocior in urbanitate brevitas"; "On the other hand brevity in wit gives greater point and speed" [14]), Christine's sally against Jean de Meun here avoids any of the more substantive criticism she would offer later during the debate on the *Rose*. At this point she ridicules him for what she sees as his preposterously over-drawn seduction of a virgin: the people, the plots and plans and pains, the posturing—are these not once more the contents of the swollen sack, filled this time with "scïences," "aventures," "gent," "peines," and "baras"? They are set in contrast to the "foible lieu," the simple "pucelle," a figure of (sometimes feigned) weakness who threads her way through Christine's writing, often acting as a foil. Since the "pucelle" is inexperienced, a contrast is implied between Jean de Meun's (acquired) learnedness, which is put to degenerate use, and the (natural) innocence of his female prey. The word *soubtiveté* (line 401), which means a kind of subtlety acquired precisely through learning, is key. Pierre-Yves Badel points out that the adjective *soutil* was applied generally to the ancient authors, whose works required study: "Une oeuvre subtile est difficile. Elle est lourde du poids de la science antique. Elle exige réflection" ("A subtle work is difficult. It is heavy with the weight of ancient learning. It demands reflection").[15] If we say that the *Roman de la Rose* is subtle, then it is to be treated like a text to be glossed. Badel maintains that if we call the *Rose* subtle, thus elevating it to the level of the classical texts, that would "contradict Christine's judgment," for she "reserves 'subtlety' for the ancient authors and opposes it to the easy writing of vernacular poets." [16] Christine's use of the word *soubtiveté* to describe Jean de Meun's assault is not an exception to Badel's observation; it stands rather as an ironic qualification.

The examples I have cited are linked thematically, rhetorically, and ideologically. Among similarities that might be mentioned is Christine's rebuke of those who put knowledge to perceivedly nefarious ends as well as of those who present hearsay and lies as knowledge: whereas the crowing paramours seated around the fire do no more than pretend to a knowledge they do not in fact have, some of Christine's other *caractères* (schoolmasters, Ovid, Jean de Meun) sin on both counts by turning their scholarship to bad account and by putting forward fallacious statements. For Christine, the abuse of knowledge in both instances is a reprehensible act, a way of dealing in false appearances, and that is something she associates with certain men, seldom with women. In the *Epistre* she criticizes misogynists for generalizing about *all* women, and she herself does not generalize, limiting her statements to apply to groups or individuals. Thus she certainly would not claim to be depicting the class of *all* men. Rather, it could be said that Christine ridicules traits that, when she does find them, she finds in men. It is nevertheless difficult, and perhaps naïve, not to think that passages from her writing like the ones discussed here are meant to return the misogynists' insults in kind. (When she depicts gossipy knights, for example, she is clearly returning to the very accusation of gossip-mongering that for so long had been leveled against women.) [17] They are buttressed by the long list of exemplary qualities that Christine attributes to women in the second half of the *Epistre*, as she studies what she herself calls the *nature de femme* (in her definition, gentleness, meekness, fear of violence, devotion, and the like) and by the equally long list of malignant qualities that she says women do *not* have (starting wars, setting fires, stealing, cheating people of their inheritance, and the like); she finds the causes of those destructive events in the ambitions of men. It might be said, therefore, that although Christine's reeducation of her antifeminist society in the main took the form of writing in defense of women, it was also part of her program to write against certain activities in which she saw men engaged far more often than women.

The *Epistre au dieu d'Amours*, with its moments of wry and perceptive psychology, is thus the first work of modern European literature to provide an explicit woman's-eye view of certain male affairs. There is surely no single, easy explanation for the long absence of Christine de Pizan's writing from modern histories of literature, nor for the lack of modern editions of her work, lacunae that modern criticism is slowly eradicating. Perhaps some who heard the strong and pointed voice of the *Epistre* did not think it funny. They may have hoped to ignore or silence it. Though Christine was subtle, it was not like her to hide the views she most cherished. For her, humor was a diversion through which she could channel her ideas, but she never lost sight of their destination.

Notes

1. A shorter version of this essay was offered as a talk at the Patristics, Medieval, and Renaissance (PMR) Conference at Villanova University, September 24, 1988. All quotations from the *Epistre au dieu d'Amours* have been taken from *Poems*

of Cupid, God of Love: Christine de Pizan's "Epistre au dieu d'Amours" and "Dit de la Rose," Thomas Hoccleve's "Letter of Cupid," with George Sewell's "Proclamation of Cupid," ed. and trans. Thelma S. Fenster and Mary Carpenter Erler (Leiden: E. J. Brill, 1990). For additional background information, see also Joseph L. Baird and John R. Kane, *La Querelle de la Rose: Letters and Documents*, University of North Carolina Studies in the Romance Languages and Literatures, no. 199 (Chapel Hill: University of North Carolina, Department of Romance Languages, 1978); Eric Hicks, "De l'histoire littéraire comme cosmogonie: La Querelle du *Roman de la Rose*," *Critique* 32 (1976): 510–19, and "Sous les pavés, le sens: Le Dire et le décorum allégoriques dans le *Roman de la Rose* de Jean de Meun," *Études de Lettres* 2–3 (1987): 113–32; and Charity Cannon Willard, "A New Look at Christine de Pizan's *Epistre au Dieu d'Amours*," in *Seconda miscellanea di studi e ricerche sul Quattrocento francese*, ed. Jonathan Beck and Gianni Mombello (Chambéry and Turin: Centre d'études franco-italien, 1981), 73–89.

2. Christine Reno, "Christine de Pizan: Feminism and Irony," in *Seconda miscellanea*, ed. Beck and Mombello, 125–33. Passage cited from p. 131; see also p. 127.

3. Cicero, *De oratore*, bk. 3, trans. E. W. Sutton, Loeb Classical Library (Cambridge, Mass.: Harvard University Press, 1979), 373, 375.

4. Quintilian, *Institutio oratoria*, bk. 6, trans. H. E. Butler, Loeb Classical Library (Cambridge, Mass.: Harvard University Press, 1966), 474–75.

5. Reno, "Christine de Pizan," 129.

6. This arrestingly self-referential metaphor has been noted before in the scholarship. In addition to Christine Reno (ibid., 130–31), Joan Ferrante, in her article "Public Postures and Private Maneuvers: Roles Medieval Women Play," in *Women and Power in the Middle Ages*, ed. Mary Erler and Maryanne Kowaleski (Athens: University of Georgia Press, 1988), 213–29, discusses Christine's use of "ganivet ou cotelet" on p. 227.

7. Eric Hicks, ed., *Le Débat sur le "Roman de la Rose,"* (Paris: Champion, 1977), 25.

8. Ibid., 149.

9. Sylvia Huot, "Seduction and Sublimation: Christine de Pizan, Jean de Meun, and Dante," *Romance Notes* 25 (1985): 361–73. Citation here is from p. 365.

10. Ibid., 369.

11. Ibid., 368–69.

12. Hicks, *Débat*, 123. Also cited by Reno, "Christine de Pizan," 130.

13. Many medieval readers of the *Roman de la Rose* treated it as a *summa,* an encyclopedic compendium of knowledge which they might dip into here and there to extract nuggets of wisdom. (See as well Sylvia Huot, "Medieval Readers of the *Roman de la Rose*: The Evidence of Marginal Notations," *Romance Philology* 43 {1990}: 400–420.) Christine, on the other hand, seems to have read and grasped the thrust of the entire work. As Professor Willard has suggested informally, Christine may have copied manuscripts for others as a livelihood, and her knowledge of the *Rose* may have come to her through her activity as a scribe. If so, it is most unlikely that she would have overlooked or forgotten the provocative disclaimer uttered by Jean de Meun's Poet.

14. Quintilian, *Institutio oratoria*, 463.

15. Pierre-Yves Badel, *Le "Roman de la Rose" au XIVe siècle: Étude de la réception de l'oeuvre* (Geneva: Droz, 1980), 138.

16. Ibid., 141.

17. I am grateful to Professor Wendy Clein for this observation.

Poetics and Antimisogynist Polemics in Christine de Pizan's *Le Livre de la Cité des Dames*

GLENDA MCLEOD

When Christine de Pizan responded to literary misogyny by structuring the *Livre de la Cité des Dames* as a universal history, she had a more profound moral and artistic purpose than has previously been suggested.[1] Literary misogyny had, after all, consistently relegated women to minor genres (in medieval literature those lacking immediate ethical utility). In rejecting this relegation with her choice of genre, Christine rejected much of the misogynist argument. Her alternative, an important moral and artistic synthesis, also reflects the ethical cast of late medieval literature. Much of this synthesis has passed without comment, but in fact, if read by the standard medieval commentaries, glosses, and *accessus ad auctores,* Christine's defense of women reveals both her indebtedness to scholastic traditions and her shrewd reappropriation of them.

While medieval Europe produced few if any works on poetics per se, scholars such as Judson Allen and Alastair Minnis have recently demonstrated that the commentaries and *accessus ad auctores* often imply a distinct and very different system for reading and writing.[2] "Literature" as *belles lettres* plays little part in this system, but "literary" texts are studied for their moral if not aesthetic content (itself a category first promulgated by Baumgarten in the eighteenth century). Obviously, texts read under such different assumptions often appear quite different. To one fourteenth-century commentator, for example, Ovid's *Heroides* taught readers how to love their wives more chastely.[3] To a recent scholar, the same text offers an intriguing commentary on literary form.[4] The latter study emphasizes aesthetics in strict formalist terms, that is, without any concern, as in Kant, for the merging of *das Schöne* with *das Gute*. But to the medieval commentator beauty is important only if it leads to virtue.

While most medieval texts on poetics were highly technical treatises on rhetoric, we do have Hermannus Alemannus's translation of Averroës' Arabic version of the *Poetics* (1256), and it does give us some theoretical approximations for this implied system. Although hardly the *Poetics* we know, Hermannus's commentary evidently suited the medieval mind, for twenty-four manuscripts survive as compared to two of William of Moerbeke's considerably more accurate version (1278).[5] This *Poetics* describes how a text embodies and exhorts the reader to ethical conduct. For example, Hermannus like Aristotle defines all poetry as either blame or praise, yet what is blamed or praised is *consuetudo* and *credulitas,* the Latin translations of Averroës' substitutions for Aristotelian plot and character. Allen translates the terms as "custom" and "belief" and claims that both, acting together in the text, provide the "representation of the true, of the universal as both enactable (*consuetudo*) and credible (*credulitas*)," in other words, describing normative behavior.[6] The relationships between text and reader, words and referents are implied by Hermannus's translation of Aristotelian *mimesis—assimilatio,* which O. B. Hardison translates as "likening." Allen has demonstrated that this "likening" could occur between many different things—a description and the object or objects described, individual *exempla* and the principles exemplified, a text and its audience, or (most profoundly) words and their referents. Like metaphoric meaning, the truth produced by this process of "likening" is "rooted in and related to particulars, for which it [*assimilatio*] generates some connection with the universal."[7] If this connection fails at any level, then the text fails as an ethical guide and hence as poetic language.

Upon this basic point Christine founds both her arguments and her artistry in *Cité des Dames*. She had done so earlier in *L'Epistre au dieu d'Amours,*[8] and her contributions to the Quarrel over the *Roman de la Rose* also apply ethically determined standards of literary criticism to the problem of misogyny. But the *Cité des Dames* pushes the critique further and shapes the response more fully than in these works, logically so since in Christine's own words, she was consciously elevating her style and subject by 1405, seeking "plus grant soubtilleté et plus haulte matiere" (*L'Avision-Christine,* 64).

The book also dramatizes rather than simply narrates the attack, appropriately so since medieval commentaries held the end of reading to be action, not knowledge. The famous opening scene where Christine encounters Matheolus's *Liber lamentationum* shows what happens internally to a woman reader confronted by the misogynist legacy. The three crowned ladies allegorically depict Christine's reactions as a reader, for on the allegorical level they represent her reason, rectitude, and sense of justice. As we might expect from Hermannus's commentary, they are mostly concerned that Christine's reading lead to moral conduct. This concern substantiates Christine just as the misogynist writers' encouragement of immoral conduct undermines their authority, an attitude that sheds valuable light on Christine's response to the *Roman de la Rose* as well.

Everything in the opening scene makes this dichotomy clear. Alone in her "celle,"[9] a monastic study, Christine comes upon Matheolus after "une longue frequentation d'estude" (616). Significantly, she comes upon him in her search for some light reading, the "dities des pouetes" (616), with which women were generally identified. By rights, Matheolus should hold authority over this woman reader. He is a clerk and scholar; *Liber lamentationum*, a medieval Latin satire, makes ample use of classical and patristic erudition to expound a venerable *topos,* that women are antithetical to a life of the mind.[10] Instead, the woman reader is associated with "estude" and Matheolus with the "dities," which have limited ethical import. In other words, from the outset Christine uses genre to enhance the status of her narrator and her gender.

She substantiates her claim first by the narrator's rejection of Matheolus and then by dramatizing what happens to her when she takes misogynist texts at their word. The narrator's first instincts are sound. *Liber lamentationum* offers nothing to people who delight not in slander, does not improve the reader, and uses obscene words and materials. In other words, it encourages an improper *assimilatio* between reader and text. But thinking of other, more prestigious authors who speak similarly, the narrator questions her first reaction and comes to accept the view of women as vile, thereby falling into a deep depression, a "tristesce de courage" (620) expressed when she asks God why he made her so flawed. Rather than virtue, Matheolus provokes *tristia,* a sinful condition. Similarly, Christine's own better instincts—the virtues—must deny him to assert their presence.

They do so by analyzing the *forma tractandi* (form of treatment) and *forma tractatus* ("form of treatise") of literary misogyny. Both are scholastic concepts, but the latter emphasizes certain features extrinsic to the text, and modern readers, perhaps too accustomed to textually immanent interpretations, must recall that Christine's work is rooted in a very different horizon of expectations. As Allen notes, the *forma tractandi* is essentially a "way of thinking."[11] He connects it—as does the writer of the Letter to Can Grande—with the five scholastic *modi:* definition, proof, refutation, division, and exemplification. Other commentaries connect it with even older terms, such as *qualitas carminis* or *modus agendi,* which can indicate things as mundane as meter or as complex as methodology (for example, allegory, metaphor).[12] By the fifteenth century, the *forma tractandi* touched upon generic matters because it concerned "the content of a work and the way words work in relation to their significations."[13] Most important, it made the author's mental state an important generic consideration. Medieval texts sought to direct their readers' "thoughts into and along the decorous tracks already determined by the nature of . . . art."[14] When Dante's Francesca and Paolo in *Inferno* 5 read and imitate Lancelot's kiss, Dante signals this connection between reading and conversion.[15] Augustine had picked up the book, read, been converted, and read no further. When Francesca and Paolo also stop reading—"quel giorno più non vi leggemmo avante" (the very words echo Augustine's text)—the characters have been converted to the wrong kind of love. Similarly, when Christine reads Matheolus, doubts the love of God, and prays, she has been converted to a wrong belief. The prayer that she utters is a sharp judgment against the ethics (or lack thereof) in Matheolus' text. The connection between reading and ethical reactions is a very close one; an author's approach, and the mental and ethical attitudes implicit there, help classify a work's genre. In fact, Allen suggests that analyzing the medieval text's outline—its *forma tractatus*—is really important only because it leads to identifying its *forma tractandi*.

Reason raises the problem of form by identifying misogyny with two kinds of writing, philosophy and poetry. By the same token and consistent with this interpenetration of genre and ethics, Reason excludes misogyny from the theological writings forming the basis of Christian rhetoric since Saint Augustine. In other words, Reason claims Christine has mistaken the *formae tractandi* of philosophy and poetry. Philosophic principles are uncertain; Aristotle disagreed with Plato, Aquinas with Aristotle. In critical terms, philosophers invoke the modes of proof and refutation but not the absolute mode of definition. Likewise, the poets' metaphoric quality (*qualitas carminis*) makes meaning difficult to detect since they use *antiphrasis,* "which means . . . if you call something bad, in fact it is good and vice versa" (7).[16]

While this beginning tactfully corrects a reader's reaction, Reason shows the reaction derives from flaws in the author's *forma tractandi*. Reason shows Christine that even if misogynists write with the perfectly laudable intent of steering others away from evil, their approach is wrong. They formulate their "arguments loosely only to make their point" (17), attempting definition without division, two *modi* habitually linked in the medieval commentaries. Likewise, poets mechanically imitate received authorities without regard to ethical purpose. They thus discuss "the behavior of women or of princes or of other people while they themselves do not know how to recognize or correct their own servile conduct and inclinations" (20).

These flawed *formae tractandi* inevitably generate Christine's succession of failed, imperfect, or even harmful *assimilationes*. Medieval commentators identified assimilations on the four levels inherited from Biblical exegesis—literal, allegorical, tropological, and anagogical. Ideally, these various levels and the reader's experience connect into a seamless whole, indicative of creation's unity. Christine indicts misogynist texts for failures on all four levels and for failing to cohere. On the literal level, Matheolus's book is full of lies. Because misogynist texts hold that God intentionally created woman as flawed, they generate no allegory that points to God's goodness. Allegorical interpretation held that the Virgin was the "new Eve" bringing salvation to man, so Christine necessarily introduces the Virgin to rule over both the City and the book that answers misogynist literature. Christine encounters even greater difficulties applying misogynist notions to behavior, thus generating a faulty tropological assimilation. If the *auctores* are correct, women must follow a pattern of depraved behavior, and men can't love them in community. Such behavior also precludes assimilation on the anagogical level of divine meaning in the community of saints. For this reason, the three allegorical virtues find misogyny incompatible with the articles of faith, as Christine's prayer so powerfully dramatizes.

To avoid the failings of literary misogyny in her own text, Christine must be sensitive to rhetorical effect, deliberate in her application of the *modi,* and inclusive in her use of *assimilatio.* The success of her efforts is evident by *Cité des Dames's forma tractatus* and *forma tractandi,* and by the *assimilationes* they generate. Medieval commentators often began with the *forma tractatus* because it generally expressed a logical relationship. Each part of a text was seen as developing arguments or definitions even if the whole text was not strictly syllogistic in form. Behind this approach lay the assumption that two parts in relationship have more to say than in isolation. Allen calls division the essential act of medieval criticism because the *forma tractatus* provides "the basis of a study of the text's wholeness, subject, and meaning." [17] For this reason, Christine goes to great lengths to correct the apparent disorganization and formlessness of one of her sources, Boccaccio's *De claris mulieribus*. There were three kinds of division recognized in the commentaries and *accessus ad auctores—dispositio, divisio,* and *distinctio.* Christine provides a clear implementation of all three.

Dispositio, usually associated with a text's beginning, provides a logical point of departure. Medieval readers expected a natural order from their books and were particularly concerned with correct beginnings. As a standard formula has it, *dispositio* "proposes, invokes, and narrates" (*proponit, invocat, narrat*). Christine's opening encounter in the study follows this order. It proposes the problem with literary misogyny and introduces the three Virtues' counterarguments. It invokes the reader's participation by setting up an identification with Christine, and it narrates the contents of the book by signaling not only these issues, but also the subsequent themes to be developed.

This opening conditions the reader to expect the content, modalities, and forms of thought associated with a *forma tractandi*. The *Cité des Dames* includes all five *modi*. Christine redefines woman's nature through division, in part indicated by the three Virtues' tasks. Her successful revision depends upon proving a new model which, by extension, refutes the misogy-

nist one. And she provides most of her proof through examples. For some
medieval readers there appears to have been a punning relationship between
these last three *modi* and poetry's basic mission of praise or blame. At least
one commentary links proof with approval (praise) and rebuttal with rebuking (blame).[18] Christine's refutation thus depends upon her censure of
certain men—misogynist authors in book 1, traitors to Church and state
in book 2, and pagan judges who condemned Christian women to death in
book 3. All five *modi* are thus present.

Divisio in the *Cité des Dames* is a more complex matter. For the moment, I
would like to leave aside the obvious division into three books and suggest
Christine also follows the six-part organization (*exordium, narratio, partitio,
confirmatio, refutatio,* and *peroratio*) outlined by Cicero in *De inventione*. Originally designed for legal pleading, this structure was especially suited to a
defense.[19] Indeed, Sir Philip Sydney adopted the form two hundred years
later in his *Defense of Poesy*.

The Ciceronian schema is clearly present. The opening confrontation between the narrator and literary misogyny constitutes the *exordium* that seeks
to make the reader well-disposed, attentive, and receptive. To this end,
it draws upon two of the four traditional *loci* of good will, the narrator's
probity and her opponents' wickedness. The visit of the three Virtues marks
the *narratio* in which Reason, Rectitude, and Justice expound Christine's
case by analyzing the narrator's reading, misogyny's methodology, and
woman's integrity. As Cicero had prescribed, they relate their objections
clearly, briefly, and with probability. The remainder of book 1 is taken
up with *exempla* illustrating women's potential. This part forms the *partitio* (wittily presented as the raising of city walls) which establishes what
Christine will seek to disprove about women's potentials.

Book 2 begins with the *confirmatio,* allegorically presented as the building
of the city and the introduction of its residents. Here Christine marshals her
arguments to lend credit, authority, and support to her case. Book 2 also
provides the *refutatio* in which Rectitude explicitly attacks misogyny by exposing inconsistencies in its arguments. She shows that the most frequent
charge against women—that they are unchaste—is false, badly defined,
shameful, and contradictory. Men expect more chastity from women than
they themselves can muster, and they specifically ignore male instances of
disloyalty such as treason.

Book 3 provides the two concluding parts of the presentation. Ruled by
Justice and devoted to the stories of Christian saints, it gives readers an
ethical digression of the kind recommended by the Greek rhetor Herma-
goras. As specified, it praises and blames individuals and compares the
case in question to another one, the repression of Christianity. In conclusion, Christine delivers a *peroratio* that sums up her conclusions, excites in-

dignation against the slanderers (*indignatio*), and arouses sympathy for the speaker and her case (*conquestio*). It thus encompasses all three traditional elements of a finale and highlights the fact that Christine's book seeks to move women to moral actions. Determining what these actions are involves identifying the *distinctio* and completing an analysis of the *forma tractatus* in the *Cité des Dames*.

In the system applied here, *distinctio* presents a thorny problem because, as Allen discusses, *distinctiones* existed in medieval commentaries both for the *forma tractatus* and *forma tractandi* of texts. The *distinctio* of the *forma tractatus* was simply a list or outline. Allen has argued, however, that the *distinctio* also existed in relationship to the *forma tractandi,* which clearly involved both "the mode *definitivus* and the mode *divisivus,*" and that its existence at both levels shows us medieval texts operated by two outlines—an "internal and intrinsic" and "external and parallel" one.[20]

Normally the two outlines were differentiated, but medieval critics recognized certain rare works united the two. The Song of Songs, for example, was singled out in this way by Aegidius Romanus.[21] I would argue that the *Livre de la Cité des Dames* also unites its *forma tractatus* and *forma tractandi*. Its *forma tractatus* is that of universal history, a fact suggested both by the title borrowed from Saint Augustine's *City of God* and by the opening *exempla* of each book, which follow the east-to-west migration typical of the *translatio studii et imperii topoi*. But the book's *forma tractandi* went to the heart of universal history, namely, salvation history or *Heilsgeschichte*. Medieval works that united their *forma tractatus* and *forma tractandi* contained literal orderings which corresponded "exactly to the order of that mental process whereby that material was invented and made significant."[22] In other words, such a book was about a way of thinking, which readers were asked to repeat in their own lives. If the audience were willing to submit to the experience, such a book assimilated its readers not only into beliefs and behaviors, but also into a mental process "intrinsic to knowledge itself."[23] I propose that the *Livre de la Cité des Dames* is such a book, collapsing the ordering of its three divisions into the mental process that invented its material. For this reason, the *distinctio* of universal history is equated with the *distinctio* of self-fashioning or moral education, which the three books jointly name. Both processes finally attain meaning in their destination, a divine community.

We can see this operation most clearly if we return to the *distinctio* of the *forma tractatus*. Book 1 is dominated by Reason, book 2 by Rectitude, and book 3 by Justice. This outline refers also to the identity formation that the narrator undergoes. Reason's mirror shows a being's true nature (reasonable reflection). Rectitude's ruler measures that nature in action (evaluation). Justice's measuring cup apportions a judgment (decision), which either aligns or separates the identity from "nature." In this case, it assimilates the individual into history, the divine city, and therefore Providence. Thus the narrator Christine not only functions as the focus of the dramatized defense but appears with the other virtuous women of the past as an *exemplum* in book 2 and in book 3 is linked implicitly to Saint Christine, a woman whom a hostile misogynist authority also tried unsuccessfully to silence. Most interesting is the image of the city itself, which lends itself beautifully and richly to assimilation on all four levels of reading. It refers to the female gender on one level, on another to the end point of history in the Augustinian City of God. There are also fascinating rhetorical implications. Rhetoricians back to classical Rome had commonly used architectural metaphors to describe composition just as Christine presents her writing of the text as the building of a city.[24] In addition, classical rhetoricians had taught speakers to memorize images, parts of speech, and moral and theological *exempla* by placing them in an imaginary building, a *loco illustri* as Martianus Capella described it in *De nuptiis Philologiae et Mercurii*.[25] In the same way Christine re-remembers history and fixes it forever by constructing a city of ladies. In short, the city represents not just the text but the mental process that creates the text—the integration of personal memory (identity) into social memory (history). By the end of the defense, then, the city represents not just the female gender and universal history but the participation of both in the narrator's self-identification.

The city was a common metaphor for self in fifteenth-century poetry. As Danielle Régnier-Bohler recently noted in volume 2 of *A History of the Private Life*, by "the close of the Middle Ages subjectivity took on spatial attributes."[26] Charles d'Orléans, for example, refers to the "citadel of self" in one of his poems. Christine's city, however, is more than a mechanical implementation of an old figure of speech. She makes the figure apt. In manuscript illuminations of the *Cité des Dames*, the city is circular and enclosed, that is, both complete and apart. Yet through its gates flows a free interchange with the outer world. Most significant, this interchange is controlled by Christine, to whom Justice gives the keys of the city. By thus assuming control of her identity, she also controls what women are allowed inside, that is, what uses are made of the tradition from which the *exempla* come. This control is as integral to the mental process that women readers are to imitate as the various *assimilationes* the text sets up. In fact, that control over self-definition is what the book offers women as their surest defense.

To return to a more medieval terminology, the *Cité des Dames* offers women a self-definition that assimilates on all four levels of reading. Christine was a sensitive observer of allegory; she criticized the *Roman de la*

Rose for the primitiveness of its allegory when compared to the *Commedia*. In this, her own work, she lavished a great deal of effort on working out the various levels of reading. The literal or historical level—Christine's encounter with the Virtues—is linked to the experience of women from pagan and sacred history, as though these figures function as allegorical types. The stories of pagan women then prefigure those of women from sacred history who are tied to experiences of historical women of the present. The tropological or moral level tied to belief and community is found in the ethical beliefs presented to the reader for imitation within this community. Finally, the divine origin of the Virtues, the reference to the City of God, and the divine sanction evident in the Virgin Mary's role as queen, guarantees the presence of an anagogical meaning as well.

As a medieval reader and writer, Christine would have felt that the merit of her art lay in its rhetorical effect on the reader. She had argued that the *imitatio* encouraged by misogynist texts pushed women into vice and error and in her own work invites a more beneficial imitation, noting that the City "is made entirely of virtue, so resplendent that you may see yourselves mirrored in it" (255). She hopes that her readers will find the City "an occasion for you to conduct yourselves honestly and with integrity and to be all the more virtuous and humble"(255). In other words, for Christine and her audience, the *Cité des Dames* is not only more polished than the misogynist texts but also more true because of it. In terms of her defense of women, the book's most important legacy may be its realization that self-images are made in part by cultural forces subject to manipulation. In its criticism of misogynist literature and its own careful craft, *Cité des Dames* demonstrates how women can change one by mastering the other.

Notes

1. For a discussion of this point, see Earl Jeffrey Richards's introduction to his translation, *The Book of the City of Ladies* (New York: Persea Books, 1982), xxx.

2. I am greatly indebted to Professor Allen's analysis in *The Ethical Poetic of the Later Middle Ages: A Decorum of Convenient Distinction* (Toronto: University of Toronto Press, 1982). I have also drawn on Alastair Minnis's excellent study, *Medieval Theory of Authorship: Scholastic Literary Attitudes in the Late Middle Ages* (London: Scolar Press, 1984). I consulted some of the original sources Allen and Minnis use, including the Averroistic version of Aristotle's *Poetics*, the *Glossa ordinaria*, Bernardus Silvestris's *Commentum super sex libros Eneidow Vergilii*, Geoffroi de Vinsauf's *Poetria nova*, Conrad of Hirsau's *Dialogus super auctores*, Pierre Bersuire's *Ovide moralisé*, and *An Anonymous Medieval Commentary on Juvenal*, ed. Robert Barrett. Most helpful for Christine's view, the material in Eric Hicks, ed., *Le Débat sur le "Roman*

de la Rose" (Paris: Champion, 1977) also offers an important glimpse of late medieval literary criticism.

3. Judson Allen in *Ethical Poetic* (28) cites this commentary, which is found in MS 302 of the Biblioteca communale, Assisi.

4. See Florence Verducci, *Ovid's Toyshop of the Heart* (Princeton, N.J.: Princeton University Press, 1984).

5. See Hermannus Alemannus, "The Middle Commentary of Averroës of Cordova on the *Poetics* of Aristotle," trans. O. B. Hardison, in *Classical and Medieval Literary Criticism*, ed. Alex Preminger, O. B. Hardison, and Kevin Kerrane (New York: Ungar, 1974), 341–83; and G. Dahan, "Notes et textes sur la poétique au moyen âge," *Archives d'histoire doctrinale et littéraire du moyen âge* 55 (1980): 171–239.

6. Allen, *Ethical Poetic*, 23–24, 27.

7. Ibid., 191.

8. This poem was composed in 1399, only three years before the accepted date for the *Cité des Dames*. Rectitude refers to it in *Cité des Dames* 2.54.

9. The text not only places the opening scene in Christine's "study," as Richards translates *celle,* but notes that scholarly research was the narrator's "usual habit" (*City of Ladies*, 3). All references to Christine's edition in the original come from Maureen Curnow's edition, "The *Livre de la Cité des Dames* by Christine de Pisan: A Critical Edition," 2 vols. (Ph.D. dissertation, Vanderbilt University, 1975). Translations are from Richards's translation, *The Book of the City of Ladies*. References to these works hereafter appear in the text.

10. Saint Jerome advances this argument, for example, in the Theophrastian excerpt of *Adversus Jovinianum*.

11. Allen, *Ethical Poetic*, 69.

12. *Modus agendi* is the term usually found in twelfth-century *accessus ad auctores; qualitas carminis* is generally listed under *modus agendi*. The scholastic period introduced into commentaries the *forma tractandi* and its association with the five modes.

13. Allen, *Ethical Poetic*, 79.

14. Ibid.

15. Robert Hollander comments upon this aspect in *Allegory in Dante's "Commedia"* (Princeton, N.J.: Princeton University Press, 1969), 106–14.

16. Perhaps Christine is being ironic here, for her opponents in the Quarrel of the Rose had invoked the same principle to denigrate her reading of Jean de Meun's work.

17. Ibid., 126.

18. Allen quotes this remark from a commentary found in Munich's Bayrische Staatsbibliothek, MS clm 6954, ff. 141^0–142^0 (ibid., 82).

19. See the contribution of Maureen Curnow in this volume for an extended discussion of legal and judicial terminology in the *Cité des dames*.

20. Allen, *Ethical Poetic*, 143, 148.

21. Ibid., 91–92.

22. Ibid., 92.

23. Ibid., 93.

24. Geoffroi of Vinsauf, for example, opens the *Poetria nova* with such a metaphor.

25. See Francis Yates, *The Art of Memory* (Chicago: University of Chicago Press, 1966) for a detailed study of this branch of classical rhetoric.

26. Danielle Régnier-Bohler, "Imagining the Self," in *Revelations of the Medieval World*, vol. 2 of *A History of the Private Life*, ed. Philippe Ariès and George Duby, trans. Arthur Goldhammer (Cambridge, Mass.: Harvard University Press, 1988), 377.

Christine de Pizan's *Livre de la Cité des Dames*: The Reconstruction of Myth

ELENI STECOPOULOS WITH
KARL D. UITTI

Christine de Pizan's *Livre de la Cité des Dames*[1] seems to present itself as a deliberate, though complex, refutation of myth. On one level—and fundamentally—Christine wishes to destroy the pernicious, and in several important respects recent, *idée reçue* according to which women cannot be considered as the indispensable historical, and equal, partners of men. Myth is refuted on another level too. In order to achieve her objective, she places all her characters within a continuum that, quite purposefully, does not distinguish between ancient and contemporary, "real" and fictitious. This decontextualization allows Christine to turn many so-called "mythic" women (who otherwise might not be considered viable examples of historical female achievement) to her advantage; she utilizes them as her coworkers in an ongoing feminine endeavor—the construction of what she calls "The City of Ladies."

When at the start of the book, Christine laments her folly in listening to the harangues of male clerkly authorities regarding women—she paid heed to these harangues despite her own experience, her *personal* and *lived* encounters as a "natural woman" (*femme naturelle*) with the virtues of other women from all social classes—she breaks new ground, as it were, in both allegorizing the reception of "masculine myths" and providing illustrations selected by herself in order to demonstrate to her audience that these prevailing and newly "authoritative" views of women are precisely myth, in the negative sense. These views, more accurately, constitute a system of lies (or perhaps more accurately, *fables*[2]) the essential purpose of which is to serve a false *parti-pris*. By citing misogynist "authorities," Christine works within the very tradition that these men of learning claim to represent. She follows this practice first in order to expose their inaccuracy and unjustified bias; she then molds their methods to her own moral and historical purpose. She thereby traps them at their own game. Moreover, "remolding" is exactly what Christine aims to accomplish in the *Livre de la Cité des Dames*. This history of the world according to Christine reflects a particularly, and indispensably noteworthy, feminine cast: her narrative consequently gives voice to participants increasingly ignored, even maligned. As we shall see, the very salvation of France—of human society—is also at issue. Myth formerly placed at the disposal of mendacity is thus pressed into the service of truth.

The selection of male writers whose work focuses specifically on women is consequently not a matter of little importance, for Christine's work represents a deliberate revision of the misogynistic canonical conception of femininity. It mimics the techniques and indeed the very tales of the misogynist authorities (*auctores*)—even while undermining their unfavorable depiction of women—in order to authorize its rectification of women's position in society. It follows logically, therefore, that it is no accident that a majority of Christine's anecdotes come directly from Boccaccio's *De claris mulieribus* (ca. 1355–59), a "humanistic" work that concludes when its author "reach[es] the women of our time, in which the number of illustrious ones is so small."[3] The *Livre de la Cité des Dames* constitutes far more profoundly a response to Boccaccio than to Matheolus, whose *Liber lamentationum* (in its early fourteenth-century French translation) is merely despicable, a miserable example of "party-line" late-medieval clerkly misogyny.

Boccaccio's "defense" of illustrious women is another matter entirely; his "authorial" misogyny—let us call it that right from the start—lies latent in the very structure of his book, or so Christine would have us believe. For example, in drawing examples of illustrious women exclusively from the realm of "pagan women"—he avoids the Christian martyrs to whom Christine devotes the third book of the *Cité des Dames*—Boccaccio "divides and conquers." He grounds his endeavor to bestow fame upon (certain) worthy women on what Christine clearly views to be his fundamentally misogynist belief that women, who are naturally weak in both body and mind, deserve all the more praise when succeeding at that to which they are not by nature inclined. For Boccaccio, womanly fame is to be construed as a function of the individual woman's *overcoming* her "nature." He compliments these women who "surpass the endowments of womankind" (33): he attributes their accomplishments to "manly courage" (*virilem animum*, 37).[4] Putting the shoe on the other foot, one might well argue—for the sake of consistency—that certain men in history merit heroic stature only to the extent that they succeed in interiorizing such traditionally feminine values as allegiance to the Couple (for example, Roland and *douce France*, Thibaut de Champagne and Blanche of Castile); of course, Boccaccio himself hardly puts forth such a claim.

It is this subversion—*corruption* would not be too harsh a word here—that Christine wishes to overcome; the desire to extirpate this corruption constitutes the textual prehistory and pretext for her own project of positive mythic restoration. The profound implications of the *Cité des Dames*, as well as the bedrock upon which this work rests, may be located in her most un-Boccaccian certainty that it is precisely in the *nature* of women to perform illustrious deeds (*gestes, faits*).[5] Exceptionality for Christine thus resides not in a woman's denial of her nature, but rather—despite the obstacles placed in her path—in the intensity and purity of her fidelity to it. What many today label Christine's "feminism" occurs, then, on two very conscious, and closely related, planes: one of positive affirmation, the other of literary (or poetic) reversal. Christine refutes by totally reversing Boccaccio's rationale in selecting worthy women. The abundant evidence of women's talents displayed and *narrated* in Christine's book, and the crucial inclusion of Christian women (among other things emblematic of her faith in the competence and worth of her contemporaries) fuel Christine's edification of a City of Ladies that is restricted neither by time nor by space. A clear universalism characterizes her fundamentally historical vision: Christine's City is open to all women, regardless, even if certain of them do not qualify as "ladies" in terms of the conventional hierarchies operative in society. Her evaluation of the characters she studies rests on their skills and contributions to society, not merely on status or ahistorical reputation; they are rendered noble through their recorded deeds—acts that demonstrate their possession of the feminine ideal (and its affirmation) that pervades the *Livre de la Cité des Dames*. To put the matter another way, Christine declares women to be authentic subjects of historiography (a status effectively denied them by *De claris mulieribus*). In a very genuine sense, then, and without running any risk of anachronism, it may be said that almost, as it were, *en passant,* she founds the study of women's history as a legitimate scholarly or clerkly discipline, and, as we take the nature of Boccaccio's male-centered "humanism" into account, we understand Christine's founding of this discipline to have constituted her well-reasoned reaction to that male-directed humanism.[6] This innovation is most significant, indeed prescient. Furthermore, by integrating this history anew into an all-encompassing historical vision, she renovates historiography *tout court* and, concomitantly, restores it to its proper wholeness.[7]

This emphasis on skill and deeds as opposed to social position or reputation marks Christine's writing when she discusses the figures from classical mythology that derive from Boccaccio's *De claris mulieribus*. As Boccaccio does when discussing goddesses, Christine informs the reader that the divinity of these figures is "fabulous," that is, not in the final analysis true. However, she utilizes their one-time designation as goddesses in order to point out that they (in history) were so outstanding in their contribution to the good of humanity, and so revered, that they were deemed to have been goddesses.[8] By expelling the mythic—the fabulous—from these heroines, Christine, very much the Christian and vernacular writer of the early fifteenth century, aligns them with her own, and her readers', reality. She effects a genuine *translatio*. By denying their deity, she reconstructs them as viable—meaningful and true—models for her age. Her authority here is scholarly, in both a profoundly medieval sense (*clergie*) and, for many readers nowadays, modern. She utilizes, and indeed fulfills, the venerable topic of *translatio studii* by appropriating it (and imbuing it with new life) in her own—to us, very innovative—way; her "originality" consists in her utilization of the inherently creative "originary."[9] The *translatio studii,* which thematizes "the historical transfer of literary culture from Athens to Rome to France,"[10] finds a natural vehicle in Christine's use of pagan mythological characters, who, by virtue of their having been recast as actual, mortal women, act as perfect examples of the continuing, and equally "natural," tradition of illustriousness so integral to Christine's concept of a feminine history fully and properly integrated into a global historiographical perspective.[11] Once again Boccaccio is subverted: his peculiar illustriousness of women—of certain women—which, somewhat ambiguously, he presents as exemplary (but to what end?), is reinterpreted as something not at all peculiar, but rather necessary and true. Christine's women are real actors in the drama of human history.[12]

Interestingly, Christine's procedure appears to mirror that of Boccaccio. He too employs portrayals of goddesses in "demythified" form. But whereas Boccaccio had insisted on the goddesses' ahistorical exemplarity— their reputation or abstract *fama*[13]—Christine commits herself to depicting the value of their "real," or "factual," contributions. The *Livre de la Cité des Dames* is noted for its often surprising vindication of figures traditionally held in low esteem, even condemned. By highlighting the virtuous deeds of these women of ill repute—virtues that had been either ignored or unfavorably construed by male authorities—Christine shows (indeed *proves*) that these women have been improperly slandered by post–*Romance of the Rose* historiography, and she articulates new functions for their experiences within her own, restorative history.

The figures of Ceres, Medea, and Minerva as found in the *Cité des Dames* activate and exemplify this difference. The goddesses are depicted, of course, as mortals who have earned the respect accorded to deities and whose deeds are fully praised by Christine. Meanwhile, one recalls, Boccaccio had held certain reservations regarding the benefits of Ceres' founding of civilization; he also implicitly diminishes the credit due the known Minerva by suggesting that her accomplishments belong to several different persons who share her name. Yet surely the most striking disparity between Boccaccio and Christine—their antagonism—resides in their respective versions of the Medea myth: the "evil-doing" witch of Boccaccio's narrative is vindicated in the *Cité des Dames* as a talented woman who uses her talents out of love but who is betrayed by the object of that love. All three illustrations actualize Christine's assertion of women's worthiness; by emphasizing the skills and deeds of Ceres, Minerva, and Medea rather than merely what has been written about them, her account salutes them as emblems of a universal vindication of women.

Let us look in some detail at Christine's treatment of each of these three personages.

Ceres may be viewed, in Christine's thought, as an overarching illustration of the specifically feminine contribution to human culture. Indeed, she stands as the very mother of culture in her role as the founder of agriculture and of cities. In both Boccaccio's and Christine's tales, Ceres is an ancient queen whom the people "exal[t] with divine honors, although . . . mortal" (35), because of her useful inventions and her congregation of men in cities. Yet Ceres' accomplishments are evaluated quite differently by Boccaccio and Christine.

Although he concedes that Ceres improved the quality of material and mental life for men, Boccaccio remains dubious about the more far-reaching effects of these apparent boons to mankind. He enumerates all the ills generated by society: poverty, slavery, war. In addition, he further decries Ceres' work by stating that because of civilization, "the door was opened to vices" (11). Boccaccio laments the past "golden centuries" when men were uncivilized, just as he considers Christianity an "unnaturalizing" force that distorts the way women naturally act. For Boccaccio, then, the community created by this feminine figure is seriously flawed; by no means does it constitute an unqualified improvement over what had existed before it.

Christine holds no such reservations concerning the good accrued to the world by Ceres' accomplishments. From her first statement on what Ceres achieved she reveals her different evaluation of the merits of civilization: she distinguishes her enumeration of Ceres' lessons to man from that of Boccaccio by specifically terming her lessons "cultivation," with all the implications of nurture present in that word. Christine's citation of "the authority of her knowledge and the great good she brought about for the world" (75) clearly reveals the unmitigated nature of her deep praise for Ceres. She points out the debt men owe to Ceres; she also qualifies her *human* achievements as specifically feminine when she declares that no man ever did more for the world than this woman. It is in this way that Christine remythifies Ceres: her encomium of this woman—a woman seen in ages past as a goddess—stresses the facts of her "life," and, in so doing, recovers the value—the meaning—of that life, reintegrating what Ceres did and who she was into the record of history.

Christine goes on to assert that men act like parasites in their display of "massive ingratitude" (76) for the advantages secured for them by women like Ceres. One must assume, of course, that she levels this charge against Boccaccio as well, since she is responding to his argument against civilization. She stands his indictment of this specifically feminine contribution on its head, charging that the ills of civilization—the defects which he attributes to civilization itself—arise not from civilization per se, but rather from those who misuse the goods with which Ceres has endowed them. Boccaccio himself is as ungrateful as those who are responsible for this unfavorable view of civilization. His lack of proper gratitude is all the more ironic in that, without Ceres, the great cultivator, there could be no forum in which writers like Boccaccio could express themselves and carry on dialogues with other practitioners of their art.

Christine's already cogent argument for Ceres becomes particularly relevant to her own era when she declares that "the more goods . . . the human creature receives from God, the better he is required to serve God" (77). What Christine subtly achieves in her linkage of the feminine deeds of a pagan woman to Christian duty both elevates and justifies Ceres within the context of her own time. In this way, as well, the potentiality of Ceres-like achievement in Christian women of Christine's time is articulated and validated. The alignment with the sacred is heightened by Christine's comment that Ceres, "called . . . the goddess of grain" (80), received a great honor with the gift of Christ's body in the form of bread. With this metaphor Christine shows that the sacred and the cultural accomplishments of Ceres are naturally connected, and Boccaccio's "pagan illustriousness" of the past becomes transposed ("translated") to the present-day Christian.[14]

Ceres may in fact be even more integral to the *Livre de la Cité des Dames* than at first strikes the eye. As the founder of the human city, the initiator of the hearth, she enables the creation (as she does that of a cultural forum for Boccaccio) of the type of feminine community exemplified by Christine's City. Her deeds "ennobl[e]" (76) mankind. Similarly, Ceres may be viewed as an analogue—a kind of equivalent or *translatio*-type basis—to the Virgin Mary herself, to the Notre Dame who comes to preside over the City of Ladies and the fruit of whose womb came into History in order to bring peace and love to mankind. Thus, Christine refutes Boccaccio's assertion that illustrious deeds are not in the nature of women by demonstrating, in her account of Ceres, the inherently feminine, and sacred, origin and quality of the ongoing cultural process symbolized by *translatio*.

An even more striking refutation of unfavorable depictions of women in Boccaccio's *De claris mulieribus* is to be found in Christine's interpretation of Medea. Whereas Boccaccio vehemently considers Medea to be a witch—"the most cruel example of ancient wickedness" (35)—Christine portrays her with sympathy as a woman of "noble and upright heart" (69), well versed in art and science. Much as feminists in our own day have rectified the traditional image of the witch,[15] Christine describes Medea's spells as the articulation of a great knowledge, not as the instruments of a nefarious personality.

The consequences of Medea's powers are construed as total disaster in Boccaccio. He sees Medea as acting on behalf of discord when she aids Jason in obtaining the Golden Fleece. Christine, on the other hand, reminds us more positively that it is "thanks to the art of her enchantments that Jason won the Golden Fleece" (69). Christine's Medea above all acts first as Jason's mentor: her effective teaching renders his brave accomplishment possible. As Christine very significantly puts it, a woman fulfills the quest of the "knight of Greece" (69). With this phrase, perhaps, in her usual subtle yet unequivocal manner, she means to convey the truth of the inherent superiority of women's "charms" over what, in a later context, she refers to as "any man's bravery" (189). In any case, however, Medea's fulfillment of Jason's quest must be understood also in the context of the relationship of *clergie* to *chevalerie*—of "learning" to "knightliness"—within the wider scope of history. Medea plays the *clerc* to Jason's *chevalier*.[16]

Her clerkliness is specifically feminine, though, in that Medea loves Jason. Thus what emerges from Christine's story is above all Medea's virtue in the unswerving absoluteness of her loving devotion: her particularly feminine *fidelity*. It is this positive love that motivates her to direct her powers toward Jason's gain of the Golden Fleece, not a negative desire to ruin her father or to commit the crimes cited by Boccaccio. Her father's ruin and her subsequent crimes are signs within the compass of Medea's narrative that underscore the totality of her love *and* the dreadful consequences of her eventual betrayal and victimization by Jason. Medea's "guilt" is (at the very least) rendered problematic by Christine: it is as great as that of any woman, or person, who has been forcibly violated and whose subsequent behavior has demonstrably been conditioned by the experience of that horror. Here Christine brings very much into play a Christian view of intentionality as determinative of sinning. She reverses Boccaccio's indictment of Medea's criminality, showing that she had been in fact cruelly betrayed by her husband who broke his marraige vow in order to leave for another woman. Medea does not "bec[o]me hateful to Jason" (190), as Boccaccio would have her be; instead, her "too great and too constant love," which had prompted her essentially to win the Golden Fleece for him, is rejected after first having been apparently accepted, even encouraged. Christine's Medea consequently is to be read as a Christian exemplar: she has done everything in her power to guarantee the sanctity and inviolability of marriage—of the supposedly not-to-be-broken couple which she and Jason had formed and which Jason betrayed. Her womanly fidelity results in tragedy, to be sure, but the tragedy is most definitely not her fault, since marriage, in the Christian view, constitutes the place, or institution, in which love for Christ could be expressed in "the highest form of moral commitment between a man and a woman." [17] The fault is Jason's. [18]

Medea's infamous deeds as a poisoner and infanticide, thoroughly documented and recounted by Boccaccio, are conspicuously absent in Christine's narrative. Medea is said to "tur[n] despondent" (190), and no mention is made of any deaths. Clearly, in purposefully removing these details Christine seeks to absolve Medea of the sort of charges—or reputation—leveled by the "authors" against her. But Christine also calls our attention to the facts that ought to be considered when we judge her (or properly understand her story): her skills and her virtue, how well she did what she did and why she did it. The same kinds of facts are to be brought to bear each time we judge any woman. [19] Christine silently alerts us to Medea's vilification by a history which, because it has vilified her, is a false history. Therefore she releases Medea from this undeserved fate in order to pay her the tribute that is due her.

Finally, the example of Minerva in the *Livre de la Cité des Dames* also reflects Christine's revisionary (and restorative) eye, although the discrepancy between Boccaccio's and her versions of this figure does not loom as large as in the cases of Medea and even Ceres. Both authors show the value of Minerva's diverse talents, which range over such varied areas as the invention of arithmetic, the development of the technique of weaving wool, the instruction of military strategy, and the making of armor. Like Ceres, Minerva is worshipped with so overwhelming a reverence that she comes to be considered a goddess: the goddess of wisdom, that is, the ruler of classic, and ultimately true, *clergie*.

Whereas Boccaccio fully accredits Minerva with this attribute—and title —of "wisdom" and admits her contributions to the military arts, Christine takes matters one step further along: to Boccaccio's description of Minerva's stature as a symbol of the wise man, Christine adds the symbolism of chivalry. This addition is of the greatest interest, on at least two major counts. First, by extending the symbol of Minerva to armed defense, Christine depicts wisdom as strength and *real* power. This revision of the Minerva tale could thus stand as an allegory for her entire work: "getting wise" to falsehoods about women's abilities will empower women to explore and to reach their true feminine potential, that is, to complete the restoration of their rightful—indeed, humanly essential—feminine power. Correspondingly, by injecting the notion of chivalry into the personage of Minerva, Christine imparts an ennobling character to her example, with all the connotations of *virtù* and rightfulness that accompany Christine's conception of nobility.

Second, and surely no less interesting, what Christine has done here constitutes a commentary—specifically her commentary among the many that were circulating during the initial decades of the fifteenth century in France —on the decline of chivalry during her time. Chivalric practice no longer lived up to the ideals it professed to serve; corruption, obviously, had set in, and the *clerc*'s job was to help put things right.[20] In keeping, then, with Christine's very traditional service of the idea and values of restoration, her "restoral" of Minerva's chivalric nature must be understood in terms of her consciously feminine clerkliness. There is nothing gratuitous about this restoral; it is vital to her entire enterprise.

Furthermore, what motivates Christine's essential redefinition of humanism is the concern she articulates for the Couple, that underlying configuration of holiness, letters, and life so characteristic of the Middle Ages. Conversely, many humanists placed the male outside the Couple, just as the so-called Renaissance of classical literature and of the myths that were the foundation of this literature brought on the enervatingly reductionist aestheticization of mythic presences such as Ceres. Thus, Ceres today is probably known best for her role in the change of seasons marked by her daughter's departure to and return from the underworld, not for her founding of culture itself. Nevertheless, Christine's effective revelation of *translatio* retains a great deal of potency even here: those who know the story of Proserpina cannot fail to see the resemblance between Ceres, whose child's return from the dead brings on the season of fertility, and the Virgin Mary, whose Son is "resurrected" every spring. While it is no less worthy a contribution in the scheme of things, Minerva's gift of the olive tree we would perhaps consider less awesome than her wonderful stature as the ruler of medieval *clergie* and *chevalerie*. Christine truly and ingeniously found in her the fulfillment of the *translatio imperii* and *studii*. Yet here too Christine's conclusions are so well founded and logically consistent that recognition of who it was that received her gift—the citizens of Athens—and of the form through which this gift was received—a contest with Poseidon over which one of them could provide the more useful and virtuous contribution to the city—must lead to confirmation of Christine's portrayal of the inherent feminization of the city and to her affirmation of female skill, even when this skill is in direct competition with that of the male. Poseidon's trident yielded but a single good, a spring, but Minerva's twisted olive tree furnished food, wood, and oil. So whereas "Boccaccian" authors present us with abstract treatises *on* women, Christine time and time again, as we have observed, reminds us that her women participate in, and indeed to some extent "preside over," the city, that is, over the communal entity, a forum, thanks to their skill, their *clergie,* and yes, their *chevalerie*—side by side, *in conjunction,* with men.

The confirmation of these conclusions is found in the fact that the Minerva of Christine's *Cité des Dames* turns out to prefigure, as it were, an actual young woman, who, a short time before Christine's death, came to take her place in the tradition of French *chevalerie*. We refer of course to Joan of Arc, whom Christine, as her *Ditié de Jeanne d'Arc* amply demonstrates, herself witnessed [21] as embodying the womanly values propounded in the *Cité des Dames*: Joan's historical mission is, with God's help and in his service, to restore chivalry to France, to put French history back on track.

In her role of feminine knight (like Minerva), Joan provides the realization of the *translatio:* both are virgins who, "through force of mind," [22] lead (and wisely guide) their people into battle, and who provide by their gift of themselves inspiration for the defense of their land.[23] By the same token, Joan can be likened to a Ceres in that she led the king to his *sacre,* thereby legitimizing him, under God, in the eyes of his united people. Christine's *Ditié* describes only what took place before this consecration at Rheims, but its prophetic logic contains what would happen, for in the *Ditié* the king of France has joyfully entered into his inheritance. Last—at once uncannily and tragically—the historical Joan of Arc may also be understood as Medea, for she was, like her mythic counterpart, also to be condemned by men and burned as a witch; the gifts with which she had been endowed by God, and which she had placed at the service of a Jason-like king, were (perhaps deliberately) misconstrued as maleficent by those who "officially" arrogated unto themselves the "truth" of history. In this respect, the *Livre de la Cité des Dames*, very sadly, is also a prophetic work.

That which should remain more resonant, however, in a comparison of Joan with these mythic analogues, is perhaps not specific similarities but certain binary configurations present in all of Christine's figures whose apparent disparity is disclosed to be, as it were, critical sites of women's characterization and of a clerkly investigation that reveals these apparent oppositions to constitute in reality merely a manifestation of, and testament to, women's multiplicity. These roles that come up again and again in Christine's characters—mother, teacher, spouse, saint (or virgin, witch, goddess)—must be nothing less than living metaphors for the idea of the Couple itself so central to Christine's thought. It is therefore fitting that she should see Woman, the guardian of the Couple, in terms of these figures—each one of them mythic and real—and herself as a woman whose life's work is definable in terms of her own devotion to the truth of partnership.

Joan is such a guardian of the Couple: as teacher, she instructs the king and the people of France as to their historical and Christian mission; as warrior, she leads the restoration of *chevalerie;* as virgin, she is divinely touched and designated as mediator; as saint, she is the Christian analogue of a goddess, whose gifts to France and Christendom merit her preeminence in Christine's City of Ladies—just as Minerva's to Athens merited making that City her namesake and her domain. Joan too is the latter-day equivalent of the Virgin Mary, as mortal girl and sacred mediator between heaven and earth. (It is significant that the metaphoric—and essentially lyric— "departure of the wintry season" ["le temps yvernage / Qui se depart," stanza 2, lines 10–11] that Christine alludes to in the *Ditié* springs directly from Joan's sacred role in bringing back the true heir to the French throne, just as the Resurrection of Man was brought about by the Son Mary gave to the world, and the initiation of springtime corresponds to Proserpina's departure from Hades effected through Ceres' influence.) But if Joan is mediator—a role traditionally ascribed to women quite probably for the nonparticipation and lack of stance within conflict that it implies—she is nevertheless a mediator with a difference: Joan not only takes up the problem of reinstating France's divine mission, she directly participates in the winning of the battle that must be understood as being merely the prologue to France's larger struggle of keeping the faith. Just as she will not settle for Charles's coronation in name alone but must lead him to the actual, more potent ritual, Joan put her own, internal struggle and mission, as dictated to her by God, into action. Joan's battle for God and country are thus dramatized and supremely elevated.

Christine's *Ditié* not only celebrates Joan but also saves her from being slandered by history. Conceived before Joan's fall from favor and consequent burning, the *Ditié* remains a document of her skills, virtue, and Christian soldiery. It could see no vilification as yet (although Christine makes several comments that appear to show her concern), and therefore has no place for any in Joan's being. Joan's condemnation did not exist —could not have existed—for Christine, even had she lived to witness her sentencing and execution. Thus, Medea-like, the Joan Christine quite beautifully leaves us with at the end of the *Ditié* is not merely historically accurate; it is, in an ultimate sense, true.

Notes

1. Quotations from the French original are taken from Maureen Curnow, "The *Livre de la Cité des Dames* by Christine de Pisan: A Critical Edition," 2 vols. (Ph.D. dissertation, Vanderbilt University, 1975), based on B.N. f. fr. 607; English translations are taken from Christine de Pizan, *The Book of the City of Ladies*, trans. Earl Jeffrey Richards (New York: Persea Books, 1982), based on British Library MS Harley 4431.

2. The term *fable* (*fabula*) is complex. Generally, it was taken to mean "untrue stories, lies." Christine tends to employ it in this sense. She also seems to be wary of the Macrobian tradition of *narratio fabulosa,* i.e., of fables—fictions—being utilized apparently in order to articulate truths. She understood the dangers inher-

ent in the use of *narratio fabulosa* in order to render the content of the fable truth-seeming and accurate. The device of *narratio fabulosa* becomes meaning and value. Consequently, or so Christine appears to be pointing out to us, fables can be manipulated—corrupted—to various, even surreptitious ends.

3. Quoted from the English version of Boccaccio's text, *Concerning Famous Women*, trans. Guido A. Guarino (New Brunswick, N.J.: Rutgers University Press, 1963), 251, which is based on the 1539 Latin edition printed by Mathias Apiarius in Berne. The standard Latin text is now *De claris mulieribus*, ed. Vittorio Zaccaria, vol. 10 of *Tutte le opere di Giovanni Boccaccio*, ed. Vittore Branca (Milan: Mondadori, 1967), 5.10. Subsequent quotations in English from Boccaccio are from Guarini's translation.

4. It is worth recalling that Boccaccio dedicated *De claris mulieribus* to a woman, Andrea de Acciaiuoli, countess of Altavilla and "egregia mulierum." Do his efforts to show examples of women who have overcome the weakness of their sex correspond to the requirements of this sort of dedication? On the other hand, he goes so far as to suggest to the countess that his book of illustrious examples might well stimulate her to emulate them and thereby proceed to better things ("in melius," p. 20). Developing a *figura etymologica* on the countess's name, he identifies her as *andres* "homines" (p. 20), and therefore by nature superior to those of the "weaker sex."

5. That this realm might be considered as the exclusive province of men—of male chivalry, let us say—was, for Christine, as much as for many of her contemporaries (e.g., Alain Chartier), belied by the dismal performance of that chivalry during the difficult and tormented times afflicting early fifteenth-century France.

6. Determining how much the humanist intellectual and political enterprise was male-directed is an extremely important and difficult question, particularly in light of the humanist critique of courtly romances as being contrary to the spirit of Christian marriage; see Robert P. Adams, "Bold Bawdry and Open Manslaughter: The English New Humanist Attack on Medieval Romance," *Huntington Library Quarterly* 23 (1959–60): 33–48; and Richards's contribution to this volume. At the same time, the male-directed characteristics of Boccaccio's humanism are particularly clear—and must have been so for Christine—and represent a strain in humanist thought which reappears in Calvin's vilification of Louise Labé. Piety and mysticism remained among the very few activities left open to educated women who wished to avoid being labeled "blue-stockings" or "harlots."

7. We note that Christine's very interesting "history" of Charles V, *Le Livre des fais et bonnes meurs du sage roy Charles V* (1404), pays close attention to him and his queen as a couple.

8. Lady Reason offers precisely this explanation in order to account for the Italians' attribution of divine status to Carmentis (1.33) and the Greeks' considering both Minerva and Ceres to be goddesses (1.34). Here is what is said concerning Minerva: "Ceste pucelle fu de tant grant excellence en engin que la folle gent de lors, pour ce que ilz ne savoyent pas bien de quelz parenz elle estoit et luy veoyent faire de[s] choses qui oncques n'avoyent esté en usaige, disdrent qu'elle estoit deesse venue du ciel. Car de tant que moins congnoissoyent sa venue, si que dit

Boccacce, de tant leur fu plus merveillable le grant savoir d'elle sur toutes femmes en son temps." ("This maiden was of such excellence of mind that the foolish people of that time, because they did not know who her parents were and saw her doing things which had never been done before, said she was a goddess descended from Heaven; for the less they knew about her ancestry, the more marvelous her great knowledge seemed to them, when compared to that of the women of her time.")

And Ceres: "Et pour l'auttorité de son savoir et le grant bien qu'elle avoit procuré au monde, les gens de lors et l'appellerent deesse des blefs." ("Because of the authority of her knowledge and the great good she brought about for the world, the people of that time worshipped her and called her the goddess of grain.")

By pointing out that Minerva and Ceres enjoyed reputations usually associated with immortals and that this status prompted their (mistaken) designation as goddesses, Christine stresses the essential humanity of their power: its naturalness. As we shall shortly see, the same kind of reasoning will be applied in Christine's depiction of Medea, a woman whose reputation had falsified her truth.

9. A similar procedure may be found in the Prologue to the *Lais* of Marie de France (ca. 1170?). Marie recounts how she undertook the composition of this work; in describing its gestation she underscores the peculiar value of her enterprise and contrasts it with the work of certain (male) predecessors, the *romanciers antiques*.

10. Richards has taken pains to remind us of the relevance of *translatio studii* to Christine's work and thought; see *City of Ladies*, xxvii.

11. The "pagans" precede, and are superseded by, the Christians, but they are not negated; they are fulfilled.

12. Something in Christine's rejection of Boccaccio's male-oriented humanism reflects her unease, expressed during the Quarrel of the *Romance of the Rose*, at what she discerned to be the "humanism" of Jean de Meun; cf. the Christian humanism of Gerson. See *City of Ladies*, trans. Richards, xxxi.

13. That is, dependent on opinion, on the judgment of others, not on incontrovertible facts. Christine, as historian, is here very much the precursor of Commynes.

14. Romantic and modern mythography have returned to these issues raised by Christine. One is reminded first of all of the notion of *Mutterrecht* as elaborated in 1861 by the Basel philologist Johan Jakob Bachofen (1809–82), for whom the "Demetrian principle" constituted the basis of civilization as we have come to know it, and who studied what he determined was the precedence of feminine—i.e., matriarchal—law over "the paternal conception of man." See J. J. Bachofen, *Myth, Religion, and Mother Right*, introduction by Joseph Campbell, Bollingen Series, no. 84 (Princeton, N.J.: Princeton University Press, 1973), esp. 69–207.

15. In her foreword to Richards's translation of the *Livre de la Cité des Dames*, Marina Warner alludes to Christine's praise of Medea "for her herbal arts and her command of the elements" as "an interesting and justifiable example of reassessing witchcraft from a positive viewpoint" (xv).

16. As part of her *clergie* in the *Heroides*, Medea recounts Jason's *gestes* upon reaching Colchis. It is clear, however, that they really serve as markers of her own

story, of *her* deeds. She reminds Jason: "That you are alive, that you take to wife one who, with the father she brings you, is of kingly station, that you have the power of being ingrate—you owe to me" (Ovid, *Heroides* 12.205–6: "quod vivis, quod habes nuptam socerumque potentis, / hoc ipsum, ingratus quod potes esse, meum est"; *"Heroides" and "Amores,"* ed. and trans. Grant Showerman, Loeb Classical Library [Cambridge, Mass.: Harvard University Press, 1947], 157–58).

17. *City of Ladies*, trans. Richards, xxix.

18. It is interesting, in light of the differences between Boccaccio's type of *auctoritas* and Christine's in regard to Medea, to consider how Ovid treats Medea when she is the subject of his story (in *Metamorphoses* 7) and when she is depicted as writing her own story in *Heroides* 12 ("Letter to Jason"). The beginning of the account of Medea and Jason in the former text is characterized by a long soliloquy (or internal monologue) in which Medea deliberates a future as Jason's mentor and wife. Yet—and to our mind, very significantly—when she finally makes the commitment to marriage she increasingly loses her voice in the narrative and is reduced to speaking solely when pronouncing spells and ultimately not at all, being henceforth referred to only as "the mother" and, finally, "the witch." Ovid would have us here see Medea as the reasoning *clerc* who engages in rational self-analysis only until she embarks upon the deeds rendered necessary by her marital fidelity, at which time he sees fit to appropriate the narrative and implicitly claim for himself the only "reliable" voice, denying Medea her own voice and right to self-vindication. Consequently, the "history" of Medea as it has come down to us through Ovid is precisely *his* story—a story that persists because he has suppressed other possible, and possibly dissenting, voices. It is therefore all the more curious that Ovid should have chosen to cast the Medea tale in yet another form: that of a letter written by Medea to Jason, in the *Heroides* (see n. 16 above). The authorial suppression evident in the *Metamorphoses* is only magnified by its contrast with Medea's very intelligent, sympathetic, and justified reproach of her husband in this most articulate letter. Repudiating the idea that guilt should accompany the acknowledgment of her aid and commitment to Jason, Medea nevertheless remains quite cognizant that it was she who chose to accept that commitment and, ultimately, those actions that are the monuments of her love for Jason and that are in the process of destroying her. Thus Medea, quite rightly, refuses to be reduced, to be "flattened out" into two dimensions; rather, she retains her virtues and her faults as a *real* and suffering woman who nevertheless remains unshaken in her conviction that she has been betrayed.

19. Christine raises this same point in her two-pronged analysis of Dido (Lady Reason: 91–95; Lady Rectitude, 188–89). Despite the calumnies heaped upon her, Dido's only guilt lies in her having loved too much and too completely; the catastrophe was in fact caused by Aeneas's betrayal of her.

20. This principle is reiterated in the works of many fourteenth- and fifteenth-century writers: Froissart, for example, in *Meliador* and in the *Chroniques*; Alain Chartier in *Le Quadrilogue invectif*. It is later taken up in the *Jehan de Saintré* of Antoine de la Sale, and also, of course, by Commynes.

21. Christine's status as *clerc* not only authorizes and validates such personal witness, but in fact also requires it of her. Interestingly (and in contrast with many of

their immediate predecessors) feminists today have increasingly come to accept the validity and truth of such personal witness.

22. Similar attributes are imparted by Christine to the ancient heroines Queen Penthesilea and Camilla, to whom she (through the persona of Lady Reason) devotes biographies (pp. 47–51, 60–61). These heroines constitute steps in the process of *translatio* leading to Joan.

23. We must remember, however, that Christine's Joan seeks to cast the English out of France *only* in order to enable France and her king to resume the proper historical mission that God has confided to them: the rescue of the Holy Land, the leadership of Christendom. The defeat of the English is thus a precondition of Joan's real goal, not the end she sought.

Fathers and Daughters: Christine de Pizan as Reader of the Male Tradition of *Clergie* in the *Dit de la Rose*

LORI WALTERS

In the *Dit de la Rose*,[1] dated February 14, 1402, Christine de Pizan continues the attack she initiated in the *Epistre au dieu d'Amours* against clerical antifeminism. In the *Epistre* Christine singles out for particular criticism Jean de Meun's section of the *Roman de la Rose* and several of Jean's classical models, Ovid's *Ars amatoria* and *Remedia amoris*.[2] Jean's work was perhaps the most seminal literary text in Old French. During the debate over the merits of the *Rose* that took place in 1401 and 1402, Christine's censure of so venerated an author created quite a stir.[3] Although Christine does not mention Jean by name, most scholars assume that in the *Dit de la Rose* she reappropriates and reworks the major metaphor of Jean's text for her own purposes. In the *Dit de la Rose* Christine presents her version of what Jean's "Rose" would have said had the character spoken in her own voice. More than a century had intervened between the composition of Jean's continuation of the *Rose* and Christine's commentary on it in the *Epistre* and the *Dit*. In the *Dit* Christine reacts not only to Jean de Meun but also to her more immediate predecessors writing in the tradition of the *Rose*. In this study I will focus on Christine's relationship to Eustache Deschamps, whom Christine proclaimed as her "master" in an epistle dated February 10, 1404. In his written response to this letter, Deschamps acknowledged Christine's erudition or clerkliness. That is, Christine was, as she might have put it herself, a *clergesce*, her own coinage in the *Cité des Dames* for a female *clerc*. Despite the obvious warmth of the bond between the paternal father figure and his literary daughter, Christine's poetry constitutes a corrective recasting of much of Deschamps's *oeuvre*.

Eustache Morel, better known as Eustache Deschamps,[4] was born around 1346. He served as court poet in the entourage of several noble figures: Philippe d'Orléans, Charles V, Charles VI, and Louis d'Orléans. Deschamps was a legal civil servant as well as a court entertainer, becoming the bailiff of Valois and then of Senlis. He died in 1406. Christine was approximately eighteen years Deschamps's junior and outlived him by twenty-five years. Deschamps had provided models for the young woman poet to follow in writing the lyric poetry that preceded her longer didactic works, of which the first was the *Epistre* composed in 1399. Charity Cannon Willard, and others, have argued that Christine followed the instructions for composing various verse forms set forth in Deschamps's *Art de dictier et de fere chançons, balades, virelais, et rondeaulx* (1392).[5] A close connection exists between Deschamps's notion of *musique naturelle* ("natural music") enunciated in the *Art de dictier* and Christine's practice in the *Epistre* and *Dit*. Deschamps defined *musique naturelle* as that produced by the human voice reciting words in various meters and in different patterns. His definition reflects the importance given to spoken poetry of the kind that characterized popular poetic contests, like those celebrating May Day and Saint Valentine's Day.[6] The *Epistre* is presented as a proclamation read out to Cupid's followers on May Day. The *Dit* is inscribed by Christine as having been "escript le jour Saint Valentin" (line 638; "written on Saint Valentine's Day").

The influence of the *Art de dictier* is more clearly evident in the *Dit de la Rose* than in the *Epistre* because the *Dit* includes three intercalated *ballades* and a *rondelet*. Moreover, the name of Christine's association, the Order of the Rose, probably draws on the title of several of Deschamps's poems. Deschamps composed three ballads on the "ordres de la fleur et de la feuille," a theme borrowed from the English to celebrate Philippa of Lancaster at a time when the French court was thinking about making her its queen.[7]

In addition to the literary references linking Deschamps and Christine, there were important historical connections between the two. Since both spent some of the same years at the Orléans court, they must have known each other personally. Deschamps was an auditor of the "cour amoureuse dite de Charles VI" ("the court of love ascribed to Charles VI"),[8] one of the models for Christine's Order of the Rose. The real "cour amoureuse," founded on Saint Valentine's Day 1400, was dedicated to the defense of women's honor.[9] In October 1400 Deschamps staged a parody of the "cour amoureuse,"[10] an act which suggests that his feelings toward the society were ambiguous at best. Furthermore, participation in the society did not necessarily prevent members from defaming women. Pierre and Gontier Col and Jean de Montrueil, Christine's adversaries in the Quarrel over the *Rose*, belonged to the association.[11]

The letters exchanged by Christine and Deschamps remain the best indicators of the nature of the relationship between the two poets. As a point of comparison we should first consider the series of poems Deschamps composed in honor of Guillaume de Machaut, whom he considered his poetic "father" (following this line of reasoning, Machaut would be Christine's literary grandfather).[12] Machaut's main contribution to the genre of lyric poetry was perhaps the *dit*, a hybrid form combining a story presented as autobiographical, general reflections on the world and writing, and lyric insertions. Machaut also helped regularize the traditional poetic forms. Even more than for defining the *formes fixes*, Machaut was responsible for popularizing them.[13]

Deschamps, whose *Art de dictier* is marked by more than one example drawn from Machaut's lyric production, was, as Poirion has suggested, a faithful disciple of Machaut. The practical morality that Machaut had reserved for his *dits* became the substance of Deschamps's lyric poetry. The personal character of Deschamps's verse grows out of Machaut's emphasis on the feelings and experiences of the poetic self. Deschamps, however, often sounds an anticourtly note foreign to Machaut's lyric verse and most of his narrative *dits*.[14] In the prologue to his complete collected works, written near the end of his life, Machaut claims that he wrote, "A l'onneur et a la loange / De toutes dames sans losange" (lines 17–18; "in honor and praise of all women without deceit"). Despite this assertion, Jacqueline Cerquiglini claims to perceive antifeminist strains in Machaut's judgment poems, and shows how the praise of women in the person of Toute-Belle in the first part of the *Voir-Dit* gives way to criticism of women in the second.[15] Whether or not Machaut was indeed expressing antifeminist sentiments, it is undeniable that he raises the problem of antifeminism in the judgment poems. In contrast to what appears in Machaut's collected works, Deschamps's antifeminism is deep and pervasive. Women and the institution of marriage are major objects of his satire. Deschamps's transformation of the tradition handed down by Machaut and others is in turn revised by Christine. She not only restores the respect for women that characterized a significant portion of Machaut's poetic output, but portrays women in a more realistic manner because she does so from the viewpoint of a woman herself.

Deschamps presents his image of Machaut in a series of three ballads composed on the occasion of the poet's death in 1377 (reprinted in his collected works 1:243–46 and 3:259–60). In two of these poems, Deschamps calls upon the collective body of lyric tradition to lament in song "la mort Machaut le noble rethorique" ("the death of Machaut, the noble rhetorician"). In presenting Machaut as the consummate rhetorician, Deschamps situates poetic composition in the vernacular squarely within the seven liberal arts, a principle he was to set forth clearly in his *Art de dictier*.

In the third ballad Deschamps again portrays Machaut as rhetorician. The first stanza of this ballad, which is addressed to Péronne d'Armentières, the anagram of Toute-Belle in the *Voir-Dit*, merits special attention:

Après Machaut qui tant vous a amé
Et qui estoit la fleur de toutes fleurs,
Noble poete eҭ faiseur renommé,
Plus qu'Ovide vray remede d'amours.
Qui m'a nourry et fait maintes douçours,
Veuillés, lui mort, pour l'onneur de celui,
Que je soie vostre loyal ami.

(After Machaut, who loved you so much, and who was the flower of all
flowers, noble poet and famed maker, more than Ovid a true remedy
of love, who nourished me and created much delight, grant, with him
dead, for his honor, that I be your loyal friend.)

I should like to make several points about the stanza. First, it is Machaut
himself rather than Péronne who is referred to as the flower, "la fleur," an
allusion to the poet as an incarnation of the flowers of rhetoric also encountered in one of the other two ballads in question (1:245–46, poem
124). With this reference Deschamps stresses Machaut's status as a *clerc* well
versed in the liberal arts. In conjunction with the term *faiseur* or "maker,"
the allusion to Machaut as rhetorician emphasizes his technical virtuosity.[16]
If Christine were familiar with Deschamps's poems on the death of Machaut
(and it is hard to believe that she would not be), then her self-presentation
as the Rose in the *Dit de la Rose* could be seen as a means by which she
legitimizes her role as a *clergesce,* in contrast to the *clerc* of Machaut and Deschamps. In other words, besides being the female object of desire of literary
tradition who now gets to speak on her own behalf, Christine as the Rose
represents as well a *clergesce* who dares to protest against injustices perpetrated against all women. Second, it is in this stanza that the term *poète* is applied to a writer of the *langue d'oïl* for the first time.[17] In connecting Machaut
directly to Ovid, Deschamps imitates Jean de Meun's linking of the *Rose* to
the school of Latin elegiac poetry headed by the same Ovid. Furthermore,
just as Jean had presented himself as the legitimate continuator of Guillaume de Lorris, so Deschamps in this passage portrays himself as Machaut's
literary son. According to Deschamps, it is Machaut "who nourished me
and created much delight" ("qui m'a nourry et fait maintes douçours").[18]
It may be this line that prompted an author of a fourteenth-century art of
second rhetoric to claim that Machaut was Deschamps's uncle.[19] My third
comment bears on Deschamps's desire to reappropriate Machaut's young
muse. On the surface an expression of Deschamps's esteem for his predecessor, it can nonetheless be taken as a sign of his envy of Machaut's achievements. It points to Deschamps's secret wish to outdo Machaut in the related
realms of love and poetic composition.[20]

Christine's letter to Deschamps dated February 10, 1404, found in Roy's
edition (2:295–301), reveals a great deal about the relationship between

the two poets. Christine's attitude toward Deschamps is one of apparent humility and deference. She feels justified approaching him only because he had previously expressed his esteem for her work (lines 5–6). Christine delineates clearly the roles of the two writers: she addresses Deschamps as her "maistre" (line 51; "master") and refers to herself as his "disciple" and "bienveillant" (line 212). The use of the term *master* is an unambiguous allusion to Dante's use of the same term to characterize his relationship to Vergil, found in Dante's first words to Vergil in *Inferno* 1.85, "tu se' lo mio maestro e il mio autore," "you are my master and my author." [21] Her deference goes hand in hand with a deep pride in her own accomplishments as *clergesce*. On the one hand, she begs Deschamps not to scorn her feminine mind or sensibility ("son feminin scens," line 29) which is small ("petis," line 34). On the other hand, she justifies her entreaty couched in the first person by claiming she learned appropriate clerical style from those who spent their time in pursuit of knowledge (lines 21–22). Her signature at the end of the letter is accompanied by the loaded phrase "handmaiden of knowledge," ("ancelle de science," *ancelle* certainly a semilearned borrowing from *ancilla,* the term used, of course, for the Virgin Mary in the Annunciation).

Christine devotes much of her letter to a criticism of contemporary French society, singling out corruption among the nobility, the clergy, and the general population. Pride, selfishness, and wantonness are the order of the day, she feels. In this environment the search for knowledge has lost its meaning (line 110). Toward the end of the letter Christine moves from an overall consideration of the shortcomings of the times to her particular problems. Citing the neglect of widows and orphans, she laments her own precarious situation following the death of her husband, a situation that continues to affect her at the time she composes the letter.

Besides her explicit praise of Deschamps, Christine expresses in other ways her indebtedness to him as poet. Like Deschamps, who had dramatized both sad and comic aspects of his own daily existence, Christine proposes herself as the subject of many of her works. Perhaps Christine also means that she learned something about writing social satire from Deschamps. To cite just one example: Christine's criticism of the France of her day recalls Deschamps's critical analysis of historical events in the *Miroir de mariage*. In this never-finished work surviving in 12,103 verses, Deschamps presents a debate between Franc-Vouloir and Folie on the relative merits of the marital state. [22] At the end of this text Deschamps enumerates the evils caused by the action of Folie throughout human history. The work breaks off in the middle of events recounted around 1360; Deschamps, his editor Raynaud argues, apparently thought it prudent to refrain from continuing his satire into his own time.

Although we possess no written testimony that Christine knew the

Miroir, there are reasons other than the general affinity to social satire that I have cited above to believe that she did. Christine and Deschamps were associated with several of the same royal patrons and undoubtedly knew each other's work well. The unfinished state of the *Miroir* could be taken as an implicit invitation to complete it with the satire of the times subsequent to the mid-fourteenth century.[23] Moreover, Deschamps appears to acknowledge tacitly Christine's elaboration in her epistle of his own unfinished satire in the *Miroir* though his comparison of her to Boethius in Pavia ("For I see you, like Boethius in Pavia, unique in your acts within the kingdom of France"; "Car je te voy, come Boece a Pavie, / Seule en tes faiz ou royaume de France," lines 35–36). This allusion echoes line 11057 of the *Miroir*: "You had Boethius imprisoned unjustly in Pavia" ("Boece fistes enmurer a Pavie contre raison").[24] In addition, despite the very different views on marriage held by Christine and Deschamps, in the *Livre des Trois Vertus* Christine criticizes some of the same social foibles exhibited by married women as does Deschamps.[25] I would also argue that the third book of the *Cité des Dames*, devoted largely to female saints, was inspired at least in part by chapter 80 of the *Miroir*, in which Deschamps gives a list of holy women including Saint Christine.

In comparing Deschamps's letter to Christine (6:251–52 of his collected works) with his ballads dedicated to Guillaume de Machaut, especially the one in which he addresses Péronne d'Armentières, one easily discerns the honor and respect in which Deschamps holds his self-proclaimed disciple. Possibly reacting to the disparity pointed out by Christine between the vices of present-day France and the virtues of antiquity, Deschamps opens his epistle by likening Christine to one of the nine Muses: "Christine, eloquent Muse among the nine, incomparable as best I know today" ("Muse eloquent entre les .ix., Christine / Nompareille que je saiche au jour d'ui"). He continues his praise of her great learning, which, he adds, is constantly increasing. Deschamps certifies Christine's intellectual pedigree. Implicitly accepting himself as her literary father figure by responding warmly to her letter, he situates Christine in the line first of the Biblical King Solomon, renowned as teacher (and often cited as an authority figure in medieval Latin and Old French literature), and second of her biological father, Thomas de Pizan. Deschamps claims to have known her father personally (line 14), which would not be surprising given the latter's prominence as court astrologer and Deschamps's own service to the monarch. Deschamps mentions Thomas's association with the city of Bologna, where he had received a medical degree from the university and remained as lecturer in medicine and astrology until 1356.[26]

Many of Deschamps's comments imply that the title of *poète* he had applied to Machaut could also be ascribed to Christine. Just as he had emphasized Machaut's status as a rhetorician, Deschamps stresses that Christine followed her father's example in studying astronomy and the other liberal arts. This assertion, in fact, appears well founded because, as Charity Cannon Willard has shown, many of Christine's astrological ideas and her concept of cosmology can be traced to her father's influence. In claiming that she was both intellectually refined and erudite ("en sens acquis et en toute dotrine"), Deschamps further implies that Christine has mastered the male tradition of *clergie,* something which, as far as Deschamps is concerned, no woman had done previously. The refrain of Deschamps's poem stresses Christine's uniqueness: she is "unique in [her] acts in the kingdom of France" ("seule en [ses] faiz ou royaume de France"). Deschamps employs the term *seule* in response to Christine's characterization of having composed her letter "seulette en m'estude" (line 205; "all alone in my study"). The designation "seulette" functions as an emblematic signature of Christine's didactic writing as well as her lyric poetry.[27] By picking up Christine's use of the term, Deschamps reinforces her identity as *clerc* and *poète.* He thereby offers her what may be the best compliment one writer can give another: he confirms the image that she projects of herself. Rather than trying to lessen her achievement, for example, by attacking her weakness as a woman, he accepts and approves of her self-designated poetic persona as a *clergesce* who must function in the world without the protection of a man.

Deschamps reserves the greatest expression of his homage to Christine for the *envoi* of his verse epistle. Reversing the master-disciple roles initially assigned by Christine, he asks to be admitted to her company in order to study under her tutelage. Unlike his imagined relationship with Toute-Belle/Péronne, who we recall was also a woman poet, he seems to consider Christine as a respected equal. If she is a daughter figure, she is one who has things to teach her father, whether he be Thomas de Pizan or Eustache Morel. Daniel Poirion treats Deschamps's request to study with Christine as a direct response to her expressed wish to receive some of his virtuous works, "oeuvres vertueuses." Deschamps's comment indicates that at the time he composed his letter to Christine he (and probably many others) already considered her as having mastered the didactic modes.[28]

There is yet another reason to believe Deschamps considered Christine to have attained the rank of *poète.* Whereas in her letter Christine cites Boethius in support of her contention that people in modern-day France should not prize material goods over virtue (lines 72–77), Deschamps in the final verses of his response compares Christine to Boethius. It is as if Christine, as a *clergesce* declaiming on subjects of philosophical import (like Carmentis, the figure to whom Christine applies the term *clergesce* in the *Cité des Dames*), had become a second Boethius. For Deschamps, Christine is a true literary authority with the status of a writer in Latin, an *auctor* in the full sense of the term.

Although Christine expresses deep admiration for Deschamps and for the tradition of vernacular writing he represents, in the *Dit de la Rose* (as well as in many of her other texts) she registers a strong protest against the antifeminist stance he often adopts. Many passages of his *Miroir de mariage* assume the character of a clerical diatribe against marriage and the evils that stem from women (11:164–65). Although arguments are offered both for and against marriage, Deschamps borrows Jean de Meun's pessimistic view of women's virtue as the controlling idea in his own work (11:219–20). Overall, he closely patterns his *Miroir de mariage* on Jean's "Miroër aux amoreus" ("Mirror for Lovers," see 11:165). Deschamps draws upon Jean's repertoire of allegorical characters as well as on his amorous terminology. He devotes an entire chapter, 57, to an elaboration on the rose as an image of the fragility and evanescence of feminine beauty; the chapter heading reads, "Comment beauté de femme est comparée a la rose qui incontinent passe, seiche et pert son odour, beauté et amortist," "How the beauty of woman is compared to the rose which passes away, dries up and loses its fragrance and beauty, and decays." The conclusion of the *Miroir* (11:290) is that *clercs* who preserve the great actions of men for posterity should dedicate themselves wholly to their vocation and not get married.

Besides the *Miroir*, Deschamps composed a large number of short poems satirizing marriage. One such poem (5:73) states that men should heed the tradition of *clercs* such as Theophrastus and Matheolus who had warned men of the dangers inherent in marriage. Christine rejected this advice from Deschamps and did not shy away from denouncing male *clercs* for their antifeminism. In the *Epistre* Christine began her crusade against the antifeminism endemic in the clerkly tradition. The immediate occasion for the construction of the City of Ladies was, of course, Christine's reaction to her reading of Matheolus's *Liber lamentationum*. Her censure of Theophrastus merits special attention. During the quarrel over the *Rose*, Jean de Montreuil compared Christine to the Greek whore who dared to correct Theophrastus. In a remark, at once condescending and patronizing, he had sniffed, "Although she does not lack intelligence at all—as much as a woman can have any—I seemed to be hearing the Greek courtesan Leontium, who as Cicero reminds us, 'dared to write against the great philosopher Theophrastus,'" ("que licet, ut est captus femineus, intellectu non careat, michi tamen audire visum est Leuntium grecam meretricem, ut refert Cicero, que 'contra Theofrastum, philosophum tantum, scribere ausa fuit'").[29] Christine's reply to Jean's attack is recorded in the *Cité des Dames*: "Leontium was a Greek woman and also such a great philosopher that she dared, for impartial and serious reasons, to correct and attack the philosopher Theophrastus who was quite famous in her time," ("Leonce, qui fu femme grecque, fu autresi si tres grant phillosophe que elle osa, par pures et vrays raisons, reprendre et redarguer le philosophe Theophraste, qui en son temps estoit renommez," 1.30.3). Christine redefines Leontium as an accomplished philosopher entirely justified in taking Theophrastus to task for his misogyny.

In many cases Christine's *Dit de la Rose* constitutes a corrective response directed toward her "master" and literary father, Eustache Deschamps. His *Conseils aux dames* ("Advice to Ladies" (2:113–14) is a good case in point. Deschamps counsels women to "be wise, guard your reputation" ("Soiez saiges, gardez vostre renom," line 3), advice with which Christine would concur entirely. If women follow my counsel, Deschamps continues, then their "good name will remain like a flower" ("le bon nom demourra comme fleur," line 28), a verse that could have helped inspire the *Dit*. Deschamps then composes a list of qualities women should have, headed by "Loyauté," the same personification who figures in the *Dit*. Overturning the association of gender and teacher-pupil roles in Deschamps's poem, Christine in the *Dit* has the female character Loyauté teach a lesson to men. In the *envoi* to the *Conseils aux dames* Deschamps insinuates that he would like to have enough respect for women to be able to obey them ("Dames, a qui je vueil de chiere lie / Comme voz serfs obeir sans folour"). Significantly, Christine's female speaker in the *Dit* is capable of leading and directing men. Her message is that it is primarily males who need reforming, not females. Her creative reworking of Deschamps's poem reveals the contradictions in his larger stance as well as the limitations of his narrowly masculine point of view.

Christine's corrective recasting of Deschamps extends even to the form of some poems. Deschamps employs a dream vision several times to speak out against problems in the kingdom of France (see 3:155–59, poems 187 and 188). In the *Dit* the dream vision is used to bring the problem of antifeminism to the attention of Christine's contemporaries. Here it is Deschamps himself who is among those being criticized.

As Sandra M. Gilbert and Susan Gubar noted, women writers often achieve literary authority by simultaneously complying with and subverting patriarchal literary standards.[30] Christine conforms to this model of literary practice first elucidated for the nineteenth century, but Christine also, it should be remembered, following the custom of medieval writers both in Latin and in the vernacular, at once continued and transformed the works of her predecessors. However, Christine's situation differed from that of a male writer in that she attempted to enlarge and to universalize the poetic tradition that she inherited. As a *clergesce* proposing nothing less than a fundamental revision of the presuppositions of literary composition, she was trying to secure women's place in literary tradition and to free the literary representation of women from misogynist conventions.

The present study emphasizes Christine's role as critic and innovator of accepted literary and social norms. Christine borrowed from Deschamps's techniques to celebrate him as her predecessor while herself making better use of them. In his now-classic study *The Anxiety of Influence: A Theory of Poetry*, Harold Bloom called attention to the rivalry often found in the relationship between a male writer and his male precursors.[31] According to Bloom's model, Deschamps's praise of Machaut may hide a subconscious desire to establish himself as the legitimate successor to the rank of *poète* he so generously accorded the earlier writer, and may reflect an even larger attempt to displace the locus of authority in the vernacular canon. If Machaut assumed the central position so often occupied by Jean de Meun in the minds of late fourteenth-century poets, then Deschamps's importance as Machaut's successor would necessarily increase. After all, Deschamps probably began work on the *Miroir de mariage*, his creative recasting of Jean de Meun's "Miroër aux amoreus," several years after composing the series of ballads on Machaut's death. Whether the kinds of anxiety that Bloom ascertained in modern texts are as omnipresent in medieval ones must remain an open question, but in Deschamps's specific case, as the documentation clearly demonstrates, the concern with portraying himself as Machaut's successor, with poetic legitimacy as a function of continuation for its own sake, seems to anticipate more modern male authors. Christine's break both with Jean de Meun—who had established a lineage of exclusively male poets from Ovid to Guillaume de Lorris—and ultimately with the lyric tradition as represented by both Machaut and Deschamps, takes on new meaning in this context.

Christine, by successfully winning Deschamps's praises, beats him at his own game.[32] She has her living precursor certify her legitimacy and prestige. Her emphasis on her feminine weakness—her famous *seulete suy et seulete veuil estre* ("I am a little lonely woman and I want to be a little lonely woman") represents a daring variation on the traditional humility topos, and as such is emblematic of Christine's substantial innovation of literary tradition—is used to advance the cause of womanhood. As for the two poets' respective relationships to Jean de Meun, it is Christine rather than Deschamps who succeeds in questioning his literary authority, much to the shock of her male contemporaries. Whereas Deschamps can only undermine Jean's prestige indirectly by setting up Machaut as Jean's rival, Christine consistently, explicitly, directly, and deliberately attacks Jean de Meun. Christine could only have pioneered as a woman poet as she did if she were free from the kind of "anxiety of influence" which so characterized Deschamps's relationship to Machaut. Her conduct during the Quarrel of the *Rose* and during her subsequent literary career offers ample proof of how she broke away from the restraints imposed on literary creativity by misogyny and suggests that such literary misogyny in fact has a corollary in works of male *clercs* concerned with establishing their literary legitimacy through mechanical continuations of petrified poetic forms rather than through innovative contributions of substance. Christine was sensitive to the frequent gender differences evident in attitudes regarding inheritances and noted in the *Cité des Dames*: "God knows how many sons of great lords and rich men long for their parents' deaths so that they can inherit their lands and wealth" (2.7.1). It fell to the daughters to care for the parents, and Christine gives many examples of filial piety. In Christine's case it fell to a daughter to restore the inherited poetic tradition to its proper status.

At the same time, not only was Christine sensitive to the differences between the behavior of daughters and sons toward fathers, but she was also especially keen throughout the Quarrel of the *Rose* to distinguish Jean de Meun and Dante. It is striking that Dante's relationship to Vergil, while of enormous complexity, is also one of extraordinary openness, free of Oedipal anxiety.[33] But the poetic tradition posited in *Inferno* 4 encompassing Homer, Vergil, Horace, Ovid, Lucan, and, finally, Dante is surely of a different order from that of the poets who died in love's service—Catullus, Tibullus, Ovid again, Guillaume de Lorris, and Jean de Meun—celebrated at the midpoint of the *Rose*.[34] Christine, at once advocate of filial piety and staunch opponent of misogyny, undoubtedly must have recognized and understood with all its ramifications the difference between Jean de Meun's and Dante's views of literary tradition when she launched her critique of the *Rose*, and in so doing, she attempted to free late medieval French literature from the misogyny and concomitant formal narcissism of so much late fourteenth-century lyric.

Notes

1. In *Oeuvres poétiques de Christine de Pisan*, ed. Maurice Roy, 3 vols. (Paris: Firmin Didot, 1886–96), 2:29–48. The *Dit* is divided into two distinct episodes. In the first the female speaker witnesses the apparition of Lady Loyalty, who establishes the Order of the Rose in a courtly gathering held at the Parisian residence of the king's younger brother, Louis d'Orléans, in January 1402. During the ceremony the twenty renowned knights and squires present learn the vow of upholding women's good name which constitutes membership in the order. In the second episode the same speaker experiences a dream vision in which Lady Loyalty enjoins her to disseminate information on the order and encourage other women to establish the order throughout the world.

2. Consult my article "The Woman Writer and Literary History: Christine de Pizan's Redefinition of the Poetic *Translatio* in the *Epistre au dieu d'Amours*," *French Literature Series* 16 (1989): 1–16.

3. See Eric Hicks, ed., *Le Débat sur le "Roman de la Rose"* (Paris: Champion, 1977); and Peter Potansky, *Der Streit um den Rosenroman* (Munich: Fink, 1972).

4. He was called Des Champs after the name of his country home. See Paul

Zumthor, "Eustache Deschamps," in *Dictionnaire des lettres françaises*, 7 vols. (Paris: Fayard, 1964), 1:267. The following biographical information on his life comes from Daniel Poirion, *Le Poète et le prince: L'Évolution du lyrisme courtois de Guillaume de Machaut à Charles d'Orléans* (Paris: Presses universitaires de France, 1965), 218–35.

5. Charity Cannon Willard, *Christine de Pizan: Her Life and Works* (New York: Persea Books, 1984), 44; see also Enid McLeod, *The Order of the Rose: The Life and Ideas of Christine de Pizan* (Totowa, N.J.: Rowman and Littlefield, 1976), 43. The *Art de dictier* is found in *Oeuvres complètes d'Eustache Deschamps*, ed. A. Queux de Saint-Hilaire and Gaston Raynaud 11 vols. (Paris: Firmin Didot, 1878–1903), 7:266–92.

6. Willard, *Christine de Pizan*, 55; Poirion, *Le Poète et le prince*, 226.

7. Poirion, *Le Poète et le prince*, 228. She in fact subsequently became the queen of Portugal. Deschamps also composed a ballad on the *ordre de la couronne* ("order of the crown," in his *Oeuvres complètes*, 2:35–36, poem 212) which corresponded to a real-life order; see also 11:27–28, 265.

8. Poirion, *Le Poète et le prince*, 227.

9. See A. Piaget, "La Cour amoureuse, dite de Charles VI," *Romania* 20 (1891): 416–54; and A. Piaget, "Un Manuscrit de la 'Cour amoureuse de Charles VI,'" *Romania* 31 (1902): 597–603.

10. Poirion, *Le Poète et le prince*, 223.

11. Piaget, "La Cour amoreuse," 447.

12. On the relationship between Christine and Machaut, see Charity Cannon Willard, "Concepts of Love According to Guillaume de Machaut, Christine de Pizan, and Pietro Bembo," in *The Spirit of the Court: Selected Proceedings of the Fourth Congress of the International Courtly Literature Society (Toronto, 1983)*, ed. Glyn S. Burgess and Robert A. Taylor (Cambridge, England: D. S. Brewer, 1985), 386–92.

13. Nigel Wilkens, *"La Louange des dames" by Guillaume de Machaut* (Edinburgh: Scottish Academic Press, 1972), 18.

14. For Deschamps's relationship to Machaut, see Poirion, *Le Poète et le prince*, 224–25, 229.

15. Jacqueline Cerquiglini, "Éthique de la totalisation et esthétique de la rupture dans le *Voir dit* de Guillaume de Machaut," in *Guillaume de Machaut: Poète et compositeur*, Actes et colloques, no. 23 (Paris: Klincksieck, 1982), 255–56.

16. See Kevin Brownlee, *Poetic Identity in Guillaume de Machaut* (Madison: University of Wisconsin Press, 1984), 8. The term *faiseur* here is synonymous for "maker," "creator."

17. Ibid., 7–9. On p. 8, Brownlee mentions how in Deschamps's poem the idea of a classical *auctor* is fused with an expanded notion of *poète* that includes vernacular writers. Besides Deschamps's ballad on Machaut, the text of several fourteenth-century manuscripts of Richard de Fournival's *Bestiaire d'amours* contains the example of an Occitanian poet (probably Bernard de Ventadour) who is assimilated to Ovid. See pp. 368–70 of my *Chrétien de Troyes and the "Romance of the Rose": Continuation and Narrative Tradition* (Ph.D. dissertation, Princeton University, 1986).

18. Poirion, *Le Poète et le prince*, 224.

19. Raynaud, writing in the introduction to vol. 11 of Deschamps's *Oeuvres com-*

plètes, 11, n. 4. The choice of the uncle and nephew relationship over that of father and son may be attributable to the well-known importance of the former in medieval French literature.

20. Poirion, *Le Poète et le prince*, 225, notes Deschamps's "strange fidelity to the courtly idea" and his "troubling behavior" (*démarche troublante*).

21. For Dante's importance to Christine, see Earl Jeffrey Richards, "Christine de Pizan and Dante: A Reexamination," *Archiv für das Studium der neueren Sprachen und Literaturen* 137 (1985): 100–111. I am grateful to Professor Richards for calling this allusion to my attention.

22. The works' editor, Raynaud, in vol. 11 of Deschamps's *Oeuvres complètes*, 199, contends that Deschamps undertook the work around 1381 and wrote the final verses sometime around 1389. In the introduction to his edition of *Les Quinze Joies de mariage* (Geneva: Droz, 1963), Jean Rychner (pp. xvi–xviii) takes issue with this dating. Relying almost exclusively on a letter Deschamps wrote to his friend Pierre Manguin, Rychner claims that all that can be stated with certainty is that the *Miroir* was composed before 1403.

23. In fact, the following rubric appears at the end of the *Miroir* in at least one manuscript: "The author did not go on to treat the subject of this book any further because of an illness which befell him, from which he died. May God pardon his soul! Amen!" ("De la matiere de ce livre ne traicta l'acteur plus avant pour maladie qui lui survint, de laquelle il mourut. Dieu lui pardoint a l'ame! Amen!") Deschamps probably did not prepare the rubrics on this manuscript. According to Poirion (*Le Poète et le prince*, 219), the only manuscript he could have prepared himself was the one he offered to Charles VI on April 18, 1383. We should note that the rubric at the end of the work is incorrect. Deschamps lived several years after penning the last verses of the *Miroir* and went on to compose other works. The rubricator suggests an analogy between Jean de Meun's continuation of the first part of the *Roman de la Rose* because of the "death" of Guillaume de Lorris and the possibilities for continuation offered by Deschamps's unfinished satire.

24. Deschamps's verse could also contain a reference to the *Rose*. It implies that Christine, akin to Jean de Meun, who completed Guillaume's poem, is a "new Boethius" who continues the work of the original philosopher-poet, perhaps a veiled reference to the *Livre de la mutacion de Fortune*.

25. Charity Cannon Willard makes this point in her forthcoming "Women and Marriage Around 1400: Three Views." In this study, Willard states her belief that Christine's allusion to the "debate on marriage" found in the *Cité des Dames* (2.13.1; English translation, p. 118) may be a reference to Deschamps's *Miroir*. Moreover, despite Raynaud's hypothesis (Deschamps, *Oeuvres complètes*, 11:105) that the *Miroir* was made public only after Deschamps's death, there is additional reason to affirm that the work circulated in some circles before 1406. Rychner (*Les Quinze Joies de mariage*, xviii) cites the letter Deschamps wrote to his friend Pierre Manguin in 1403 in which he reproaches him for not following his advice on marriage: "You have little considered our writings and the books we have composed" ("Tu as po compté a nos dis / Et aux livres que faiz avons"). Rychner maintains that this remark is almost certainly an allusion to the *Miroir*. I am grateful to Professor Willard for bringing this last point to my attention.

26. See Charity Cannon Willard, "Christine de Pizan: The Astrologer's Daughter," in *Mélanges à la mémoire de Franco Simone: France et Italie dans la culture européenne* (Geneva: Slatkine, 1980), 1:95–111.

27. See Jacqueline Cerquiglini's introduction to her edition of Christine's *Cent ballades d'Amant et de Dame* (Paris: Union générale d'éditions, 1982), 10–11, and Poirion's remarks on the term, *Le Poète et le prince*, 253.

28. Poirion, *Le Poète et le prince*, 228. On p. 237 Poirion notes that Deschamps here acknowledges that Christine's reputation as a poet was solidly established by this time. Furthermore, in the *Avision-Christine* (1405), Christine states her pleasure at having finally discovered the personal style that expressed her deepest aspirations, a didactic style inspired by Boethius and others. See Charity Cannon Willard, "Christine de Pizan and the Order of the Rose," in *Ideals for Women in the Works of Christine de Pizan*, ed. Diane Bornstein, Medieval and Renaissance Monograph Series, no. 1 (Detroit: Michigan Consortium for Medieval and Early Modern Studies, 1981), 63.

29. Eric Hicks, *Débat*, 42.

30. Sandra M. Gilbert and Susan Gubar, *The Madwoman in the Attic: The Woman Writer and the Nineteenth-Century Literary Imagination* (New Haven, Conn.: Yale University Press, 1979), 73.

31. Harold Bloom, *The Anxiety of Influence: A Theory of Poetry* (New York: Oxford University Press, 1973). Sheila Delany has also applied a Bloomian model to Christine; her arguments, however, lack cogency because they fail to integrate Christine into the tradition of medieval French poetry. See her "Rewriting Women Good: Gender and Anxiety of Influence in Two Late-Medieval Texts," in *Chaucer in the Eighties*, ed. Julian Wassermann and Robert J. Blanch (Syracuse, N.Y.: Syracuse University Press, 1986), 75–92.

32. The question remains why in his epistle Deschamps accords Christine unreserved praise despite her earlier strong criticism of the antifeminist attitudes espoused by male writers, including himself. I would tentatively suggest the following reasons, which tend in some important ways to contrast with the Bloomian model: when Deschamps drafted his response to Christine, he was an old man, with only a year left to live, who may have wanted to encourage Christine as his continuator in the area of social criticism, not exactly a lyrical convention. Perhaps Christine's story of her own misfortunes struck a responsive chord in Deschamps, who had himself been beset with financial problems stemming from family responsibilities. Both he and Christine had their differences with Louis d'Orléans (see Willard, "Christine de Pizan and the Order of the Rose," 62). These common points of interest and contact would suggest that their own relationship was not particularly anxiety-ridden.

33. See Robert Hollander, *Il Virgilio Dantesco: Tragedia nella "Commedia"* (Florence: Leo S. Olschki, 1983).

34. My thanks to Professor Richards for noting this to me.

A Mirror for Misogynists: John of Salisbury's *Policraticus* (8.11) in the Translation of Denis Foulechat (1372)

ERIC HICKS

In what is one of the finest passages in fifteenth-century prose, that exordium of the *City of Ladies* in which Christine gives what might be termed a classic portrait of the alienation of the female scholar,[1] special injury attaches to the fact that doctors are at one with fools in waxing eloquent against the second sex:

> Mais nonobstant . . . j'arguoye fort contre les femmes, disant que trop fort seroit que tant de si renommez hommes—si sollempnelz clercs de tant hault et grant entendement, si clerveans en toutes choses, comme il semble que ceulx fussent—en eussent parlé mençongieusement et en tant de lieux, que a paine trouvoye volume morale, qui qu'en soit l'atteur, que quant que je l'aye tout leu, que je n'y voye aucuns chappitres ou certaines clauses au blasme d'elles. Ceste seule rayson brief et court me faisoit conclurre que, quoyque mon entendement pour sa simplesce et ignorance ne sceust congnoistre les grans deffaultes de moy meismes et semblablement des autres femmes, que vrayement, toutevoye, couvenoit il que ainsi fust. Et ainsi m'en rapportoye plus au jugement d'autruy ad ce que moy meismes en sentoye et savoye.

> (Yet I still argued vehemently against women, saying that it would be impossible that so many famous men—such solemn scholars, possessed of deep and great understanding, so clear-sighted in all things, as it seemed—could have spoken falsely on so many occasions that I could hardly find a book on morals where, even before I had read it in its entirety, I did not find several chapters or certain sections attacking women, no matter who the author was. This reason alone, in short, made me conclude that, although my intellect did not perceive my own great faults and, likewise, those of other women because of its simpleness and ignorance, it was however truly fitting that such was the case. And so I relied more on the judgment of others than on what I myself felt and knew.)[2]

Although much of Christine's subsequent argumentation will tend to illustrate that doctors can be at times the most consummate of fools, the issues involved by the point are serious, and as with most things serious and medieval, at bottom theological.

One of the touchstones of antifeminist Christian thinking is the celebrated treatise by Jerome against Jovinianus, who held that human sexuality was not necessarily an evil, nor virginity necessarily a state of preeminence. Spurred on by his fervor for virgins, Jerome embarked upon one of the grandest diatribes against women ever penned, lapsing into misogyny, as it has been aptly put, for the sake of virtue.[3] Jerome found ample inspiration for this vein in the writings of the ancients, and it has been said that the entire *Adversus Jovinianum* is only a rehashing of Seneca's *De matrimonio*.[4] Our attention will focus, however, on a lost work by Theophrastus, the *Liber aureolus de nuptiis*, preserved for medieval clerics in the paraphrase given by Jerome, and for the twelfth century and beyond, by the insertion of the relevant passages in the influential *Policraticus* of John of Salisbury.

The *Adversus Jovinianum* was known to Abelard and has long been acknowledged as the principal source of the critique of marriage attributed to Heloise in the lovers' correspondence.[5] That John of Salisbury was once Abelard's disciple is interesting in this light, although a scholar of his stature probably had no need of Abelard to be introduced to Saint Jerome. It is certain, at any rate, that the *Policraticus* quickly became the standard reference for the sayings of Theophrastus on marriage.[6]

The *Policraticus* was known to Christine, who cites it as one of the works translated on royal commission during the reign of Charles V.[7] Most scholars believe that Christine had access to the king's library in the Louvre, and it thus seems plausible that the translation by Denis Foulechat, completed in the year 1372, was available to her there.[8] It is not certain just how well Christine knew this text, as the *Policraticus* was an extremely popular work, quoted or excerpted in many quarters. Ultimately, with its allegory of the "body politick," it was to supply the framework for Christine's *Livre du corps de policie*, perhaps by way of the *De regimine principum* of Egidio Colonna (Giles de Rome).[9] Explicit references to the *Policraticus* are to be found in several of Christine's works; it seems to have been, in particular, an accepted source on princely generosity.[10] The most important traces of the work are, however, the allusions to Theophrastus in *The City of Ladies* on the subject of female ingratitude (2.13), the argument being that greater confidence can be placed in the gratitude of a faithful servant than in one's wife: the allusion to the source is clear and the subject matter sufficiently developed to imply direct knowledge of the text.

The *Policraticus* is far more important for the appreciation of medieval attitudes than for any inherent intertextuality: as a diatribe against women, "Theophrastus" on marriage is beyond compare.[11] The text combines a fundamental male suspicion of female sexuality with peculiarly medieval notions of sexuality as sin, tempered at times by humor—for there is much here that is exploited ironically in a paradoxical mode. Also included in the chapter is the story of the Ephesian wife, a paradigm for many such tales, not the least of which is Chrétien's *Yvain*. No direct influence is to be implied here, but attention should be drawn to this articulate narrative complex as a broad cultural phenomenon with clear ideological overtones, topical in both the technical and the ordinary sense of the word:

> S'il est un conte usé, commun et rebattu,
> C'est celui qu'en ces vers j'accommode à ma guise.
>
> (La Fontaine, *La Matrone d'Ephèse*, lines 1–2)

The misogynist compendium presented here, half philosophy and half satire, embodies perhaps more than any other work Christine might have read those complex tendencies of medieval "wisdom" which led her to wonder, as one evening in her *cele* she took up, then put down, a small book of light poetry,

> quelle peut estre la cause, ne dont ce peut venir, que tant de divers hommes, clercs et autres, ont esté, et sont, sy enclins a dire de bouche et en leur traittiez et escrips tant de diableries et de vituperes de femmes et de leurs condicions. Et nom mie seulement un ou deux ne cestuy Matheolus, qui entre les livres n'a aucune reputacion et qui traitte en maniere de truffereie, mais generaument aucques en tous traittiez philosophes, pouettes, tous orateurs desquelz les nommes [H. dire] seroit longue chose, semble que tous parlent par une meismes bouche et tous accordent une semblable conclusion, determinant les meurs femenins enclins et plains de tous les vices.

> (. . . how it happened that so many different men—and learned men among them—have been and are so inclined to express both in speaking and in their treatises and writings so many wicked insults about women and their behavior. Not only one or two and not even just this Matheolus, for this book had a bad name anyway and was intended as a satire, but more generally, judging from the treatises of all philosophers and poets and from all the orators—it would take too long to mention their names—it seems that they all concur in one conclusion: that the behavior of women is inclined to and full of every vice.)[12]

Manuscripts and Editions

The three known copies of the Foulechat *Policraticus* have been adequately described by Charles Brucker in his partial editions of the text.[13] They are:

> N: Bibl. nat. fr., MS 24287
> A: Bibl. de l'Arsenal, MS 2682
> G: Bibl. Sainte-Geneviève, MS 1144–1145.

Indications of intermediate copies, on the basis of paleographical evidence, are strong. Brucker has also established that a fragment of a manuscript now lost has been included in MS N,[14] and a fragment of still another manuscript is contained in MS Bibl. nat. lat. 6416.[15] The stemma proposed by Brucker posits the existence of at least four other copies.

Of the surviving manuscripts, two are incomplete. The Arsenal copy need not detain us here, as books 7 and 8 are lacking in this volume; book 6 is missing from manuscript G, which gives a reasonably good copy of our text (8.11). The remaining manuscript, N, with its full page portrait of Charles V,[16] is a magnificent volume, well known to paleographers and to students of the medieval book. We follow Brucker in basing our transcription on this, the oldest of the three copies, listed in the inventory established by Giles Malet in 1373.[17]

Neither of the available manuscripts is beyond reproach. Ordinary scribal errors appear sporadically in both, and a case could be made—at least on the basis of the chapter edited here—for using either text as a base manuscript. N is marred by several short omissions, one of which is an obvious case of homoeoteleuton; most of its defects, however, reflect inattention to syntactical detail. The comparison of the two manuscripts yields several instances of simple word reversal, but it would be difficult to say, in any given case, that the reading of one is clearly better than the other. Orthography is perhaps more systematic in N, whose text seems generally more reliable on finer points: it is, at any rate, closer to what modern readers of Middle French are accustomed to reading. Where the manuscripts clearly diverge, reference to the Latin original generally suffices to settle any doubts, as in note 55 below (see pages 94, 105), where N reads *prendre*, against *pendre* in G (for the Latin *crucibus jussit affigi*).

Our choice of N has largely been determined by the question of coherence: nothing appreciable could be gained, and much lost, by choosing a base manuscript other than the one edited by Brucker.

We have not considered it useful to give a complete listing of variant readings. Corrections to N are given *in extenso,* along with such variants of

G as might bear on meaning or, ultimately, textual criticism. On the basis of the chapter edited here, it is certain that G was corrected by a revisor: the interlinear or marginal hand consistently follows the readings for N. In one particular passage, plainly corrupt, N's reading has been reproduced in a space originally left blank. This would imply that the scribe of G did not feel he could follow the reading of his exemplar, and that a decision was deferred on the passage until revision. The model for this revision was either N or a manuscript closely related to it.

On the Translations

Foulechat, like most other medieval translators, tends to the literal.[18] Vocabulary is Latinate, and closeness in meaning is sought—in a manner quite unlike the genius of later French—in profusion rather than concision. The resulting syntax is often burdensome to the modern ear and carries a decidedly legalistic ring. The ubiquitous *and*s, *however*s, and *yet*s of our own translation reflect an attempt to render the feel of the Middle French and thus mirror, after a fashion, the efforts of Foulechat himself. At times perhaps, in our translation as in his, the meaning may get lost in the shuffle, since like sums of words do not necessarily add up to like sums of meaning. There are also times when the original French translation obviously runs afoul of the Latin, and it is plain enough that the translator has not always understood his text. This is particularly true where the original *Policraticus* lapses into allusion, as in quotations from classical authors woven into the textual fabric. In all such instances we have followed Foulechat, not John of Salisbury, for it has not been our intention to give a new translation of the *Policraticus* (however desirable this may be),[19] but a translation *of a translation*, as a guide to a Middle French text.

8.11. Des molestés et des charges de mariages selon saint Jerome et selon les autres philosophes; et de la fauseté de luxure; et de la foy de la femme de Ephese et de ses semblables

Si comme sobrieté est nécessaire es disners, tout aussi mesure et attrempance est necessaire en toutes choses. Car c'est certain que a personne saoule et remplie vient luxure, et de luxure vient ordure et plusseurs autres viltéz. Et de ces choses ici ne s'ensuit riens fors que doleur de repentance (et est[20] faite grant courtoisie aus pleurans se leur repentance est d'aucun fruit). Dont il me semble que le cuer et l'entendement est bien hebeté et bien avugle qui tient l'opinion que parfaite delectacion ne puet estre diffinie sanz acomplir la luxure, si comme l'en dit que Epicurus a tenue ceste opinion. Mais quelconques gruiment ou vilain cri icés truies si getent, je ne croy point que ceste opinion ait pleu a quelconques philosophe, tant est vilaine et orde; et je croi[21] que elle ne pleust onques a Epicure, qui fu si grant entre les philosophes que il ot grans escoles et grant suite. Et si comme racompte Seneque, plusseurs choses[22] nobles sont faites et venues de li que l'en puet trouver et veoir legierement et souvent estre dites et racontees des philosophes, et bien clerement expres[247c]ses et mises bien et ordenees ou livre qui est appellé *Des traces des philosophes* ou *De l'enseignement des philosophes*. La sentence Silvain[23] l'ancien veillart—et a miex lire, la fole opinion et forsennerie de li, car il fu plus rude et bestial que n'estoit l'asne qui le portoit— si se y acordoit aucunement et mauvestié le traioit a ce dire. Et par aventure les ficcions des paiens monstrent aucunement celle opinion en soy y acordant, quant il racomptent le viellart tout plain de vin et tout boullant (pris de Lotide plus et par dessus les autres, s'acordans a nature et reposans leurs corps traveilliéz); et lequel viellart fu finablement rappellé et ramené de son asne et enseignié de son rude cri, au ris et a la mocquerie de toutes gens, pour ce que ne l'aage ne honte le pooit refrener fors que son asne.

Toute delectacion de luxure doncques est laide, fors que celle qui est excusee par le lien de mariage: quar par le benefice du congié donné par mariage, elle muce tout ce qui puet tourner a honte. Et pour ce noz sages anciens ont dit que noces estoient dites de «nuer», car elles mucent aussi come souz une nue oscure les secréz honteus par la vertu du congié de la loy, si comme dit Nonius Marcellus. La coustume aussi est ja passee par lonc usage que ceulz que l'auctorité[24] de l'Eglise joint en mariage charnel si soient mis souz le voile et le poile de l'autel, ou souz[25] ·i· autre institué de l'Eglise, afin que le lit qui par l'ordenance de Jhesu Crist est institué au mariage si cuevre et muce le fait de fragilité par la foy de chasteté, et que il soit innocent et ne sente rien de chose honteuse ne laide. La sont portéz

On the Ills and Burdens of Marriage According to Saint Jerome and Other Philosophers; on the Deceptions of Lust; and of the Fidelity of the Ephesian Woman and Her Like

As sobriety is necessary at table, so are moderation and temperance required in all things. For it is certain that those who are sated and stuffed are prone to sensuality, and that lechery and other such filth follows upon sensuality, and upon such things as these there follows nothing but the pangs of remorse (yet great blessings are bestowed upon penitents if their remorse bear fruit). Hence I believe that the hearts and minds of those who hold that the heights of pleasure cannot be attained without sensuality must be either stunned or blind, as perhaps was the case of Epicurus, who is said to have held this doctrine. But however the swine[68] may grunt and grovel in the vileness of their cries, I cannot believe that so unworthy and lowly an opinion ever found favor with any philosopher, and thus profess that it found none with Epicurus, who was such a noted philosopher that he founded a school and attracted many followers. Seneca relates[69] that several worthy opinions were first held by him; they can easily be found among the different sayings of the philosophers who took them up, and are plainly set forth with methodical treatment in the work entitled *The Footprints* (or *Teachings*) *of the Philosophers*.[70] It was rather the aged dotard Silvanus[71] who held this opinion—which it were better to term prejudice or madness—, for he was more of a brute or beast than the ass who bore him, and it was out of wickedness that he came to profess such things. Perchance this is what pagan myth seeks to express when it portrays the old man as a drunkard full of wine and lust, more easily taken with Lotis than were the others (who were, according to the dictates of nature, resting their weary bodies), for in the end this dotard was recalled to reason and taken to task by the raucous braying of his ass, so that he whom neither age nor shame could restrain was finally halted by a jackass, and held up to ridicule by all.

All delight in sensuality is therefore vile, except where condoned by the bond of marriage, since the privilege of the wedded state allows dissimulation of all that might redound to shame. Thus did the sages of old set forth that "nuptials" derived from "nebulous," since the privilege granted by law conceals as beneath a heavy cloud the secrets of shame, as Nonius Marcellus[72] has said. A venerable custom further prescribes that those whom the authority of the Church has joined in human marriage are clothed by the altar veil or by such a veil as the Church may provide,[73] so that the marriage bed, consecrated by the authority of Jesus Christ, may cover and conceal human weakness through the law of modesty, so that purity remain firm

tortiz, chandelles brandans touz [247*d*] ardans devant le lit, car le double lit qui est paré pour les noces—et non pas pour acomplir la delectacion de luxure ne par ardeur charnelle, mes par honneste consentement de bonne et pure volenté des parties—, ycelui lit est ennobli de la biauté du bien de mariage. Car Himeneus si aime la lumiere et le lie la harpe o instrumens;[26] et l'enfant qui atise au feu[27] convoiteux la larrecineuse et secrete flambe, si quiert clotéz et angles pour soy mucier.

Et combien que la couple[28] de mariage soit honneste et profitable, toutes-voies il y a plus de tristece que de lieesce. Car la femme si enfante a grant doleur, et point ne fait fruit que l'amertume ne aille par avant ou ne l'ensuive. Car Valerius racompte que un jenne homme demanda a Socrates lequel par son conseil il feroit: ou se il espouseroit femme, ou se il se tendroit de en espouser quelconque. Et Socrates li respondi, «aussi comme un respons terrien de humaine sapience, que quelconque partie il prist il en feroit penitence. Et dit de l'un faire—c'est dire, se tu ne prens femme—, "tu demourras tout seul, tu seras orphelin, ton linage faudra et un estrange sera ton hoir et prendra ton heritage; et se tu fais l'autre—que tu pregnes femme—, tu auras pardurable sollicitude et cure, un fessel de complaintes, reproche de douaire, male chiere de tes affins et parens, femme genglerresse, langue qui determinera des autres mariages,[29] incertaine fortune de tes enfans." Et pas ne s'accorde que le jenne homme en telle multitude de choses aspres fist eleccion de si perilleuse chose».

Toute la compaiginie des philosophes si se acorde ensuivant droite philosophie, et chante en telle maniere [248*a*] que se il y a personne qui redoubte la rigueur de la crestienne religion, si apreigne chasteté a l'exemple[30] des paiens. Et je ne veul pas blasmer la chasteté de mariage, mais combien que le nombre de ·100· et de ·60· si vieigne de la racine de ·30·, toutes-voies je ne veul pas pour ce comparer le fruit ·100me· et le fruit ·60e· au fruit ·30e·, qui est donné aus mariés. Zeno, Epitectus, Aristote, Crittolaus et plusseurs des Epicures, si comme l'en a escript, si ont baillié et publié ceste sentence a leurs successeurs. Et selon le tesmoing saint Jerome, l'en raconte ou livre *Des noces* que Aureolus Theophrasti demande «se c'est bon que homme qui est sage preigne femme a espouse».[31] Et quant il ot diffini et determiné en disant que se elle estoit belle et de bonnes meurs et de honnestes parens, et se l'omme estoit sain et riche, par telle voie ces choses trouvees, que le sage homme se pooit bien marier, il y ajousta tantost aprés: et certes, dist il, toutes ces choses se pooient a paine trouver toutes ensemble, et pour ce donques le sage homme ne doit point espouser femme. Pour ce premierement que l'estude de philosophie en seroit empeeschie, et que aussi personne ne puet entendre ensemble aus livres et a sa femme; et que plusseurs choses sont que il faut as femmes pour leur usage, comme sont robes precieuses, or, argent, pierres precieuses, despens, coustanges,

and neither shame nor disgrace burst forth. For flaming torches are brought out and candles displayed before the couch, as the twofold bed of marriage decked out for wedlock, not for lecherous pleasure or the fulfillment of carnal delight, but to honor the lawful consent and pure faith of the parties' troth: such is the bed graced by the beauty of the marital state. For Hymen so loves the light and joins in harps and instruments, and Cupid, who fans the secret and furtive flames of desire, seeks out nooks and crannies in which to hide.[74]

And although the conjugal state is decent and useful, yet it contains more sadness than joy. For the woman gives birth in great pain,[75] and there is no issue that is not preceded or followed by bitterness. Thus Valerius Maximus[76] tells us of the youth who asked Socrates for advice on the matter of taking a wife or refraining from doing so. "And Socrates, like an earthly oracle of human wisdom, replied that whatever choice he made, he would repent of it. For he said that on the one hand—that is, should you not take a wife—'you will live alone, with no family; your line will die out and a stranger to your family will be your heir and take possession of your estate. If, on the other hand, you do take a wife, you will endure eternal anguish and worry, complaints by the bushel, reproaches for her dowry, ungracious conduct toward your friends and relatives, a gossiping woman, discussion of other people's households, and uncertainty as to what will come of your children.' And therefore he is of the opinion that in the face of all these adversities, one should not elect so dangerous a course."

The entire chorus of philosophers, of one accord with right thinking, chants in unison that, if anyone fear the strictness of the Christian faith, he should learn chastity from the example of the pagans.[77] Not that I would take it upon myself to condemn the purity of marriage; still, although the yield of a hundred or sixty both stem from the root of thirty, I cannot compare a hundredfold or sixtyfold with the yield of thirty which is accorded to the wedded.[78]

Zeno, Epictetus, Aristotle, Critolaus, and several of the Epicureans, as it is written,[79] professed this doctrine and established it to be kept among their followers. It is further related, according to Saint Jerome, that Aureolus put the question to Theophrastus[80] "as to whether or not it is a good thing for the sage to take a wife. Having made qualifications and reservations to the effect that, 'if she is beautiful, of good conduct and a reputable family, and if the man himself is healthy and rich, under such circumstances a wise man may well marry'; he added immediately thereafter: 'yet since it is hardly possible to meet all these conditions at one and the same time, the sage would do better not to take a wife. First of all, the study of philosophy must suffer, since no one can look at the same time to both a wife and books. Again, there are many things with which women must be provided, such

damoiselles, divers paremens et riches couvertures, littieres, mesnages dorés; et puis tout au lonc de la nuit gengleries et diverses demandes. Dont elle dira: "Celle la s'en va par les rues moult hautement paree; celle la est honnoree de toutes gens et [248b] en toute la compaignie des femmes: je sui la plus chaitive et plus despitee! Pour quoy regardiez vous au jour d'ui tant nostre voisine? Que avez vous tant parlé a nostre chamberiere? Que m'avez vous au jour d'ui aporté du marchié?" Nous ne poons avoir un bon ami; nous ne poons trouver loyal compaignie. Et briefment elle souppeçonne tout estre contre soy et repute l'amour que elle pense sur l'autre femme estre sa propre haine. Se il a en chascune cité un tres sage doctor, il te dira tantost que nous ne poons nostre femme laissier, et si ne poons trop grant fessel porter.

»C'est forte chose de povre femme nourir; et riche femme souffrir si est trop grief tourment. Et y adjouste[32] que de prendre femme n'a point de eleccion, mais doit l'en prendre telle femme comme au devant venra. Car se elle est haineuse et noiserresse—ou fole, ou laide, ou ourgeilleuse, ou puante, ou de quelconque autre vice entachiee—, nous ne le[33] sarons jusques après les noces. Mais un cheval, ·i· asne, ·i· beuf, un chien et toutes viles choses—robes, chaudieres,[34] banc, huches, escrins, pos, henaps— sont premierement esprouvéz et puis achatéz: et la femme est musciee et non esprouvee, afin que elle ne desplaise avant que on l'espouse.

»On la doit tout temps regarder en la face et loer sa biauté, afin que se tu regardes une autre, elle ne cuide que elle desplaise.[35] On la doit appeller dame, et li doit on faire feste le jour de sa nativité,—et doit l'en jurer par son sauvement, et desirer que elle vive longuement, honnorer la nourrice et celle qui la porta. L'en doit prisier et amer son varlet, son serjant, son perrain, son escuier bel et cointe et sa jolive damoi[248c]selle, et le procureur jolis et bien pignié, et l'escuier chastré et esbarbé qui la sert hors bouté pour longuement garder sa luxure et plus seurement maintenir, et touz les autres soulz lesquiex pour leurs noms et leurs offices les avoultres et les ribaux prennent leur titre et l'occasion de leur luxure muscier. Et brievement touz ceulz que elle aura amé ou amera, combien que il soient malgracieux, il les faut loer et amer.

»Se tu li bailles et commés toute ta maison a gouverner, l'en doit servir a son plaisir. Et se tu gardes et reserves aucune chose pour en faire ton plaisir, elle dira que tu n'auras point fiance en lui et s'en prendra a toy hair et toy tencier; et se tu ne t'en avises, elle t'appareillera venin. Se tu entroduis en ton hostel aucune veille ou aucun orfevre ou enchanteur ou marcheant de pierres precieuses, de draps de soie, de jouaux ou de robes, tout ce sera en peril de chasteté[36] perdre; et se tu ne les veulz introduire, tu li feras injure en donnant souppeçon.

»Mais pourquoi doit l'en baillier garde a femme? Car se elle est ribaude,

as expensive clothing, gold, silver, precious gems, allowances, expenses, servants, bedclothes and other such covers, litters, or furniture inlaid with gold. And then, all night long they nag and make all kinds of demands. She will say for example: 'So-and-so goes out decked in the best of finery; so-and-so is admired by everyone and looked up to by all the women there are, while I am the poorest and most neglected of all! Why were you looking so intently at the woman next door? Why did you talk so long with our maidservant? What did you bring me home from the market today?' We cannot have a close friend; we cannot keep good company. The long and the short of it is that she suspects everyone is against her, and believes that the love she thinks another woman enjoys means so much scorn for herself. If you find a learned man in any city, he will tell you it is impossible for us to do without our wives, yet we cannot bear so great a burden as to stay with them.

"It is a difficult thing to provide for a poor wife, and insufferable pain to put up with a rich one." He adds that "there is no point in choosing a wife at all, but that you should simply take the first one that comes along. For if she is ill-tempered and nagging—or mad, or ugly, or proud, or mean, or a prey to any other vice—we learn of it only after the ceremony. A horse, an ass, an ox, a dog, all articles for ordinary use—clothing, cauldrons, benches, chests, coffers, pots, goblets—are first tried and then purchased: but a woman is not shown or tried out, so that she not displease before marriage.

"You must constantly gaze upon her features and praise her beauty, so that she not find herself ugly, should you chance to gaze upon another. You must not forget to call her 'My Lady,' or to celebrate her birthday—you have to swear by her salvation and wish her long life, revere her nurse and her who bore her. You have to hold in esteem and affection her boy, her servant, her godfather, her squire so elegant and handsome and her cavorting handmaiden, her lusty majordomo with his neatly combed hair, and the castrated squire with the clean chin who serves her from afar, keeping her senses safely and durably aroused, as well as all the others who find an opportunity in their titles and duties to conceal the lechery of adulterers or fornicators. In short, you must praise and love all those who have found or may find favor with her, however repugnant they may be.

"Should you entrust her the charge of directing your household, you must of needs serve at her pleasure. And should you keep anything at your own disposal, she will say you have no confidence in her, and set to hating and scolding you; if you are not wary enough, she will soon be brewing poison. Should you bring into the house any old merchant, or a goldsmith, a magician or some vendor of precious stones, silks, jewelry or clothing, it will all be at the risk of her chastity; should you however refuse their admittance, she will find insult in your suspicions.

on ne la puet garder, et se elle est chaaste, elle se gardera bien. Et vraiement la garde de chasteté est neccessité de pou de fiance; et a proprement parler, la femme est vraiement chaste qui a eu grant occasion et pooir de pechier et point n'a pechié.

»Belle femme est tantost amee et convoitiee; et laide femme legierement convoite et s'enflambe moult tost. Et c'est fort de garder ce que plusseurs aiment; et c'est tres grief tourment de tenir ce que nul ne daigne avoir. Mais toutesvoies a mendre meschief l'en tient la laide, que l'en ne garde la belle, pour ce que rien [248d] n'est seur ou les desirs de tout le peuple souspirent. Car l'un l'atrait pour sa biauté, l'autre par biau langage, l'autre par son engin, l'autre par courtoisie: et ainssi on la sollicite et assaut de toutes pars, et par aucune maniere est gaaignié le chastel qui est de toutes pars assailli.

»Et se pour le bon gouvernement[37] de l'ostel et la dispensacion des biens, et les esbatemens et soulas d'aucune langueur et pour eschiver vie solitaire aucun prent femme, certes je di que un loyal serjant gouverne trop miex l'ostel et plus sagement despense les biens et obeist a l'auctorité du seigneur, que ne fait la femme,—qui se tient en l'ostel pour dame et qui contre la volenté du seigneur fera ce que il li plaist, et non pas ce qui li est commandé. Les amis puent plus assister et mieux acompagnier le seigneur se il est malade—et par especial ceulz qui sont obligiéz par les benefices receuz et les varléz néz en l'ostel—que la femme qui nous imputes lermes et qui pour l'esperance de l'eritage[38] si vent son ordure et qui, en soy vantant de sa diligence, si trouble le cuer du malade jusques a desesperance. Et se elle est aucunement deshaistiee, il couvient[39] estre malade avec li, et nullement soy departir de son lit ne de sa compaignie.

»Et se il avient que la femme est bonne et douce et soueve—laquelle chose n'avient pas souvent, car c'est ·i· oysel chier et estrange et que l'en treuve a tart—, il couvient[40] pleurer quant elle enfante; et se elle meure, il faut souffrir tourment.

»Selon la verité, le sage ne puet onques estre seul. Car il a avec li touz ceulz qui sont qui onques furent bons, et si [249a] transporte son cuer franc quelconques part il veult. Et la chose qu'il ne puet faire par force de corps, il acomplist par sa prudence et supplie par son engin. Et se compaignie d'ommes li faut, il parlera a Dieu. Il ne sera onques moins seul que il est quant il est tout seul.

»Certes prendre femme pour avoir ligniee—ou pour cause que le linage ne tourne a noient, ou pour cause d'avoir aide et confort en temps de viellesce et d'avoir certains hoirs et améz—, si est chose tres sotte. Que avons nous a faire quant nous sommes mors et quant nous nous departons de ce monde, se un autre est appellé de nostre nom, puis que le filz ne raporte pas si tost le nom du pere et il en y a plusseurs et sans nombre qui portent tel nom? Et quelz confors et aides de viellesce est ce de nourrir en son hostel celi

"Yet what boots it to put a woman under guard? If she is lecherous, there will be no guarding her; if she is chaste, she will guard herself. The obligation to protect chastity is indeed of doubtful issue, and at bottom, she is truly chaste who does not sin when she is given all power and opportunity to do so.

"A beautiful woman readily inspires love and desire; an ugly one is filled with her own desire and easily surrenders to passion. Difficult it is to protect what many desire, but it is grievous torment indeed to guard what none deign possess. Still there is less damage done in keeping an ugly woman than in protecting a beautiful one, for nothing can be safely guarded when the entire population is panting with desire. One man will attract her by his handsomeness, the other by his elegant speech, the next one by his intelligence, still another by his fine manners. She will thus be attacked and solicited on all sides, and a fortress besieged on all fronts will always be taken, one way or another.

"And if you would take a wife to govern your household and disburse your wealth, or for pleasure, or for care in sickness or to avoid a solitary life, I must admit that a faithful servant will better administer the household, tend to expenses, and obey the will of the master than any wife can do. For a wife imagines herself the master and will do as she pleases, rather than following orders and doing as she is told. When the master is sick, friends are better suited to help him and keep him company—especially those obligated by past benefits and the youths born in the house—than a woman, who will serve you up with tears, selling yourself in hopes of an inheritance, and who, glorying in her solicitude, will perturb the spirits of her sick husband and drive him to despair. Should however she herself fall out of sorts, we must be sick along with her, and constantly remain by her bedside to keep her company.

"If however the wife is a good, sweet, and loving one—a most infrequent occurrence and a rare, costly, and exotic bird indeed [81]—you must still weep at the pangs of her labor, and should she die, bear heavy grief.

"But in truth the wise man is never alone. For he has in his company all who ever were just, and his free spirit may err wherever he will. If his physical force prove unequal to some task, he can accomplish it through wisdom and compensate with his mind. Should ever the company of men fail him, he can converse with God. Never will he be less alone than when he is all alone. [82]

"To take a wife for the sake of offspring—either to keep your line from dying out or for aid and comfort in time of old age or for the sake of true and cherished heirs—surely this is utter folly. What good is it when we are dead and have departed this world if someone bears our name, especially since sons need not immediately take the name of their father, and when many

qui par aventure mourra avant que le viel homme, ou qui sera de tres fausse nature et tres mauvaises meurs, ou qui par aventure quant il sera venu a perfait aage, il li sera grief que son viel pere vive si longuement? Il n'est si bons hoirs ne si certains comme les amis et prochains, lesquiex tu esliras par bon jugement; et miex valent pour toy que ceulz que, veulles ou ne veulles, il escouvient qu'il soient tes hoirs, et a ce tu es contraint et tenu de souffrir. Et combien que ton heritage soit certain tant comme tu es en vie et que tu en pues bien user, toutesvoies il faut que celi meismes que tu as aquis, tu laisses en non certains usages.

»Ces paroles dit Theophrastus, et plusseurs autres semblables,—les- quelles sont souffisans pour declairier les povretés et miseres de la grant douceur des mari[249b]ages.»

L'en raconte que P. Clodius si dist que pour ce qu'il avoit malcourtoise- ment accusé Neptunus qui avoit la seconde foiz trebuchié et plungié sa nef en la mer et cassee, il respondi: «Et ne seroit ce pas plus noblement dit de celui que malcourtoisement il blasme et argue Luxure comme adversaire, et prent et espouse la seconde femme?» Et qui sera celui qui ara pitié de l'ome qui est une fois deslié des liens et puis aprés retourne pour estre lié de chaiennes? Vraiement celui est bien nondigne de l'onneur de franchise et de repos avoir, qui retourne au servage et au truage et misere duquel il s'est getté. Dont je dis que celui est semblable aus monstres et figmens, qui se donne le nom non pas seulement de philosophe, mais qui plus est, de religion, et s'attribue saintité et si ne puet estre refrené et ne se puet tenir d'embracemens[41] et compagnie de femmes.

Il avient souvent que aucuns, avant qu'il facent profession en religion ou en philosophie—et ainsi parlé je pour veoir se religion et philosophie sont choses diverses, pour ce que personne ne puet droitement estre fait philo- sophe sanz tenir religion—, il est doncques que celui dessus dit a vescu par avant tres chastement; et quant il est promeu a aucun degré et est mis a repos, il prent le premier et le souverain point de toute son estude en eslire belle femme et la prendre pour soy, ou—qui pis vault—de considerer les mariages d'entour li et de damoiseller les jennes femmes d'entour li[42] et les prier et traire a son plaisir, et sanz quelconques honte les traire a pechié.

Et aucunesfoiz[43] la deshontee ardeur de femme s'esmeut et passe route. Car aussi comme escript Hero[249c]dotus, «quant femme despoille sa robe elle despoille toute honte»; elle se met avant et se embat et desordene, baude et hardie, sanz honte, en la face du pueple raysonnable et honteus; et la elle revelle et desnue tous les secréz du noble lit de mariage[44] et se com- plaint de la froidure de son mari et allegue cause souffisant et clere que elle doit estre departie de tel mariage. Car homme imparfait et qui n'est que demi homme, et qui n'est prest de faire fais de mariage et de nature, n'est pas profitable ne souffisant a mariage: ainçois est indigne de femme avoir. Et

and numerous are those who bear the selfsame name! What aid and comfort is it in old age when the child brought up in our household dies before his aging father, or if he is of mean character or criminal in his conduct, or if—when he is come of age—he should find it grievous that his old father live so long? No better nor more dependable heirs can be found than friends and acquaintances chosen by your own good judgment: they will do better by you than those who are heirs whether you want them or not, and whom you are obliged and constrained to tolerate. So long as you are alive and can tend wisely to your estate, so long will it be safe: still you must leave to uncertainty whatever you have acquired."

Such and similar are the words of Theophrastus, which should suffice to recount what calamities and misery lie in the bliss of marriage.

It is told of P. Claudius that, having arrogantly accused Neptune of twice capsizing, wrecking, and sinking his ship,[83] he retorted: "And would not they more rightly be called arrogant, who take lust to task as their enemy, while going off to marry a second wife?" Who indeed would take pity on the man who, once liberated from his bonds, returns to be set again in chains? Truly unworthy of the honor of freedom and peace is he who returns to slavery, accepting the tribute of misery he has just thrown off. I must therefore hold that the man is rather a monster or a freak who not only calls himself a philosopher but—proclaiming himself holy—claims to be a man of religion while remaining incapable of containing himself or resisting the embraces of women and foregoing their company.

It often happens that a man, before taking vows of religion and philosophy—for I hold it true that although religion and philosophy are not one and the same thing, no one can rightly become a philosopher without religion—it happens then that such a person often will live chastely for a long time; then, when promoted to some high estate and a life of leisure, he will make the first and foremost aim of all his efforts to have some beautiful woman as his own. Or, worse still, he will survey the marriages around him and court young women on all sides, soliciting them and impressing them in his pleasures, and, without the slightest hint of shame, drag them down to sin.

It also happens at times that the shameless lust of women breaks forth and runs amok. For Herodotus writes:[84] "A woman who removes her clothing also removes all shame." She will strut around with no decency, immodest and provocative, divest of all retinue, before a sober and modest throng. There will she reveal and unclothe all the secrets of the marriage bed, complaining that her husband is frigid and alleging this due and sufficient cause to free her from wedlock, for an imperfect man is only half a man, and he who cannot accomplish the conjugal work of nature is useless and inadequate in marriage; indeed he is unworthy of having a wife. One

certes Goffroy de Villeher, mon familier, en confondi une foiz la hardiesce de une telle et en tel cas tres noblement. Car on li avoit baillié en patron de par le juge pour ordener la departie et la dessevrance[45] du mariage—si comme l'en pensoit a faire—, et la femme belle et gracieuse en la presence de ses amis qui estoient pour li et li aidoient, et un advocat, afin que elle exposast et declairast miex les circumstances de la cause. Le sage homme li demanda se elle avoit onques eu autre mari; et elle dit que non. Et lors il li demanda se elle estoit vierge, en li disant qu'il estoit de neccessité de savoir ce point et que on le devoit demander, afin que le juge ne la prist a paroles par aucune occasion. Et elle l'afferma toute honteuse pour ce que on ne la crooit pas bien. Et aprés il li demanda se il avoient eu de coustume de dormir ensemble, et s'entrebaisier et entrebracier; et elle recognut que oyl et que ainsi estoit. Et lors le patron li demanda en disant: «Et tres douce vierge, tres sage et tres chaaste et tres honteuse, dont [249d] vient ce que ton mari n'a acompli ce fait de mariage avec toy et n'a paié les drois de mariage? Qui t'a apris quelle chose est le fait charnel de l'omme avec femme, quant tu dis maintenant que entre tant de baisiers et de embrace-mens il n'a point eu a faire a toy, et t'a eu tant de foiz a son plaisir et t'a manié ton corps si comme il a voulu par le congié de mariage? Car c'est cer-taine chose que aucunes bestes sont qui en soy entrebaisant, il cognoissent l'une l'autre et conçoivent; et les autres en soy un petit touchant, il conçoi-vent; et aucunes sont qui par l'ardeur de leur chaleur sont emprainses[46] et conçoivent de l'attrempance de l'air et font fruit de leur espece.» Et celle damoiselle fu finablement esbahie en disant seulement, toute honteuse, que elle n'avoit chose que elle sceust dire a ces arguments. Mais au jour d'ui la besoigne se porte bien et courtoisement avec les philosophes, c'est a dire avec les clers, car l'en ne treuve entre eulz nul froit, ou qui soit semons ne appellé devant juge pour telle tache.

Ciceron fu prié que quant il ot repudié Terence, il espousast la suer Hircius. Et il n'en voult rien faire, et dit qu'il ne pooit mettre son entente a femme et a philosophie ensemble.

La femme de Phelippe le roy de Macedoine, contre lequel les dittéz De-mostenes si crient, une fois ainsi comme elle estoit courrouciee et yceli Phelippe le roy entroit[47] en sa chambre pour dormir comme il avoit de cous-tume, elle courrouciee le bouta et enchaça hors de sa chambre, et li ferma l'uis. Et quant il se vit ainsi exclus et hors bouté, il se tust et se reconforta et passa son injure par une chançon et la dissimula.[250a]

Un retheur appellé Gargias si composa un tres biau livre de concorde et pais et d'amistié du peuple qui par devant estoit a descort, et le recita en commun, devant le peuple assemblé pour veoir les jeux de Jupiter. Et un sien adversaire appellé Melancius li reprocha en disant: «Cesti ci nous chante son livre de concorde, qui onques ne pot ensamble acorder ·iii· per-

of my acquaintances, Godfrey of Hérouville,[85] once confuted quite properly the brazenness of such a woman in a case of this sort. The judge had in fact appointed him executor in the separation and annulment of a marriage—and they were proceeding with this intent. The wife, all beauty and grace, was attended by friends who had come to serve as witnesses, and a lawyer as well, so that she might expose and explain as best she could the circumstances of her case. Counsel, a man of experience, asked if she had ever had another husband; she replied in the negative. Then he asked if she were a virgin, explaining it was necessary to be informed on this point and that if he did not bring it up, the judge might find occasion to take her to task. She then affirmed she was, not without embarrassment, since no one was disposed to believe her. Then he asked if it was their habit to sleep in one bed, to kiss and caress each other. She answered in the affirmative, admitting it was so. Then counsel asked her, saying, "My sweet young maiden, so prudent, chaste, and modest, how can it be that your husband has not performed the act of marriage with you and paid the conjugal debt? Who has taught you the nature of carnal knowledge between a man and a woman, when you maintain straight off that with all this kissing and caressing he never did anything with you, having you so often at his disposal and at his will to do with you as he cared, according to the dispositions of marriage? For it is well established that certain animals know each other and conceive by kissing; that others conceive by touching each other ever so lightly; that still others are impregnated by the heat of their own desire and conceive by the warmth of the air, producing thus the offspring of their species." At this point the young lady was confounded and could only admit with embarrassment that she had nothing to reply to such arguments. But nowadays it's all for the best with philosophers—that is to say with clerics—for there is not a frigid man among them, nor anyone who could be hauled before the judge for a vice of this kind!

Cicero[86] was entreated, upon his repudiation of Terentia, to marry the sister of Hirtius. But he would have none of it, saying that he could not attend to both a wife and philosophy.

The wife of Philip,[87] the king of Macedonia impugned in the writings of Demosthenes, fell angry one evening when the aforementioned Philip came into the chamber as usual to go to bed, and driving him out of the room, locked the door. Reflecting on the way he had been driven away and shut out, he said nothing, taking comfort in a quotation from a tragedy, and glossing over the offense.

A rhetorician by the name of Gorgias[88] wrote for the people, who had been up to that time in conflict, an excellent book on peace, concord, and friendship, reading it aloud before the entire population assembled to see the Olympic games. One of his enemies, Melanthius by name, rebuked

sonnes: soy, sa femme et sa chamberiere.» Car sa femme avoit tres grant envie sur sa chamberiere, pour ce que elle estoit moult belle; et son mari estoit tres chastes hons, si ne cessoit de tencier puis l'un puis l'autre. Et pour ce afin que envie cesse et que l'en ait pais en mariage, les riches gens ont de coustume de non avoir en leur hostel plus belle femme que la leur.

Une foiz Socrates voult accorder ·ii· femmes qui s'entretençoient. Et finablement elles tournerent toute la tempeste sur li et l'assaillirent. Et lors il s'en fui et elles le suivirent moult longuement en tençant, et après elles getterent sur li leur orine de la fenestre du solier ou elles demouroient.

Les aucteurs ont escript plusseurs choses de la chaitive legereté des femmes. Et par aventure plusseurs faussetéz en sont controuvees, mais ce n'est pas que pour ce aucunesfoiz ne die[48] l'en bien voir en riant et en moquant et en fables, lesquelles aucunes foiz[49] philosophie ne deffent pas: l'en dit bien aucunes choses[50] qui pourroient aidier et nuire aus bonnes meurs. Par ces choses il appert comment elles aiment legierement et comment elles heent a petite occasion et combien tost elles oublient leur amour. Et souventesfoiz[51] toute nature oubliee, elles s'arment contre leur filz et aucunesfoiz contre leur cuer et leur corps. [250b] Aucunes sont tres chaastes, ja soit ce que un courtois chanteur si dist[52] que «c'est ·i· oysel que l'on treuve a tart sur terre, et que autant en est comme de cines noirs» qui soient de parfaite et esprouvee chaasté. Un chanteur de dittiéz si dit qu'il n'est femme si chaaste qui ne soit ardant et eschaufee de longue luxure jusques a forsener.

Petronius racompte que une matrone fu en Ephese, et de si noble chasteté et de si honneste renommee que les femmes de tout le pays d'entour la desiroient a veoir. Ceste dame, quant son mari fu mort, elle ne fu pas contente de poursuivre le corps selon la commune maniere, mes les cheveux destreciéz et espenduz et melléz, et la robe deciree et le piz descouvert devant le peuple, elle poursuivi le corps jusques au sepulcre. Et quant il fu mis ou tombel et mucié selon la maniere des Grex, elle se prist[53] a le garder et le pleurer jours et nuis, en soy si tourmentant come celle qui par mesaise pourchace sa mort, ne ses parens ne la pooient oster ne faire departir, ne autres gens; et les princes et les maistres après y vindrent, mais il n'i firent rien. Et la povre femme toute pleurant come femme de singuliere exemple et que le peuple plaignoit tres grandement, si fu la jusques au ·ve· jour[54] sanz viande prendre; et sa tres loyale chamberiere estoit avecques elle et plouroit avec sa maistresse, et toutes fois que la lumiere que elles avoient portee au tombel failloit, elle la renouvelloit. Et de ce couroit une fable par toute la cité que la seule et vraie exemple d'amour et de chasteté avoit en ce fait noblement resplendi, et les gens de touz estaz le disoient et tesmoin[250c]gnoient.

Et en ce temps l'empereour commenda a pendre[55] touz les larrons de la province en telle robe comme le dit mort estoit ou sepulcre, que celle femme

him, saying, "Here is a man who declaims his book on peace, yet has been quite incapable of establishing harmony among three individuals: himself, his wife, and the maid." His wife was in fact extremely jealous of the maid, a most beautiful woman, and even though her husband was of irreproachable conduct, they could never leave off their quarreling. And so, to put an end to jealousy and promote domestic peace, it has become the custom among the rich to have no woman in the house more beautiful than the wife.

It happened that Socrates [89] attempted to reconcile two women who were quarreling with each other. But they ended up directing their fury against him and fell upon him together. He took flight, and they pursued him hotly, screaming all the while. They finally drenched him with urine thrown down from the window of the upper story where they lived.

Ancient authors have written at length on the deplorable fickleness of women. And although it may be that much of it is pure invention, this does not mean that truth cannot be expressed in laughter,[90] satire, or allegory: philosophy does not condemn such writing, for many things so expressed can influence morals, for better or for worse. Such works clearly demonstrate that women are easily moved to love, that their hatred is aroused at the slightest provocation, and that their love is quick to die. At times, mindless of nature, they will wreak violence upon their children, or even upon their own souls and bodies. Some of them are chaste, but as a gentleman poet[91] puts it, those whose chastity is tried and true are birds rarely found in this world, and as plentiful as the black swan. A dramatic poet[92] further states that there exists no woman so chaste as cannot be driven out of her mind by the flames of persistent desire.

Petronius tells us of a woman who lived at Ephesus,[93] whose irreproachable chastity and reputation for modesty were such that women flocked from all around to see her. When her husband died, this woman was not content to follow the bier in the ordinary manner, but with her hair disheveled, tangled, and torn, her clothes tattered and her breast bared for all to see, she accompanied her husband to the grave. And when he had been entombed and covered with earth according to the manner of the Greeks, she began watching over him night and day, weeping and tormenting herself as one who would die of grief. Neither family nor others could remove her or turn her away, and though princes and lords also came, they met with no greater success. The poor woman remained there for five days, taking no nourishment, giving singular witness to her grief and eliciting from all the utmost pity. Her faithful maid accompanied her, weeping at one with her lady, and every time the lamp they brought with them would die out, she would light it anew. The news spread throughout the town how this unique and veritable paragon of love and chastity had so nobly shown forth, and people from all estates talked and bore witness to the fact.

plouroit tant. Lors la nuit prochaine, le chevalier qui gardoit les penduz si
vint veoir que nul homme peust venir aus penduz pour oster aucun mort:
si apperçut entre les sepulcres une lumiere clerement resplendissant et vint
veoir que c'estoit. Si oÿ le cri et les pleurs de celle femme, et lors il con-
voita—selon le vice de humain desir—a savoir qui c'estoit et que elle faisoit
la; si descendi aval vers la fosse et vit une tres belle femme. Et adonques
troublé et esbahi aussi come se ce fust un monstre ou aucun esperit d'enfer
qui eust pris corps de femme, il s'arresta, et quant il vit et aperçut le corps [56]
gisant et les lermes de la plourant et la face toute desciree de ses ongles,
considerant ce qui estoit en verité que celle femme ne pooit porter le grant
desir et la doleur de son mari mort, il s'aprocha d'elle pour la reconforter,
et se prist a preschier et amonnester la femme pleurant. Et li dist que elle
ne pourroit tant perseverer en telle doleur vaine et sanz profit, et que elle
se romproit le chief et le cuer se elle n'i prenoit garde, et que il failloit que
toute personne passast par tel pas et par la mort, qui ainssi dessiroit [57] son
cuer et sa pensee pour noient. Et lors celle femme qui ne cognoissoit le con-
fortant, et aucunement touchiee et ferue, si se prist plus fort a descirer son
pis et arrachier les cheveux et les espandre sur le pis du corps mort. Mais
toutesvoies le chevalier ne s'en departi pas pour ce; ainçois il persevera en
son amonicion et se prist a donner [250*d*] a mengier a celle femme, et tant
que la chamberiere, qui fu prise de la grant oudeur du vin, a la volenté du
priant premierement prist le vin aussi comme a force. Et quant elle ot pris la
viande et le vin, elle commença a blasmer sa dame en disant: «Et quel profit
aurez vous, dame, se vous fendez et tailliez vostre cuer et vostre corps en ·ii·
pieces, se l'en vous ensevelist toute vive, se vous rendez vostre esperit non
condampné avant que les diex l'appellent ou avant que il aient determiné
vostre mort? "Cuidiez vous que ce que vous faites puisse guerir les mors,
et ceulz qui ja sont tournéz en cendre?" Et, tres chiere dame et douce creature, veulz tu que le mort si revive contre la volenté des dieux? Veulz tu que
tant comme il plaira aus diex et a toy vivre en joie de lumiere, hors mise
et hors boutee ton erreur feminine? Le propre corps du mort te doit amonnester a ce faire et donner volenté de vivre? Il n'est personne qui doie oïr
en desplaisance la priere de prendre sa substance et soustenance se elle veut
vivre.» [58]

Et lors celle femme, traveilliee de celle abstinence de plusseurs jours, si
se mua de la durté de son cuer, et menga aussi fort et ardanment comme
sa chamberiere, qui avoit esté premierement vaincue. Et après, vous savez
quelle chose puet et seult tempter et acompaignier personne saoule! Et pour
ce, de telles paroles douces comme il avoit empetré que celle dame vousist
vivre, il l'assailli de son corps avoir a plaisir. Et ce jennes homs ne sembloit pas lait a celle dame, ainçois li sembloit bel et bien parlant; et aussi
la chamberiere li looit grandement et racomptoit ses graces, et li disoit:

Meanwhile, the emperor executed a sentence of hanging on all the thieves in the province where the man this woman so mourned had been buried. The following night, the soldier appointed to guard the corpses came to make certain that no one would approach the gallows and carry off any of the dead. He noticed among the tombs a light shining brightly and came to see what it was. Hearing the women crying and sobbing, he was taken—as is only human—with curiosity and, wondering who she was and how she came to be there, climbed down into the vault and fell upon a woman of extreme beauty. Surprised and taken aback, he paused for a moment, fearing it might be some phantom or spirit of the underworld appearing in the shape of a woman. Then his gaze fell upon the corpse lying there, the woman's face all scratched by her nails and flooded with tears; he then realized the simple fact was the woman was in unbearable grief at the death of her husband, and he set about admonishing and consoling her. He told her it was impossible to persevere in such useless and empty mourning, that she would lose her mind and spirits if she did not take care, that it was inevitable for all human beings to suffer the fate of death, and that she was devastating her heart and soul for nothing. Then, somewhat shocked and moved by this man she had never seen come to comfort her, she began rending her breast all the more, tearing out locks of her hair and throwing them on the breast of the corpse. But this did not convince the stranger to leave: rather he continued to admonish her and prevailed upon her to eat. Finally, her maid, vanquished by the fragrance of the wine, surrendered to the offer and accepted first, as against her will, to drink. When she had taken some food and wine, she began rebuking her mistress, saying, "And what good will it do you, My Lady, if you rend your body and soul in two, if they bury you alive, if you surrender before the time allotted you by the gods a soul unclaimed by death? 'Do you believe[94] you can cure the dead and bring back those who have turned to dust?' O sweetest and most beloved of women, would you have the dead revived against the gods' own will? Will you not put off womanly folly and accept to live in the joy of light so long as it please you and the will of the gods? This very corpse instructs you so and admonishes you to love life! There is no one as should be offended at being implored to take food and sustenance, if he would live."

Weakened by several days' abstinence, the woman softened her heart, eating as much and as heartily as the maid, who had been the first to succumb. As for the rest, you well know what temptation comes to those who have fully dined. And so, with that same sweet speech he had used to convince the lady to live, he pressed her to yield her body to his will. As she looked upon the young man, she did not find him entirely displeasing, but handsome and fine-spoken; the maid too praised him greatly and counted his charms, saying to her mistress: "Most noble lady, 'would you

«Et tres gente damoiselle, "veulz tu guerroier contre la douce et plaisant amour? Et point ne vient en pensee ne en memoire en quel champ tu te soies esbatue?"» Et que demourrai je plus longuement? Ceste femme ne se contint point quant a ceste partie de son corps, et ainsi celi chevalier ot victoire [59] et l'amonesta de ces ·ii· poins. Et furent ensemble non pas tant seulement icelle ·i· nuit que il firent les noces, mais les nuis d'aprés. Et furent les portes du sepulcre fermees, et en tant que toute personne, tant de sa cognoissance comme non, si cuidoit que celle tres chaaste femme et tres loyal fust morte et eust rendu l'esperit sur le corps de son mari.

Et aprés, ce chevalier prist grant plaisir et grant delectacion en la biauté de celle femme et tout ce que par son argent il pooit avoir, il achetoit secretement et la premiere nuit ensuivant il le portoit au sepulcre. Si avint que une nuit les parens de l'un des penduz apperçurent qu'il n'i avoit point de garde qui entendist aus pendus: si deslierent l'un des penduz et l'envoierent au souverain de la justice. Et ainsi comme yceli chevalier s'estoit reposé, tantost aprés s'apperçut que il y avoit une crois et n'i avoit point de corps. [60] Il ot tres grant paour de la justice: si recognust et desclaira a sa femme ce qui li estoit avenu; et li dist que il n'atendroit point la sentence du juge, et que il avoit plus chier de prendre de son espee le droit et la punicion pour cause de sa charnalité, en li priant que elle li appareillast un lieu et li feist ·i· sepulcre tel comme pour son familier mari. Et la femme, qui n'estoit pas moins misericorde que chaaste, si dit: «Ja les diex ne veullent souffrir que en ·i· temps que je doie recevoir la mort de mes ·ii· tres chiers maris. J'ay plus chier a baillier le premier mari mort que laissier mourir celi qui est en vie.» Et selon ce parler, elle [251b] commenda a lever le corps de son mari mort, et pendre et atachier au gibet qui avoit esté vuidié;[61] et ainsi le chevalier usa du conseil de sa tres sage femme. Et le jour ensuivant le peuple se merveilla grandement par quelle maniere le mort fust alé a la crois et au gibet.

Se tu veulz, tu reputeras ce compte pour fable ou pour vraie hystoire, si comme il te plaira. Toutesvoies Petronius le racompte, et Flavianus en est aucteur qui dit qu'il avint de fait en Effese: et dist que la femme si le compara et fu punie de son deffaut, pour sa mauvaistié et du pechié de l'omicide et de l'avoultire.

Et Petronius n'est pas tout seul qui se moque et racompte les chaitivetéz des femmes, car saint Jerome si escript que toutes les chançons et dittiéz de Erripides sur les femmes sont maldissons, et que Epicurus, combien que Metodorus son disciple eust pris Leoncion a femme, toutesvoies il dit que tout sage se doit garder de marier, car plusseurs grans dommages et desplaisirs si viennent de noces et de mariages. Et aussi escript il comment richesces et honneurs et santé de corps et plusseurs autres choses que nous appellons indifferens ne sont ne bonnes ne mauvaises, mais aussi

fight[95] against love so sweet and pleasant? Have you no thought or feeling for the country where you have landed?' " Need I dwell upon the matter? The woman observed no greater abstinence regarding that other part of her body, and the soldier, advising her equally well in both areas, carried the day. They were together not only on this their wedding night, but also on the night that followed. And with the portals of the tomb all closed, the city believed—those who had known her and those who had not—that this most chaste and excellent of women had given up the ghost over the corpse of her departed husband.

Then the soldier, so delighting with gladness in the beauty of this woman, secretly purchased all that his money could buy and brought it to her in the sepulchre the following night. Then one night it happened that one of the relatives of the hanged men noticed there was no one guarding the gallows; so he took down one of the bodies and sent it to the supreme judge of the court. The soldier, wakening shortly thereafter from his rest, noticed immediately that one of the crosses had no body. In extreme fright of the law, he came and confessed to the woman what had befallen him, saying it was not his intention to wait for a judge's sentence, but he would rather let his own sword exact vengeance and punish him for his lust, begging her to prepare him a resting place and to create for him a tomb such as she had given her dead husband. But the lady, every bit as forgiving as she was chaste, replied: "May it never please the gods that I suffer at one and the same time the deaths of both my beloved husbands! I prefer to surrender the body of the dead one than to let die the one who is alive!" Putting her words into action, she ordered the body of her husband to be disinterred and hanged on the empty gallows: thus did the soldier benefit from the counsel of this most prudent wife. The following day, the population was astounded to see how a dead man had ascended to the gallows of the cross.

You can take this story as you will, for fiction or for a true account, accordingly. Still it is Petronius who tells it, Flavian being its original author; he affirms that it truly did happen at Ephesus and further says that the woman paid for her misdeed and was punished for the vile sins of homicide and adultery.[96]

Petronius is not the only one to poke fun at the foibles of women. Saint Jerome tells us[97] that practically all the plays and poems of Euripides are diatribes against women, and Epicurus, albeit his disciple Metrodorus had Leontium as his wife, still held[98] that the wise man shies away from marriage, since many great ills and pains are attendant to the marital state. He writes as well that riches, honors, bodily health and many others of the things we call indifferent are neither good nor bad, but lying as it were in the middle of the road, are good or bad depending on the conditions of their

comme mises au milieu du champ, elles sont faites bonne ou mauvaises [62] par usage ou par aucune occasion: aussi sont femmes demourans en voisinage de bonnes gens ou de mauvaises personnes. Et certes c'est chose grieve et ennuieuse a personne sage de soy mettre en doubte se il prendra bonne femme ou mauvaise; se donques il a si grant molesté et de ennuis es noces— qui sont bonnes et instituees de Dieu—que tout sage homme les redoubte, qui est celui qui appreuve la delectacion d'icelles, fors que celi qui est hors du sens—lequel y met son cuer et le tourne en celle ordure et qui est {251c} deffendue et que les gens blasment, et laquelle sera condampnee de Dieu sanz quelconques doubtance!

Car ces ·ii· delectacions (c'est a dire de gloutonnie et de luxure) sont en aucune maniere appartenans aus bestes mues: l'une (c'est assavoir gloutonnie) semble [63] garder et suivre l'ordure du porc; et l'autre (c'est luxure) semble tenir la puantise du bouc; car aussi comme chasteté resplendist entre les vertus, aussi ribaudie est la plus vile et laide entre les vices. Et comment que elle apartiengne aus ·ii· sexes [64] de homme et de femme, toutesvoies elle deshonnore plus la femme que l'omme. Vraiement le dit d'un tres sage homme si fu que au premier l'en doit garder par devant tout chaasté, laquelle perdue, toute vertu trebuche. La principalité des vertus feminines si est contenue en elle: elle loe et donne grace a la povre et eslieve la riche; et rachate [65] et excuse la laide et aorne la belle; elle reçoit grande merite et grant deserte des greigneurs, desquelz [66] elle ne deshonore pas le sanc par ligniee larrecineusement procree ne faussement engendree. La besoigne va bien des enfans, qui n'ont point de honte de leur mere et point ne doubtent de leur pere. Et premierement, il va bien a elles meismes quant le vilté et laidure d'estrange corps n'i a point de droit conquesté. Il n'est plus grant doleur de chaitiveté que quant personne est traite a luxure d'autrui. Eloquence et belle parole ennoblist et honneure les sages hommes conseilleurs, et gloire de chevalerie si donne nom perdurable et conferme les victoires de la nouvelle gent, et plusseurs choses sont qui ennoblissent les soutilz et clers engins et entendemens: mais propre[251d]ment chasteté est la vertu des femmes. Saint Jerome tesmoigne que avant que la religion crestienne resplendist [67] ou monde, les matrones qui n'avoient eu que un mari si avoient grant honneur, et par elles les sacrifices appartenans a la fortune des femmes estoient acoustuméz a faire. Nul prestre estoit bigame, et aussi nul prestre des paiens si estoit ·ii· foiz marié; et les sains parleurs d'Athaines si se chastroient par lonc usage de cigue, et depuis qu'il fussent esleuz et fais evesques, il delaissoient a estre hommes.

Se je veul plus parler de ce propos, la page et l'escripture si croistra sanz mesure. Car les ditteurs, les chanteurs de geste, les conteurs de biaux fais et de lais et des histoires et les poetes en sont touz plains, sanz ce que je y amaine philosophes naturelz ne moralz ne theologiens. Et toutesvoies je ne

use: so it is with women, as they are found in the company of good or bad people. But surely it is a grievous and unbearable risk for a wise man to take a chance on marrying a good or a bad woman. If the ills and pains of marriage are therefore such—even though the state itself is good and instituted by God—that the wise must fear it, who can therefore approve its sensual pleasures, except those who are out of their senses, whose hearts are won to evil and given over to a corruption that all do censure and that will be condemned, beyond a doubt, by God.

For these two temptations, that is, gluttony and lust, are so to speak specific to dumb animals: the first, that is, gluttony, is redolent of the filth of swine; the second, that is, lust, reminds us of the stench of goats. For as chastity is preeminent among virtues, so is wantonness the ugliest and vilest of sins. And although it occurs in both the male and the female sex, yet it is more repugnant in women than in men. It was indeed the word of a very wise man[99] who said that chastity must be maintained above all, for if it be lost, all virtue crumbles. The very principle of feminine virtue is contained therein: chastity commends and graces the poor; it extols the rich; it redeems and excuses the ugly; it adorns the beautiful. It is especially meritorious and prized in the noble, whose blood is not dishonored by a lineage spawned in thievery or fraudulently begot. It is to the advantage of progeny, who have neither to be ashamed of their mothers nor to wonder about their fathers. But above all, chastity becomes women themselves, for the disgrace and indignity of another's body have earned no title to them, and there is no greater pain or humiliation than to be bound to another by lust. Eloquence and oratory ennoble and honor men of state; military glory lends eternal fame to soldiers and confirms the feats of the unseasoned; there are many things which grace quick and noble minds or the understanding of men: chastity however is the singular virtue of women. Saint Jerome declares that in the time before the Christian religion came to lighten the world, matrons who had had but one husband were held in great respect, and the custom was that all sacrificial rights pertaining to women belonged to them. No priest was bigamous, nor was any pagan priest permitted to remarry, while the holy doctors of Athens castrated themselves by repeated doses of hemlock and, elected to the rank of bishop, ceased to be men.

Were I to dwell longer on these matters, my leaves and script would grow beyond measure. For the authors of tragedies, epic poets, chroniclers of great deeds, singers of lays, historians, and the works of poets abound on the subject, not to mention philosophers of nature or ethics and theologians. Still I doubt that all these and others too would be equal to the task—I cannot say of containing such evil—but of describing it adequately. Yet were I only to say that the flintstone[100] does no less harm to the foot than stones which are born on the shoulders of servants, the malice of women is

croy point que touz ceulz ici et touz les autres puissent souffire pour ceste malice, non pas seullement d'effacier ne reprimer et refraindre, mais il ne souffiroient pas a la exposer ne desclairer. Se je di que plusseurs ont esprou- véz que le caillou dont le feu saut n'est pas meilleur aus piéz que la pierre portee sus le col de ses serjans, tantost la malice des femmes si calumpniera, et dira que c'est en leur injure! Et certes il n'est rien meilleur ne plus profit- able que femme chaaste est; il n'est riens plus joieus ne plus plaisant a ceulz qui ne se pueent garder ou contenir ou qui ne le veullent faire. Mais celi est pou sage qui a foy ne esperance en celles qui plus—a droit dire—deservent avoir pardon miex que gloire.

Toutesvoies ces paroles sont entendues, [252a] que les choses dessus dittes si soient ordenees et attrempees par le bien de mesure. Car autre- ment, non pas le pardon, mais la honte et la paine de luxure de ·ii· parties si engendreroit vilenne tache et honteux diffame,—se ce n'estoit que par aucune aventure l'en deust tenir celui pour bel et pour honneste qui seroit transformé en ·i· bouc, et pour belle celle qui seroit muee en une truie.

such that they would claim it an insult. Still there is nothing better in this world than a chaste woman, and nothing more pleasant or ridiculous than those who cannot contain themselves or do not wish to do so. The man has very little sense indeed who would put his hope and faith in those who—if the truth be known—are more deserving of forgiveness than of fame.

These words, however, are so intended that the foregoing be tempered and ordered by the virtue of moderation. Otherwise, not forgiveness but repugnant vices and shameful infamy would spring from the shame and pains of lust—unless perchance we would repute as an honest man him who would transform himself into a goat, or as a beautiful woman, her who would become a sow.

Notes

1. See Thérèse Moreau and Eric Hicks, introduction to the modern French translation of *La Cité des Dames*, trans. Moreau and Hicks (Paris: Stock, 1986), 13ff.

2. Cited from Curnow's edition. Quotations are from the English translation by Earl Jeffrey Richards, *The Book of the City of Ladies* (New York: Persea Books, 1982), 4.

3. P. Delhaye, "Le Dossier anti-matrimonial de l'*Adversus Jovinianum* et son influence sur quelques écrits latins du XIIe siècle," *Mediaeval Studies* 13 (1951): 65.

4. C. Webb, in the notes to his edition of the *Policraticus* (*Ioannis Saresberiensis episcopi Carnotensis Policratici, sive De nugis curialium et vestigiis philosophorum*, 2 vols. [Oxford: Clarendon Press, 1909], 2:296).

5. Etienne Gilson, *Héloïse et Abélard* (Paris: Vrin, 1964), 37ff.

6. Some of the argumentation given by Jean de Meun's Mari Jalous derives from this source. Cf. *Le Roman de la Rose*, ed. Félix Lecoy, Classiques français du moyen âge (Paris: Champion, 1965–70), 2:272–74. Theophrastus is mentioned in conjunction with Leuntion in the Debate on the *Roman de la Rose*; see my edition, *Le débat sur le "Roman de la Rose,"* Bibliothèque au XVe siècle, no. 43 (Paris: Champion, 1977), 42 and 207n.; the quip by Jean de Montreuil, taken from Cicero by way of Petrarch, is not entirely flattering: perhaps this explains why Christine makes a fleeting reference to Leuntion (and Theophrastus!) in her *City of Ladies* (1.30).

7. See the inventory given by Christine in *Le Livre des fais et bonnes meurs du sage roy Charles V*, 2 vols., ed. Suzanne Solente (Paris: Champion, 1936–40), 2:44. The list is also cited in *Le Livre de la Paix*, ed. Charity Cannon Willard (The Hague: Mouton, 1958), 142.

8. Cf. *Livre de la Paix*, ed. Willard, 200 (note to bk. 3, chap. 2; p. 117, line 21).

9. Christine de Pizan, *Le Livre du corps de policie*, ed. R. Lucas (Geneva: Droz, 1967), xxiff. The importance of the apocryphal letter of Trajan on the state as a political body, consigned in the *Policraticus*, has been discussed by Sandra Hindman, *Christine de Pizan's "Epistre Othéa": Painting and Politics at the Court of Charles VI*, Texts and Studies, no. 77 (Toronto: Pontifical Institute of Mediaeval Studies, 1986), 28–29; cf. p. 71.

10. See *Le Livre des Trois Vertus*, ed. Charity Cannon Willard and Eric Hicks, Bibliothèque du XVe siècle, no. 50 (Paris: Champion, 1989), 1.20.15ff.: "Et ce tesmoigne Jehan de Salberieuse en son *Policratice*, ou tiers livre ou xiii chapitre: a monstrer que la vertu de largece. . . ." The same reference is made in the *Livre du corps de policie*, 44–45. In *Le Livre des fais et bonnes meurs du sage roy Charles V*, the passage preceding the catalog of translations alludes to the generosity of Titus, known through the *Policraticus*. A quotation from the work also appears in *Le Livre du chemin de long estude*, lines 4263ff., on the subject of the knight's duty to defend the Church (ed. R. Püschel, Berlin, 1877; reprint, Geneva, 1974).

11. It is worth noting that Christine, like Jean de Meun, associates "Theophrastus" with another well-known antifeminist satire, the "Valerius" of G. Map's *De nugis curialium* (*City of Ladies*, trans. Richards, 118; cf. *De nugis curialium*, ed. and trans. H. R. James [Oxford: Clarendon Press, 1983]). There are many points in common, particularly regarding *loci communes*, briefly noted, between John of Salisbury's chapter and the *dissuasio* against marriage by Map.

12. *City of Ladies*, trans. Richards, 3–4.

13. Most recently in *Le Moyen Français* 21 (1987): Denis Foulechat, trans., *Tyrans, princes, et prêtres (Jean de Salisbury, Policratique IV et VIII)*. A diplomatic edition of book 4 was earlier published by the same editor: *Le "Policratique" de Jean de Salisbury traduit par Denis Foulechat (1372), Livre IV*, Travaux de C.R.A.L., no. 3 (Nancy: Presses universitaires de Nancy, 1985). Books 1–3 were edited as the author's *doctorat de 3e cycle* in 1969: "Le *Policraticus* de Jean de Salisbury traduit par Denis Foulechat en 1372."

14. Charles Bruckner, "Le *Policratique*: Un fragment de manuscrit dans le ms. B. N. fr. 24287," *Bibliothèque d'Humanisme et de Renaissance* 34 (1972): 269–74.

15. Ibid., 273.

16. Often reproduced. See, among others, *La librairie de Charles V* (Paris: Bibliothèque nationale, 1968), cover; and the excellent handbook of medieval literature by Michèle Gally et Christiane Marchello-Nizia, *Littératures de l'Europe médiévale* (Paris: Magnard, 1985), 389. See also Claire Sherman, *The Portraits of Charles V (1338–1380)*, Monographs on Archaeology and Fine Arts, no. 20 (New York: New York University Press for the College Art Association of America, 1969).

17. L. Delisle, *Recherches sur la librairie de Charles V*, 4 vols. (Paris: Champion, 1907), 1:263–64. On Giles Malet, see the bio-bibliographical notice, 1:10–20. The book was given to "Monsieur d'Anjou" (son of Charles V) on October 7, 1380; it does not appear in subsequent inventories (ibid.; cf. Brucker, *Le "Policratique,"* Livre IV, xix–xx).

18. On the style of the Foulechat translation, see Charles Brucker, "Quelques aspects du style de Denis Foulechat, traducteur de Charles V," *Zeitschrift für französische Sprache und Literatur* 80 (1970): 97–106.

19. Two translations are available in English: *The Statesman's Book of John of Salisbury, Being the Fourth, Fifth, and Sixth Books and Selections from the Seventh and Eighth Books of the "Policraticus,"* trans. John Dickinson, Political Science Classics, no. 12 (New York: Knopf, 1927); and Joseph B. Pike, *Frivolities of Courtiers and Footprints of Philosophers* (Minneapolis: University of Minnesota Press, 1938).

20. est] *om. N*

21. je croi] i croi *N*

22. plusseurs c.] plus c. *N*

23. Silvain] Silvein *G / Lat.* Sillenus

24. c. que l'a.] c. de l'a. *N*

25. l'a. ou souz] l'a. ouz souz *N*

26. et le lie la harpe o instrumens] *NG corrupt; G. s. m. (originally blank) / Lat.* alacer faretra puer Cupido

27. feu] *om. N.*

28. couple] coulpe *G.*

29. des a. m.] autre *N.*

30. chasteté a l'e.] chaste exemple *N.*

31. a espouse] et e. *N.*

32. y adjouste] adjoustez *N* (adjustez *corrected,* adjouste *G*)

33. le] *om. N / G s.m.*

34. chaudieres] *G. s.m. (originally blank)*

35. desplaise] despaise *N.*

36. chasteté] *ad.* i *N.*

37. bon gouvernement] g. bon *N.*

38. l'eritage] *s.m. (over erasure).*

39. il couvient] escouvient *G.*

40. il couvient] escouvient *G.*

41. embracemens] embrasemens *N.*

42. d'entour li] de tour li *N.*

43. aucunefoiz] aucune foiz *N.*

44. lit de mariage] *om. N. / G.s.m.*

45. dessevrance] decevance *G.*

46. emprainses] emprenees *G.*

47. le roy entroit] le r. estoit et entroit *G.*

48. ne die] ne dise *G.*

49. aucunesfoiz] aucune foiz *N.*

50. aucunes choses] aucune chose *N. /* aucune *G.*

51. souventesfoiz] souvente foiz *N.*

52. si dist] si dise *G.*

53. se prist] se i prist *N.*

54. au ·v^e· jour]a ·v· jours *G.*

55. pendre] prendre *N.*

56. le corps] les c. *N.*

57. dessiroit] desiroit *N.*

58. Il n'est personne . . . vivre] *om. N.*

59. ot victoire] ot la victoire *G.*

60. corps] *ad.* pendu *G.*

61. avoit esté roidié] *N*

62. mais . . . mauvaises] *om. N.*

63. gloutonnie semble] g. ensemble *G.*

64. a. aux ·ii· s.] a. a deux s. *G.*

65. la riche et r.] richece et la r. *G.*

66. desquelz] desquelles *N.*

67. resplendist] si replendist *G.*

68. Proverbial: Horace refers to himself as a "hog from the herd of Epicurus" (*Epistulae* 1.4.16).

69. *Epistulae morales* 8.8; 21.9.

70. A lost work by Flavian. Also quoted in *Policraticus* 2.26.460b (ed. Webb, 1:141). Webb refers to C. Schaarschmidt, *Johannes Saresberiensis nach Leben und Studien, Schriften, und Philosophie* (Leipzig: Teubner, 1862), 103–6. The identification of "Flavianus" remains problematic: cf. Peter van Moos, *Geschichte als Topik: Das rhetorische Exemplum von der Antike zur Neuzeit und die "historiae" in "Policraticus" Johanns von Salisbury* (Hildesheim: Ohms, 1988), 222–23.

71. That is, Silenus. The original text of the *Policraticus* is somewhat enigmatic; the translation compounds its allusiveness. The episode, as related by Ovid in his *Fasti* (1.391–440), is as follows: at the feast of Bacchus, the Pans, satyrs, and nymphs were joined by Priapus and Silenus (riding on his ass). One of the nymphs, Lotis, scorned the advances of Priapus (not Silenus); at nightfall, weary with reveling, she fell asleep. Priapus stole upon her and was preparing to take her by force when the ass began to bray. Lotis awoke and fled with the other nymphs, leaving Priapus held up to ridicule. The ass was slaughtered and became the sacrificial animal "dear to the Hellespontian god."

72. Unidentified quotation.

73. On the altar veil, Webb cites Pope Nicolas I, *Responsa ad consulta Bulgarum* (*PL* 119.980) and the article *palla altaris* in Ducange.

74. The original reads: "For it is Hymen that loves light; it is Cupid with his swift shafts that kindles the furtive flame and lurks in nooks and corners" (Pike, *Frivolities*, 355.) I have tried to render as closely as possible the flavor of the translation, which makes little sense as it stands. Cf. Ovid, *Metamorphoses* 10.525; Martianus Capella, 8.804.

75. Cf. Genesis 3:16.

76. *Factorum et dictorum memorabilium* 7.2, ext. 1.

77. Cf. Jerome, *Adversus Jovinianum* 1.47 (*PL* 23:289).

78. Cf. Matthew 13:22 (parable of the sower). Jerome interprets the passage as applying to virginity, widowhood, and the marital state, in decreasing order (*Adversus Jovinianum* 1.3 [*PL* 23:223). The interpretation is based on the manner of counting on fingers in late antiquity (ibid., n. 2).

79. Sources unknown.

80. The translator has not recognized *Aureolus* as part of the book's title. From "Theophrastus" to "such and similar are the words of Theophrastus," verbatim from Jerome, presumably verbatim from the lost *De nuptiis.*

81. Proverbial; cf. Juvenal, *Satires* 6.165.

82. A saying attributed to Publius Scipio Africanus by Cato, as quoted by Cicero, *De officiis* 3.1.1; cf. *De re publica* 1.18.27.

83. That is, Publilius Syrus. Quoted in Gellius, *Noctes Atticae* 17.14.4, and Macrobius, *Saturnalia* 2.7.11. The translator has not recognized the gnomic char-

acter of the quotation, nor the limits of its syntax. Cf. Pike: "It is arrogant of one twice shipwrecked to blame Neptune."

84. Quoted by Jerome in *Adversus Jovinianum* 1.48 (*PL* 23:292); cf. Herodotus, 1.8.

85. Hérouville in the Calvados (arr. Caen); Webb cites three persons with this place name, but none of them of the Christian name Godfrey.

86. A well-known "witticism"; quoted by Jerome, *Adversus Jovinianum* 1.48 (*PL* 23:291).

87. Verbatim from Jerome (ibid.).

88. Ibid.

89. The anecdote is in Jerome (ibid.), here slightly abridged.

90. Proverbial; cf. Horace, *Satires* 1.1.24.

91. Juvenal(!), *Satires* 6.165; the same verse as quoted above, n. 14.

92. John refers to the Eumolpus of the *Satyricon* (110).

93. Verbatim from the *Satyricon* (111).

94. Addressed to Dido; *Aeneid* 4.34.

95. Ibid., line 38.

96. John of Salisbury is alone in this opinion. Lichas, one of Petronius's characters, comments that a just emperor would have put the dead husband back in the tomb and his wife on the cross.

97. Jerome, *Adversus Jovinianum* 1.48 (*PL* 23:292).

98. To "a bad woman," verbatim from Jerome, *Adversus Jovinianum*, PL 23:293.

99. Jerome, *Adversus Jovinianum* 1.49 (*PL* 23:294), to "the singular virtue of women," verbatim. What follows is from the same paragraph, to the end of book 1 ("ceased to be men").

100. The translator has garbled text and quotation. The lines are from Juvenal (*Satires* 6.350–51), and are to the effect that she whose foot "beats the stones of the pavement" is no different from her "who is borne on the shoulders of slaves." The conclusion continues in this oblique vein: "a ceulz" (line 410) is perhaps an error for the comparative; translated thus.

PART TWO

Christine

AND MEDIEVAL FRENCH

LITERATURE

Elegant Closures: The Use of the Diminutive in Christine de Pizan and Jean de Meun

NADIA MARGOLIS

Notre langue est tellement ployable à toutes sortes de mignardises
—HENRI ESTIENNE

In her compact yet still monumental survey of Christine de Pizan's literary career, Suzanne Solente points to the poet's abundant use of diminutives as an important stylistic trait. In so doing, Solente supplements the earlier remarks by Gay and Bruins, all three of whom perceive this tendency as a product of Christine's Italian background and to some extent of her femininity. Solente states the second factor most directly when discussing the presence of diminutives in the poetry of Christine's time ("les femmes en usent volontiers") and leaves it at that, as though unaware of the provocative nature of her observation.[1]

I should therefore like to begin where Solente and others have left off, in order to understand why a female poet would use them and whether such outwardly banal stylistics can be seen to transcend the *dolce stil nuovo* of her beloved "Dant de Flourence" and stereotyped *mignardise* characterizing later medieval through early seventeenth-century French lyric poetry, especially pastoral. We already know that Christine composed excellent examples of traditional *forme fixe* lyric poetry and *pastourelle,* whose verses teem with diminutives, as listed in detail by Bruins. What strikes us in addition is their presence in Christine's more serious poetry and even in some of her prose polemics, as though she may have experimented with them toward more specific ends as she developed her unique literary voice. In this way, the humble diminutive might be viewed as a microcosmic facet of her thematic and stylistic evolution into what Poirion has numbered among the "masters" of later medieval poetry.[2]

Various scholars continue to uncover the extent of her borrowing from male authors, despite their often misogynistic messages, as a necessary step toward becoming their equal, to be taken seriously by both sexes. Conversely, some evidence exists of her influence over her male contemporaries and successors. One of her main sources of thematic inspiration is, of all people, Jean de Meun in his continuation of the *Roman de la Rose* (ca. 1275).[3] Given Jean de Meun's aptitude for a poetics of contrast and toying with dissonant contexts and ironic wordplay,[4] it would not be surprising for Christine, who never shrank from erudite neologisms and tonal variation, to have foraged among the recesses of his text. Because one usually associates Jean de Meun's addition with amplification, "bourgeois realism"[5]—to say nothing of the antifeminism that Christine would later deplore—and other forms of irreverent expansiveness, one does not think of him as resorting to usage as dainty as the diminutive, a bias we shall soon dispel.

To begin our actual analysis, we may divide Christine's diminutives into three categories: (1) the most conventional, indistinguishable from those contained in the work of the *chansonniers* and other lyric poets; (2) those presenting a noticeable departure from traditional stereotypes—a solitary shepherdess with a different allure; (3) the most inventive and complex, often bivocal and oppositional in that they juxtapose the dominant male terminology with that of the minority female, in the latter's attempt to thwart the more powerful group by means of its own discourse.[6] In general, chronology does not figure into these groupings, although there is no true example of the third category in her earliest lyrics.

Bruins cites most of those assignable to our first two categories, finding the majority of them, understandably enough as they are both pastoral, in the *Dit de Poissy* (1400) and *Dit de la Pastoure* (1403). Not only does he note a greater number of diminutives in these than in comparable poems by other authors, Bruins also judges the relatively low proportion of the often desperate kind of end-rhyme diminutives in Christine's lyric poems to be a mark of her proficiency in relation to her fellow poets.[7] He goes on to characterize the *Poissy* as more personal and psychological than the *Pastoure*. A sympathetic but nonetheless masculine reader, Bruins explains all of this in terms of his subject's greater "emotion" as a poet in contrast to Deschamps and others. This quality, along with her "finesse," he attributes to her gender and Italian origins. He does mention, although superficially, Christine's effective incorporation of spoken language, particularly in her predilection for "les petits mots,"[8] which we can also suggest as a source for her diminutives.

Because of the profusion of diminutives listed by Gay, Bruins, and Solente, it may be best to focus on a specific cluster associated with a central concept in Christine's writing and trace its ramifications at key points in her career. Since the theme of women and their status permeates her work, a worthwhile cluster would involve the figures of *pucellette/fillette/femmelette* with their contingent motifs, often signaled by diminutives in themselves.

Pucellette certainly prevails as a first-category diminutive in Christine's most conventional, especially pastoral, poems from her early period. She associates with *bergerete* ("little shepherdess"), *berbiete* ("little lamb"), and *flourete* ("flowerlet") among others in the standard pastoral repertory. *Fillette* can also be found in this idyllic setting, as both terms betoken the innocence and charm of a young girl about to be smitten with an equally comely shepherd. Both are thus female archetypes as seen through admiring masculine eyes that objectify every attribute: hair *crespellet*, often covered with a *chapellet*, adorning a face described as *doulcet*, whose *mentonet* is *sadinet* and whose cheeks are *vermeillez*. The lustful *jouvencel* does not neglect her body, with its *corselet greillet*, down to her little feet *doulcetement chauciez*. In such a pre-*précieux* idyll, few parts of speech are spared the cloying suffix. Even *seulete*, to be treated as intrinsically second category because of its significance for Christine's self-imposed destiny, originates in this register of which she soon tired.

Yet if we turn to the other end of Christine's career, to the *Ditié de Jehanne d'Arc* (1429), we note how *pucellette* attains a different significance, somewhere between the second and third of our categories, since its meaning is more exclusively tied to Christine's being and self-expression. We have only to look at stanza 50, depicting Charles's victorious entry and coronation at Rheims:

> Avecques lui la *Pucellette*
> En retournant par son païs,
> Cité ne chastel ne *villette*
> Ne remaint. . . .

(Lines 393–95)

(. . . with the little Maid. As he returns through his country, neither city nor castle nor small town can hold out against them.)[9]

Kevin Brownlee, in his discussion of the passage immediately preceding this one, rightly acknowledges its emphasis on Joan's invincibility via the merging of temporal and textual present.[10] We can add to this assessment by focusing on the rhyming of the two diminutives as part of the enhancement of the Maid's invincibility, a strategy of contrast through which Christine magnifies Joan's exploits through lexical minimizing. The fact that she, a "little maid," has recaptured what mighty men have lost proves her election by God. On a strictly mundane level, "little village"—at first glance a metric filler and convenient rhyme for line 395—also ends the succession of demolished, emblematic structures, decreasing in stature (city–castle–hamlet), annihilated by "ni . . . ni . . ." syntax as much as by the battles themselves.

Pucellette also conveys a variety of voices as used here: the lyric literate voice versus the popular diminutive of spoken language, and the common, somewhat condescending view of outsiders versus the singular purpose within the heroine's own mind. She is obliged to label herself in the same terms for lack of what we would now call gendered nomenclature.

Christine has already prepared us for the townspeople's opinion in such passages as that from stanza 35, referring to Joan as a *fillette:*

> Une fillette de XVI ans
> (N'est-ce pas chose fors nature?)
> A qui armes ne sont pesans . . .   (Lines 273–75)
>
> (A little girl of sixteen [isn't this something quite supernatural?] who
> does not even notice the weight of the arms she bears . . .)

Here, the poet's use of the diminutive has departed from the vulgar connotation of prostitute [11] as well as that of the pastoral while retaining a vernacular aura: Joan in the words of the common folk moved by awe and elation. The Maid's supernatural side has itself been presaged by previous allusions to the prophecies of "Merlin, the Sibyl and Bede" (line 241) and contrasts with her humble origins as evoked in line 198 ("A woman—a simple shepherdess"). The real-life figure of Joan thus not only legitimizes Christine's ideal for the militant woman improving the world corrupted by men, but also informs the poet's discursive shift from the passive, vulnerable *filete* of the *Dit de la Pastoure* (line 419) to the active, though still pure *fillette* celebrated in the poet's last known work. Moreover, in referring to the Maid by diminutives, Christine mimes the divine viewpoint: we are all lesser creatures before God, who decides our destiny. Finally, these elegant locutions open up the possibility of the poet's private self-identification with her heroine, beyond the public promulgation of feminine ideal, thus rendering them closer to the third category.

Diminutives appearing in her prose works, such as the *Cité des Dames* (1405), often belong to the higher categories as well. Perhaps the most interesting example from the *Cité des Dames* occurs in the story of the life of Saint Christine, twice referred to as *enfancelle* or *enfancellette,* [12] whose lyrical textual existence can be traced to the *enfançon* describing the shepherd's son of the *Dit de la Pastoure* (line 1354). In an example from the *Cité des Dames*, the gender shifts to the more appropriate feminine, linking it to holy martyrdom. As Charity Cannon Willard has noted, Christine is very aware of the onomastic kinship between herself and the saint,[13] yet unlike similar terms labeling Joan of Arc, the diminutives here emphasize the vulnerability of female purity—or, if we wish, the more passive invincibility typifying martyrs—as her fragile, virgin flesh is offered up to cruel torture: "Le cruel pere, [plus forcené], fist apporter une roue que il avoit fait faire, et fist celle doulce *enfancelle* estre liee dedens et mettre feu dessoubz, et puis fist gitter huile boulant a grant plenté sur son corps." (3.10.1, p. 1003;

"The cruel father, [madder than ever], ordered a wheel to be brought which he had had made, and had this sweet child bound within it and then set afire, and then had plenty of boiling oil thrown over her body" [translation mine].) *Enfancelle* here underscores her innocence rather than actual infancy, since she was really a young woman at this moment.

We also observe examples deriving from the courtly love register, as in the story of Pyramus and Thisbe. The two children growing up are depicted as *grandelés* (2.57.1, p. 933); a charming usage serving to portend their personal charm and destiny as lovers, forced to communicate through an opening in a *quignet* ("little corner"), a common form (for example, compare Guillaume de Lorris, lines 452, 3803). The delicate restraint of these forms subtly echoes the same quality within the ideal lover. Christine had previously rendered the same story in verse, in the *Debat des deux amants* (1400?), again using diminutives such as *fontenelle* ("little fountain")—the site of their deaths—to contribute a bittersweet tonality to the amorous hagiography of Ovid's *enfant cortois* and *la jeunete pucelle* ("courtly child" and "tender young maiden," lines 671–73) within a less didactic context than that of the *Cité des Dames*.

There are more words that are closely related, presented in diminutive form, within the *pucellette/fillette/femmelette* progression, notably *seulette*, which appears on at least five occasions. The most famous instance, of course, initiates ballad II of the *Cent ballades*. Although one of Christine's earliest efforts (1395), "Seulete suy" remains one of the most unique and psychologically charged, in part because of its proximity to her tragic bereavement in the death of her husband five years earlier. Very much in the voice of the simple soul, the poem's anaphoric relentlessness reminds us that this is a solitary, tender woman wronged by fate. Her self-awareness as martyr to virtuous love reflects itself farther on in the same sequence (ballad 14):

> Seulete m'a laissié en grant martyre
> En ce desert monde plein de tristece.

> (Alone he's left me to my great martyrdom in this barren world full of sadness).[14]

A more explicit gloss of the same experience, this ballad thereby loses some of the trenchant simplicity of the previous one, even though the poignant diminutive is retained.

On the other hand, the most pedestrian example of *seulette* is found in one of her later works, the *Cent ballades d'Amant et de Dame* (1409–10). Yet even this conventionalism serves a purpose, since ballad 79 distinguishes itself from the surrounding, more abstract ones in its focus on nature's beauty in a pastoral setting. Like the *Dit de la Pastoure*, this work is a pastourelle related through the woman's point of view. Furthermore, the addition of this genre to the total sequence, comprised of a variety of short lyric forms, enables Christine to put her virtuosity at the discourse of love through its paces.

Within the *Dit de la Pastoure* itself, each of the three occurrences of *seulette* marks a stage in Marotele's emotional progression.[15] First,

> Et comme d'amours rebelle
> Vouloye la *seulete* estre   (Lines 458–59)
>
> (And like a rebel against love, I wished to be alone)

offers a defiant, coquettish alternative to Christine's usual solitary sufferer, as in "Seulete suy," cited earlier. Each "solitary little woman" voluntarily chooses her situation. In the second phase, the shepherdess's solitude becomes more wistful than willful, as she (*seulete*) sings to herself and devotes her understanding (*entente*) to gathering flowerlets near a fountain (lines 828–32). The third stage most closely resembles the narrator in "Seulete suy," in that Marotele laments the departure of the lover to whom she has finally succumbed, "Pleurant seulete en destour" (line 2057; "weeping all alone in isolation") while praying to "saints et sainttes." All of these aspects: femaleness, solitude, sadness, saintliness—recur as in the other texts examined.

So far, in our survey of first- and second-category diminutive usages, the heroine remains a passive object of misfortune or even divine election, as in the case of Joan of Arc. The inner will manifested aims more at endurance or obedience than true self-revelation and active engagement (even Joan acted under God's orders). In the term *femmelete,* however, we witness a more self-contained, yet aggressive persona. For this reason, this appellation best characterizes Christine's mature voice as a female author. Although all narrative first persons can be viewed as extensions of the poet's own self-consciousness as well as the protagonist's in some sense or other, Christine's self-image and self-confidence display themselves most sharply in the choice of *femmelette.*

As in the case of other key themes in Christine's work, this word/theme is first assayed in her early poetry, then further developed in usually at least one other work, often in a different context. *Femmelette* originates in the *Epistre au dieu d'Amours* (1399), Christine's verse rebuttal to Jean de Meun's *Roman de la Rose* and Ovid. That *femmelette* does not have its roots in her pastoral poems or other short lyrics—and is thus already extracted from its usual context—immediately distinguishes it from the poet's other diminutives. Because, as Willard notes, the *Epistre* is her first occasion to incorporate legalistic, "official" style into her writing,[16] the presence of this typically lighter form jars all the more. Closer reading, however, reveals that this jolting effect is calculated to mime the woman's emotional crisis upon realizing that she has been deceived in love:

> On peut vaincre une chose simplete,
> Une ignorant petite femmelete.   (Lines 549–50)

> ('Tis easy to conquer a simple little thing,
> An innocent little womanling.)

As in the *pucellette/fillette* figures from the *Ditié de Jehanne d'Arc*, there operates within *femmellette* a *dédoublement* of images and voices centered on the subject, which, because one is the reaction of the powerful, collective other and the second signifies the lone individual being perceived, replicates the relation between the narrator-object and her (here, subjugating) milieu. This dominant group (men) also inevitably governs the narrator's self-image, if by no other means than by controlling the language used to label herself: her *a priori* smallness or inadequacy, even if affectionate, has become a reality. Her status as *femmelette,* because that is exclusively how she sees herself, causes her to be already vanquished lexically, making physical possession by a man virtually inevitable. Although this example from the *Epistre* approximates the second more than the third category, it is Christine's first attempt at writing about the plight of women in official style [17]—the learned language of lawmakers and leaders, not lustful shepherds—and a major step in her development. She has embarked upon the path of beating male writers at their own game.

Her use of bivocal, sharply ironic *femmelette* reflects her increased confidence of two years later when, during the famous Quarrel of the *Roman de la Rose*, she assails Jean de Meun's misogyny and Pierre Col's defense of him: "O entendement ofusqué! O congnoissance pervertie . . . qui juges . . . laidure orrible estre biautey solacieuse; de qui une simple fammelette, avec la doctrine de sainte Esglise, puet reprandre ton erreur!" ("Oh obfuscated understanding! Oh perverted knowledge . . . that judges . . . a horrible ugliness to be consoling beauty; whose error can be taken on by a simple little woman [*fammelette*] with the aid of the Holy Church's doctrine!") [18] Here we have a true third-category diminutive, in that it is distinctly bivocal, or even multivocal—the first voice "heard" being not that of the speaker but that of those reproaching the speaker and all of her gender daring to enter the Parisian humanist intellectual circle. This constitutes a fine example of oppositional irony, of the kind forged by Jean de Meun, to be explored later. [19]

Her own, self-deprecating voice in the statement cited above has already surfaced, yet without irony at that point, in Christine's epistles introducing the Debate. Although cast in legal diction, they contain such self-minimizing phrases as "I, a simple and ignorant woman" (p. 5), "I, Christine, of feeble understanding and the least of all women" (7), "woman ignorant of understanding and of scant feeling" (12), "my little intellect" (*mon petit engin,* 12), which contribute toward a modest, nonthreatening panoply from behind which she might attack. The letter to Col, situated toward the end of the Debate, maintains this initial façade despite the respectful opening formulae employed by Christine's adversaries toward her in their letters. She sees through such superficial praise and reacts instead to insults into which they lapse in the heat of argumentation, such as Pierre Col's charge: "Tu as parlé par oppinion ou presumpcion oultrageuse. . . . O parole trop tost yssue et sans avis de bouche de fame!"; "Garde que tu ne rassambles le corbel, lequel, pour ce que on loua son chant, se prist a chanter plus fort qu'il n'avoit acoustumé et laissa cheoir sa bouchié." ("You speak out of biased opinion or outrageous presumption . . . Oh heedless and all too hasty words issuing from the mouth of woman!" [p. 100]; "Take care not to resemble the crow who, because they praised his voice, began to sing more loudly than usual and thus let fall his morsel" [p. 110, also cited in Willard, *Christine de Pizan,* 84–85]). Singing shepherdesses are acceptable, but not women engaging in serious, learned debate. Such strictures recall the "unnaturalness" of the Maid who forsook her lambs and took up arms: both ideas and arms are too weighty for these frail creatures of feeble mind.

Diminutives play a part in representing both sides of this deeper dispute. While male authors continue to use them to condescend, Christine arms hers with dissonant context. For example, when Pierre Col summarily refers to her literary endeavors as *chosettes* ("little things," 89), it is not the same as when Christine calls her own works "little treatise," and so on. She also retorts by using diminutives in disarming fashion, as when, in the midst of a passionate invective, she then shifts into a demure tone to portray herself as a "little twig against a mighty stalk," then a "little cricket" (*gresillon*), beating its "winglets" (*elettes*) in comparison to the "delightful song of graceful birds"—that is, more gifted writers (146). After more forensic fervor, she again retreats into another self-portrait as a solitary, studious woman who enjoys picking *flourettes* from which she makes dainty little crowns (*chapellés*).[20] Christine the verbal tactician has so far taken the reader through various moods within this single epistle, by turns lulling her male reader into a false sense of superiority, only to sting him again. It is in this manner that she effectively deploys a diminutive in the midst of an outwardly prissy admonition: "Car tu sces que toutes chose sont meues a certaing temps, ne riens n'est long envers l'espace des ans; et souvent avient que par une petite pointelette est curey une grant enflure." ("For you know that all things are changed at a certain time, nor does anything last long compared to eternity; and thus it often happens that a great swelling is pierced by a tiny needle [*pointelette*]," 149). All of the above quotations subliminally feminize the David-and-Goliath theme noted earlier, with the aid of diminutives. The forcefulness of Christine's technique seems not to have been lost on Col, who in turn tries one himself in the final document to the Debate. Alluding to Christine's self-depicting "little twig" (146), he instead delicately calls it a *branchette* and proceeds to accuse her of false modesty: "How many people there are who belittle themselves . . . in order to magnify themselves! I see you call yourself a *little branch*" (154). Unfortunately, Col's letter breaks off in midinvective in the manuscript. For her part, Christine was not to be deterred from her polemical use of diminutives. In the *Livre de la Paix*, for example, the same little crown of *fleurectes* discussed above resurfaces as a symbol of Christine's humble wisdom exhorting the duke of Guyenne toward virtue (69)—deriving from her evocation of his "belle juenece flourissant" (63)—ten years after the *Rose* Debate.

In any case, we have demonstrated the subtle and highly individualized usage of these usually innocuous structures and how they reflect Christine's protean persona. Yet whatever the nuance in context and message, the diminutive has been revitalized by its transformed role from that of masculine term for female objects to vehicle for expressing feminine subjectivity, without descending to *grossierté* for shock value. As she presents the woman's viewpoint, she is reacting not merely to certain of her contemporaries and both *Rose* authors; she is discursively defending her sex against the entire misogynistic tradition in learning and literature, whose perpetrators she was forced to assimilate, *faute de mieux*; to whose typologies she too had naïvely succumbed in her studies, especially that of women's "lesser wit" and moral weakness.[21]

Christine has therefore enhanced the artful usage of diminutives but did not invent it. Her most notable precursor in this respect might be the late tenth-century German nun, Hrotsvita of Gandersheim. Peter Dronke has demonstrated her success in conveying Christian morality via unlikely rhetorical models, principally Terence. More specifically, Dronke appreciates her use of ironic, disarming diminutives as gleaned from pagan authors.[22] Just as Christine was to do, she not only alludes to her *ingeniolum* ("little wit") as part of an advantageous didactic strategy, she also shows herself adept at miming the crude male characters' attitudes toward women via such supposedly harmless, though actually degrading locutions as *puellulae* ("little girlies"), and *mulierculi* ("little broads") in the context of the drama *Dulcitius*, for example. Coincidentally, the heroines in Hrotsvita's plays are Christian female martyrs to the brutality of their pagan male captors.

At this point we might draw an analogy between the female authors and their relationship to their sources: as Hrotsvita is to Terence et al., so Christine is to Jean de Meun and his tradition. Although the scope of this study neither requires nor permits a complete enumeration of the *Rose* continuator's diminutives and their significance, preliminary investigation of both authors reveals pertinent features of their particular usage of them.

To summarize these findings, it can first be stated that, although Guillaume de Lorris's romance is often considered the "courtly" version in contrast to Jean de Meun's "bourgeois" reworking, it contains proportionately fewer diminutives than Jean de Meun's section. None of these is really tinged with irony in the way the latter author so often uses them. Jean de Meun's diminutives mock their traditional background just as his didactic message debunks theological teachings, by assuming the guise of innocence (that is, diminutive suffixes) and then delivering a twist at the end in various ways. For example, Jean de Meun is perfectly capable of including diminutives modeled on those of Guillaume de Lorris to describe the beauty of the amorous setting. But he also playfully lists diseases and other unpleasantries in the same terms, so that boils, pustules, and toads become adorable (lines 13294, 17815, 5135).

Furthermore, although they appear to be stylistic amenities designed to close out a verse or an idea, they invite opening, just as Guillaume de Lorris does in a larger sense when he claims that the art of love is "all enclosed" in his romance (line 38).[23] The clearest case of this practice is when Jean de Meun, to take his central image, having appropriated the *bouton* ("bud") of Guillaume de Lorris's *rose* or *rosette,* proceeds to encapsulate it even more as a *boutonet*—repeatedly (lines 21691, 21695, 21699) at the moment in the story when the Lover is about to possess (open) the rose:

> A la parfin, tant vos an di,
> Un po de greine i espandi,
> quant j'oi le *bouton* elloichié.
> Ce fu quant dedanz l'oi toichié
> por les *fueilletes* reverchier,
> car je vouloie tout cerchier
> jusques au fonz du *boutonet,*
> si con moi samble que bon et.
> Si fis lors si meiller les greines
> qu'el se desmellassent a peines,
> si que tout le *boutonet* tandre
> an fis ellargir et estandre.   (Lines 21689–700)

(Finally, I scattered a little seed on the *bud* when I shook it, when I touched it within in order to pore over the *little petals*. For the *little rosebud* seemed so fair to me that I wanted to examine everything right down to the bottom. As a result, I so mixed the seeds that they could hardly be separated; and thus made the whole tender *little bud* widen and lengthen.)[24]

Jean de Meun thus combines the erotic charm of pastoral with the glossator's lust to learn-and-tell, which of course forms the thematic justification for his entire work. Other diminutives serve this same purpose to a lesser extent, such as the obligatory narrow *santele* ("little passage," line 21607) the Lover had to penetrate to enter the garden. Borrowed from the epic register, this form subtly spoofs its own momentousness as well as Saint Matthew's "strait is the gate." Even the continuator's own name as once given in the text, Chopinel, resembles a diminutive of proto-Rabelaisian self-effacement ("little boozer," line 10535) and, because of his scandalous ideas and methods of presentation, self-defense. Other authors, like Machaut and Deschamps, imitated this enormously influential poet, yet none before Christine took issue with his ideas while incorporating his techniques. But then, they were not female tropological readers. If other male authors, most notably Jean Gerson, deplored Jean de Meun, they resisted using him as a stylistic model. More research needs to be done on the extent of Christine's debt to the *Rose*, although whatever the result, one aspect— one discursive weapon—she never procured for her polemical arsenal was ribald language, against which Guillaume de Lorris also cautioned (lines 2097–2100). While herself impounding the early humanists' discourse in order to winnow out its inherent prejudices, she never accepts the Rhodophiles' defense of vulgar speech for ostensibly the same moral purpose (compare the infamous castration of Saturn allusion, lines 5507–8),[25] as her letters in the *Rose* Debate aver. Both Jean de Meun and Christine vow *exprimer proprement,* yet for her no degree of clever or elegant trivialization—even via diminutives—can redeem blasphemy, especially since such speech is so strongly linked to the denigration of women.

Notes

1. Suzanne Solente, "Christine de Pisan," in *Histoire littéraire de la France* (Paris: Klincksieck, 1969), 40:83; Lucy M. Gay, "On the Language of Christine de Pisan," *Modern Philology* 6 (1908–9): 69–96; Jan Gerard Bruins, *Observations sur la langue d'Eustache Deschamps et de Christine de Pisan* (Dordrecht: Dordrechtsche Drukkerrij, 1925), 117–33.

2. Daniel Poirion, *Le Poète et le prince: L'Evolution du lyrisme courtois de Guillaume de Machaut à Charles d'Orléans* (Paris: Presses universitaires de France, 1965), esp. 248–51.

3. Christine de Pizan, *Le Livre de la mutacion de Fortune,* ed. Suzanne Solente, 4 vols. (Paris: Picard, 1959–66), 1:xxxix–xli, discusses her borrowing of False Seeming in the *Mutacion.* For her influence on others, aside from the numerous translations of her works into other languages as attested in various critical editions, including Solente, see, for influence in England, Diane Bornstein, "French

Influence on Fifteenth-Century English Prose as Exemplified by the Translation of Christine de Pisan's *Livre du corps de policie*," *Medieval Studies* 39 (1977): 369–86; P. G. C. Campbell, "Christine de Pisan en Angleterre," *Revue de Littérature Comparée* 5 (1925): 659–70; for influence on contemporary French politics and rhetoric, Alfred Coville, "Sur une ballade de Christine de Pisan," *Entre camarades* (1901): 181–94, plus others.

4. See, among others, Nancy Regalado, " 'Des contraires choses': La Fonction poétique de la citation et des *exempla* dans le *Roman de la Rose* de Jean de Meun," *Littérature* 41 (1981): 62–81.

5. For this term and its implications see Lionel Friedman, "Jean de Meun's Antifeminism and Bourgeois Realism," *Modern Philology* 57 (1959): 13–23.

6. For this line of thought and its accompanying terminology, I am indebted to Marie Maclean, "Oppositional Practices in Women's Traditional Narrative," *New Literary History* 19 (1987): 37–50, who in turn has taken her guiding concept from Michel de Certeau, "On the Oppositional Practices of Everyday Life," trans. F. Jameson and C. Lovitt, *Social Text* 3 (1980): 3–43.

7. Bruins, *Observations*, 125–26.

8. Ibid., 137.

9. All quotations from *Ditié de Jehanne d'Arc*, ed. Angus J. Kennedy and Kenneth Varty (Oxford: Society for the Study of Mediaeval Languages and Literature, 1977); translation theirs.

10. Kevin Brownlee, "Structures of Authority in Christine de Pizan's *Ditié de Jehanne d'Arc*," typescript kindly provided by the author, p. 160.

11. F. Godefroy, *Dictionnaire de l'ancienne langue française*, 10 vols. (Paris: Ministère de l'instruction publique, 1892; reprint, Leichtenstein: Kraus, 1969), vol. 4, gives the first definition for *fillette* as "prostitute" during the early fifteenth century.

12. All references from Maureen Curnow, "The *Livre de la Cité des Dames* by Christine de Pisan: A Critical Edition," 2 vols. (Ph.D. dissertation, Vanderbilt University, 1975).

13. Charity Cannon Willard, *Christine de Pizan: Her Life and Works* (New York: Persea Books, 1984), 144.

14. All quotations from Christine de Pizan, *Oeuvres poétiques de Christine de Pizan*, ed. Maurice Roy, 3 vols. (Paris: Firmin Didot, 1886–96), 1:15; translations mine.

15. Willard, ibid., 69, remarks on Christine's originality in reworking this classical and medieval vernacular genre from the woman's viewpoint.

16. Ibid., 47.

17. Ibid.

18. All references to documents from the Debate of the *Rose* are taken from Eric Hicks, ed., *Le Débat sur le "Roman de la Rose"* (Paris: Champion, 1977). This passage translated from pp. 131–32.

19. For Jean de Meun's irony, see Vladimir R. Rossman, *Perspectives of Irony in Medieval French Literature* (The Hague: Mouton, 1975), esp. 157; Michael D. Cherniss, "Irony and Authority: The Ending of the *Roman de la Rose*," *Modern Language Quarterly* 36 (1975): 227–38, among others.

20. Hicks, *Débat*, 227–28, notes the presence of the crown of flowers in two of Christine's later works: the *Avision* (*Lavision-Christine*, ed. Mary Louise Towner

[Washington, D.C.: Catholic University of America, 1932], 187) and the *Livre de la paix* (ed. Charity Cannon Willard [The Hague: Mouton, 1958], 64), composed in 1405–6 and 1412–13, respectively. We note furthermore that the diminutive form of this imagery occurs only in the *Paix* and even then only with the word *fleurecte,* which then compensates by appearing in the same paragraph three times, apparently the sole diminutive to intrude upon the soberly Latinate diction throughout the entire work. The absence of this lighter form for the same image in the *Avision* may be explained by the fact that Christine, speaking as Philosophy, associates it with the ascetic, saintly life: from the "flowering honors" of Saint Ambrose's life (186) to her subtle insinuation of the crown of thorns via allusion to Saint John (187); while in the *Paix,* Christine addresses her "flowerlets" to a lofty, though secular, personage. The form *chappelet* itself reappears in the *Mutacion* (ed. Solente, 1.5.729) as Christine describes her crown containing a magic stone from her mother.

21. One has only to look at such favorite sources as the French translation of Boccaccio's *Concerning Famous Women* (BN MS. fr. 12420), proclaiming how most women are "slow-witted" (*de tardif engin*) "by nature" and are "weak in character" in comparison to the "great intellect" (*grant engin*) of men, so that those few female exceptions must be honored because of their "great and subtle wit and virtue" (f. 23r); Brunetto Latini makes a strange comment about the "covetousness" due to the *feminité* (here: "femaleness") of a goshawk (!) (*Li Livres dou Tresor,* ed. F. J. Carmody (Berkeley and Los Angeles: University of California Press, 1948), 1.146.5, p. 137); there are of course many other authors of this type.

22. Peter Dronke, *Woman Writers of the Middle Ages: A Critical Study of Texts from Perpetua to Marguerite Porete* (Cambridge, U.K.: Cambridge University Press, 1984), 55–83. I am grateful to Professor Elizabeth Petroff for calling this reference to my attention.

23. For the concept of closure versus forced continuation in Lorris, see David F. Hult, *Self-Fulfilling Prophecies: Readership and Authority in the First "Roman de la Rose"* (Cambridge: Cambridge University Press, 1986).

24. I have borrowed (and reworked to show diminutives) from Charles Dahlberg's monumental translation of the *Roman de la Rose* (Princeton, N.J.: Princeton University Press, 1971; reprint, Hanover, N.H.: University Press of New England, 1983), 353.

25. Much has been written on the question of Jean de Meun's propriety in this episode since the Debate. Most helpful perhaps is still Daniel Poirion, "Les mots et les choses selon Jean de Meun," *L'Information Littéraire* 26 (1974): 7–11, which concisely discusses the literary historical context.

Stylistic Conventions in *Le Livre de la mutacion de Fortune*

JEANETTE M. A. BEER

 Christine de Pizan provided an author's statement of intent for *Le Livre de la mutacion de Fortune* when she identified two components of the composition process as abridgement and truth:

> Et qui de bien rimer se charge,
> Ce n'est mie petite charge,
> Et par especial histoires
> Abriger en parolles voires! [1]

(And if anyone undertakes to rhyme well, it is no small task, especially abbreviating histories in true words.)

It is not clear why Christine should find the poeticization of "histories" so challenging. Of course, from the early thirteenth century onward, a long tradition had associated prose with fact and verse with fancy. It is hard to believe, however, that Christine equated her allegorical poem of Fortune's workings with history proper. At all events, her conception of the whole, formulated at a time when both author and work were faltering,[2] remained unaltered throughout, as was demonstrated by her constant guarantees of truth and her assertions of abridgement. Indeed those two banal devices acquired such personal significance that they provide a key to all of Christine's literary decisions in *La Mutacion de Fortune*.

Traditionally an assertion of truth had been of considerable importance toward the validation of a medieval narrative. Truth, according to Isidore of Seville, separated history from fable.[3] Truth was claimed also for fictional works, so that by the fifteenth century some authors were exploiting truth claims for the most paradoxical circumstances.[4]

Aware that the author-narrator stance and the eye-witness guarantee had become voguish ploys, justifying dream-visions and other fantasies, Christine explicitly dissociated her autobiography from such works,[5] perhaps thinking specifically of *Le Roman de la Rose* or *Le Livre du Voir-Dit*. Reiterated truth claims guaranteed that *La Mutacion de Fortune* was neither dream nor invention:

Or vueil compter une aventure,
Qui semblera, par avanture,
A plusieurs impossible a croire;
Mais, quoyqu'aucuns veulent mescroire,
Si est verité prouvee,
Evident et toute esprouvee,
Et a moy proprement avint

.   .   .   .

. . . ne fu pas songe
Quant ce m'avint, et, sanz mençonge,
Je raconteray grant merveille.   (Lines 50–56, 59–61)

(Now I want to recount an event that will seem, perhaps, to many
impossible to believe. But although some may wish to disbelieve, it is
proven truth, evident, and completely demonstrated, and it happened
to me myself . . . nor was it a dream when it happened to me, and
without lies, I will recount a great wonder.)

The projected composition was ambitious and complex. It incorporated
Christine's personal misfortune (her husband's death) into a universal history of global calamities. Indubitably an exercise in self-consolation, it was
surely intended also to enhance Christine's literary stature, allying her with
a range of medieval "greats" from Ovid and Boethius to Jean de Meun
and Dante. Autobiography blended with allegory, history with mythology.
And the entire saga of Fortune began with a *merveille,* guaranteed as truth
(lines 50–61, cited above). This miracle was the author's physical metamorphosis, "corps et voult" ("body and face") from woman to man.

The degree of literality of the claim was obviously questionable, but
another categorical truth assertion—"Homme suis, je ne ment pas" (line
147, "I am a man, I am not lying")—reinforced the *merveille.* The usefulness of the truth device to Christine's purpose was already apparent even in
these early examples. She could by this means justify subject matter which
was, at first sight, improbable, simultaneously imposing upon her narrative
a heroic dimension that would otherwise have been lacking. *La Mutacion
de Fortune* could enjoy the advantages of both fact and fiction. As Christine
lucidly explained:

Verité est ce que je dis;
Mais, je diray, par ficcion,
Le fait de la mutacion.   (Lines 150–52)

(What I am saying is the truth, but I will tell, with fiction, the fact of
the change.)

Allegorical truth was obviously the author's intention, and it served more
than once to enhance her autobiography. Actuality was concealed beneath
its *integumentum* as Christine's mother was characterized as "Dame Nature":

> Qui fut grant et lee
> Et plus preux que Panthasellee
> (Dieu proprement la compassa).   (Lines 339–41)

> (Who was great and generous, and more brave than Penthesilea [God
> amply endowed her].)

This heroic specimen wanted a daughter like herself and, as Christine asserted, "si fu nee fille, sanz fable" (392; "so, without telling a tale, I was born a girl"). Sex aside, however, her resemblance was to her father and, for his characterization as well, factual biography and allegorical truth were welded together by a truth claim. Christine's father possessed magic stones plucked from a spring on Mount Parnassus.

> Ne le dy pour lui alouser,
> Mais pour voir dire, sanz ruser.   (Lines 327–28; italics mine)

> (I do not say it to boast about him, but to speak truthfully, without
> artifice.)

Allegory would be justified later in *La Mutacion de Fortune* by the important truth assertion:

> Et si n'est mençonge, ne fable,
> A parler selon methafore,
> Qui pas ne met verité fore.   (Lines 1032–34)

> (And therefore it is neither lie nor fable to speak by metaphor, which
> does not exclude the truth.)

Metaphorical discourse brought even poets and historians together:

> Les poëtes, qui l'aviserent,
> En poësie deviserent
> Ses fais; Ovide en recorde,
> Qui a la vraye histoire accorde
> A parler selon methafore.   (Lines 13913–17)

> (The poets who had this in mind recounted his deeds in poetry; Ovid
> records some of them, and, in accord with "the true history," speaks in
> metaphor.)

"La vraye histoire" here signified an authenticated and reliable source and was Christine's usual designation for the *Histoire ancienne jusqu'à César*.[6] "Ovide" here refers to the *Ovide moralisé*. The subject upon which both works concurred was their narration of Hercules' descent into the underworld, which truth Christine regarded as allegorical, prefiguring Christ's descent into hell. Thus Christian and pagan truth blended in the labors of a classical hero[7] and the significance of *La Mutacion de Fortune* was made more profound.

The appropriate medium for a work of such import was unquestionably verse. Christine's lapse into prose at line 8749 is therefore unexpected, if not shocking. The immediate reason, of course, was the illness which prevented her from wrestling with the technical difficulties of poetry:

> . . . ne puis muser
> A rimer, pour fievre soubdaine
> Qui m'a seurpris, dont suis en peine.

> (nor can I think to rhyme, because of a sudden fever which has overtaken me and with which I am afflicted.)

When Christine was restored to health, however, she made no effort to unify the format of her narrative by converting the disparate chunk of prose to poetry. What considerations could have been more important to her than the artistic unity of the whole?

The explanation, in fact, was already contained in her observations about Jewish history, observations that reveal both her ambivalence and her unease with this subject. Her work hitherto had been unified by the centrality of Fortune. A new and higher conception of truth than the Fortune allegory must now dominate *La Mutacion de Fortune*, however, because the vicissitudes of the Jews must not be presented as resulting from Fortune's random machinations:

> Car leurs fais et prosperitez,
> Ou leurs grandes adversitez
> A Fortune je n'enjoing mie.   (Lines 8421–23)

> (For I do not connect their deeds and their prosperities nor their great adversities to Fortune.)

God had determined the course of Jewish history, punishing and rewarding according to the deserts of the Jews. Fortune was no more than the executioner. Judgment was the Lord's:

> Car Dieux, cui la loy ert amie,
> Les punissoit et meritoit,
> Selon leur dessarte, et metoit
> Puis hault ou bas, selon leur vice
> Ou merite, par sa justice.   (Lines 8424–28)

> (For God, to whom the Law was friend, punished and rewarded them according to what they deserved, and with his justice raised or lowered them according to their vice or merit.)

This shift in the characterization of Fortune, from omnipotently willful deity to subservient instrument of God's providential plan, resulted in several structural retakes and in methodological ambivalence. Christine's conflicting resolutions, necessary to ensure the completeness of the work as a whole, were as follows:

> Affin que mon oeuvre accomplie
> Soit, et que riens je n'y oublie   (Lines 8413–14)

> (so that my work be finished and that I forget nothing.)

Her overall approach of abridging true histories would be maintained:

> En touchant les vrayes histoires
> Des Juïfs anciennes et voires   (Lines 8419–20)

> (regarding the true histories of the Jews, histories both ancient and authenticated.)

The inclusion of Jewish history was, nevertheless, an amplification or "dilatation" (in other words, the opposite rhetorical process to abbreviation):[8] "Ancore un pou dilateray / Mon propos" (lines 8415–16; "I will again expand my account a little.")

Another reason—this one unacknowledged—may have undermined Christine's interest in the subject, namely, a change of sources. Her preferred authority, the *Histoire ancienne*, was in her view almost as authoritative as "la vraye sainte Escripture." Indeed, the two frequently merged in her recollection.[9] Her temporary recourse to another source (Bernard Gui's translation of the *Flores chronicorum*) apparently inspired no great enthusiasm—picturesque detail and all narrative excitement disappeared. Thus it was not until her narration of the heroic episodes of Judith and of Esther (once more from the *Histoire ancienne* and once more in poetic narrative) that Christine displayed any interest in the history of the Jews.[10]

Thus as indicators of authorial intention, assertions of truth revealed Christine's unmitigatedly serious attitude to her subject. But intentions could not always suffice. *La Mutacion de Fortune* was an ambitious project, and technical difficulties often threatened its proper realization. At those times, also, truth assertions were able to serve a purpose, providing convenient solutions which were at least appropriate, if not ideal.

Christine's handling of the octosyllabic couplet was uneven. The meter was an obvious choice in its century, but a longer narrative line might have occasioned less difficulty.[11] When one line did not suffice, yet two lines were excessive for the content, Christine usually resorted to the addition of a short phrase which, while not irrelevant, was in fact not vital to the whole. *La Mutacion de Fortune* contains numerous instances of these *chevilles*, many of them variants of the truth formula:[12] "à voir dire" ("to tell the truth"), "sachiés de vray" ("you should know for a fact"), "(ce) n'est pas fable" ("it is not a tale"), "sanz fable" ("without telling a tale"), "c'est voir" ("it is true"), "c'est chose voire" ("it is a true fact"), "en verité" ("in truth"), "(je croy) de voir" ("[I believe] for a fact"). They occur with frequency and in all contexts except Christine's fourteen paragraphs in prose.

The fact that most *chevilles* were identical in their truth content could be regarded as a demonstration of the author's concern for artistic unity. Were they thematic reminders of her overall schema? The reality of composition was surely otherwise: the guarantee of truth in short form was useful in the versification of *La Mutacion de Fortune*, and Christine employed it without reservation as an aid "bien rimer."

Other variations of the device allowed Christine to manipulate her public in more unusual ways. Her description of the "siege des nobles" veered away from sources into frequent moralizing. Included in this section was a seemingly tentative "se je ne mens" (line 5183; "if I do not lie"), which licensed the personal additions:

> si fais excés
> Apprenoit le sage Ulixés
> Aux chevaliers, de boire aux pos
> Quant ilz estoient a repos;
> Se je ne mens, ainsi faisoient
> Les bons, qui de valeur usoient.
> Ha! Gloutonnie la perverse!   (Lines 5179–85)

(The wise Ulysses taught the knights such excesses—to drink from bowls while reclining; and if I do not lie, the good men acted accordingly, abusing their valour. Oh perverse Gluttony!)

A less ingenuous "que je ne vous mente pas" in the description of Hymenaeus's court allowed her to reprove the corrupt Spanish clergy in passing:

> de gent d'eglise n'a cure,
> Vers lui ne mettroient le pas,
> Mais, que je ne vous mente pas,
> Bien oÿ dire que d'Espaigne
> En avoit en sa compaigne.   (Lines 842–46)

(He has no care for ecclesiastics and they would take no step toward him, but—don't let me lie to you—I have in fact heard that he had several Spaniards in his company.)

Whether in condensed form or fully articulated, the truth device never undermined the author's fundamental seriousness of purpose.

Linked to Christine's desire for "parolles voires" was her intention to abbreviate: "abriger." Her combinative phrase, "abriger en
parolles voires" was not borrowed from contemporary prologues and might
even be considered something of a paradox in its time. Truthful description more usually implied a listing of appropriate attributes and was enu-
merative rather than selective. Since the formulaic means used by Christine
to signal her abridgements *were* conventional, however, it is important to
understand what *abriger* could possibly signify to the author of a twenty-
four-thousand-line allegory.

Abbreviatio as interpreted by the Latin rhetoricians comprised about half a
dozen procedures,[13] most of which were irrelevant to French. Edmond Faral
in his edition of the *artes poetriae* went so far as to suggest that the whole
process of *abbreviatio* was of no interest to vernacular writers, who saw no
particular virtue in brevity: "Cette théorie ne paraît pas intéresser beaucoup
la littérature en langue vulgaire, non seulement parce que tous les procédés
qu'elle recommande n'y sont pas applicables, mais aussi parce que la briè-
veté n'y est pas souvent recherchée" ("This theory does not seem to pertain
to vernacular literature, not only because all the techniques recommended
are not applicable, but also because brevity is not often sought there").[14]

Christine's expressed intention to "abriger" obviously was not meaningless, and it occurs with tedious regularity. Source materials were being
sifted for their relevance to her principal subject, Fortune. For that reason,
as was seen above, she termed Jewish history "dilatation," since its histories,
although true, were irrelevant to her demonstration of the reverses endured
randomly because of Fortune.

On a smaller scale *abriger* implied a constant surveillance of minutiae
and a curtailment of enumeration that served no immediate purpose. It is
arguable whether Christine achieved her goals. As with her assertions of
truth, her statements of intent are nevertheless informative about much
more than the mere abridgement process.

Their form was variable. When developed in full, they could be formulated as a declaration, question, command, or hypothesis. Details of the in-
ternecine struggles in Carthage after Hannibal's era were avoided by means
of the declarative affirmation: "mais de leur joye ou grieté / Je me passeray
pour briefté" (lines 4597–98; "but for brevity's sake I will pass over their
joy or grief"). Slaughter at Troy was curtailed with two questions:

> Que vous diroye brief et court?
> Occis y fu et tous les siens
> Que vous en iroy je comptant?   (Lines 18098–99, 18107)

> (What should I tell you in brief and in short? He was killed and all of
> his own. . . . Why shall I go on telling you?)

Christine's public was directed toward the main theme of Fortune's dominance with a didactic imperative:

> Car, de vray, sachiés brief et court
> Qu'il n'est prince qui a sa court
> Ne serve.   (Lines 7127–29)

(For, in truth, you should know in brief and in short, there is no prince who does not serve at her court.)

Lavish description of the city of Nineveh was not provided because, as Christine explained in the following hypothesis:

> Se je vouloie tout descripre
> De la ville la grant noblece,
> La beauté, la force et richece,
> A tout dire trop tarderoye
> Et mon propos retarderoye.   (Lines 8806–10)

(If I wanted to describe everything, the great nobility of the city, its beauty, its power and riches, I would delay too much by telling everything, and would slow down my account.)

Not all assertions were as complex but were themselves abbreviated: "a brief parler" (line 17733; "to speak briefly"), "a vous faire brief" (17185; "to make it brief for you"), "a vous dire briefve / Raison" (21300–301; "to tell you it in brief"), "a vous dire en brief" (21962; "to tell you in brief").

Generally, however, the intention to abbreviate was articulated at length and even with fugal variations. The Trojan War aroused multiple declarations of intent to abbreviate, all of them differently formulated and none of them obviously decisive. Even before Hector had been killed Christine had already declared:

> Mais de ce lairay or ester,
> Car d'abriger m'esteut haster.   (Lines 16172–73)

(But I will let this be, for I must hurry to abbreviate.)

> . . . de les nombrer
> Couvendroit lonc temps encombrer   (Lines 16181–82)

(to enumerate them would take too much time)

> Mais n'en quier grant narracïon
> Faire, car mon entencïon
> N'est fors des principaulx fais dire,
> Si comme il touche a la matire.   (Lines 16207–10)

(But I will not try to make a long narration, for my intention is nothing
except to tell the principal deeds as relevant to the subject.)

Pour ce, vous dis, en brief   (Line 16213)

(For this, I will tell you in brief)

Du demourant me tais adés,
Pour cause de briefté.   (Lines 16222–24)

(I will now pass over the rest in silence, for the sake of brevity.)

Mais, or est temps que je me tire
A dire sa piteuse fin,
Pour la matiere traire a fin.   (Lines 16230–32)

(But, now it is time to drag myself away from telling his piteous end, in
order to bring the matter to a close.)

The context in which abridgement formulae were inserted varied greatly.
They could be opulent, as is the description of Dame Richece:

Mais jamais n'en vendroie a chief,
Se je l'avoie entrepris,
De raconter son tres grant pris.   (Lines 1626–28)

(But I would never come to the end if I had undertaken to tell of his
great worth.)

They could be disagreeable, as is the narration of the misfortunes of those
who live behind Poverty's door:

Que vous en yroye disant?
Je vous ennuyeroie en lisant
De trestous leurs maulx raconter.   (Lines 3479–81)

(Why should I go on telling you; I would bore you reading about all
their misfortunes.)

They could be bizarre, as is the enumeration of the strange creatures, mon-
sters and pygmies, in the perilous regions of Fortune's dungeon:

Tant sont estranges leurs façons,
Et pour ce, en brief nous passons.   (Lines 3997–98)

(Their manners are so strange, and for this reason, we pass over them
in brief.)

Or they could be neutral, as is Christine's account of the founding of Rome:

> Or vous ay je dit en brief comme
> Vint le commencement de Romme.   (Lines 18667–68)

(Now I have told you in brief how the beginning of Rome came about.)

Frequently cited as reasons for the abridgement were the author's boredom; (anticipated) boredom on the part of the audience; the author's inadequacy because of lack of time, memory, or inclination; (anticipated) incredulity on the part of the audience; irrelevance of the material; and the structural demands of the work.[15]

Not cited but fundamentally important was the factor of audience expectation. If Christine felt impelled to signal abridgement six times in less than one hundred lines, as in her summary of the Trojan War cited above, it was undoubtedly because a battle scene was conventionally a context for expansion, not abbreviation. (Compunction toward a mutilated source would have been another reason if Christine had been punctilious in this regard. However, she used most of her sources casually, citing them without a specific attribution and claiming that she worked from memory—a convenient explanation, whether true or false!)[16]

Other contexts where audience expectancy was high included listings of kings and princes (ancient or modern), individual combat, fortification, plunder, machines of war, feasting, and deprivations. On all of these subjects Christine habitually curtailed—with a statement of intention—what might have been an elegant amplification.

Sometimes her audience had certain narrative expectations because of their prior knowledge of her sources. After mentioning Cain's murder of Abel, Christine therefore explained:

> Je ne pense pas tout a dire,
> Quanque la Bible nous tesmoigne,
> Trop emprendroye grant besoigne!   (Lines 8238–40)

(I'm not intending to tell everything that the Bible recounts; I would be undertaking too much.)

Of similar popularity was *Li Fet des Romains*, to which she perhaps referred in the following passage:

> A la fin, a faire brief conte,
> Sanz que tous leur faiz je raconte,
> Femmes, enfens, tous i occirent
> Rommains, onques de la n'yssirent.   (Lines 21353–56)

(Finally, to make a brief account, without my telling you all their deeds,

the Romans there killed the women and children, everyone, they never
escaped from there.)

Statements of abridgement accompanied her avoidance of that work's explanations of Rome's political offices, of Pompey's conquests, and indeed of
almost all explanations of military tactics anywhere.[17]

Thus the assertions of truth and abridgement in *La Mutacion de Fortune*
may be viewed as the facilitators for an author's personal communication
with her public. The means were not infinitely variable—although Christine obviously worked on their variation! Their usefulness was rather that
they were an acceptable pretext for disclosure: of beliefs and prejudices,
tastes and foibles, sickness and health.

Sometimes the disclosure is unwelcome. Christine's consistent reduction
of Rome's politics—for example, her assessment of the reasons for Rome's
civil war—revealed more about Christine than about the careers of Caesar
and his son-in-law.

> Or couvient que je meine a chief
> Mon ystoire. A vous dire en brief,
> Julïus Cesar et Pompee
> Qui tant ot conquis a l'espee,
> Mie grandement ne s'amoyent.   (Lines 21961–65)

(Now I must bring my story to an end. To tell you in brief, Julius Caesar
and Pompey, who had conquered so much with the sword, never loved
each other very much.)

Her disdainful rejection of Jewish history (although typical of her century)
is, now, not only offensive, but it is also aesthetically disastrous, sabotaging
the unity of *La Mutacion de Fortune* and calling into question the characterization of Fortune as its Prime Mover.

Least welcome of all is the revelation at line 16660 that even the author
is tired of her book.

> . . . en brief, vous dirons
> Ce qu'il s'ensuivi aprés
> Car m'euvre encore est longue tres.   (Lines 16660–62)

(in brief, we will tell you what happened afterward, because my work is
already very long.)

The discrepancy between the banality of the device and the intensity of personal signification imposed upon it is almost shocking. But however tedious
Christine may have found the process of composition, *Le Livre de la mutacion de Fortune* merits close attention. This work was no trivial pursuit but a
serious, often laborious, stage in the literary apprenticeship of its author.

Notes

1. French text is from Christine de Pisan, *Le Livre de la mutacion de Fortune*, ed. Suzanne Solente, 4 vols. (Paris: Picard, 1959–66). All translations are my own.

2. Illness apparently interrupted her work (see below).

3. "Historiae sunt res verae quae factae sunt" ("Histories are true things which took place"), *Etymologiae* 1.44.

4. Cf. Jeanette Beer, *Narrative Conventions of Truth* (Geneva: Droz, 1981), esp. chap. 6.

5. Christine would soon turn to the dream-vision format, however, in her ambitious full-length autobiography entitled *L'Avision-Christine*.

6. For Christine's sources, see Solente's edition, xxx–xcviii.

7. Respect for the heroes of classical antiquity, described by Isidore of Seville as "viri quasi aerii et caelo digni propter sapientiam et fortitudinem" ("lofty men worthy of heaven thanks to wisdom and strength," *Etymologiae* 1.29.9) was hardly new. From the earliest centuries A.D. pagan history and fable could be justified if they prefigured Christian truth. For the prefiguration of Christ in Hercules it may be relevant to note that among the titles inserted into some manuscripts of Claudian (late fourth–early fifth centuries A.D.) were "de salvatore," "miracula Christi," and "laus Herculis." Of the writers contemporary with Christine, Dante was the most illustrious literary exponent of the pagan-Christian concatenation. See Robert Hollander, *Allegory in Dante's "Commedia"* (Princeton, N.J.: Princeton University Press, 1969), esp. chap. 5; and Earl Jeffrey Richards, "Christine de Pizan and Dante: A Reexamination," *Archiv für das Studium der neueren Sprachen und Literaturen* 137 (1985): 100–111.

8. Christine's understanding of the term *dilatation* provides an excellent example of its meaning in medieval (as opposed to ancient) rhetoric. No longer did it signify the ennobling of a subject but, rather, its lengthening. As Edmond Faral explains in *Les Arts poétiques du XIIe et du XIIIe siècle* (Paris: Champion, 1962), 61, concerning "amplificatio, dilatatio": "Par 'amplifier' les anciens entendaient 're-hausser [une idée], la faire valoir': ainsi font encore, à une époque tardive, certains de leurs imitateurs directs, comme Alcuin. Mais les théoriciens du XIIe et XIIIe siècle entendent par là 'développer, allonger [un sujet]' " ("By 'amplify' the ancients meant 'to bring out [an idea], to emphasize it': certain of their direct imitators, like Alcuin, are still doing the same even at a relatively late date. But the theoreticians of the twelfth and thirteenth century mean 'to develop, lengthen [a subject]' "). Christine's attitude toward Jewish history was somewhat patronizing, and her inclusion of it in *La Mutacion de Fortune* was certainly not for its ennobling influence. Obviously she believed, however, that her work would be less than complete without it, hence the amplification (or as she calls it, significantly, "dilatation").

9. For example, in her narration of the story of Esther, and in some other episodes of Jewish history.

10. Christine's interest in such Jewish *clarae* or illustrious women as Esther and Judith was, however, genuine, as is demonstrated by her narration of their exploits on behalf of their people in the *Cité des Dames* 2.31.1; 2.32.1 and 2.

11. This hypothesis becomes particularly pertinent in the context of Christine's

narration of battles, where she makes extensive use of epic devices. Such imitative phrases as "la les veissiés" (line 17156, "there you would have seen them") or "Atant es vous Hector venir" (line 15491, "See Hector coming") are obviously more suited to an expansive decasyllable or to the alexandrine than to her primly tidy octosyllabic couplets.

12. Her other preferred formula is that of abridgement. See below.

13. Geoffroi de Vinsauf identified seven, Evrard four, and Jean de Garlande five.

14. Faral, *Les Arts poétiques*, 85.

15. See, for example, lines 709–14, 967, 3538–39, 8745–48, 14994, 18897–98.

16. Compare the more rigorous methods of one of her sources, *Li Fet des Romains*, in which sources are named and shifts between sources are signaled.

17. The avoidance of these subjects may appear surprising in an author who would later produce *Le Livre des fais d'armes et de chevalerie*. It was, however, essential to Christine's purpose of portraying the vicissitudes of Fortune. In *Li Fet des Romains*, on the other hand, Fortune was only one of a number of factors that contributed to Rome's history. More important as a unifying theme in that work was the role of Roman "sens et proece" ("intellect and valor"). See Jeanette Beer, *A Medieval Caesar* (Geneva: Droz, 1976), xiii–xix and 193ff.

Reopening the Case: Machaut's *Jugement* Poems as a Source in Christine de Pizan

BARBARA K. ALTMANN

Among the various types of *dits amoureux* written by Guillaume de Machaut, the *jugement* poem was a clever innovation. Building on the tradition of twelfth- and thirteenth-century debate poetry, it provided not only a very satisfying form of flattery for a current patron— by putting words of wisdom in his mouth and a host of excellent qualities at his command—but also a format eminently suitable for the examination of the subtleties of love as practiced, or at least discussed, in aristocratic society. What more suitable forum for intricate argument than a court-room scene, where a minimum of plot could supply a certain amount of tension as to outcome and where characters of allegorical or human nature could quite justifiably defend conflicting opinions at length? Machaut's first "judgment," the *Jugement dou Roy de Behaigne*, was clearly a success: it engendered a sequel, the *Jugement dou Roy de Navarre*, and both poems took their places as major works in fourteenth-century as well as modern collections of Machaut's narrative poetry.[1]

Their popularity is attested to in the fifteenth century as well,[2] and they must have been known to Christine de Pizan, who produced a group of three debate poems, the *Debat de Deux Amans*, the *Livre des Trois Jugemens* and the *Livre du Dit de Poissy*,[3] which were obviously influenced by Machaut's works. While only the *Dit de Poissy* can be dated precisely (by internal evidence) to April 1400,[4] the other two may well have been written the same year.[5] All three belong to the transitional period of Christine's career, after she had produced the bulk of her short lyric poetry and before she launched into the long didactic books to follow. It was hardly surprising to see judgment poetry resurfacing at the turn of the century, given the renewed enthusiasm for love casuistry as edifying entertainment that resulted in the founding of a Court of Love in 1400 under the auspices of Charles VI, the purpose of which was to render decisions on poetic debates concerning fine points of the lovers' code.[6] Nor is it surprising that in writing works of this sort, Christine should, in the best tradition of medieval writers in general, draw upon the appropriate examples available to her in the poetry of her literary predecessors.

Without going into great detail, the following outline gives the essential content of her three debates. All of them begin and end with an appeal from Christine the narrator/poet to a nobleman; she asks him to agree to judge the cases, involving a dispute about love, that the debaters have asked her to write about. The *Livre des Trois Jugemens* then recounts three arguments, back to back, in each of which one member of a couple feels he or she has been unjustly accused of infidelity by the other. The specific circumstances each case proposes are of a sort that could be found in any compendium of twelfth- and thirteenth-century "jeux-partis."[7] All three disputes in this work actually probe the issue of what kind of provocation justifies abandoning a lover to whom one has sworn loyalty. By contrast, the *Debat de Deux Amans* is much more theoretical in nature, recording the dispute between a world-weary knight of mature years and an optimistic young squire; the former feels that service to Love brings much more grief than good, while his opponent holds the contrary. There is a third speaker in this debate whose short speech puts the issue into perspective, but we will come back to her role later. The *Dit de Poissy*, finally, upsets the pattern unexpectedly by announcing a debate but using almost half its length to desribe a visit to the Dominican convent of Poissy, even before introducing its speakers. Once the conversation is underway, it examines the question of which of the debaters may legitimately feel more aggrieved, the knight who has been spurned by his lady or the lady whose knight has been imprisoned abroad with little hope of release.

The resonances of Machaut's two judgment poems are immediately apparent. The *Dit de Poissy* particularly has been singled out as derivative of the *Jugement dou Roy de Behaigne*, but all three of Christine's poems reproduce certain aspects of the earlier works. From the brief plot summaries above, it may be noted that the first obvious parallel is the device of selecting a patron to be the judge of the cases presented. Christine does not use the adjudicator's name in the title of her poems as Machaut did, but she names him in a dedicatory prologue. The *Debat de Deux Amans* is addressed to the duke of Orléans, *Trois Jugemens* to the seneschal of Hainaut. *Poissy* is not quite so explicit: Roy assumed, as many modern critics do, that it, too, was dedicated to Jean de Werchin, but Charity Cannon Willard points out that this supposition is inconsistent with information given in the poem and suggests that it was likely sent to either the marshal Boucicaut or Jean de Châteaumorand, instead.[8] Other similarities are equally striking. For example, all three of Christine's works use the meter found in *Behaigne*, that is, quatrains of three ten-syllable lines followed by one line of four syllables. Two of them, the *Debat de Deux Amans* and *Poissy*, use quasi-realistic settings, as background for the debate, which recall Machaut's description in *Behaigne* of his sylvan hiding place and Durbuy Castle, and the long chroniclelike opening of *Navarre* that tells of the Black Plague. Further, in all three of Christine's works, the narrator/poet figure is similar to her counterpart in *Behaigne*, witnessing the arguments and playing what Barton Palmer calls "master of ceremonies" in controlling the progress of the action.[9] Even in their closings Christine's poems recall Machaut's, in that each uses the same sort of anagram one finds in *Behaigne*, where the author's name can be puzzled out of the last line.

In terms of the content of the poems, it has been pointed out that the contestants in the *Debat de Deux Amans* buttress their arguments with many of the same examples from classical, mythological, and vernacular stories that appear in the *Navarre*.[10] And the generous borrowings *Poissy* makes from *Behaigne* have been made the subject of an article by Annie Reese Pugh (published in 1894, soon after the first complete edition of *Poissy* was available) and a section of J. C. Schilperoort's 1936 comparative study of Machaut and Christine.[11]

Indeed it is hard to overlook the intertextual links between the conversations of unhappy knight and lady that take up the second half of *Poissy* and the first half of *Behaigne*. The dramatic situation behind their sorry tales is strikingly similar: in both stories, the knight has been rejected by a young woman who had initially seemed inclined to favor him, while the lady's lover has been taken from her, by death in *Behaigne* and by imprisonment in *Poissy*. Their determined suffering gives rise to exactly the same gratifyingly melancholy question in both texts: Which of the two may rightly claim to be the more unhappy?[12] Both Pugh and Schilperoort devote a large part of their discussions to a line-by-line comparison of the passages involved, demonstrating how closely Christine's work follows Machaut's in leading into the conversation, in describing the lady's distress, and especially in drawing verbal portraits of the lovers of each participant. It is particularly the pictures that the knights paint of their beloveds that closely resemble each other.

Having seen briefly how Christine appropriated various aspects of the material provided by Machaut, we can now turn to the perhaps more interesting and fruitful discussion of how and to what purpose she reworked her source. The major differences between her *débats* and Machaut's are again easily discerned. The first, not unexpectedly, is that Christine puts the lady back into the text by permitting her to tell her side of the story.

This redistribution of parts is a distinctive characteristic of Christine's whole corpus. Her ladies are active participants and sometimes as frank as their male counterparts in their expression of physical desire. One thinks immediately, for example, of Marotele, heroine of *Le Dit de la Pastoure*.[13] In this poem, unlike other *pastourelles*, Marotele, rather than the knight, is the narrator, and far from behaving like an unsophisticated country girl, her actions and feelings are entirely courtly, more than a match for those of the nobleman with whom she falls in love. She is undeniably attracted by the knight's physical appearance, although she resists him at first. When at last she agrees to accept him as her lover, she enjoys herself wholeheartedly during their trysts.[14] During his absence, she appeases her desire by embracing him in her thoughts, remembering how they would lie together (lines 1769–75). When he returns, they embrace each other more closely than ever Tristan did Yseut, for whom he died (lines 2156–60). And so on.

None of Christine's other heroines is quite so explicit, or speaks of love-making in quite such extended passages. Nevertheless, the lady of the *Cent ballades d'Amant et de Dame* tells her knight, once he has promised to respect her wishes:

> Et quant a moy, cuer et corps et pouoir,
> M'onneur gardant, du tout vous abandon
> Tres bel et bon, toudis vueilliez m'avoir
> En loyauté, et je tiens qu'a bandon
> De doulz plaisirs arons en cel espoir;
> Toute m'amour je vous octroye en don.[15]

(And as for me, while safeguarding my honor, I give over to you completely my heart, my body and my power. . . . Fair and good friend, be faithful to me always and I promise that we shall have sweet pleasures freely in this hope. I grant you the gift of all my love.)

And later, at the height of their romance:

> Doulz ami, mon cuer se pasme
> En tes bras; t'alaine entiere
> Me flaire plus doulz que basme,
> Baisiez moy, doulce amour chiere.[16]

(Sweet friend, my heart is fainting in your arms; your pure breath smells sweeter to me than balm; kiss me, my sweet, dear love.)

In the judgment poems, the women involved in the debates are quite assertive and do not hesitate to speak up. The young lady in the third of the *Trois Jugemens* wants her case heard by "les dames" (lines 1492–96) before a judgment is made on it (perhaps assuming that a jury of her peers might be more sympathetic than a male judge?). In *Deux Amans*, the female speaker who takes the floor midway through the poem politely but openly contradicts the opinion of the knight who spoke before her. The lady's increased participation is most evident, however, in the *Dit de Poissy*. While the dialogue between the debaters in both *Poissy* and *Behaigne* takes approximately 1,200 lines, the lady in Machaut is allotted only 120 lines to tell her tale while the knight takes a generous 850. In *Poissy* the lady expounds much more fully on her subject, taking 300 lines as compared with the knight's 480. Moreover, she is not content to recount her woes passively. She states strong, unequivocal opinions on the subject of the evil *Basac* and the crusade to Nicopolis, during which her lover was taken hostage. She openly criticizes her lover's family for failing him:

> Car leur devoir en font mal, a voir dire
> Comme il me semble,
> Tous ses parens, dont mon cuer de dueil tremble,
> Car leurs terres deussent tous vendre ensemble
> Ains qu'ilz n'eussent cil qui angel ressemble.   (Lines 1303–7)

> (It seems to me, to speak the truth, that all his relatives are negligent in their duty to him, which makes my heart tremble with grief; for all of them together would have to sell their lands before they recover the one who looks like an angel.)

Not content to sit idly by, she herself would be willing to sell her entire holdings and would brave all the hardships entailed to travel to the prison where he is kept in an attempt to have him released (lines 1309–28).

Another striking feature of her speech, and one that reminds us of her sister heroines such as Marotele, is the full-length description she gives of her knight. Just like her adversary in debate, she speaks for about ninety-five lines on the topic of the physical beauty she was drawn to in her beloved. While Machaut's lady dismisses her lover's appearance in three lines, and therefore necessarily in very general terms, Christine's lady draws the exact masculine equivalent of the standard portrait of female beauty, very like the one that her interlocutor gives of his mistress. Following the standard format, her picture and the one the knight gives work their way from hair to toes, leaving very few traits unexplored on the way. Accordingly, once the knight has reached his mistress's torso, he describes her breasts, chest, and hips; the surprise here is that the lady does the same thing, dwelling on chest, stomach, hips, buttocks, and thighs, matching her male friend's description detail by detail. Of her lover's broad chest (*beau pis,* line 1146) she says,

> Quant m'en souvient j'en sue
> De grant doulour, car maintes fois receue
> Par amour fine
> G'y ay esté   (Lines 1146–49)

> (I sweat with great sorrow when I remember it, for many time was I received there with tender love).

The sensual nature of the physical portraits caused a *frisson* of disapprobation among early twentieth-century critics who found the explicit nature of the descriptions unseemly, particularly because they were written by a woman. Marie-Josèphe Pinet, who acts as an apologist for Christine by pointing out that she does nothing but follow the rules for such depictions, quotes E. -M. -D. Robineau, who was less objective: "Robineau, pourtant fervent admirateur de Christine, paraït [sic] un peu scandalisé de sa liberté de langage. C'est à propos du réalisme de la description du chevalier et de la dame, dans le *Dit de Poissy*, 'La description est complète, dit-il, et d'une naïveté effrayante. Comment devaient parler les dames à une époque où une Christine de Pisan écrivait ainsi!' " [17] ("Robineau, although a fervent admirer of Christine, appears somewhat scandalized by the freedom of her language. Concerning the realism of the description of the knight and the lady in the *Dit de Poissy*, he says, 'The description is complete and frightfully naïve. How must ladies have spoken in an age where a Christine de Pisan wrote in such a way.' ") However politely or explicitly the ladies of Christine's day expressed themselves, they must surely have spoken more than Machaut's ladies are allowed to do.

Aside from the reintegration into the love story of the female point of view, Christine makes other major changes to her model by leaving out two elements integral to Machaut's debates. These are the participation of allegorical personifications and the rendering of a decision on the case at the end. While these obvious omissions have generally been remarked on by those who discuss Christine's debt to Machaut, their significance has not been addressed in terms of Christine's concept of love or in determining the status of these three works in her corpus. In Schilperoort's opinion, the lack of judgments indicates simply a greater interest on the author's part in the poem as a presentation piece for a particular patron. She says: "Pour Christine c'est le choix du juge qui est le point capital; elle s'adresse à lui au commencement, dans le corps et à la fin du Dit, tout en le comblant de louanges; elle lui expose le débat, mais la sentence lui est égale; l'affaire litigieuse fait absolument défaut." [18] ("For Christine, the choice of judge is the essential point; she addresses him at the beginning, in the middle and at the end of the *Dit*, while showering him with praise; she relates the debate to him, but the outcome is of little concern to her; the legal dispute is completely lacking.")

Christine certainly does transform the way in which the narrator of *Behaigne* courteously selects a judge for his fellow characters. She uses an elaborate dedicatory framework and then embeds the debate into this rhetorical structure. As I have argued elsewhere, this device is an essential element in binding together the two very different segments of the *Dit de Poissy*. [19] And while I agree that Christine cares little about the outcome of the disputes she presents, it seems to me that this apparent disregard cannot help but influence a reading of the works, particularly in the face of the enormous importance placed on the decision in Machaut. In my opinion, the elimination of decisions and personified abstractions from Christine's three poems is symptomatic of the attitude she takes toward her subject matter. As such, these changes made to the form she inherited are related to other, less conspicuous alterations that on closer investigation can be discerned in each piece.

A first such alteration is illustrated in *Poissy*, where, for all its similarities to the *Behaigne*, the dramatic situation has been rendered much more innocuous. Gone are two of the crucial points that determine the verdict, namely, the death of the lady's lover and the fickleness of the knight's lady. Annie Reese Pugh notes the second change and reasons: "Christine n'admet pas facilement qu'une dame puisse être *fausse*" [20] ("Christine does not easily admit that a woman can be *false*"). This claim must surely be the case—examples of infidelity on the part of a woman are difficult to find in Christine's corpus. But this fact does not account for the decision to make the lady-debater's knight a prisoner after the disastrous crusade to Nicopolis, rather than one of the many who lost their lives there. I read both changes as a decision to take the sting out of the dilemma, to even up the sides. The death of a loved one is a loaded issue in Christine's poetry, given the autobiographical circumstances that inspired her lyric poems about the sorrow of widowhood. With no death and no betrayal in *Poissy*, there can be no debate over which of these two adversities is the harder to bear, the question which, after all, is ostensibly the subject of discussion in both *Behaigne* and *Navarre*.

This defusing of the contentious issue effectively reduces the points of doctrine under discussion. It limits the argument to just one aspect of the wrangling in *Behaigne*, that is, the effect on the unhappy partner of seeing or not seeing the loved one. In *Poissy* as in *Behaigne*, the lady tries to convince the knight that he is more fortunate than she because he can at least see his beloved from time to time. He, in turn, insists that this only exacerbates his pain, while in her case, distance and time will soon lessen her misery.[21] This juxtaposition of views, however, is the full extent of the debate. Without the intervention of advocates such as *Behaigne*'s Raison and Loyauté on one side and Jeunesse and Amour on the other, no course of action is suggested for either of the debaters, nor do more fundamental issues arise. While Machaut's interest lies primarily in ideological issues, Christine's does not.

In fact, we have come to one of the essential differences between Christine's and Machaut's debates: whereas Machaut uses a set of personal circumstances to launch a discussion of the tenets of love, Christine uses the debate format as an excuse to elaborate on personal circumstances. As Douglas Kelly says with regard to Machaut, "the immediate question is a convenient pretext for exemplifying important ideas and sentiments that determine the arguments and the final judgment."[22] From *Behaigne* to *Navarre*, Machaut's concept of "bonne amour" is transformed, in Kelly's view, by a Boethian idealism, from one in which love is bound by desire and tied to the vagaries of Fortune into one in which love is sustained by hope.[23] In Christine's debates, however, there is no such evolution in philosophy, nor does optimism reign. In *Poissy*, as far as we can see, desire still drives the characters and Fortune still dictates their fate.[24] In the *Trois Jugemens* one finds a twenty-line passage about the mutability of all things, including love (lines 1293–1312). But these brief statements are as far as Christine's theorizing goes in the debates. She is not concerned with the intellectual aspect of the courtly game, but rather with the rules, making sure that the players behave honorably, and with the effect that love's disappointments have on the participants.

One might assume that what attracted Christine to *Behaigne* as a model was not the scene at the court of Durbuy but the anecdotal quality of the conversation between the lady and knight. In effect, she simply re-created this portion and bypassed the part that is of greater importance in Machaut. *Poissy* comes very close to being neither a judgment nor a debate. Certainly the argument as such, assertion followed by contradiction, takes only a very limited number of lines—approximately 130 of more than 2,000.[25] The *Livre des Trois Jugemens* is similarly constructed; in each of the three segments, there is a passage of verbal sparring between members of the feuding couple, but as in *Poissy*, the greater part of each story is spent recounting their case histories.

In this tendency *Poissy* and the *Trois Jugemens* show a manifest affinity with Christine's *ballade* sequences, both of those to be found in her early poetry and the later *Cent ballades d'Amant et de Dame*, as well as with the *Livre du Duc des Vrais Amans*. All of these stories trace the development and failure of a love relationship. As Charity Cannon Willard has demonstrated, the sad and thorny alliances described in *Poissy* and the *Trois Jugemens* reinforce the opinion of *fin'amor* found elsewhere in Christine's work as something that will invariably lead to disaster and despair, particularly for the woman involved.[26]

This disapproval of courtly dalliance is not made explicit in either of these works or in the *Deux Amans*, but all contain implicit statements, hints about the author's attitude toward her material. In all three poems Christine completely discarded the abstract arguments put forward in the court scenes of Machaut's debates by his cast of allegorical counselors. Without personifying the character, she does, however, seem to espouse the teachings of Raison. In *Behaigne*, Raison agreed with her fellow courtiers that the knight was the more unfortunate of the two lovers; but while sympathetic to his case, she also stated that he remained loyal to his unfaithful love against her, Reason's, advice and that he could and should abandon the foolish pining that is causing his grief.[27] In Christine's poems, while not given a speaking role, the presence or absence of reason appears to determine a character's well-being. In the *Trois Jugemens* it is a healing, moderating force. For example, when the lady in the first case decides to give up her fickle, unattentive lover, she returns to rationality: "le sien cuer a raison se revint" (line 358; "her heart returned to reason"). In a time of great unhappiness for the lady in the second case, reason prevents her from falling into despair:

> . . . n'autres armes
> N'avoit d'espoir
> Qui gardassent encontre desespoir
> Son dolent cuer, et cheoite y fust apoir
> Se grant raison, qui en a le pouoir,
> Ne l'eust gardé.
>
> (Lines 845–52)

(She had no other weapons of hope that would protect her heart from despair, and she would have succumbed to it soon, had great reason, which has the power to do so, not saved her.)

Similarly, the young squire in *Deux Amans* implies that it was unreasonable, intemperate behavior that caused the deaths of the famous lovers cited earlier by the disenchanted knight: "leur fole maniere / Les fist morir" (lines 1378–79; "their foolish manner caused their death"). He asserts that even a positive force such as love must be channeled wisely: "Ne peut on pas de toute chose bonne / Trés mal user?" (lines 1393–94; "Cannot one abuse every good thing?"). The squire's companion, the young lady, goes so far as to praise the speech of Raison in the *Roman de la Rose* (objected to so vehemently elsewhere in Christine's writings, on other grounds), for its sensible advice to the lover:

> Bien en parla le *Romans de la Rose*
> A grant procès et aucques ainsi glose
> Ycelle amour, com vous avez desclose
> En ceste place,
> Ou chapitre Raison qui moult menace
> Le fol amant, qui tel amour enlace,
> Et trop bien dit que pou vault et tost passe
> La plus grant joye
> D'ycelle amour, et conseille la voie
> De s'en oster. . . .
>
> (Lines 961–70)

(The *Romance of the Rose* speaks of it well at some length and thus explicates this love, as you have described in this place, where Reason rebukes and scolds the foolish lover, who embraces such love, and states most accurately that the greatest joy of that love is worth little and quickly passes, and advises how to rid oneself of it.)[28]

The key words in the suffering of Christine's characters are *fole amour* and *trop amer* (with the connotation of loving excessively), both of which come up repeatedly.[29] The sort of love they desire is not a sufficient end in itself, nor is it self-sustaining. The narrator's voice in *Trois Jugemens* tells us:

> Fole amour est tout vent
> Qui peu dure et les cuers va decevant
> Et un espoir dont après ensuivent
> Va joye vaine. . . .   (Lines 1309–12)

(Foolish love is nothing but wind that lasts but briefly and deceives hearts, a hope that is followed by empty joy.)

The *Trois Jugemens* in its entirety is actually an elaboration of the question, when should one reasonably give up on love? The implied answer is, quickly. Good sense prohibits placing much faith in earnestly professed but ill-founded love and loyalty.

This disavowal of love is reinforced by the status and role of the narrator in Christine's poems, which emphasize her detachment from the debates themselves. There is a fundamental shift in the character of the narrator figure from Machaut's work to the equivalent construct in Christine's.[30] Machaut's narrator is always engaged in the service of Love, whether as lover and protagonist or as clerk reporting on the love relationships of others. In the *Behaigne*, for example, he identifies himself in both the prologue and the closing as a lover. Christine the narrator, for her part, deliberately dissociates herself from any personal involvement in courtly love and any desire to participate. This practice is evident as early as her first *ballade* cycle, the *Cent ballades*, in which she insists both at the halfway point and in the final poem that the *ditz d'amours* she is writing should be read as entertainments and must not be interpreted as her own experience, for her heart is elsewhere.[31]

In the *Debat de Deux Amans*, the narrator's unwillingness to identify with the *fins amans* about whom she writes is vividly demonstrated by her physical separation from them at the party where the story begins. She sits on the periphery, on a window seat, immersed in thoughts of her widowhood (lines 145–61), until she is drawn into conversation with an unhappy knight. Even when she agrees to accompany the knight and a young squire into the garden for their discussion on love, she restricts her role to that of silent witness and reporter.

In the *Trois Jugemens* the narrator is presented as someone with a reputation for wisdom: all three couples seek her out to ask her if she will judge their case or at least recommend to them someone who might. She declines the invitation to act as arbiter, however, asserting that she is too little versed in the matters of love to serve as a good judge. Part of her protestations can be dismissed as the modesty topos: her small wisdom cannot compare to that of her patron. Nevertheless, one observes that she goes to some lengths to establish her position as a disinterested party. To the seneschal of Hainaut, to whom the poem is dedicated, she says that she presents the cases to him because she herself knows too little about the subject to decide fairly ("trop peu sçay pour en bien jugier," line 26); when the first couple approaches her, she states that she has no desire to please one partner at the expense of angering the other, and what is more, she would not know how to begin to judge such a debate, so little versed is she in such things (lines 665–72). To the second and third couples she replies simply that they could certainly find a much better judge than she, and that the best possible person to ask for help would, of course, be the seneschal (lines 1243–61, 1504–11). In each case she agrees to act only as an intermediary. Her flat refusal to become involved in their cases to any greater extent contrasts strongly with Machaut's *Behaigne*, in which the narrator figure approaches the debaters, eager to participate, and even more strikingly with the *Navarre*, where the narrator himself assumes a major role as the defendant in the proceedings.

Poissy begins with a prologue very similar to that of *Behaigne*. Like Machaut's narrator, who sets off into the spring morning to hear the birds with thoughts of love on his mind, Christine sets off into the forest in April, hears the same delightful bird song, and converses about love with her companions. But her motivation for undertaking this outing is unlike his: she is going to visit her daughter in a convent. The amorous and the maternal are two very different sources of inspiration! This shift is an excellent example of Christine's ability to manipulate traditional forms to express an unexpected message, to subvert a commonplace or, at the very least, to assimilate it for use with uncommon topics. Neither Christine's nor Machaut's narrators stay in the spotlight after these opening sequences. But while Machaut's lover/poet makes the transition from apparent protagonist to witness by hiding in a bush for the duration of the conversation between the knight and the lady, Christine's removal from the debate to come is not so literal. In her case, it is the result of her clear ties to another realm of experience, the engagement of her heart in familial and religious matters rather than matters of love.

For all the narrator's detachment and purported neutrality in the matter of the debates she recounts, however, she does not refrain from taking sides. In the *Trois Jugemens* she makes frequent editorial comments, as in the following:

> A brief parler, du tout en tout desroute
> Celle amour fu,

> Et la laissa et la mist en reffu
> Le faulz amant, que fust il ars en feu!   (Lines 1375–78)

(To put it briefly, that love was completely misguided, and the unfaithful lover abandoned and rejected her, may he roast in flames.)

She freely uses pejorative expressions to describe the knights in the first and third cases. The first chevalier, for example, is called *le desloyal* (line 309) and a *mençongier* (line 312); he makes excuses to his lady *pour la decepvoir* (line 299), and lies to her (line 309). It is obvious that she sympathizes with the warning given to other ladies by the first heroine: having been abandoned after three months by her knight, this heroine admonishes:

> Si soit mon fait exemple a toutes dames
> De croire pou ceulz qui jurent leurs ames,
> Car ce n'est tout fors pour decepvoir femmes.   (Lines 261–63)

(May my case be an example to all ladies, to believe little those who promise their souls, for it is all only to deceive women.)

This message is the same lesson that is delivered more forcefully some time later in the *Duc des Vrais Amans* and in the *Livre des Trois Vertus*. It certainly also constitutes an indirect reply, along with the negative presentation of the knights in the first and third cases, to Machaut's assertions in *Navarre* about the fickle nature of women. As Earl Jeffrey Richards has pointed out with regard to the *Cité des Dames*, Christine does not challenge misogynist slander head on in her defense of women, preferring a more nuanced refutation: "Her idealization of women does not represent an automatic antithesis to the demonization of women found in misogynist writers. She is not a prisoner of the literary clichés of her sources and of her opponents. Her refutation of such clichés is accomplished in a masterfully understated way." [32] The *Trois Jugemens*, like the *Cité des Dames*, uses counterexamples that point out the falseness of accusations such as Machaut's. The first knight levels a charge of infidelity against his lady, who has taken another lover, while it was actually his abandonment of her that provoked her action. In the third case, the knight is dismayed when the young lady he had loved refuses to take him back after he left her to serve a woman of higher status for a short time. Without stating categorically that women are faithful while men are not, Christine suggests that her ladies have acted honorably and with good sense in the face of often irresponsible behavior from the knights they loved.

Unlike the *Trois Jugemens*, *Deux Amans* cannot be construed as a cautionary tale because both the knight and squire speak in general, theoretical terms, however much their respective points of view are the result of personal experience. In this poem, the most sophisticated and learned of Christine's judgments, the debaters are well matched; both make skilful, sustained arguments and use many authoritative examples, drawn from mythological and classical compendia as well as from contemporary courtly circles. Declaring a winner in their dispute would be difficult, although the knight's experience compared with the youth's earnest and rather naïve enthusiasm might weigh the balance in the older man's favor. But despite this evenhandedness, Christine's attitude is again apparent, this time in the most explicit statement on the subject to be found in any of her three debate poems.

This statement takes the form of a short speech by the lady whom the narrator, the knight, and squire invite into the garden with them for the sake of appearances. As Charity Cannon Willard has said of this young woman, "One suspects she is Christine's mouthpiece."[33] In a brisk address of eighty-six lines (915–1000), she politely but firmly debunks the knight's assertions that men suffer terrible pain because of love. She does not believe that men are ever so taken with women as they say. This situation might have been true in the past, but not today. No one could withstand the torments described by the knight; at least, she adds with a flash of humor, she has never heard tell of the cemeteries where lie those "qu'amours entiere / A mis a mort" (lines 989–90, "whom loyal love has put to death").[34] In her opinion, "ce n'est qu'usage / D'ainsi parler d'amours par rigolage / Et passer temps" (lines 942–44; "it is simply common practice to speak thus about love for amusement and to pass the time"). There it is, stated baldly: talking about love is nothing but a pastime. This lady means specifically the exaggerated tales of woe with which knights ply ladies and try to win sympathy. Her dispassionate skepticism undermines the argument not only of the knight who speaks immediately before her, but also of the knights in *Poissy* and *Behaigne*. In a broader sense, however, it also undermines the value of debate poems and "jugements," reducing them from the level of serious and learned pursuit to that of entertainment.

Christine's practice here might best be explained as a return of the debate to its origins. Machaut had adapted the mechanism of debate for much the same purpose as Andreas Capellanus or Jean de Meun had, that is, as a device used to give structure to a treatise on important issues. His *dits amoureux* as a group, including the two "jugements," engage in a discourse which, as Daniel Poirion suggests, "cherche à dégager une sagesse pratique des conventions de l'amour courtois" ("tries to establish a practical knowledge of the conventions of courtly love"),[35] an "ars amatoria" of sorts, developed anecdotally. Christine, on the other hand, used other formats to express the ideas most important to her. The debates fall into the category of what Willard calls her "society poetry."[36] She employed them much as the earlier *trouvères* had: the debate formula allowed her to display her skill at argumentation and the portrayal of sentiment, and there were many models available for her to draw on for inspiration. She was also well aware that love stories were the most reliable of topics; in the fiftieth of the *Cent ballades* she had written:

> Car qui se veult de faire ditz chargier
> Biaulz et plaisans, soient ou longs ou cours,
> Le sentement qui est le plus legier,
> Et qui mieulx plaist a tous de commun cours,
> C'est d'amours.   (Lines 9–13)

> (Because, for anyone who wants to undertake the writing of fine and pleasing tales, be they long or short, the topic that is lightest and generally pleases everyone best is love.)

Poems treating fine points of chivalric love were certain to amuse the patrons whom she was hoping to please.

If we can posit that Christine's debate poems were written primarily as entertainments for her patrons, the changes she makes to Machaut's models are readily accounted for. It would explain why she did not rise in any direct way to the misogynistic bait of the narrator's arguments in *Navarre*, even though she was engaged around this time in the epistolary war over the *Roman de la Rose*. It would elucidate the absence in her debates of the allegorical characters she does not hesitate to employ elsewhere at this stage of her career, as shown by the figures Cupido in the *Epistre au dieu d'Amour*, written in 1399, and the goddess Loyauté in the *Dit de la Rose* of 1402. If she prefers to deal with the debates in a more realistic way than Machaut does, it is probably because she reserved the use of allegorical personifications for stating a more serious message in a different sort of poem. The debate as entertainment theory may also throw light on the missing judgments. Why bother answering an inconsequential question? There may be more fun in asking it skillfully than in discussing a solution.

The amusement provided by posing a conundrum does not, however, deny the implied warning about treating such games seriously. The lovers in these poems recount adventures that started joyfully but have stalled in sadness and/or dissent. The omission of judgments means that there is no resolution to their laments. Christine's characters and readers have to forego the satisfaction of the happy ending that Machaut provided for his.

Let us analyze these endings briefly. *Behaigne* moves from dispute in a garden to resolution at court. To quote William Calin, the first section shows two lovers "alone, unhappy, secretive, enslaved to their passions." In the second, at the castle, "we observe a dynamic community, working together in relative harmony."[37] *Poissy* stands this structure on its head. The harmonious, dynamic community at the convent described in the first half gives way to the static, melancholy world of secret sorrows in the second. Machaut's lovers may not be cured of their pain by the denouement of *Behaigne*, but their debate ends with a decision and they receive consolation for their distress in the form of material comfort and reintegration into good company. What is more, the losing party, that is, the lady, has powerful allies who appeal the verdict in a sequel, the *Navarre*, from which she emerges vindicated. Even then, her opponent the knight has the solace of knowing that although the first decision is overturned, he still has the support of the narrator.

Christine's lovers are left hanging. The *Dit de Poissy* is written carefully enough to ensure closure on other levels (for example: the appeal to the patron is brought full circle, the company leaves from and returns to Paris, the lady and squire rejoin their group after riding in isolation for the length of the conversation), but their dilemma remains open-ended. While Christine's outing is successful, the debaters' is not. Without a decision, *Poissy*, the *Trois Jugemens*, and the *Debat de Deux Amans* cannot end on the optimistic, productive note established by Machaut's poems; instead they end ambiguously, with tensions unresolved, on a note of both bewilderment and despair.

This practice reinforces a contention made by Charity Cannon Willard that there is greater coherence of ideas across Christine's poetry than has often been assumed. As Willard says, "[Christine's] attack on courtly love as practised by her contemporaries is one of her most persistent themes,"[38] and the alert reader should not be surprised to find it surfacing in these works from Christine's transitional period as well as in works of more serious didactic intent.

Machaut felt strongly enough about his *Behaigne* and the ideas it expressed to write what purports to be a palinode, and the revised judgment of the second work demands the creation of yet another poem. Christine's debates contain nothing controversial enough in her eyes to inspire either retraction or elaboration. What does give rise to more poetry in her work is a later, much bolder statement of a notion only adumbrated in the debates and early *ballade* cycles. In a very clever twist on Machaut, she uses his devices of recanting a previously expressed opinion and paying a fine that consists of more poetry in the prologue to her *Cent ballades d'Amant et de Dame*.[39] In the introductory poem she states that, although she would rather be engaged in work of a more learned nature, she has been obliged by a noble person to undertake the composition of one hundred *ballades* about love. This penalty has been imposed for having said, "que traire / En sus se doit d'amoureux pensement / Toute dame d'onneur" (lines 21–23), that is, for having said that honorable ladies should give up all thoughts of love. The first irony is that she does not recant any more than Machaut does:

while writing "Cent ballades d'amoureux sentement" (8 and refrain) as a punishment for trying to turn ladies away from love, she continues to do just that with yet another example of an unhappy love affair.[40] *Ballade* 100 makes this explicit. The lady is dying of grief, and states:

> De toutes dames soit sceue
> Ceste exemple, a fin que leurs
> Cuers, si faicte amour, ne mue,
> Car ja me deffault li cuers.   (Lines 13–16)

> (Let this example be known to all ladies, so that such love does not sway their hearts, for my heart already fails me.)

The second irony is that she uses Machaut's artifice in exhorting ladies to reject precisely the kind of involvement that he advocates and takes as subject in his poetry.

In evaluating Machaut's borrowings from the *Roman de la Rose*, R. Barton Palmer says: "These indicate not Machaut's inability to go beyond the mastery of that popular model but rather his desire to anchor the meaning of the present poem to a solid and richly signifying base. Machaut insists that we read the *Judgment of the King of Bohemia* through the *Romance of the Rose*."[41] If Machaut's work must be read through the *Rose*, we must similarly read Christine's work through Machaut. Christine is indeed reopening the case. She never does reply to the initial question that launches *Behaigne* and *Navarre* (the issue of grief associated with loss by death versus loss by infidelity), but several works in her corpus, both before and after the debates, address the other issues for which Machaut's narrator in *Navarre* is condemned: rudeness to women and glibness of speech meant to deceive. Her adaptation of his debate poem structures makes an ironic comment on his works. She sets up expectations and then derails them, both by treating lightly the form in which he placed serious discussion and by criticizing the subject matter that he considered of great importance. Just as Guillaume de Machaut reverses his first decision, she reverses them both, in favor of quite a different attitude toward love.

Notes

An earlier version of this paper was read at the 23d International Congress on Medieval Studies at Western Michigan University in May 1988.

1. *Oeuvres de Guillaume de Machaut*, ed. Ernest Hoepffner, vol. 1 (Paris: Firmin Didot, 1908). *Behaigne*, pp. 57–135; *Navarre*, pp. 137–291. See also Guillaume de Machaut, *The Judgment of the King of Bohemia (Le Jugement du Roy de Behaigne)*, trans. and ed. R. Barton Palmer (New York: Garland, 1984) and Guillaume de Machaut,

The Judgment of the King of Navarre (New York: Garland, 1988); and *"Le Jugement du Roy de Behaigne" and "Remede de Fortune,"* ed. James I. Wimsatt and William W. Kibler, music ed. Rebecca A. Baltzer (Athens: University of Georgia Press, 1988). In this paper, all line references for Machaut's poems refer to Hoepffner's edition.

2. On the subject of *Behaigne*'s popularity, see *Oeuvres*, 1:lxiv.

3. *Oeuvres poétiques de Christine de Pisan*, ed. Maurice Roy, vol. 2 (Paris: Firmin Didot, 1891). *Debat de Deux Amans*, 49–109; *Livre des Trois Jugemens*, 111–57; *Dit de Poissy*, 159–222. Line numbers for quotations taken from these and other works in Roy's edition will be given in the text.

4. *Dit de Poissy*, lines 37–39.

5. Enid McLeod states that the *Debat de Deux Amans* can be dated to 1401 on the basis of internal evidence (*The Order of the Rose: The Life and Ideas of Christine de Pizan* [London: Chatto and Windus, 1976], 58). Concerning the relative dating of the three debate poems, it might be of interest to note that in the five early fifteenth-century manuscripts in which all three of the works appear, the *Deux Amans* appears first, followed (immediately, in two cases) by *Trois Jugemens*, which is in turn followed (always immediately) by the *Dit de Poissy*. For manuscript and folio numbers, see the appropriate entries in Angus J. Kennedy, *Christine de Pizan: A Bibliographical Guide*, Research Bibliographies and Checklists, no. 42 (London: Grant and Cutler, 1984), 69, 71, 106–7.

6. See Daniel Poirion, *Le Poète et le prince: L'Évolution du lyrisme courtois de Guillaume de Machaut à Charles d'Orléans* (Paris: Presses universitaires de France, 1965), 37–38.

7. See, for example, Artur Långfors, *Recueil général des jeux-partis français* (Paris: Champion, 1926). In Långfors's compendium, no. 114 poses the question: "Un amant, après avoir fidèlement servi sa dame pendant sept ans, sans en avoir reçu merci, peut-il l'abandonner et chercher consolation auprès d'une autre?" (p. 55, "After having loyally served his lady for seven years without receiving her mercy, can a lover abandon her and seek consolation with another?"). No. 135 debates the following: "Supposez que j'aime une femme belle, sage et ornée d'autres qualités précieuses; dois-je l'abandonner dans le cas où je trouverais l'occasion d'obtenir l'amour d'une femme d'une qualité supérieure?" (p. 138, "Suppose that I love a woman who is beautiful, wise and endowed with other precious qualities; should I leave her if I have the opportunity to win the love of a lady of greater worth?"). This collection also includes one poem (no. 110) addressed to Adam de la Halle, that asks the exact question debated in *Deux Amans*: "L'amour apporte-t-il à un amant loyal plus de bien que de mal?" (p. 41, "Does love bring a faithful lover more good than harm?").

8. The question turns on which patron was absent from Paris when *Dit de Poissy* was written, because the text stresses that it is addressed to someone who is *loings de ci* ("far from here," line 10). Willard draws attention to the fact that Werchin's pilgrimage to Santiago de Compostella, which he is said to have undertaken at the time the poem was composed, did not take place until the summer of 1402. Boucicaut and Jean de Châteaumorand, on the other hand, were both in Constantinople in the spring of 1400. See Charity Cannon Willard, *Christine de Pizan: Her Life and Works* (New York: Persea Books, 1984), 64–65, 68.

9. Machaut, *King of Bohemia*, trans. and ed. Palmer, p. xxv.

10. See Johanna Catharina Schilperoort, *Guillaume de Machaut et Christine de Pisan: Etude comparative* (The Hague: Mouton, 1936), 61–65; and Charity Cannon Willard, "Concepts of Love According to Guillaume de Machaut, Christine de Pizan, and Pietro Bembo," in *The Spirit of the Court: Selected Proceedings of the Fourth Congress of the International Courtly Literature Society (Toronto, 1983)*, ed. Glyn S. Burgess and Robert A. Taylor (Dover, N.H.: D. S. Brewer, 1985), 388. It should be noted, however, that Christine does not limit her examples to those found in *Navarre*; she uses far more than Machaut did.

11. See Annie Reese Pugh, "*Le Jugement du Roy de Behaigne* et le *Dit de Poissy* de Christine de Pisan," *Romania* 23 (1894): 581–86; and Schilperoort, *Guillaume de Machaut et Christine de Pisan*.

12. In *Dit de Poissy* Christine and the debaters ask her patron: "Pour droit jugier / Lequel par droit doit avoir plus legier / Mal a porter ou en doit plus chargier / Et qui plus vit en peine et en dongier / Des deux parties" (lines 2048–52, "To judge correctly which of the two parties must by rights have the lighter grief to bear or is more burdened by it, and which one lives in greater pain and difficulty"). In *Behaigne* a similar formulation is put in the judge's words: addressing his courtiers (Loiauté, Amour, Jeunesse, and Raison), he says: "Et jugement vuelent oïr de mi, / Li quels a plus de mal et de sousci" (lines 1630–31, "And you want to hear from me a judgment as to which has more suffering and care"). See also *Behaigne*, lines 1285–88, 1160–63.

13. Ed. Roy, 2:223–94.

14. For example:

> La se seoit couste mi
> Mon trés savoureux ami,
> Que j'ay maint jour attendu,
> Ou gisoit tout estendu
> Sus l'erbete qui venoit,
> Et en mon giron tenoit
> Sa teste et j'aplanioye
> Son chief et aonnyoye,
> Puis je lui mettoye au col
> Les deux braz dont je l'acol.

> (Lines 1604–13, "There my delectable lover, whom I had awaited for many days, sat at my side or lay stretched out on the new grass, and I held his head in my lap, caressing and smoothing his hair, and then I put my two arms, with which I embrace him, around his neck.")

15. Christine de Pizan, *Cent ballades d'Amant et de Dame*, ed. Jacqueline Cerquiglini (Paris: Union générale d'éditions, 1982), ballade 26, lines 21–22, 25–28; translation mine.

16. Ibid., 39.28–31.

17. Marie-Josèphe Pinet, *Christine de Pisan, 1364–1430: Étude biographique et littéraire* (Paris: Champion, 1927), 79 n. 1. She quotes from E.-M.-D. Robineau,

Christine de Pisan: Sa vie, ses oeuvres (Saint-Omer: Fleury-Lemaire, 1882), 67. Schilperoort, who refers to both Pinet and Robineau, adds: "Il faut convenir que la description de Guillaume concernant les beautés corporelles de la dame est plus décente et plus discrète que celle de Christine" ("One must admit that Guillaume's description concerning the physical beauties of the lady is more proper and discreet than Christine's," p. 37).

18. Schilperoort, *Guillaume de Machaut et Christine de Pizan*, 34.

19. Barbara Altmann, "Diversity and Coherence in Christine de Pizan's *Dit de Poissy*," *French Forum* 12 (1987): 261–70.

20. Pugh, "*Roy de Behaine* et *Dit de Poissy*," 581; italics hers.

21. On the role of sight in *Behaigne*, see Douglas Kelly, *Medieval Imagination: Rhetoric and the Poetry of Courtly Love* (Madison: University of Wisconsin Press, 1978), 138.

22. Kelly, *Medieval Imagination*, 139. See also Barton Palmer, who says of *Behaigne*: "The debate itself concerns what proves ultimately an empty question that, at John's court, is turned toward the important issue underlying it" (Machaut, *King of Bohemia*, xxxvi). The important issue he refers to is "the reconciliation of emotional idealism with the practical necessity of living in the world" (p. xxxvi).

23. See Kelly's chapter on "The Transition from the *Behaigne* to the *Navarre*," in his *Medieval Imagination*, 137–44.

24. See, for example, *Dit de Poissy*, lines 1962–68.

25. *Dit de Poissy*, lines 1873–2006.

26. See Charity Cannon Willard, "Concepts of Love," and "Lovers' Dialogues in Christine de Pizan's Lyric Poetry from the *Cent ballades* to the *Cent ballades d'Amant et de Dame*," *Fifteenth-Century Studies* 4 (1981): 167–80.

27. Raison's speech takes lines 1663–1784 in the *Behaigne*.

28. For a discussion of how Christine "corrects" Jeun de Meun's portrait of Reason in her *Epistre au Dieu d'Amour*, see Lori Walters, "The Woman Writer and Literary History: Christine de Pizan's Redefinition of the Poetic *Translatio* in the *Epistre au Dieu d'Amours*," *French Literature Studies* 16 (1989): 1–16.

29. *Fole amour* occurs three times in *Trois Jugemens*: lines 313, 1309, 1443; *trop amer* occurs in *Trois Jugemens* at lines 718, 1304, in *Dit de Poissy* at lines 1066, 1398, and in *Deux Amans* at lines 206, 319, 597, 680, 706, 1000, 1334.

30. On Machaut's narrator figure, see Kevin Brownlee, *Poetic Identity in Guillaume de Machaut* (Madison: University of Wisconsin Press, 1984). Of particular interest on this question is the very useful discussion of *Behaigne* in ch. 4, "Poet-Narrator as Witness-Participant" (pp. 158–71).

31. See *Cent ballades* 50 and 100 (ed. Roy, 1:51 and 100).

32. Christine de Pizan, *The Book of the City of Ladies*, trans. Earl Jeffrey Richards (New York: Persea Books, 1982), xxxiii.

33. Willard, "Concepts of Love," 390.

34. This becomes a lovely irony when compared with René d'Anjou's cemetery for loyal lovers, to be found on the "île du dieu d'Amours," in which one finds buried, among others, "Machault, poethe renommé." See *Le Livre du cuer d'amours espris*, ed. Susan Wharton, (Paris: Union générale d'éditions, 1980), 142–43. My thanks to Professor Charity Cannon Willard for pointing out this reference.

35. Daniel Poirion, *Le Moyen Âge: 1300–1480* (Paris: Arthaud, 1971), 192.

36. Willard, "Concepts of Love," 388.

37. William Calin, *Poet at the Fountain: Essays on the Narrative Verse of Guillaume de Machaut* (Lexington: University Press of Kentucky, 1974), 53.

38. Willard makes this observation with regard to Christine's *Cent ballades d'Amant et de Dame* in her article "Christine de Pizan: *Cent ballades d'Amant et de Dame*: Criticism of Courtly Love," in *Court and Poet: Selected Proceedings of the Third Congress of the International Courtly Literature Society (Liverpool, 1980)*, ed. Glyn S. Burgess (Liverpool: Francis Cairns, 1981), 357.

39. See *Cent ballades d'Amant*, ed. Cerquiglini, 31–32.

40. See Willard, "Lovers' Dialogues." Christine has been ordered to write these ballades as punishment, but "The sequence . . . shows her quite unrepentant in her views, for in this dialogue the affair is seen to go as badly as ever" (176).

41. *King of Bohemia*, xxix.

"La Pioche d'Inquisicion": Legal-Judicial Content and Style in Christine de Pizan's *Livre de la Cité des Dames*

MAUREEN CHENEY CURNOW

During the period of her primary formation as a professional writer —from approximately 1390 to 1404—Christine de Pizan was involved in a series of legal situations in an effort to stabilize her finances and obtain the pensions and rents due her and her children as the widow of a royal secretary and daughter of a deceased court official. Her involvement with the legal-judicial structures of the period and her knowledge of her husband's professional activity as a notary and royal secretary contributed to her use of legal and judicial stylistic structures and content in her written works. This practice is particularly evident in her *Livre de la Cité des Dames*, written 1404–5. In appreciating the extent of legal knowledge and terminology in Christine's work, it is helpful to review Christine's own personal experience with the law and the use of judicial style in the *Cité des Dames* itself. Given the close ties between rhetorical and legal education in medieval universities, judicial language in Christine's works is a clear touchstone of erudition, further proof of the affinity of women for learning. Moreover, Christine's use of legal terminology is part of a larger argument of the affinity of women for the law itself, a profession from which they were, of course, barred in her day.

I. Christine's Experience with the Law

The presence of judicial language in her work is all the more striking given her lack of formal training in the law. However, she gained knowledge of legal lore from both her father and husband, and from the legal disputes she was involved with after their deaths. Christine's father's positions as lecturer at the University of Bologna, counselor of the Venetian Republic, and court astrologer for Charles V of France made him a well-known man of letters. He encouraged Christine's education, and through him she had access to the Royal Library at the Louvre. In the *Cité des Dames*, Christine comments that her father was pleased with her interest in study- ing and did not believe that women were less worthy when educated. Dame Droiture speaks: "Ton pere, qui fu grant naturien et phillosophe, n'oppinoit pas que femmes vaulsissent pis par science apprendre, ainsi de ce qu'encline te veoit aux lettres, si que tu sces, grant plaisir y prenoit." (2.36, par. 186; "Your father, who was a great scientist and philosopher, did not believe that women were worth less by knowing science; rather, as you know, he took great pleasure from seeing your inclination to learning.")[1] Although Christine's mother was the daughter of Thomas Mondini, a counselor of the Venetian Republic, she did not share her husband's enthusiasm for Christine's education. In the same chapter of the *Cité des Dames* (2.36, par. 186), Christine comments that her mother preferred that she occupy her- self with learning household responsibilities, which Christine describes as "fillasses"—a play on the spinning activity and the pejorative suffix *-asses* attached to the word *fille,* that is, stupid activities for girls.

Christine's husband's position as a royal secretary also contributed to Christine's knowledge. Estienne de Castel was selected as her husband when she was fifteen years old. He was of a good family from Picardy, but she later comments that he was more intelligent and charming than wealthy. His university education as a notary and his prestigious position as a court secretary meant that he prepared letters and legal acts on behalf of the king and represented the king on diplomatic missions. Estienne died in 1390 while on a diplomatic mission for the king, leaving Christine a widow at the age of twenty-five with three young children, a niece, and a mother to sup- port.[2] Through her husband's work, Christine was familiar with the highly stylized, Latinate chancery style and structure of official acts and letters. There is evidence that Christine herself transcribed some manuscripts of her own works, and Charity Cannon Willard suggests that Christine may have worked as a copyist of official acts and letters for a period of time in order to support her family. Autograph notes in Christine's hand show that she knew the official bookhand and chancery hand of the period.[3]

After the deaths of her husband and father, Christine spent fourteen years in legal court battles in order to straighten out her difficult and com- plex financial situation. She describes her experiences in detail in the *Avi- sion*. Christine poignantly relates her shame at having her goods seized by sergeants of the court: "Mes chosetes m'estoient levees par sergens," her dismay at being mocked by drunkards, and her fear that a response to the taunts might worsen her case (*L'Avision-Christine*, 156–57). In her biogra- phy of Christine, Charity Cannon Willard recounts some of the legal battles in which Christine was involved: collecting bonuses and salary due her hus- band from the royal court, trying to recoup her children's educational funds from a dishonest investor, disengagement from payment responsibilities for properties acquired by her husband, and sales of properties that she inherited from her husband and father—such as the Château de Mémorant inherited from her father and sold to Philippe de Mézières.[4]

In a number of her works, Christine comments that because she was a female, she did not receive a complete enough education to address the problems that faced her. Undoubtedly this disadvantaged position prompted her later to undertake the detailed program of self-education that she describes in her *L'Avision*.

Again in *L'Avision*, she reflects on the period of her legal trials, sounding a bitter note that it was not customary for a husband to keep his wife informed about the family's financial affairs and that she, herself, understood that problems ensued from this lack of communication: "car comme se soit la coustume commune des hommes mariez de non dire et declairier leurs affaires entierement a leurs femmes, de laquelle chose vient souvent mal comme il m'appert par experience" (154; "as it is the common custom of married men not to tell and to explain their affairs completely to their wives, from which frequently arises misfortune, as it seems to me from experience"). Christine continues this discussion in the *Avision*, stating that as was often the case for widows, legal complaints and judicial trials surrounded her ("Et comme ce soient les mes des veusves, plais et proces m'avironnerent de touz lez," 154). As she states, at one time she was simultaneously involved as the defendant in four different Parisian courts: "Je vi le temps que a .iiii, cours de Paris estoye en plait et procés defferderresse." (155; "I saw the time that in four courts in Paris I was the defendant in proceedings and trials.") She comments that during these fourteen years of legal battles, she frequently encountered deception and dishonesty, and she often yielded because she was not educated enough to master these situations and was by nature peaceful. She indicates that it ended when she had nothing left to lose: "que plus a perdre n'avoye" (156).

At this point, one should comment that Christine did not complain of the injustice of the law vis-à-vis the inheritance rights of women and their rights to have matters heard in court. During the fifteenth century France was still governed by a complex structure of laws and policies that combined aspects of Roman law, canon law and Germanic law. As Régine Pernoud comments in *La Femme au temps des cathédrales,* until the end of the fifteenth century women enjoyed a "capacité juridique"—they could legally inherit and hold goods, participate in legal actions and even act for a husband if he was absent or incapacitated. It was not until the rigid codification of French laws in the sixteenth century that women were defined as juridically incapable.[5]

Christine's primary complaints underscore the dishonesty of those involved in her legal struggles. She later seems to have felt some consolation in knowing that judges would be judged. In her *Enseignemens moraux à son fils* she warned him that if he ever became involved in the affairs of justice, he should judge carefully, for he would one day go before the great judge (God):

> Se tu as estat ou office
> Dont tu mesles de justice;
> Gardes comment tu jugeras,
> Car devant le grant juge yrass.[6]

> (If you hold estate or office which deals with the law, take care how you judge, for you will go before the Great Judge.)

As an aside, it is interesting to note that her son Jehan de Castel did become a notary and royal secretary like his father. He followed the Dauphin Louis de Guyenne into exile in Bourges, was appointed ambassador to the Court of Castille, and preceded his mother in death. His own first son, also named Jehan de Castel, followed the same career pattern, and the second son (also named Jehan) was a royal historian.[7] Some Renaissance critics later attributed Christine's works to her grandson, the royal historian.

In a number of Christine's works, she expressed her disappointment that France no longer was a place where widows could find comfort and friendship and that the property of widows was often taken from them. One of her poems, a ballad, is a direct reflection of her legal battles:

> Helas! Ou dont trouveront reconfort
> Povres vesves, de leurs biens despoullees?
> —Puis qu'en France, qui seult estre le port
> de leur salu, et ou les exilees
> Veulent fuir, et les desconseillees.   (*L'Avision-Christine*, 159)

> (Alas! Where then can poor widows, despoiled of their goods, find comfort? Except for France, which is usually the port of their salvation, and where exiles and the disconsolate want to flee.)

In her *Trésor de la Cité des Dames, ou Le Livre des Trois Vertus*, she advises women to avoid involvement in legal affairs. She then counsels widows on how to proceed in legal matters, telling them to seek the advice of wise lawyers and clerks, to exercise great care and diligence in pursuing the cases, and finally to have enough money to do it.[8] Her advice that women work diligently in preparing the details of their cases undoubtedly reflects her own situation.

II. Legal Vocabulary and Style in the
Livre de la Cité des Dames

Christine had probably concluded most of her legal cases before writing the *Livre de la Cité des Dames*, but the structures, style, and content of that work show that she is still very concerned with legal-judicial issues. In Marie-Josèphe Pinet's general comments on Christine's style, she notes that Christine was indebted to the legal language and style of her period and that this influence is evident in her biography of Charles V: "Christine, lorsqu'elle écrivit les *Fais et bonnes meurs* en "stille prosal," contrairement à ce qu'elle avait fait jusqu'alors, a voulu adopter et embellir le langage des chancelleries qu'avait écrit son mari et que devraient écrire ses enfants.[9]

The *Cité des Dames* presents Christine's boldest didactic writing in defense of women and her most thorough contribution to the literature of the *querelle des femmes*. In this work she argues that women are basically virtuous and have the same intellectual capacities as men. She analyzes and refutes past criticisms of women, discussing Theophrastus, Ovid, Jean de Meun, Cecco D'Ascoli, Matheolus, and numerous other writers and popular sayings about women. Christine comments that many of these criticisms are generalizations based on observation of a few women. Pragmatist that she is, Christine states that some women are immoral and weak—just as some men are. She notes that men and women are ordained to different roles in life, but contends that women can be as capable as men, and even surpass them in government, letters, sciences, arts, and religion. She declares that women are faithful to those they love, keep them securely, and counsel them wisely, and that women are also capable of great love and service to God and his saints. In order to prove these contentions, Christine discusses some two hundred women; she relates biographies from ancient history, mythology, the Bible, hagiography, French history, and contemporary Europe.

The content development of the literary work the *Cité des Dames* is described in terms of the building of a physical city—the allegorical City of Ladies. The basic literary structure is that of a dream vision in which the daughters of God—the personified three Virtues, Raison, Droiture, Justice—direct Christine in constructing this defense of women. The discussion of the qualities of women and the biographical *exempla* take place in a legal framework of accusation, reply and illustration, then conclusion.

Parenthetically, I would note that Christine also used legal-judicial frameworks in a number of her other works. To mention only a few of them, we note that in her *Chemin de long estude*, the allegorical figure Raison hears arguments in her court and finally asks Christine to transmit the arguments to earth, where they can be judged by the princes of France. In the course of Christine's literary debate with the supporters of the *Roman de la Rose*, Christine had copies of all the letters sent to Queen Isabeau de Bavière and Guillaume de Tignonville, provost of Paris, asking them for a judgment concerning the quarrel. Her *Epistre au Dieu d'Amours* is structured as a situation in a legal court where Cupid hears complaints from women that they are unjustly defamed and criticized; he concurs and judges that those who defame women thus should be punished.

In the *Cité des Dames*, Christine's replies to attacks on women and her positive ideas are usually presented in this form of a legal defense: accusation or argument, reply and illustration, then judgment or conclusion. She first states the basic argument, then one of the Virtues replies to it, giving examples that illustrate and prove the reply. Christine often concludes with a general summation or a statement of agreement with the reply given by the Virtue. This stylistic procedure is seen in part 1, chapter 14. Christine begins by agreeing with Dame Raison's conclusion concerning the previous topic. Christine then presents the argument that women are allegedly inferior because they are physically weaker than men. Raison replies, saying: "Fille chiere, ceste consequence n'est point bonne et ne fait a soustenir" (par. 51; "My dear daughter, such a deduction is totally invalid and unsupported"). Raison continues, arguing that when Nature forms something with some type of weakness, she compensates by adding a strength. Dame Raison then gives the example of Aristotle, who, according to medieval tradition, had one eye lower than the other; his great mind made up for his ugliness. She also speaks of Alexander the Great, whose virtues compensated for his ugliness. Dame Raison continues, generalizing from the evidence, noting that a strong and large body does not cause a person to be virtuous and courageous, but that virtue and courage are from God and he allows Nature to give them to some reasonable creatures more than to others: "Et ainsi est-il de mains autres. Si te promés, belle amie, que le grant et fort corpsage ne fait mie le vertueulx poyssant couraige: ains vient d'une viguer vertueuse naturelle qui est don de Dieu qu'il concede a Nature empraindre es unes creatures raisonnables plus que es autres." (1.14.2, par. 52; "Fair friend, I assure you that a large and strong body never makes a strong and virtuous heart but comes from a natural and virtuous vigor which is a boon from God, which he allows Nature to imprint in one reasonable creature more than in another.") Dame Raison further develops the arguments, saying that some big men are weak and some small men are bold and vigorous. She then comments that some women have had strong bodies and have shown courage and boldness in action; this argument is then supported by numerous examples, beginning with Semiramis of Baby-

Ionia and then passing to the Amazons who allegedly lived in Asia Minor during the classical Greek period.

Christine is extremely skilled at using the forms of legal debate and argument. On at least one occasion, she sets up a syllogism that leads to such a faulty conclusion that anyone would be forced to disagree with it, thereby agreeing with her. She argues that one could respond to her that because women attract men by their virtue and purity and because some believe that it is wrong for men to be attracted to women, therefore it would be better if women were less good. She states that is patently not so, and that good things should not be set aside, just because some people misuse them. Dame Droiture speaks:

> Sy me pourroit doncques estre respondu, puisque femmes attrayent les hommes par leur vertu et honnesteté, puisque c'est mal qu'ilz soyent attraiz, mieulx vauldroit que moins bonnes feussent. Mais cest arguement riens n'y vauldroit: car les bonnes et prouffitables choses ne doivent pas estre laissiees a cultiver et a acroistre pourtant se les folz mal en usent; et chascun doit faire son devoir en bien faisant quoy que avenir doye. (2.64.1, par. 239)

> (One could answer that, since women attract men with virtue and integrity and since it is bad that men be attracted, it would be better if women were less good. But of course this argument has no validity at all, for one should not neglect the cultivation and advancement of the good in spite of however much fools abuse it, and everyone must do his duty by acting well regardless of what might happen.)

In discussing Christine's style, one must recall that she was a prolific writer of both poetry and prose and that her subject matter varies from love poems and laments to political treatises, to defenses of women, to works of personal religious sentiment. Her style varies greatly according to the genre and the content of a particular work or passage. The highly Latinized official style of the chancery, reminiscent of legal acts and letters, is most frequently seen in her longer prose works such as the *Cité des Dames*. Here, as in other works, however, she is also capable of writing a clear, concise prose style. This feature is particularly evident when she is asserting a philosophical principle, as seen in the following statement that he or she who has the highest level of virtue is the most noble and that nobility and baseness are not determined by the sex of the person but are the result of a perfection of morals and virtues: "Celuy ou celle en qui plus a vertus est le plus hault; ne la haulteur ou abaissement des gens ne gist mie es corps selonc le sexe, mais en la parfeccion des meurs et des vertus." (1.9.3, par. 28; "The man or the woman in whom resides greater virtue is the higher; neither the loftiness nor the lowliness of a person lies in the body according to the sex, but in the perfection of conduct and virtues.")

She frequently states her conclusions and personal beliefs with startling realism and absolute clarity, as can be seen in her response to the accusation that women like to be raped. In her conclusion to the story of the rape of Lucretia, she comments that an appropriate, just, and holy law resulted from that incident. She clearly believes that death is an appropriate punishment for rape. "Et a cause de cel oultraige fait a Lucresce, comme dient aucuns, vint la loy que homme mourroit pour prendre femme a force; laquelle loy est couvenable, juste et sainte." (2.44.1, par. 195a; "And because of this outrage perpetrated on Lucretia, so some claim, a law was enacted whereby a man would be executed for raping a woman, a law which is fitting, just and holy.") Christine commonly uses a simple syntax when she cites her own words in the dialogues with the Virtues. Her most complex, legalistic, pedantic sentences usually result from her desire to have the three Virtues speak an elevated style that Christine perceives as noble.

Christine is however acutely conscious of different styles of writing. In the *Livre de la Paix*, she characterized her writing as "stille vulgal et rural" ("a commonplace, countrylike style") and speaks of other writers who are "remplis de clergie, orateurs sages stillés en rethorique, droit et raison" ("full of ecclesiastical knowledge, wise orators with styles characterized by rhetoric, law, and reason").[10] In her *Avision*, Christine describes how she studied historical works and sought to refine her style and content, "amendant mon stille en plus grant soubtilleté" (164). With a mixture of humor, bitterness, and pride, she notes that some say that her works must have been written by clerics or men of religion, as they could not come from a woman's mind: "Car les aucuns dient que clers ou religieux les te forgent et que de sentement de femme venir ne pourroyent" (*L'Avision-Christine*, 143). Christine admires Boccaccio's periods—his long, highly stylized sentences —and frequently takes whole passages from his text when she is using his works as a source for the *Cité des Dames*. In reality, some of these long periods are the translator's expansion of passages from Boccaccio (those of Laurent de Premierfait, for example), but these sentences may also serve her as models. In order to look at Christine's own style, one must clearly know when she is writing original passages and when her style primarily reflects her sources.

Her syntax is the most complex when she writes in the Latinized style of the courts and clerics of her epoch. Her prose is sometimes very studied, and her desire to imitate Latin sentence structure often leads her to write extremely complex sentences. Occasionally, her tendency to multiply subordinate clauses becomes so overwhelming that the sense of direction is lost and she completes neither the sentence nor the idea that she began.

In an early passage of the *Cité des Dames* (1.3.3, par. 7), Dame Raison explains that the three Virtues have come to ask Christine to build a defense of women. There is no syntactical conclusion to the clause that she began with the two uses of the subordinating conjunction *que:* ". . . sy saiches que, pour forclorre du monde . . . et que les dames . . . puissent . . . avoir aucun retrait. . . ." After numerous involved clauses and full sentences, Christine finally completes the idea that she began with those subordinating conjunctions, saying, "nous trois dames . . . te sommes venues adnoncier un certain ediffice . . . qui a toy a ffaire est predestinee. . . ." Although the idea is complete, the initial sentence structure is not, and in punctuating the text one is forced to end this forty-three-line sentence with marks of ellipsis, noting that it is syntactically incomplete.

In using this Latinate period, Christine frequently interjects parenthetical material into her sentences in order to add a personal reflection, or to insert a rhetorical question, or to expand an idea—giving examples and explanation. She usually tries to conclude with a resumptive phrase that returns the reader to the basic idea and enables Christine then to complete the content and structure of her sentence. This stylistic trait is seen as Dame Raison explains that the City of Ladies will be eternal and will not be like the kingdom of the Amazons, which eventually collapsed. The resumptive use of "mais nonpourtant" forces the reader back to the basic "neantmoins," and Christine then completes the sentence with relative clarity: "Et neantmoins, tout fussent ycelles de grant force et puissance et que ou temps de leur dominacion grant partie de tout Orient conquisdrent et toutes les terres voysines espoverterent, et meesmement les redouterent ceulx du pays de Grece qui adonc estoit la fleur des contrees du monde, mais nonpourtant a chief de temps, [failli] la puissance d'icelluy royaume." (1.4.3, par. 10; "Yet, although they were strong and powerful and had conquered a large part of the entire Orient in the course of their rule and terrified all the neighboring lands [even the Greeks, who were then the flower of all countries in the world, feared them], nevertheless, after a time, the power of this kingdom declined.")

In his discussion of syntactical structures in Old French, Lucien Foulet comments on the "principe du moindre effort," saying: "Le moyen âge n'a pas connu, en grammaire et en syntaxe cette passion raisonnante et raisonneuse qui nous possède. . . . Nous ne sommes jamais trop pressés pour revenir sur nos pas et analyser le cas: le moyen âge pousse droit devant lui. Il applique volontiers le principe du moindre effort. Si la langue lui tend un piége, il trouve plus commode de tomber dedans quitte à s'en dépêtrer, que de faire un détour pour l'éviter."[11] Foulet's principle is very evident in Christine's structure—either because of enthusiastic involvement in the subject or else because she and others of her period considered this style appropriate and even elegant. Except for Christine's use of a resumptive phrase, she is constantly moving forward, and her sentences are stylistic spirals, rather than statically formed blocks. As she writes, she retains a basic subject or a basic verbal structure in mind and frequently does not repeat the syntactical elements that we might now consider essential. One verb, for example, will suffice for three clauses, even though the second clause is a complete sentence. She also dislocates the elements of a clause in order to control the emphasis in a sentence. Thus, her fondness for the Latin period—the style of legal acts and letters, her tendency to intercalate explanations and comments into the middle of a sentence, her assumptions that syntactical elements can be carried forward in the reader's mind, and her manipulation of word order all combine to make certain prose sentences some of the most complex examples of the era.

The vocabulary that Christine uses in the *Cité des Dames* reflects the legal language and style of her period. In choosing this type of diction, she is constantly seeking to convince the reader that she is presenting a quasi-legal defense of women. The Virgin Mary is described as the "deffenderresse" and "protectarresse" or "protestaresce" of women (3.1.2, par. 261). Christine digs into the antifeminist attacks with the "pioche d'inquisicion"—the spade of inquiry (1.8.1, par. 15). Dame Raison speaks of the "preuves" that she has presented and refers to the "deposicion de mes autres deux suers" (1.48.1, par. 123; "the deposition of my two sisters"). Dame Droiture also uses legal terms—trial, producing testimony—when she speaks in the following passage: "Mais comme de toutes dyre entrepris n'aye et seroit infini procés, me souffist sans plus que je produise en tesmoingnaige pour contredit a ce que tu m'a proposé que aucuns hommes dient" (par. 22). The very names of the allegorical figures themselves that Christine has chosen for her defense of women reflect the reason, righteousness, and justice of her cause—Raison, Droiture, Justice.

Some of the Biblical and popular sayings that Christine cites in the *Cité des Dames* also reflect her preoccupation with a legal style and content: "Qui maine procés sans partie bien a son ayse plaide" (2.13.1, par. 153; "Whoever goes to court without an opponent pleads very much at his ease"); "Mais or est temps que leur juste cause soit mise hors des mains de Pharaon" (1.3.3, par. 7; "Now it is time for their just cause to be taken from Pharaoh's hands"); "L'entencion juge l'omme (1.8.3, par. 16a; "Intention judges the man"); "Le tesmoingnaige de plusieurs fait a croire" (1.1.2, par. 2; "The testimony of two or three witnesses lends credence").

Christine also uses a stylistic redundancy—which has characterized legal documents since the time of William the Conqueror and other rulers who found it necessary to list terms from two languages in order to ensure clarity. This practice is seen in forms of address: "Tres hault et honnouree dame"

(1.11, par. 40), and in a variety of types of passages in the *Cité des Dames*. An example of this repeated stylistic usage of doublets is seen in the following very rhythmical passage in which Christine basically says that she had read so many criticisms of women that she was starting to believe them:

> Mais nonobstant que pour chose que je y peusse congnoistre, tant longuement y sceusse viser ne esplucier, je ne apperceusse ne cogneusse telz jugemens estre vrays encontre les naturelz meurs et condicions femenines, j'arguoye fort contre les femmes, disant que trop fort seroit que tant de si renommez hommes—si sollempnelz clercs de tant hault et grant entendement, si clerveans en toutes choses, comme il semble que ceulx fussent—en eussent parlé mencongieusement. (1.1.1, par. 1)

> (To the best of my knowledge, no matter how long I confronted or dissected the problem, I could not see or realize how their claims could be true when compared to the natural behavior and character of women. Yet I still argued vehemently against women, saying that it would be impossible that so many famous men—such solemn scholars, possessed of such deep and great understanding, so clear-sighted in all things, as it seemed—could have spoken falsely . . .)

This stylistic redundancy gives a certain rhythm to her sentences, but it also makes them rather heavy at times.

As typical of a legal-judicial style, Christine begins each chapter with a rather formal definition of the situation and the persons. The references to herself, the forms of address she uses to address the allegorical figures, and her descriptions of titles and relationships are presented with the stylistic precision of legal documents. Throughout the text she opens paragraphs with a brief formulaic description typical of the official language of the chancellery: "Je Christine," "Moi, Christine." She is particularly precise in her mention of official titles and relationships when she is speaking in praise of outstanding French noblewomen and her patrons and patronesses of the French royal houses. She describes, for example, Jeanne d'Evreux, queen of France (third wife and widow of Charles IV, whom Christine met when she first came to France), saying, "Tu veÿs en ton enffance la royne Jehanne, vesve du roy Charles .iiij^e. du nom," and then continues, detailing that queen's reputation for order and justice (1.13.3, par. 45).

As Christine introduces her praise of the duchess of Anjou, the need for legal precision is clear—given the complex family relationships of the duchess of Anjou: "Et que puet on dire de la vaillant et saige duchesce d'Anjou, fille jadiz de saint Charles, duc de Bretaigne, et feu femme de l'ainsné frere aprés lui du saige roy Charles de France, lequel duc fu puis roy de cecille?" (1.13.6, par. 48; "What can one say of the valiant and wise duchess of Anjou, late daughter of Saint Charles of Blois, duke of Brittany, and late wife of the second oldest brother of the wise King Charles of France, who was then king of Sicily?")

The content of the *Cité des Dames* includes a number of passages dealing with aspects of laws and judicial systems. It does not, however, attempt to provide advice to women on how to deal with legal situations. As noted above, Christine provided some advice on that topic in the following work: the *Trésor de la Cité des Dames*.

III. Women and the Law in Christine's Work

In the *Cité des Dames* Christine comments on some judicial practices, makes some philosophical statements concerning the nature of law, and in her biographical *exempla* mentions a woman associated with the legal profession and other women who made wise laws and governed according to them.

One of the detractors whose works provoked Christine into writing the *Cité des Dames* was a lawyer named Matheolus. In his *Liber lamentationum* he explains that women are not allowed in the legal profession because they, like the legendary Cafurnia, cannot control their talking and speak unwisely. He also mentions that canon law bars women from public office because of their basic iniquity. Christine first comments that all women should not be condemned because of the sins of one woman and then proceeds to discuss the positive things that have resulted from the speech of women. She then discusses why women do not sit in courts of law in part 1, chapter 11, entitled "Demande Christine a Raison pourquoy ce est que femmes ne sieent en siege de plaidoyerie; et responce" ("Christine asks Reason why women are not in the seats of legal counsel; and Reason's response"). Christine asks Dame Raison "pourquoy ce est que les femmes ne tiennent plaidoyerie en cours de justice, ne congnoissent des causes, ne font jugemens" (1.11.1, par. 40; "why women do not plead law cases in the courts of justice, are unfamiliar with legal disputes, and do not hand down judgments"). Christine notes that men say it is because women would not conduct themselves wisely. Raison responds that it is simply because God established certain roles for men and others for women. She then continues, commenting that it is logical that men who make judicial rules have the physical force to enforce those rules, and women do not usually have that physical force, nor are they inclined to the bold action that it takes to sit in judgment in courts.

Christine hastens to add that women have the intelligence to learn laws. She then cites an example and discusses the daughter of Giovanni Andrea ("Jehan Andry"). He was a professor and legislator at Bologna in the fourteenth century who wrote commentaries on canon law and whose reputation must have been known to Christine's father when he studied and taught at Bologna. Christine says that Giovanni Andrea was not of the opinion that it was bad for women to be educated and that his daughter, Novella, was so advanced in the study of letters and law that she read lessons to his students in his place and thus lightened his burdens. She spoke from behind a curtain so that her beauty would not distract the students. Christine continues, stating that the father wanted to inscribe the daughter's name in memory and thus named one of his law volumes after her—*La Nouvelle*. The passage reads:

> Jehan Andry, le sollempnel legiste a Boulongne la Grace, n'a mie soixante ans, n'estoit pas d'oppinion que mal fust que femmes fussent lettrees. Quand a sa belle et bonne fille que il tant ama, qui ot nom Nouvelle, fist apprendre lettres et si avant es loys que, quant il estoit occuppez d'aucun essoine par quoy ne povoit vaquier a lire les lecons a ces escolliers, il envoyait sa fille en son lieu lire aux escolles en chayere. Ed adfin que la biauté d'elle n'empeschast la penssee des ouyans, elle avoit une petite courtine au devant d'elle. Et par celle maniere supploit et allegoit les occupacions de son pere. Lequel l'ama tant que, pour mettre le nom d'elle en memoire, fist une nottable letture d'un livre de lois que il nomma du nom de sa fille, *La Nouvelle* (2.36.3, par. 185).

> (Giovanni Andrea, a solemn law professor in Bologna not quite sixty years ago, was not of the opinion that it was bad for women to be educated. He had a fair and good daughter, named Novella, who was educated in the law to such an advanced degree that when he was occupied by some task and not at leisure to present his lectures to his students, he would send Novella, his daughter, in his place to lecture to the students from his chair. And to prevent her beauty from distracting the concentration of her audience, she had a little curtain drawn in front of her. In this manner she could on occasion supplement and lighten her father's occupation. He loved her so much that, to commemorate her name, he wrote a book of remarkable lectures on the law which he entitled *Novella super decretalium*, after his daughter's name.)

One must note that in a recent article entitled "Learned Women of Early Modern Italy," Oskar Kristeller accepts this story with some hesitation,[12] but Christine's own knowledge of the story did enable her to make a point concerning women's intellectual capacities to learn, and even teach, legal concepts.

Christine also gives details from the lives of a number of women from antiquity who instituted laws and governed according to them. She speaks, for example, of Nicaula, who is described as empress of the kingdom of Arabia, Ethiopia, Egypt, and the island of Meroë, noting that "ceste dame fu celle qui premierement commenca a vivre en son raigne selonc lois et pollicie ordonee ("during her rule this lady was the first to begin to live according to laws and cordiated policies"). Christine continues, commenting that "elle fu tant saige et de tant grant gouvernement que meismes la saint Escripture parle de sa grant vertu. Elle meismes institua loys tres droitturieres pour gouverner son puepple. (1.12, par. 42; "She was so wise and so capable a ruler that even the Holy Scriptures speak of her great virtue. She herself instituted laws of far-reaching justice for governing her people.") The subject is then expanded to include a description of a number of women from antiquity and French history who governed strongly and wisely with justice and law—mentioning among those of France, Queen Fredegonde; Queen Blanche, mother of Saint Louis; Queen Jeanne, widow of Charles IV; her daughter the duchess of Orléans; Blanche, wife of King John; the duchess of Anjou; and Christine's contemporary the countess of La Marche (1.13.7, par. 43).

Christine often considers the nature of laws and legal concepts. She states that there is a natural law of physical attraction between men and women that causes them to love each other: "Dame, il cuert au monde une loy naturelle des hommes aux femmes et des femmes aux hommes, non mie loy faitte par inclinacion charnelle par laquelle ilz s'entreaiment de tres grant et enfforciee amour." (2.54.1, par. 219; "My lady, a natural behavior of men toward women and of women toward men prevails in the world which is not brought about by human institutions but by the inclination of the flesh, and in which men and women love one another with a very strong love strengthened in turn by foolish pleasure.") Christine then cites those who say that women are not loyal to this natural law, and Dame Droiture gives her biographical examples of women who were known for their great love.

Christine also states that laws (or the absence of them) are relative and reflect the mores of a particular society. She comments on the widowed Semiramis of Babylonia, who had an incestuous relationship with her son Ninus. Christine rather lamely explains that Semiramis is not to be condemned as there was not yet written law; instead they followed the laws of nature: "Pour ce adonc n'estoit encores point de loy escripte: ains vovoyent les gens a loy de nature" (1.15.2, par. 56; "Because at this time there was still no written law, and people lived according to the law of Nature").

As noted above, in the discussion of the passage on the rape of Lucretia, Christine understands that new laws arise because of an incident of abuse through which it is recognized that a group or individual needs protection. She firmly states that the capital punishment is appropriate in circumstances of rape: "Laquelle loy est couvenable, juste et saine" (2.44.1, par. 195a).

The legal question of intention is also of interest to Christine. Christine asks Dame Raison if men who criticize women are to be excused in that their intentions were good—"bonne entencion les y a meus"—and they thus wanted to convince men to stay away from bad women. Through Dame Raison, Christine gives us a very clear statement that the intention is not a sufficient excuse for negative actions, noting by analogy that if one acted with good intentions, but through carelessness killed a person, the intention would not be sufficient to compensate for the death (1.8.3, par. 16a).

Thus, from the examples cited above, one can conclude that Christine's education and her relationships with her father, husband, and other persons at the royal court were combined with her own experience in legal situations and thus influenced her work. The content, structures, style, and language of the *Cité des Dames* reflect Christine's interest in and use of the legal and judicial structures of her period.

Notes

1. Citations from *Le Livre de la Cité des Dames* are by part, chapter, and paragraph from my forthcoming edition based on my previous work "The 'Livre de la Cité des Dames' of Christine de Pisan: A Critical Edition," 2 vols. (Ph.D. dissertation, Vanderbilt University, 1975). English translations are taken from Earl Jeffrey Richards's translation, *The Book of the City of Ladies* (New York: Persea Books, 1982). See also the modern French translation by Thérèse Moreau and Eric Hicks, *La Cité des Dames* (Paris: Stock, 1986).

2. Christine spoke of her husband throughout her works—particularly in her autobiographical *L'Avision-Christine*, ed. Mary Louise Towner (Washington, D.C.: Catholic University of America, 1932; reprint, New York: AMS Press, 1969), 151–54. Citations of *L'Avision-Christine* in the text are to page numbers in this edition. For details on Estienne de Castel, I am also indebted to Charity Cannon Willard's definitive biography, *Christine de Pizan: Her Life and Works* (New York: Persea Books, 1984), 34–35.

3. On Christine's possible work as a copyist, see Willard, *Christine de Pizan*, 46–47. Concerning autograph manuscripts by Christine, see Gilbert Ouy and Christine Reno, "Identification des autographes de Christine de Pizan," *Scriptorium* 34 (1980): 221–38.

4. Willard, *Christine de Pizan*, 46–47.

5. Régine Pernoud, *La Femme au temps des cathédrales* (Paris: Stock, 1980), 234.

6. *Oeuvres poétiques de Christine de Pisan*, ed. Maurice Roy, 3 vols. (Paris: Firmin Didot, 1886–96), 3:27–44.

7. Willard, *Christine de Pizan*, 196, 207–8.

8. Cf. *The Treasure of the City of Ladies; or, The Book of the Three Virtues*, trans. Sarah Lawson (Harmondsworth, U.K.: Penguin Books, 1985), 158–59.

9. Marie-Josèphe Pinet, *Christine de Pisan, 1364–1430: Etude biographique et littéraire* (Paris: Champion, 1927), 449.

10. The *Livre de la Paix*, ed. Charity Cannon Willard (The Hague: Mouton, 1958), 60; translation mine.

11. Lucien Foulet, *Petite Syntaxe de l'ancien français*, 3d ed. (Paris: Champion, 1958), 340–41.

12. The story of Novella is discussed by Paul O. Kristeller, "Learned Women of Early Modern Italy: Humanists and University Scholars," in *Beyond Their Sex: Learned Women of the European Past*, ed. P. H. Labalme (New York: New York University Press, 1984), 102–14.

Christine de Pizan and Antoine de la Sale: The Dangers of Love in Theory and Fiction

ALLISON KELLY

The possibility that Antoine de la Sale read works of Christine de Pizan has recently been raised independently by Karl D. Uitti and Charity Cannon Willard.[1] Many years ago, Georges Doutrepont noticed certain similarities in their works without pinpointing any direct influence of Christine. Her prolific work, produced mainly between 1399 and 1414, would have been available to a reader during the mid-fifteenth century in numerous manuscripts, some of which would almost certainly have been known in the courts of Anjou and Luxembourg, where Antoine (1385–1461) spent most of his life.[2] As a tutor to Jean de Calabre and later, to the children of the court of Luxembourg, Antoine was interested in education, as evidenced by his own *La Salade* (1442) and *La Salle* (1451), encyclopedias written for pedagogical purposes. He must have taken an interest in Christine's own treatise on moral education, the *Epistre d'Othéa* (1400) and perhaps other of her works as well—the *Enseignemens moraux* (ca. 1400), for example.[3] Moreover, he came into contact with people who would have known Christine's work, for the court of Anjou would have favorably received Christine's praise of Marie de Blois in the *Livre de la Cité des Dames* (1405).[4] Marie was the mother of Antoine's first patron, Louis II of Anjou, and she figures in Christine's work as a noble and wise ruler. She must have been an influential person at the court of Anjou when the young Antoine arrived there in 1400, for after being widowed in 1384 when her son was only six years old, she had governed until Louis was able to assume power as duke of Anjou. It is not unlikely that Antoine would have known at least this work in which she is mentioned.

These scholars have proposed that Antoine de la Sale may have been familiar with Christine's reputation and with specific works, namely the *Livre de la Cité des Dames*, the *Epistre d'Othéa* and the *Livre des Trois Vertus* (1405), and this judgment is based on some remarkable likenesses.[5] Above all, they have argued that Antoine's most memorable and puzzling charac-

ter, the Dame des Belles Cousines in *Jehan de Saintré* (1456) might reflect the
influence of Christine. To be sure, the fictional character is vastly different
from Christine herself, and Christine never created any character closely resembling the Belles Cousines of the final part of *Saintré*. Yet as Doutrepont
remarked, almost no other woman of the fifteenth century was known to
display the breadth of learning that Belles Cousines does in her education of
Jehan.[6] Willard has very aptly recalled Christine's *Epistre d'Othéa* in relation
to *Saintré*, for both works depict a very learned woman instructing an ado-
lescent boy in morals, religion, and chivalric customs. Other parallels that
have been noted include *Saintré*'s insistence on Belles Cousines' status as a
widow and Christine's own widowhood, as well as her interest in the special
problems that widows face, and a mutual concern with slander and reputation. These and other similarities are best made apparent by comparing
Saintré with the *Cité des Dames* and the *Trois Vertus*—comparisons already
made by Uitti and Willard, but which deserve further study.

As indicated above, many influences of Christine on Antoine's *Saintré* can
be traced, but of particular interest is the treatment of *fin'amor* in *Saintré*,
which in some ways recalls Christine's work. Indeed, to my mind, their
common concern about the degeneration of a courtly ideal of love is of great
importance to any discussion of possible influences of Christine on Antoine
de la Sale. A brief review of the role of *fin'amor* in Antoine's work is necessary, and as the central character in *Saintré*, Belles Cousines and her fate constitute the focal point for our study of Christine's influence and of Antoine's
attitude toward love, especially *fin'amor*. She is a complex character, not
easily understood, and critics have interpreted her in contradictory ways,
both as an essentially courtly lady who is wronged by her lover and as a
scheming *fabliau* woman.[7] Belles Cousines has quite rightfully been labeled
the source of the ambiguity which has long intrigued readers of *Saintré*.[8] The
narrator of the work (Acteur) presents her in a deliberately ambiguous way,
insisting on her virtuousness while also undercutting and then reaffirming
her good character. At the beginning of *Saintré*, the Acteur describes her
high position at court and likens her to the praiseworthy widows of ancient Rome who never remarried.[9] In an abrupt reversal, he counters his examples of good widows with the tale of one who married twenty-two times,
perhaps casting doubt on Belles Cousines' character, and certainly adding
a humorous note to his Christine-like praise of virtuous women. Yet he
continues to portray Belles Cousines as an honorable lady, and he presents
only worthy motivations for her involvement with Jehan. As a still-young
childless widow, she decides to devote herself to an all-consuming project:
"Ceste dame, comme dit est, aiant emprins, pour quelconque occasion que
ce fust, de jamais plus soy marier, et non obstant ce, elle aiant son cuer en
diverses pensees, entre lesquelles par maintes fois se pensa qu'elle vouloit en

ce monde faire d'aucun josne chevalier ou escuier un homme renommé, et
en celle pensee s'arresta totalement." (p. 6; "This lady, as has been said, was
resolved never to remarry, no matter what occasion might present itself;
but nevertheless, she had in her heart various ideas, among which she often
thought that she wanted to make of some young knight or squire a man of
renown, and she fixed her thoughts on this idea.")

While Belles Cousines' relationship with Jehan consists initially of education, she includes in her teaching many remarks on the necessity of loving
a lady and explains the service and obedience that a knight must render
to his lady in order to be successful both in love and war. She echoes the
idea, found in some of Christine's early works (though Christine considerably modified her views later)[10] and in many Old French romances, that
some men have been inspired to great deeds by the love of a lady; Belles
Cousines here appears to believe in *fin'amor*. This evocation of *fin'amor* is not
an anomaly in *Saintré*, for the idea is developed throughout the work. As
Jehan grows older, their teacher/pupil status evolves into a love relationship in which Belles Cousines accepts and expects the traditional givens of
fin'amor, that is, if she loves Jehan, he will love, serve, and obey her. In
Saintré, Jehan obeys and serves Belles Cousines while reaping the very considerable material benefits of her patronage. Yet a real *fin'amor* relationship
never fully develops, for Jehan shows less and less interest in his lady as
the work progresses, and the Acteur devotes increasingly more attention
to long and detailed accounts of Jehan's jousting exploits, often relegating
Belles Cousines to a minor role. Eventually Jehan leaves court to undertake
his own expedition, against the will of Belles Cousines and the king, while
the apparently heartbroken Belles Cousines retires to the countryside only
to begin a disgraceful affair with a vulgar abbot. The *fin'amor* framework
that Belles Cousines had tried to establish at the beginning of the work
breaks down entirely.[11]

An examination of Christine de Pizan's treatment of the question of
fin'amor will show how this portrayal of love in *Saintré* reflects her influence
on Antoine's work. Christine approaches the relationship between men and
women cautiously, affirming the value of love in marriage while trying to
warn women about the dangers of illicit love. Her early poetry exhibits
familiarity with the *fin'amor* tradition, and as Douglas Kelly has shown, she
attempts to distinguish between *fole amour* and *fin'amor* in her early works.[12]
In her letter (1402) to Pierre Col in the debate over the *Roman de la Rose*, she
praises married love and asserts that *fin'amor,* which she narrowly defines
as pure, chaste love without marriage, can be achieved.[13] This love en-
riches the men who are able to live up to the high standards of *fin'amor,*
and Christine gives examples of knights who became valiant and famous
because of their love for a lady. In her subsequent *Cité des Dames* and *Livre*

des Trois Vertus, Christine appears to be more pragmatic and more skeptical about the viability of *fin'amor* in the real world. While she continues to praise love in marriage, she insists that love outside of marriage is dangerous, for it is difficult to distinguish between honorable and foolish love. Indeed, she argues that even love intended to be honorable may turn into *fole amour,* for given the realities of the society in which they live, women cannot depend on men to live up to those idealistic notions of love that were at the heart of so many romances. In these works, particularly in *Trois Vertus*, where she is addressing women of all classes of society, Christine's practical advice to them is to avoid any love outside of marriage, particularly because of the possible harm it may cause to a woman's reputation.

This work, which warns most vehemently against the folly of illicit love, contains a letter warning a highborn lady (in this case a married woman) against the dangers of secret love. As Charity Cannon Willard has noted, this letter is especially interesting for a study of Christine's influence on Antoine, especially in regard to *fin'amor* since it encapsulates Christine's major objections to this kind of love.[14] The letter included in *Trois Vertus* originally appeared in the *Livre du Duc des Vrais Amants*, and it is possible that Antoine may have read either work. Since, however, as Willard has shown, the *Duc des Vrais Amants* survives in only two manuscripts, it is more likely that Antoine knew the widely read and frequently copied *Trois Vertus*.[15] It seems that this work enjoyed increasing popularity throughout the fifteenth century,[16] and ladies read it as a sort of guide book to proper conduct.[17]

The letter contained in this work is of particular relevance to *Saintré*, which illustrates every dangerous consequence outlined by Christine in her cautions against *fin'amor*. An older woman, Sebille de Monthault, dame de la Tour, who had served as a governess or lady-in-waiting, writes this letter and addresses her advice to a young noblewoman or princess. She reminds her that even though she may have good intentions, taking a lover is foolish. The governess assumes that the lady wants an honorable relationship, mentioning in particular that a lady might take a lover with the idea of making him valiant, that is, for his benefit and not for her own selfish desires. Indeed, she explains that many ladies have expressed this very thought and warns against it: "Et ne vous fiez es foles pensees que pluseurs joennes femmes ont, qui se donnent a croire que ce n'est point de mal d'amer par amours, mais qu'il n'y ait villennie—car je me rens certaine que autrement ne le vouldriez penser pour mourir—, et que on vit plus lieement et que de ce faire on fait un homme devenir vaillant et renommé a tousjours mais." (p. 100; "Do not trust in vain thoughts, which many young women have, who persuade themselves that it is not wrong to take a lover provided that there is no wickedness [for I feel certain that otherwise you would never consider doing so], for a lady is happier with a lover and she can make a man valiant and renowned forever.")[18] Of course, as noted above, Belles Cousines has exactly this motive for choosing Jehan as her servant and lover. The writer of the letter in *Trois Vertus* warns of the pitfalls of love and of the erroneous ideas about love that the younger woman might hold, and Belles Cousines encounters each problem that is warned against, falling into every trap as if to demonstrate the veracity of Christine's objections to *fin'amor*.

In *Trois Vertus*, the governess suggests that a younger lady might convince herself that taking a lover is an honorable endeavor by saying to herself: "Tu es joenne, il ne te fault que plaisance, tu puez bien amer sans villennie, ce n'est point de mal puisqu'il n'y a pechié: tu feras un vaillant homme, ou n'en sera riens. Tu en vivras plus joyeusement et auras acquis un vray serviteur et loyal ami,—et ainsi toutes telz choses." (p. 108; " 'You are young and nothing matters but your pleasure. You can easily love without any wrongdoing. It is not wrong, since there is no sin, and you will make a man valiant. No one will know anything about it, you will live more happily for it and you will have acquired a true servant and loyal friend,' and so on and so forth," pp. 101–2.) However, the older woman objects to such reasoning on many grounds, for she predicts dire consequences, all of which are illustrated in *Saintré*. She insists that from such a love, a lady will find more suffering than pleasure: "Ha! ma chiere dame, pour Dieu! soiez avisee que telles folles opinions ne vous deçoivent, quar quant a la plaisance, soiez certaine qu'en amours a cent mille fois plus de dueil, cuisançons, et dongiers perilleux, par especial du cousté des dames, qu'il n'y a de plaisance." (p. 108; "Oh, my lady, for God's sake do not be deceived by such mad ideas! As for pleasure, you may be certain that in love there is twice as much sorrow, pain, and perilous danger [especially on the side of the ladies] as there is pleasure," p. 102.) In *Saintré* Belles Cousines' pleasure in her love for Jehan is always countered by trials and suffering. She worries about Jehan constantly, fainting from anxiety when he is in combat, wearing hair shirts when he is away, while Jehan never suffers at all. In fact, when Jehan leaves Belles Cousines to pursue his own glory, Belles Cousines is stricken ill, and the doctor pronounces a diagnosis of acute and life-threatening heartsickness.

The letter in Christine's *Trois Vertus* also points out that a lady who takes a lover will always have to worry about her love being discovered, for her reputation is at stake in such an affair. Again, Belles Cousines demonstrates exactly this concern, for she tries to take precautions to keep her love of Jehan secret, often constructing elaborate schemes to hide her meetings with him, arranging secret signals to alert him, and above all, impressing upon Jehan the importance of discretion. She makes him take a very

serious oath never to reveal their relationship: "Or ça, comme bon crestien
et gentil homme que vous estes, vous me promectez, sur Dieu, sur vostre
foy de crestien et sur vostre honneur—cy n'a que vous et moy qui nous
puisse oÿr—que, de chose que je vous die, a personne qui puisse vivre
ne morir, par quelque façon que ce soit, vous ne direz, descouverrez ne
ferez savoir ce que je vous diray presentement ne autrefoys, et que ainsin
de vostre main a la mienne le me promectez?" (pp. 35–36; "Well now, as
the good Christian and gentleman that you are, promise me, by God, on
your faith as a Christian and on your honor—there is no one here except you
and me who can hear us—that concerning the things that I tell you, you
will never, by any means, say, uncover or make known that which I will tell
you soon—or at any other time; and with your hand in mine do you promise
me this?"). Belles Cousines demonstrates that she fears for her reputation,
and, as Christine would have warned, her fears are justified, for in the end
Jehan breaks his promise to her.

The letter writer raises another objection to the secret love affair that
the young lady in *Trois Vertus* proposes. She insists that though the younger
lady may intend to commit no sin and to keep her love honorable and discreet, it is difficult to control the course that love might take: "Ne soit
nul ne nulle si asseure de soy qu'elle se rende certaine de soy, quelque bon
propos qu'elle ait de garder tousjours mesure en si faicte amour" (p. 108;
"Neither men nor women may be so sure of themselves that they can be certain always to love in moderation," p. 102). Belles Cousines' words to Jehan
similarly indicate that she intends their love to be beyond reproach: "Sire,
devez vous choisir dame qui soit de hault et noble sang, saige, et qui ait de
quoy vous aidier et mectre sus a voz besoings, et celle tant servir et loial-
ment amer, pour quelque peine que en aiez a souffrir, qu'elle cognoise bien
la parfaite amour que sans deshonneur lui pourtez" (p. 16; "Sire, you must
choose yourself a wise lady of high and noble blood, who has the means
to help you and take care of your needs, and serve her and so loyally love
her, that despite whatever pain that you might suffer for her, she would
know the perfect love that you bring to her without dishonor"). However,
Belles Cousines, while apparently remaining chaste, becomes passionately
involved in her love for Jehan, and she demonstrates, as the *Trois Vertus* letter claims, that it is difficult to love in moderation.

Christine's letter writer insists that the young lady cannot depend on her
lover to remain a faithful servant, for he is likely to put his own needs before
hers: "Mais ilz sont aucuns qui dient qu'ilz servent leur dames quant ilz font
beaucoup de choses, soit en armes ou aultres fais. Mais je dy qu'ilz servent
eulx mesmes, car l'onneur et le preu leur en demeure et non mie a la dame"
(p. 109; "There are some men who say that they serve their ladies when they
do many things, be it in arms or other deeds. But I say that they are serving

only themselves, for the honour and the benefit remain with them and not with the lady," p. 102).

Christine's exhortations that men should change their ways and that women should be alerted to possible harm from love had appeared in several of her earlier works as well. In the *Epistre au dieu d'Amours*,[19] she chastises the French, who used to be exemplary defenders of women; however, with a few exceptions whom she mentions by name, they have failed to live up to their former deeds. In the *Cité des Dames*, Dame Raison tells Christine that women must protect themselves, for men's neglect has left them vulnerable; their City of Ladies must be built so that "les dames et toutes vaillans femmes puissent d'ores en avant avoir aucun retrait et closture de deffence contre tant de divers assaillans, lesquelles dites dames ont par si longtemps [esté] delaissies, descloses comme champ sans haye, sans trouver champion aucun qui pour leur deffence comparust souffisantment, nonobstant les nobles hommes qui par ordenance de droit deffendre les deussent, qui par negligence et nonchaloir les ont souffertes foller" (1.3.3, p. 629; "From now on, ladies and all valiant women may have a refuge and defense against the various assailants, those ladies who have been abandoned for so long, exposed like a field without a surrounding hedge, without finding a champion to afford them an adequate defense, notwithstanding those noble men who are required by order of law to protect them, who by negligence and apathy have allowed them to be mistreated").

It is exactly this sort of negligence and apathy that allows Jehan to pursue his own interests without regard for Belles Cousines. Again, Belles Cousines' experience of love illustrates the precepts of the governess in *Trois Vertus*, for Jehan does put his own desire to joust before Belles Cousines' need for him to stay at court with her. Christine reiterates in *Trois Vertus* that many men do not act as they should toward women, for though they may swear to love faithfully and eternally, their love cannot always be trusted. Her distrust of *fin'amor,* and specifically her opinion that some men do not live up to their own high standards of behavior toward women, results first from the less-than-praiseworthy conduct of the courtiers of early fifteenth-century France who still professed a belief in *fin'amor,* and second from the slanderous, and to her mind uncourtly, accusations of misogynistic writers such as Jean de Meun and Matheolus.[20]

The governess warns that women should protect their reputations; indeed, combatting slander was Christine's purpose in writing the *Cité des Dames*, and in *Trois Vertus* she supplies practical advice to women on ways to avoid slander, arguing against illicit love largely because women and their reputations will likely be hurt by it. In this work, she cautions that widows especially must avoid situations that could lead to slander, for they are left vulnerable to malicious accusations. Christine warns that men will defame their ladies once their love has ended, even though they may have promised to be discreet. In Antoine de la Sale's work, Belles Cousines finds herself in a situation closely resembling the hypothetical one outlined in the *Trois Vertus* letter. Despite her frequent insistence on the secrecy and permanence of their relationship, and despite Jehan's swearing to remain faithful and discreet, Jehan cruelly reveals not only Belles Cousines' affair with the abbot but also her love for him, a relationship that had lasted for many years. In the final scene of *Saintré*, Jehan, jealous of Belles Cousines' involvement with the abbot, tells only his side of the story, and then, he asks each woman in turn to give her opinion of the unnamed lady's guilt or innocence. He then openly blames her, transgressing any code of honorable behavior. Of course Belles Cousines is guilty of her dalliance with the abbot, but by asking the ladies to judge on the basis of his simplified and slanted story, he deflects their attention from his possible guilt.

Finally, the overall purpose of the governess's letter in *Trois Vertus* is to warn women against the dangers of love, since as Christine claims, women are never cautioned against the deceitfulness of men. Like Christine, who directs her advice to women of both high and low social status, the Acteur, at the end of *Saintré*, warns women of all classes to learn from the example of Belles Cousines, who threw her life away because of her love: "Et cy commenceray la fin de ce compte, priant, requerant et suppliant a toutes dames et damoiselles, bourgoises et autres, de quelque estat que soient, que toutes prenent exemple a ceste si tres noble dame oiseuse qui par druerie se perdist" (p. 307; "And here will begin the end of this tale, praying, requesting and beseeching every lady and maiden, goodwives and others, from whatever estate that they might be, that all of them make an example of this very noble, idle lady who was lost through love"). The governess in *Trois Vertus* warns that no woman should risk her reputation for a lover: "Certes, je dy que c'est trop grant folie de soy destruire pour accroistre un aultre" (p. 108; "It is assuredly a very great folly to destroy oneself in order to advance another," p. 102), advice that Belles Cousines validates through her own folly.

The relationship between men and women described here recalls another significant point of comparison, that of Belles Cousines and the Dido depicted in the *Cité des Dames*. Uitti has shown that Dido bears a marked resemblance to Belles Cousines, for one can read both women as putting too much trust in the men they love; they fell victim to their passion, and both self-destruct when they realize that they have been betrayed.[21] Christine discusses Dido twice in the *Cité des Dames*: once as a powerful ruler and a second time as a woman who loved Aeneas too much and who is betrayed by her love. As Uitti has demonstrated, in both cases she resembles Belles Cousines;[22] in the first, her capable and knowledgeable comportment can be likened to that of the Belles Cousines who teaches Jehan and who knows how to manipulate the court so that no one suspects her patronage. In the second case the resemblance is even closer. Christine remarks in this passage that, though men say that women are fickle, women are never warned against the duplicity of men—who frequently deceive women. She then goes on to discuss Dido, who loved Aeneas far more than he loved her: "Car nonobstant que il luy eust la foy baillee que jamais autre femme que elle ne prendroit et qu'a tousjours mais sien seroit, il s'en parti aprés ce que elle [l']ot tout reffait et enrichi d'avoir et d'aise, ses nefs refraischies, reffaictes et ordonnees, plain de tresor et de biens, comme celle qui n'avoit espargné l'avoir la ou le cuer estoit mis (2.55.1, pp. 930–31; "For even though he had given her his pledge never to take any other woman and to be hers forever, he left after she had restored and enriched him with property and ease, his ships refreshed, repaired, and placed in order, filled with treasure and wealth, like a woman who had spared no expense where her heart was involved.") Christine's portrayal of Dido anticipates Belles Cousines, for Jehan's lady loves him with unreciprocated fervor, and as signs of her love, she, like Dido, generously supplies his every material need and spares no expense.

Following Christine's description of Dido's tale, we can see just how closely Belles Cousines is modeled on such a scenario. According to the *Cité des Dames*, Aeneas "s'en ala sans congié prendre de nuit en recellee traytreusement, sans le sceu d'elle; et ainsi paya son hoste" ("He departed at night, secretly and treacherously, without farewells and without her knowledge. This was how he repaid his hostess.") Though Jehan gives Belles Cousines some warning, his departure on his own expedition was against her will, and unlike his other tournaments, where he had participated only at Belles Cousines' bidding, this expedition was conceived and born in secrecy and only announced to the king, the court, and Belles Cousines after all preparations had been made. Finally, Christine remarks on Dido's fate: "Et ainsi piteusement fina la noble royne Dido, qui tant honnouree avoit esté [que elle] passoit en renommee toutes les femmes de son temps" ("And so the noble queen Dido died in such a pitiful manner, who has been honored so greatly that her fame has surpassed that of all other women of her time"). Once abandoned by Jehan, Belles Cousines, for all practical purposes, commits suicide. She has nothing to live for, and she willfully destroys her reputation and her life by her self-imposed exile from court and her affair with the abbot.

In the *Cité des Dames*, Christine uses Dido's story as an example of a woman who loves faithfully. She does not condemn her actions, but she does include the story in order to alert women to the dangers of love, much as the letter in *Trois Vertus* does. She shows that even a strong and honorable woman such as the wise ruler Dido, as she depicts her in her first account, can be victimized by love. Her only censure of Dido, that she loved Aeneas too much, is also praise, for in this work Christine is countering claims by men that women are inconstant in love. Of course in the *Livre des Trois Vertus* Christine takes a harder line, since here she is giving more concrete and practical advice to contemporary women who may fall victim to slander— a significant concern of Christine's.[23]

Christine's influence is clearly apparent in Antoine de la Sale's work as demonstrated by the parallels between Belles Cousines' conduct and the *Livre des Trois Vertus*, as well as by her resemblance to Christine's Dido. Yet Antoine uses Christine's ideas and characters in a very liberal fashion, always allowing for multiple readings. While *Saintré* essentially shows that Christine is justified in her wariness of *fin'amor* (at least as practiced in the fifteenth century), it does so in a way quite different from Christine. The Belles Cousines of the beginning of the work may imitate Christine's didactic tone, but her discourse is tempered by that of the Acteur and by the humor of the work. In addition, *Saintré*'s irony renders any message highly problematic, for as the divided and even contradictory criticism of the work has shown, *Saintré* refuses any facile reading.

Antoine de la Sale demonstrates the truth of Christine's warnings—that men will slander women, and like Christine, the Acteur avoids any clearcut condemnation of Belles Cousines' actions, that is, while Jehan may slander his lady, the Acteur's judgment of her remains ambiguous. Certainly, the work does not entirely vindicate Belles Cousines, for unlike Dido, who, when frustrated in love kills herself in a pitiful, but still somehow noble, act, Belles Cousines reacts in a much more blameworthy fashion in taking the abbot as her lover. She gives Jehan a reason to condemn her; her actions even appear to confirm the accusations of slanderers that women are fickle in love, accusations always combatted by Christine. Indeed, the work appears to give credence to Christine's defense of women and her distrust of men's actions, while at the same time poking fun at the idea of virtuous women that Christine propagates. For example, *Saintré* seems to echo *Trois Vertus*, which argues that women can be harmed by their lovers: "Et! pouvres dames, comment estes vous abusees de voz amoureux, en pluseurs desquelz n'est pas en ce cas toute loiaulté envers sa dame" ("Poor ladies, how you are abused by your lovers, some of whom do not show true loyalty"). Yet these words, spoken by the abbot, who is not the most admirable character in the work, may or may not be read as authoritative by the reader.

In *Saintré*, when Jehan discovers Belles Cousines' treachery with the abbot, he relates a one-sided tale of a knight who faithfully loved a lady so much that he went on an expedition to gain glory for her. However, while he was away, his lady deceived and betrayed him by cavorting with an unworthy cleric; of course, he is referring here to Belles Cousines and the abbot, and he deliberately incriminates his former lady. Yet, Jehan is interrupted by the Acteur's poem about fortune, a poem which renders Jehan's version of the story ambiguous: he blames the lady, whereas the poem implies that fortune is responsible. The Acteur's poem suggests that multiple readings of the situation are possible, for it is clear that Jehan is not totally correct. Indeed, here again, Belles Cousines can be read in the light of Christine's Dido, for she also blames Dido's fate on Fortune, who "luy destampa a la parfin trop dur buvraige" (1.46.3, p. 775; "mixed too harsh a brew for her in the end"). But *Saintré* again refuses too close an identification with Christine and her work, for despite the obvious parallel between Dido and Belles Cousines, the Acteur still allows for ambiguity. He refers to Dido in the beginning of *Saintré* as a virtuous widow who remained faithful to her first husband and clearly compares her to Belles Cousines. However, in an apparently deliberate reversal of Christine's portrayal of Dido, he insists that Aeneas loved Dido, but Dido ignored his love because of her love for her husband. The implications of this version of Dido's tale for *Saintré* are complicated, but one might assume that Belles Cousines does not value Jehan's love just as, for the Acteur, Dido did not value that of Aeneas.

Finally, the last pages of *Saintré* emphasize the Acteur's ambiguous treatment of Christine's ideas, both affirming her point of view and voicing the misogynistic opinions of her opponents as well. According to Christine, women who engage in illicit love affairs act foolishly, for they should realize that, despite their honorable intentions, they risk their reputations: "car feu n'est point sans fumee, mais fumee est souvent sans feu" (p. 108; "for there is no fire without smoke, although there is quite often smoke without fire," p. 102). Yet Christine does not condemn such women; rather, she condemns their illicit love, tries to outline standards for proper conduct as she does in *Trois Vertus*, and warns against too readily trusting men. In other of her works she insists that if a man is loyal, his lady will be as well, so that much of the blame lies with men who fail to act as they should. The Acteur of *Saintré* takes the opposite position in his assessment of Belles Cousines and seems to condemn women and to agree with Jehan's accusations of Belles Cousines by using the same proverb that Christine employs to discuss the problem of women's guilt or blame and the fragility of their reputations.

> Onques ne fut feu sans fumee, tant fust il en terre parfont. C'est a entendre que onques ne fut bien ou mal, tant fust il secret, repost ne obscur, que a la fin ne soit sceu, car ainsin l'a ordonné le vray et trestout puissant juge de toutes choses, auquel ne fault ne on ne puet riens celer, pour meriter les justes et les bons, et pour pugnir les pecheurs et les mauvais, soit en ame, soit en corps ou en honneur, ainsin qu'il fist de

ceste dame, et de mains autres hommes et femmes, pugnis par leurs desordonnees volentez. (p. 307)

(There was never fire without smoke, no matter how deep in the ground it was. That is, there was never good nor evil, no matter how secret or obscure, that was not known in the end; for the true and all-powerful judge of everything, from whom nothing can or should be hidden, has ordained it to be as such, so that he can reward the just and the good and punish the sinners and the bad—either in soul, in body or in honor— as he did to this lady and to many other men and women, punished for their inordinate willfullness.)

However, after appearing to reiterate Jehan's condemnation of Belles Cousines, he then counters with the idea, expressed by Christine, that many have their reputations destroyed unjustly: "Ils sont bien des fumees sans feu, c'est a entendre que sont maintes faulses langues desliees de flacteurs a gecter les fumees sans feu, c'est a dire porter et rapporter faulses et mauvaises renommees a hommes et a femmes sans cause et contre raison, mais elles ne peuent porter le feu, c'est la veritable preuve" (pp. 307–8; "There are indeed smokes without fire; that is to say that there are many false tongues of flatterers which are unloosed to give forth smokes without fire; that is to say, to bear and report false and bad tales about men and women without cause or basis in truth, but they cannot bring the fire which is the real proof"). In this passage he casts doubt on his earlier accusation of Belles Cousines, and throughout the work he protects her reputation from slanderers by keeping her anonymous.

Much of the interest of *Saintré* lies in its creative reworking of Christine's ideas in a very different and ironic framework, illustrating the problems with *fin'amor* that Christine had earlier discussed. Though Antoine de la Sale never directly cites Christine, her influence is apparent,[24] and a rereading of *Saintré* in light of her work offers a greater understanding of its most puzzling character, Belles Cousines. For both authors, *fin'amor* as practiced in the courts of the late Middle Ages posed grave dangers to women and their reputations, and both point to "courtly" relationships as unsatisfactory, especially because of the failure of many men to value women as they should. In the *Epistre au dieu d'Amours*,[25] Christine urges men to remember the importance of woman: "C'est sa mere, c'est sa suer, c'est s'amie" ("she is his mother, she is his sister, she is his lover")—roles that *Saintré* denies the frustrated Belles Cousines, with, as Christine would have predicted, tragic consequences.

Notes

1. Karl D. Uitti, "Renewal and Undermining of Old French Romance: *Jehan de Saintré*," in *Romance: Generic Transformation from Chrétien de Troyes to Cervantes*, ed. Kevin Brownlee and Marina Scordilis Brownlee (Hanover, N.H.: University Press of New England, 1985), 135–54. Charity Cannon Willard discussed this subject in "Antoine de la Sale, Reader of Christine de Pizan" (Paper delivered at the Southeastern Medieval Association meeting, University of Georgia, October 1986). This article cites a typescript of Willard's paper which will be published in a forthcoming volume on Christine de Pizan's readers, *Visitors to the City: Readers of Christine de Pizan*, ed. Glenda McLeod. See also Georges Doutrepont, *La Littérature française à la cour des ducs de Bourgogne: Philippe le Hardi, Jean sans Peur, Philippe le Bon, Charles le Téméraire* (Paris: Champion, 1909), 97.

2. Willard ("Antoine de la Sale," 3–4) notes that Jehan Miélot, an important copyist for the duke of Burgundy, finished a revision of Christine's *Epistre d'Othéa* in 1455, while Antoine de la Sale's *Jehan de Saintré* was completed in 1456.

3. Willard, in "Antoine de la Sale," 3, mentions Antoine de la Sale's probable interest in such treatises.

4. See Maureen Curnow, "The *Livre de la Cité des Dames*: A Critical Edition, 2 vols. (Ph.D. dissertation, Vanderbilt University, 1975), 670–71. All French quotations of this work are taken from the Curnow edition. See also *The Book of the City of Ladies*, trans. Earl Jeffrey Richards (New York: Persea Books, 1982), 34–35. English translations of quotations from the *Cité des Dames* are taken from Richards. Charles A. Knudson mentions this connection in "The Historical Saintré," in *Jean Misrahi Memorial Volume: Studies in Medieval Literature*, ed. Hans R. Runte, Henri Niedzielski, and William L. Hendrickson (Columbia, S.C.: French Literature Publications, 1977), 303.

5. Uitti ("Renewal and Undermining," 145–47, 153) compares la Dame des Belles Cousines in *Saintré* to the Dido of Christine de Pizan's *Cité des Dames*, while Willard ("Antoine de la Sale," 2) sees a possible influence of the *Cité des Dames* and the *Epistre d'Othéa* on *Saintré* and suggests also that Antoine may have also known the *Livre des Trois Vertus* and possibly the *Livre du Duc des Vrais Amants*.

6. See Doutrepont, *Littérature française*, 97, also cited by Willard, "Antoine de la Sale," 1.

7. See Clifton Cherpack, "*Le Petit Jehan de Saintré*: The Archetypal Background," *Journal of Medieval and Renaissance Studies* 5 (1975): 244–45; Janet Ferrier, *Forerunners of the French Novel* (Manchester, U.K.: Manchester University Press, 1954), 64; Jane H. M. Taylor, "The Pattern of Perfection: *Jehan de Saintré* and the Chivalric Ideal," *Medium Aevum* 53 (1984): 208.

8. Emma Stojkovic Mazzariol calls Belles Cousines "la matrice prima dell'ambivalenza del romanzo," in *L'occhio e il piede: Lettura critica del "Petit Jehan de Saintré" di Antoine de la Sale* (Vicenza, Italy: Neri Pozza Editore, 1979), 36. Julia Kristeva remarks on the ambivalence of Belles Cousines' discourse in: *Le Texte du roman: Approche sémiologique d'une structure discursive transformationelle*, Approaches to Semiotics, no. 6, ed. T. A. Sebeok (The Hague: Mouton, 1976), 117.

9. Antoine de la Sale, *Jehan de Saintré*, ed. Jehan Misrahi and Charles A. Knud-

son (Geneva: Droz, 1978), 3. All further references to *Saintré* are from this edition. The English translations of *Saintré* given here are my own.

10. See below for a discussion of Christine's attitude on this subject.

11. This discussion of *fin'amor* in *Saintré* was developed in my paper "Love and Chivalry: Antoine de la Sale's Ideal of *Conjointure*," which was delivered at the Modern Language Association Convention, San Francisco, December 1987, and which is being revised for publication.

12. F. Douglas Kelly, "Reflections on the Role of Christine de Pisan as a Feminist Writer," *Sub-Stance* 2 (1972): 67.

13. See Christine's reply to Pierre Col in Eric Hicks, ed., *Le Débat sur le "Roman de la Rose"* (Paris: Champion, 1977), 129. See also Charity Cannon Willard, *Christine de Pizan: Her Life and Works* (New York: Persea Books, 1984), 60–61.

14. Willard, "Antoine de la Sale," 8–9, notes that this letter applies to the situation of Belles Cousines and Jehan, an interesting suggestion which I propose to develop here.

15. Willard, "Antoine de la Sale," 9.

16. See Charity Cannon Willard, "The Manuscript Tradition of the *Livre des Trois Vertus* and Christine de Pizan's Audience," *Journal of the History of Ideas* 27 (1966): 436.

17. Interestingly, while Antoine de la Sale's work is ostensibly dedicated to a man, Jean de Calabre, at least one manuscript of *Saintré* is known to have belonged to a woman, Marie de Luxembourg. It is not unlikely that the ladies who read Antoine's works would also have been familiar with Christine's *Trois Vertus*.

18. Christine de Pizan, *Le Livre des Trois Vertus*, ed. Charity Cannon Willard (Paris: Champion, 1989). Professor Willard graciously allowed me to cite galley proofs of her edition of *Trois Vertus* before its publication. All French quotations of this work are taken from the Willard edition. English translations of this work are from *The Treasure of the City of Ladies, or; The Book of the Three Virtues*, trans. Sarah Lawson (Harmondsworth, U.K.: Penguin Books, 1985). Citations of this work indicate first the page number from the Willard edition and, following the translation, the page number from the Lawson translation.

19. *Epistre au dieu d'Amours*, in *Oeuvres poétiques de Christine de Pisan*, ed. Maurice Roy, 3 vols. (Paris: Firmin Didot, 1886–96), 2:1–27. See especially pp. 2–8.

20. The *Cité des dames* constitutes a protest against such accusations. Cf. also Willard, *Christine de Pizan*, 150.

21. Uitti, "Renewal and Undermining," 146–47.

22. Ibid., 153.

23. See Charity Cannon Willard, "Christine de Pizan's *Livre des Trois Vertus*: Feminine Ideal or Practical Advice?" in *Ideals for Women in the Works of Christine de Pizan*, ed. Diane Bornstein, Medieval and Renaissance Monograph Series, no. 1 (Detroit: Michigan Consortium for Medieval and Early Modern Studies, 1981), 91–116.

24. Though *Saintré* contains many direct quotations from other works, all of them are from ancient authors or from the Bible. Antoine de la Sale rarely cites contemporary vernacular works.

25. *Oeuvres poétiques*, ed. Roy, 24, line 733.

Christine de Pizan and the House of Savoy

GIANNI MOMBELLO

TRANSLATED AND EDITED BY

NADIA MARGOLIS

The above title represents a wager. In fact, Christine's relations with the lords of Savoy were rather tenuous, if not nonexistent. Savoy is not mentioned in the works of this woman writer, although she passed through its lands in order to go from northern Italy to Paris in 1368. Born around 1363, she was too little to have been able to retain a lasting memory of her crossing of the "lofty Alps." [1] Although the last counts and then the first duke of Savoy pursued a policy of close ties with the kings of France [2] and took French princesses as wives, Christine paid scarcely any attention to them in her writings. Nevertheless, a certain number of her works belonged to the members of the House of Savoy.

Despite these strongly pessimistic considerations, it is appropriate to devote a few pages to this subject in a volume of studies dedicated to Charity Cannon Willard, who has expended all of her tireless energies as a scholar to elucidate and make better known the life and works of this engaging woman writer.

To begin at the beginning, we must recall that relations between the counts of Savoy and Christine go back to her father. In fact, Thomas of Bologna, or of Pizzano (henceforth: "de Pizan"), received from Amadeus VI, the Green Count, the sum of forty gold francs in 1377. This detail, reported by Suzanne Solente in her edition of *Livre des fais et bonnes meurs du sage roy Charles V* as well as in her essay of 1969, is not mentioned in the excellent biography that Professor Willard has devoted to Christine de Pizan. [3]

How do we explain this absence? Those who have read this book know, from experience, that Professor Willard verifies everything. Indeed, the credibility of what she writes is founded upon an impressive return to primary sources and the care she takes in accounting for every detail.

Yet there is also another reason for the reader's initial surprise. If we compare the concise essay by Suzanne Solente with the much more extensive biography by Professor Willard, we notice the latter never misses the opportunity to anchor Christine soundly within her historical context. We might now wonder why she judged it proper to remain silent on this detail concerning the poet's father.

We shall devote the first part of our contribution to this problem. In the second part, we shall provide the list of manuscripts of Christine de Pizan's works which belonged to the members of the House of Savoy or which are still preserved today in Turin.

I. The Historical Context of Christine's Ties to the House of Savoy

In the introduction to her edition of the *Livre des fais et bonnes meurs du sage roy Charles V*, Suzanne Solente thus relates the event of interest to us: "In 1377 Amadeus VI of Savoy resorted to the science of Thomas de Pizan. It involved the choice of a favorable time for the wedding of the young Amadeus, his son, and of Bonne, the daughter of Duke Jean de Berry. The astrologer to Charles V cast the horoscope for the count of Savoy and received as compensation forty gold francs. The marriage took place at the Hotel Saint-Pol, in the presence of Charles V, January 18, 1377." [4] In her essay of 1969, this event is reported in almost the same terms. [5] Solente had taken this detail from a work by Jean Cordey. This historian related the wedding of Amadeus VII, the Red Count, to Bonne de Berry, in these terms: "The wedding was celebrated a few days later, January 18th, in the chapel of the Hotel Saint-Pol. The hour had been chosen most carefully in advance. Amadeus VI had consulted on this matter the royal astrologer, Thomas of Bologna, father of Christine de Pizan, who cast the horoscope for him." [6] The detail regarding the forty francs paid to Thomas de Pizan is absent from this text, so that Solente must have resorted to the source given by Cordey, that is, two works by Luigi Cibrario: *Origine e progressi delle istituzioni della monarchia di Savoia sino alla costituzione del Regno d'Italia* [7] and *Dell'economia politica del Medio Evo.* [8]

In the latter work, first published in 1839, Cibrario recalls the gift in a chapter dealing with different medieval marriage customs. He wrote on this matter: "It was still the custom to consult astrologers in order to know the propitious hour for the union; and Amadeus VII, in 1377, when he married Bonne de Berry in Paris, sought advice in this from Master Thomas of Bologna, astronomer to the king of France, and gave him forty gold francs" (1:389–90). As is apparent, the detail regarding the gift made to Thomas de Pizan as given here, though Cibrario does not exactly say that Christine's father cast the horoscope for this wedding, but only that it was the custom at this time to consult astrologers in choosing the most propitious hour for celebrating a wedding and that his young lord had followed this practice.

In the *Specchio cronologico*, which constitutes the second volume of his *Orig-*

ine e progressi delle istituzioni della monarchia di Savoia, Cibrario reports the same event in these terms: "Gift of forty gold francs from the count of Savoy to Thomas of Bologna, astronomer to the king in Paris, for casting the horoscope for the hour at which the wedding of My Lord Amadeus (for so the hereditary prince of Savoy was called) to Bonne de Berry was supposed to occur. The gold franc was worth fifteen Tournese gross [*grossi tornesi*], a fifth more than the genuine florin. The wedding took place on January 18th of that year. To betake himself from Chambéry to Paris Amadeus took nine days." [9] The relationship between the gift of forty gold francs and the fact that Thomas of Pizan cast the horoscope for the marriage of Amadeus VII seems to be well established in this text. Solente therefore expressly quotes from this latter work of Cibrario in her edition of the *Livre des fais* for her version of the events reported.

In his *Specchio chronologico* Cibrario does not indicate his source, but he cites it in another work, in a note, in the following terms: "Accounts of the General Treasurer of Savoy" (*Conti del tesoriere generale di Savoia*). This reference is useless for—or rather, made purposely to discourage—any curious scholar wishing to verify this detail.

In fact, the records of the treasury of Savoy are preserved within the "Combined Divisions" (*Sezioni riunite*) of the state archives (*Archivio di stato*) of Turin (abbreviated as AST), among those of the "Chamber of Accounts of Savoy." [10] The holdings in this series are described in a handwritten register referring to various "inventories." [11] The inventories of potential interest to us are numerous. [12] We thus consulted quite a few packets and rolls without finding anything. But Cibrario did not invent this fact; he simply confined himself to interpreting it to suit his needs. It is actually recorded in Inventory 38, folio 21, packet 11, roll 68.

This roll is so bulging and filled with names and figures as to challenge the good intentions of the most tenacious researcher. Finally, at the bottom of *membrana* VI^{xx}X, exactly on lines 46–48, we have found the notation of interest to us. It reads: "Item, ibidem [scilicet "Parisius"] dicta die [die .xxvi. januarii, anno M.CCC.lxx septimo], Magistro Thome de Bononia estronomiano Regis Franchorum, dono sibi facto per Dominum - xl franch.auri." ("*Item,* at the same place as above [Paris], on the said day [that is, on the 26th day of January, in the year 1377], to Master Thomas of Bologna, astronomer to the king of France, gift made to him by my lord of forty gold francs.") That is all. That Thomas de Pizan received a gratuity from Amadeus VI is certain; whether he received it because he had cast the horoscope in order to select the most propitious hour for Amadeus VII's marriage is a highly probable conjecture, but only a conjecture. History is also made, sometimes, by gently nudging evidence into place.

We have no idea whether Professor Willard has attempted this verification herself, but she certainly did well to refrain from mentioning a detail which, in our opinion, has been somewhat skewed.

It is clearly rather difficult for us to appreciate the commercial value of an astrologer's services in the fourteenth century. If we are prepared to accept the idea that Thomas de Pizan, esteemed member of the court of Charles V, was able to command an exorbitant fee for his collaboration and that Amadeus VI, in good humor because of the circumstances, did not look at the expenditure, the bill seems to us a bit padded, even if it is not a question here of an honorarium, but of a present.

However, since a present, bestowed by a lord, was not purely a gift— and, in this case, it was to correspond to a service rendered by the recipient—we, as literary scholars and not accountants, have allowed ourselves to make a few amateur calculations on this matter. They have yielded the following results. The franc in the time of Charles V weighed 3.87 grams of fine gold. Gold being worth, these days, $410 an ounce (as long as these values do not change too quickly before this volume appears), this value will give us $410 divided by 30 equals $13.60 as the price of gold per gram; $13.60 multiplied by 3.87 equals $52.63 per gold franc at that time, so that, for 40 gold francs, $2,105.28 was the value of the gift received by Thomas de Pizan. A hefty reward for a horoscope.

Because we distrust the validity of our calculations, we shall provide readers with other information that may give a less problematical idea of the value of the forty gold francs received by Thomas de Pizan and the importance of the obligation he fulfilled for the count of Savoy.

On February 1, 1377, Amadeus VI in fact gave forty gold francs to Master Henri de Marle, advocate, "quod dictavit et fecit memorialem colleccionis facte in dieta Domini tenuta coram rege die ultima januarii" ("because he dictated and took the minutes of the assembly called at the meeting of My Lord held in the presence of the king on the last day of January").[13] The drafting of a brief for presentation to the king of France must have been rather important work.

During his stay in Paris, Count Amadeus had given various sums of money to several advocates he had consulted concerning a dispute opposing him to the marquis of Saluzzo. These payments usually ranged from fifteen to thirty gold francs.[14] This count also gave thirty gold francs to the canons of Saint Maurice of Paris: "pro faciendo unum reliquarium [sic] argenti ad tendendum modicum de osso brachii sancti Maricii [sic] per Dominum, die presenti [prima decembris, anno 1376] sibi datum, et qui canonici tenentur imperpetuum facere commemoracionem in eorum ecclesia, singulis septimanis, pro Domino et eius successoribus" ("for the making of a silver reliquary to hold a little piece of the bone of the arm of Saint Maurice by My Lord given to them on this day [first of December, 1376] and the canons are obliged in perpetuity to make a commemoration in their church every week for My Lord and his successors").[15] Finally, we recall that Christine de Pizan had received from John the Fearless, in 1407, 1408, and 1412, fifty, one hundred, and fifty gold francs, respectively, "in compensation for several [notable] books in parchment"[16] presented by her to the duke. Unfortunately, these payments specify nothing more, but we know that fifty or one hundred gold francs must have corresponded to the price of more than one handsome manuscript in parchment, perhaps illuminated, even if a "book" does not necessarily signify a volume but also a work divided into several parts.

In conclusion, while it is certain that Thomas de Pizan received forty francs from Amadeus VI, we prefer nevertheless to say that we do not know the reason for this gift, leaving to the exactitude or fancy of another historian the problem of uncovering the real reason for it. In our opinion, Thomas de Pizan perhaps did not limit himself to casting a horoscope in these circumstances.

The marriage having been celebrated, the newlyweds were separated. Their parents judged them too young to be allowed to "behave seriously," as Cognasso adds jestingly.[17] Bonne returned to Bourges, back to Mother, and My Lord Amadeus began his journey back toward Savoy, equipped with a splendid falcon, a gift from Bureau de la Rivière, chamberlain of Charles V. He wandered from Nevers to Cluny, without being able to come any closer to his beloved. He must not have seen her again until March 1381. The reunion of the married couple took place at Pont-d'Ain, "and on that night they sang, danced, and feasted until midnight, when the castle caught fire and burned everything," adds Cabaret,[18] who must have obtained this detail from a good source. When the Red Count gets married, he literally sets the world on fire. It is high time to take leave of our newlyweds in order to begin the next part of our account.

II. Manuscripts of Christine's Works Recorded in the Savoy

It is not surprising that the first mention of a manuscript containing the works of Christine de Pizan that belonged to a member of the House of Savoy leads us to a daughter of Amadeus VII. It concerns the second child of the Red Count, Bonne, born in 1388, married in 1405 to Louis of Achaia and deceased at Stupinigi on March 4, 1432.

An inventory compiled April 10 at Stupinigi notes that listed among the princess's books was "a romance by Crestina."[19] We have no difficulty at all in removing the question mark that Sheila Edmunds placed next to the identification of this "Crestina." It indeed involves a work by our woman writer, without our being able to identify it. The Savoy inventories, drafted in haste, are often rather sketchy.

The second reference concerns a French princess: Yolande of France, daughter of Charles VII, born September 23, 1434, and deceased at Moncrivello (Vercelli) August 29, 1478. She had married, in 1452, Amadeus IX the Blessed and had administered the duchy well before the abdication of her husband, who, sickly and very pious, scarcely enjoyed dealing with the affairs of this earth.

The inventory conducted after his death, in April 1479 at Vigone castle (thirty-six kilometers southwest of Turin), informs us that Yolande possessed three works by Christine:

> 48. *Item:* a book in paper of the *Othéa*.
> 67. *Item: Le Livre de Crestine* ("The Book of Christine"), covered in gold brocade, in parchment, with one clasp.
> 73. *Item: La Vision de Cristine*, in parchment, with a silver clasp.[20]

Just before *Le Livre de Crestine* (no. 67), this inventory mentions "*Les sept pheaumes* in French done on parchment" (no. 68). We should not exclude the possibility that this work is *Les sept psaumes allegorisés* by our author.[21]

The richest and most detailed medieval inventory of books once belonging to the House of Savoy was composed at Chambéry from October 25, 1498, onward, in the beginning of the reign of Philibert II the Fair. The library of the "lower alcove" or "wardrobe" (*garde roube basse*) of Chambéry castle comprised five manuscripts containing the works of Christine de Pizan:

> 22. Then another thick book in paper, in large format, treating the *Faictz d'armes de chevalerie* and beginning with a large initial: "Cy commence," written in prose, by hand, covered with wooden boards and white hide.
> 102. Then a medium-sized book handwritten in French in prose, named *La Destruction de Jherusalem*, beginning with a large initial: "Cy dit," etc., treating *Othea [Hotea]*, covered with wooden boards and black hide with a brass clasp.
> 121. Then another medium-sized book in parchment, in prose, handwritten in French, called *La Cité des Dames*, historiated and illuminated in gold and azure, beginning with a large initial: "Selon la maniere," etc., covered with wooden boards and tanned leather with small studs and brass clasps.

141. Another medium-sized book in parchment written by hand in French, historiated and illuminated in gold and azure, named *La Division de Crestine*, beginning: "Pour ouvrir la voye," covered with wooden boards and tanned leather with a gilded silver clasp.

254. Another in parchment named *Perpetua*, written in French, historiated and illuminated in gold, treating the *Fais d'armes et chivallerie*, beginning: "Pour ce que hardiement est," etc., covered with wooden boards and white hide with a brass clasp.[22]

Without being as well represented as in other French libraries of the fifteenth century, Christine occupies an honorable enough place in this collection.

The rich library that the counts and then the dukes of Savoy gathered at Chambéry must have been dispersed thereafter. We know that a certain number of Savoyard manuscripts were taken to the Netherlands by Marguerite of Austria, second wife of Philibert the Fair.[23] According to an inventory drafted at Mechlin, in July 1516, this princess possessed two works of Christine de Pizan: "Another small book in parchment, in small handwriting, covered and fitted with iron in the same way, entitled *Livre des Trois Vertus à l'enseignement des dames et demoiselles* . . . [and] *Le Livre des fais d'armes et de chevalerye*."[24]

The manuscript, described in the first article cited, came from the collection of Charles de Croy, prince of Chimay, from whom Marguerite of Austria purchased it in 1511.[25] It is impossible to know whether the second article refers to one of the two copies of this work of Christine de Pizan that were at the ducal library of Savoy.

The majority of the manuscripts in the Savoy collection perished during the political and military vicissitudes of the sixteenth century and especially, we believe, as a result of the long occupation by French militia of the duchy's territories beyond the Alps.[26] However, an inventory made at Nice in 1538 permits us to know that Beatrice of Portugal, wife of the unfortunate Charles II (III) and mother of Emmanuel-Philibert, possessed "a book in Spanish called *espello de Christina* ["mirror of Christine"]."[27] This reference denotes the edition of 1518 (Hernão de Campos) of the Portuguese translation of the *Livre des Trois Vertus*.[28]

Scarcely had he returned to his estates when Duke Emmanuel-Philibert also reorganized his library, at Rivoli castle. An inventory from 1561[29] informs us that Christine's works are not included among the few hundred volumes assembled by the sovereign in this temporary abode, at the moment when Turin was still being occupied and Chambéry was still the official capital of the duchy.

Nor are Christine's works explicitly numbered in the ducal library inventory made by Giulio Torrini in 1659.[30] This hastily done catalogue accounts for about nine thousand volumes. It is, however, possible that the incunabula and a manuscript containing Christine's *Livre des fais d'armes et de chevalerie* are lurking beneath the nine articles describing the French translation of the *Epitoma institutorum rei militaris* ("Handbook of Training in Military Affairs") by Vegetius.[31]

The ducal library, appreciably enriched over the second half of the sixteenth century and of the first half of the following century, was seriously damaged by fire in 1667.[32] The books that were saved were crowded into the rooms of the ducal palace. During their trips to Italy, Mabillon (1685) and Montfaucon (1709) found books and manuscripts still gathered "in a heap" and "jammed together without order." [33]

It was not until 1709 that Victor Amadeus II, who was soon to become king of Sicily, appointed Philibert-Marie Machet to reorganize the library. In 1713 Machet composed an inventory, which has come down to us.[34] Although the name Christine de Pizan is not noted in the document, we know that some incunabula and most probably a manuscript of the *Livres des fais d'armes et de chevalerie* were located in Turin at this time, thanks to the call number assigned by this librarian to each volume.

This inventory lists five editions and three manuscripts of Vegetius in French, plus a manuscript containing the French translation of Frontinus.[35] We have thus been able to identify two copies of the Verard edition of 1488 of the *Livre des fais d'armes et de chevalerie*.[36] They are now kept in the holdings of the Museo storico of the Turin archives (Sezione prima; call number J. b. IV. 17) and at the National and University Library of the same city (call number XV. VII. 155). These copies still bear the numbers 41 and 42, respectively, from the Machet inventory, who describes them thus: "Vegetius on Military Arts."

This same inventory lists, immediately afterwards, three manuscripts, of which one might refer to a copy of the *Livre des fais d'armes et de chevalerie*: *Vegece de l'art militaire*, MS 332; and *Vegece art de chevalerie*, MS 333, 334.[37] Upon verification, the MS J. b. II. 19 of the Museo storico of the Archives of the State of Turin, containing the French translation of the *Handbook of Military Affairs* of Vegetius by Jean de Meun, indeed bears the number 334 from the Machet catalogue. Yet the "Old Library" (*Biblioteca antica*) section of the same archives retains, under the call number J. b. II. 15 and J. b. VI. 11, two other works in French attributed to Vegetius. The first in fact contains the *Livre des fais d'armes et de chevalerie* of Christine de Pizan and the second the *Handbook of Military Affairs* of Vegetius, translated by Jean de Meun.

These two manuscripts no longer bear the call numbers of Machet (332 and 333), which had most likely been written on some insets glued onto the endpapers. Unfortunately these labels have not survived,[38] but the identification of these two manuscripts, with the articles from Machet's inventory, seems most likely to us.

Despite what Leena Löfstedt wrote in 1977,[39] the Turin archives possesses, most likely since the second half of the seventeenth century, two manuscript copies of the French translation of Vegetius by Jean de Meun. The first is manuscript J. b. II. 19, in parchment, from the fourteenth century, and the second is the manuscript J. b. VI. 11, in paper, from the fifteenth century. It is not possible for us to describe this latter copy here in detail—it contains a somewhat reworked version of the Jean de Meun translation (additions and omissions)—but comparison of its contents with the text provided by Löfstedt's edition, assures us of the work's identity. We intend to speak of it elsewhere.

As we see, of the nine volumes (printed and manuscript) described as containing the works of Vegetius in French and noted in the Torrini inventory of 1659, eight were still present in the library of the king of Sicily in 1713. Only one had disappeared in the fire of 1667.

Aside from the three manuscripts of Vegetius, the Biblioteca antica of the Turin archives holds a copy of the translation of Frontinus, executed by Jean de Rovroy for Charles VII, around 1440. It bears the call number J. b. VI. 21. We note the existence of this manuscript, which escaped the learned scholarship of Robert Bossuat.[40]

III. Current Manuscript and Incunabula Holdings of Christine's Works in the Savoy

At the end of the last century, Pietro Vayra had devoted several pages to the MS J. b. II. 15 containing the *Livre des fais d'armes et de chevalerie*.[41] We should have liked to provide a detailed description of this handsome manuscript, but there is not enough space. We are thus limiting ourselves to the most essential codicological data:

—Vellum and parchment (306 × 225 mm) of 2 + 97 ff. (The modern foliation, in pencil, counts 96, but there is one folio 81b). Two leaves have been removed from between the currently numbered 4–5 and 36–37.
—The binding is contemporary with the text, with boards covered in badly damaged green damask. The two sides are decorated with five brass nails and four copper corners. These corners are connected on the back side by a fillet of the same metal. The

outer borders of the covers are attached by a copper clasp. One can still see, on the front side, two brass plates which were supposed to affix to the board some bands equipped with an eyelet to be held by a rosette fastener still present on the back cover. On the upper portion of the back cover, a copper label holder affixes to the board a thin sheet of horn that protects the title, written in Gothic letters: "Vegece de l'art de chevalerie." The title has also been written on the back, by a recent hand: "Flave Vegece de l'Art de Chevalerie." Gilt-edged pages.

—The volume contains fourteen quires arranged thus: after the two flyleaves, there is a binion in vellum containing, on ff. 1r–3v, the tables; f. 4 is blank on both sides. There follow a quaternion (ff. 5–11) whose first leaf is mutilated, a ternion (ff. 12–17), and two quaternions (ff. 18–33). The following ternion (ff. 34–37) is composed of one singulion and two leaves with stubs. There is a lacuna in the text only between ff. 36 and 37. This ternion was thus imperfect from the moment the book was put together (absence of the counterleaf for f. 34).

—Eight quaternions follow (ff. 38–92). All of the first (ff. 38–45) as well as the central singulion (ff. 49–50) of the second quaternion (ff. 46–53) are of vellum; the remaining six are of parchment. The volume ends with a binion of parchment (ff. 93–96) which contains, glued at the beginning, the stub of parchment from an old flyleaf which has disappeared. The leaves 95^v and 96^{rv} are blank.

—Justification: 190–200 × 140–150 mm, written in two columns of 190–200 × 61–65 mm and thirty lines, spaced 5–6 mm. Lines ruled in violet ink. Ample lower margin.

The quires carry neither signatures nor catchwords. This MS has two large initials (approximately 25 × 30 mm), decorated in azure with flowerlets on a gold background, at the beginning of the third and fourth parts (ff. 64r and 83r) of the work; many gold capitals on filigreed blue or garnet-red backgrounds; blue paragraph marks on filigreed background or gold ones on black filigreed background. Numerous headings in red.

—The volume must have contained, originally, four illuminations.

—Two of them remain on ff. 64^r and 83^r. The first, occupying a full page (280 × 198 mm), is bordered by a floral decoration in Flemish style. In the center (160 × 140 mm), two people converse in a meadow beside a stream. In the background can be seen a rustic landscape, a stream furrowed with boats and a windmill. At the bottom, eight lines of handwriting in two columns.

—The second illumination (145 × 145 mm) portrays a duel within a closed field. Crowding around the field are armed soldiers. In the background one sees rocks, meadows, and groves. The combat scene is framed by the same type of decoration (280 × 203 mm) as the preceding illumination and recalls the style of the Bruges workshops. The execution of this manuscript seems to date back to the third quarter of the fifteenth century. On col. b of f. 95ʳ have been traced the two devices of Antoine, Great Bastard of Burgundy. On the bottom of f. 4v can be read, with ultraviolet light, the signature of another former owner of this manuscript. Since it is Liliane Dulac who has made this discovery, we believe it is for her to publish it. The text of the *Livre des fais d'armes et de chevalerie* begins on f. 5ra with these words: "[pro]fit d'en escripre et en faire aucun livre. Mais afin que ceste presente oeuvre par aucuns envieux, en quelque temps, ne puist estre reprouché que, en la mettant sus l'occupacion de y avoir vaqué ait esté perte de temps, comme de traittier chose non licite."

—This passage is found almost at the beginning of chapter 2 of the first book.

—The *explicit* is found on f.95r: ". . . et d'icestes couleurs differenciees toutes armes et banieres par diverses devises furent prinses par haultesce, des le temps tres ancien. Explicit Vegece."

The Royal Library of Turin[42] possesses two copies of the Vérard edition (1488) of the *Livre des fais d'armes et de chevalerie*. They bear the call numbers III. 23. and V. 7.[43] The purchase of the first incunabulum appears to date back to the reign of Charles-Albert (1831–49). It in fact bears, on the second flyleaf, the notation of the two English sales dated 1819 and 1823.[44] The second copy was part of the library of Cesare Saluzzo, count of Monesiglio (1778–1853) and belonged next to that of his ward and third child of Charles-Albert, Ferdinand of Savoy, duke of Genoa (1822–55) and then to the son of the latter, Thomas-Albert (1854–1931).

The books of Cesare Saluzzo, which merged with the library of the duke of Genoa, were purchased by the Italian government in 1952.[45] Among the eight hundred manuscripts composing these holdings, two contain the *Livre des fais d'armes et de chevalerie*. These are MSS 17 and 328 of the Saluzzo Collection (*Raccolta Saluzzo*).

MS 328 is a copy executed, during the nineteenth century, from the MSS fr. 607 (anc. 7087) and 1241 (anc. 7434²⁻², Colbert 1876) in the Bibliothèque nationale in Paris. They contain only the first three parts of this work by Christine de Pizan.

MS 17, fifteenth century, merits a more detailed description:

—Paper (280 × 200 mm), 2 + 1 + 12 + II–CCxlii + 2 leaves.
Folio 1 has been removed. Numeral CCxxiiii has been omitted
from the original foliation in red ink. After the two initial flyleaves there is a ruled page containing, on the *recto,* numerous
inscriptions. There follow twenty-two quires arranged in this
way. The first twelve are senions (ff. [12] + II–Cxxxi). The first,
not numbered, bears the tables of contents. The second (ff. II–
XII) has lost the first leaf. The thirteenth fascicle (ff. Cxxxii–Cxli)
is a quinion, while fascicles from fourteen to twenty are senions
(ff. Cxlii–Cxxvi). The twenty-first (ff. CCxxvii–CCxxxvi) is a
quinion, while the last is composed of 4 + 2 leaves. Folio CCxlii is
written only on the recto. The volume ends with two flyleaves.
—After the fascicle containing the table of contents, whose
leaves carry no foliation, all the others carry an older foliation in
red ink from II to CCxlii. All the quires, except the first and the
thirteenth, bear catchwords often trimmed off by the binding.
—This volume was badly damaged by humidity and was restored, in 1981–82, with Japanese vellum. The paper of the
manuscript bears, in watermark, the simple gothic letter P,
whose downstroke is crossed by the bifurcated form of a lobster
claw, very closely resembling no. 8571 in Briquet's *Dictionnaire*
(Antwerp, 1468; Paris, 1472; Douai, 1473; Nantes, 1473; Basel,
1473–78; Solothurn, 1477; Leyden, 1478).
—Binding in natural calf, with arms and monograms of
Claude V, Molé on the boards and back, which also bears the
title, *Faits d'armes et de cheval.*[46]
—Page edges flecked in blue and red.
—Execution of this manuscript dates to the second half of the
fifteenth century.
—The text, on a full page (justification: 165–170 × 118–
122 mm), laid out over twenty-two lines (spaced 7–8 mm). It
is decorated with large (30 × 30 mm), medium and small letters decorated blue and red on filigreed maroon background.
Numerous headings in red; red and blue line endings.
—The *Livre des fais d'armes et de chevalerie* begins on f. 11 recto: "et
propos deliberé de allegier la paine des bons corages vertueulx,
quy a la perfection du loable stille d'armes desirent pourfiter et en
icelluy leur jeunesse emploier [heading in red]. Cy aprés s'ensuit
le livre des fais d'armes et de chevalerie lequel est devisé en quatre
parties. La premiere desquelles parle de la maniere que princes s'y
doibvent tenir au fait de leurs guerres et batailles . . ."
—It ends on the recto of f. CCxxxix: ". . . Item, l'autre couleur

d'armoyerie est vert que on dit sinople quy signifie bois, champs et prez et pour ce que n'est mie bien comptee est [*sic*] quatre ele-mens, seroit reputee la mains noble et d'icelles .VI. couleurs sont differencyees touttes armes et banieres par diverses divises prises par haultesse des le tamps tres anchien. Explicit." Folios CCxxxix verso–CCxlii recto contain thirteen paragraphs relating episodes concerning siege tactics. Here is the first: "D'ung Rommain quy trahy une flesche ou il avoit attachié une lectre en une ville assegee, pour ce qu'il ne povoit entrer en la ville pour l'ost quy le siege tenoit entour" ("Of a Roman who shot an arrow, to which he had attached a letter, into a besieged city, since he could not enter the city because of the enemy laying siege all around it").

—The volume is decorated with three illustrations, traced in black ink and colored on ff. lxxvi verso (95 × 115 mm), Cxlii recto (92 × 126 mm), at the beginning of the different parts of the work. The first depicts two squads of soldiers advancing against each other. The second, an interior. Two clerks: one seated, the other standing, are surrounded by their books placed upon a desk and a shelf. In between can be seen a rustic landscape through the open door and window. The last scene shows two armed soldiers who carry a letter to a clerk seated in his study. We see, in the background, a rustic landscape and a town. There must have been a fourth illustration on f. 1r, now lost.

—The former owners of the manuscript left many inscriptions. One reads, on the front cover board, "Tremet 1758"; "B.N. 7435–7087"; "Bel. Lett. No. 62" (in ink); and "Bibl. Baluze No. 505" (in pencil). One label reads: "Libri di Cesare Saluzzo." In the center and below, there is a long inscription from the nine-teenth century which we have provided in a note.[47] On the recto of the first unnumbered, ruled leaf is read: "I took this book from the castle of Lannoy in Flanders as My Lord the duke of Anguyen [*mod.* Enghien] captured it in 1646" (this castle was taken by the Grand Condé's army in early June 1646).[48] Thereafter, Cesare Saluzzo annotated in his hand: "This book came to me from Paris, in 1824, purchased on my account by Hugh (Igomette [*sic*]) the Bookseller. For this I paid . . . Cesar of Saluzzo. It is thought that the author of this work was Louis XI, marquis of Saluzzo." Another hand has added: "The approximate date of this book is indicated, fol. X. verso by these words: 'Of this path the good and wise King Charles, fifth of this name, father of him who rules at present, gives good example, etc.' " On the recto of the first leaf of the unnumbered senion, which contains headings in red, we read: "Tremet, canon of the treasury of the church of Troyes, 1758." The same hand has written, on f. CCxlii recto: "Tremet, 1758."

We note, incidentally, that the Saluzzo Collection preserves, under the number 188, a precious manuscript containing an anonymous version of Vegetius executed in 1380.[49]

As we can confirm, if a certain number of works by Christine de Pizan entered the Savoyard collection at the end of the Middle Ages, it seems to be due essentially to the interest taken by certain princesses in her literary production. In the course of the modern era, the rulers of this reigning house have paid attention to her works only through a preference for Vegetius. Indeed, the only work that seemed to interest them is the *Livre des fais d'armes et de chevalerie*, transmitted to us as anonymous by the Verard edition and a certain number of manuscripts, among which are those currently kept at Turin.

If Christine de Pizan had not really concerned herself with the lords of Savoy, they forgot her in their book purchasing as well. Chance has willed it that there are now two copies of the *Livre des fais d'armes et de chevalerie* at Turin. These two manuscripts have nothing to do with the two copies of Christine's work that were preserved in the library of the "lower alcove" (*garde roube basse*) in the castle of Chambéry in 1498.

Notes

1. Christine de Pizan, *Lavision-Christine*, ed. Mary Louise Towner (Washington, D.C.: Catholic University of America, 1932), 76, line 11.

2. J. Cordey, *Les Comtes de Savoie et les rois de France pendant la guerre de Cent Ans (1329–1391)*, Bibliothèque de l'Ecole des Hautes Études, fasc. 189 (Paris: Champion, 1907); and F. Cognasso, "L'influenza francese nello stato sabaudo durante la minorità di Amedeo VIII," *Mélanges d'Archéologie et d'Histoire publiés par l'École française de Rome* 35 (1916): 257–326.

3. Charity Cannon Willard, *Christine de Pizan: Her Life and Works* (New York: Persea Books, 1984).

4. Christine de Pizan, *Le Livre des fais et bonnes meurs du sage roy Charles V*, 2 vols., ed. Suzanne Solente (Paris: Champion, 1936–40), 1:viii.

5. Suzanne Solente, "Christine de Pisan," in *Histoire littéraire de la France* (Paris: Klincksieck, 1969), 40:4.

6. Cordey, *Comtes de Savoie*, 214.

7. Quoted from the edition of 1869, 2 vols. (Florence: Cellini, 1869). The first edition is dated 1854–55.

8. Quoted from the fifth edition, 2 vols. (Turin: Eredi Bocca, 1861). The first edition dates from 1839 with the same publisher.

9. Cibrario, *Origine e progressi*, 2:142.

10. The nature of the documents pertaining to the county of Nice and the county-duchy of Savoy have been fully described by Vittoria Bernachini, who describes the holdings remaining in Turin and those brought back to France after the last war in R. M. Borsarelli and M. V. Bernachini, *Archivio di Stato di Torino: Serie di Nizza e della Savoia: Inventario*, Pubblicazioni degli Archivi di stato 17, no. 40 (Rome: Ministero dell'interno, 1954–62). The first volume contains the inventory of documents assembled in the "Sezione corte" and the second those of the "Sezione camerale." It is the second that concerns us.

11. Archivio di Stato di Torino (abbreviated AST), Sezioni riunite, Inventory 201: *Index général des titres du duché de Savoie*.

12. AST, Sezione riunite, Inventory 16: *Comptes et pièces des trésoriers généraux de la Savoie (1297–1790)*; Inventory 38: *Comptes des dépenses extraordinaires pour le service des princes et pour l'entretien des gardes du corps (1269–1619)*; Inventory 39: *Comptes et dépenses de la maison des souverains de Savoye, des assignations et pensions aux princes et princesses de Savoye (1298–1640)*.

13. AST, Sezione riunite, Inventory 38, fol. 21, packet 11, roll 68, membrana VI^{xx}X, lines 71–74 and VI^{xx}XI, lines 1–2.

14. Ibid., roll 68, membrana VI^{xx}VI, lines 73–82: "*Item*, at the same place [Paris] on September 25, same year as above [1367], on the instructions of My Lord, were given to Pierre de Ficigny, Doctor of Laws, retained for the counsel of my Lord, in his lawsuit against the dauphin of Vienne over the earldom of Saluzzo on the reference of Masters Girard d'Estrés and Pierre des Murs, twenty gold francs. *Item*, at the same place on the said day, on the instruction and reference mentioned above, were given Master Oddard de Mauly, lawyer, retained for the counsel of My Lord for the said lawsuit, fifteen gold francs of good weight"; membrana VI^{xx}VII, lines 1–5: "*Item*, at the same place, on the last but one day of September, on the aforementioned instruction and reference, were given to Master Jean de Mares, Doctor of Laws, advocate of the king of France, retained to advise my Lord against the traitor the marquis of Saluzzo, thirty gold francs"; ibid., lines 37–42, thirty gold francs given to Oddard de Mauly, November 24, 1376, for the same reason. On January 8, 1377, Amadeus again paid one hundred gold francs to Pierre de Ficigny and eighty gold francs to Oddard de Mauly, advocates, for the same reason (ibid., membrana VI^{xx}VIII, lines 34–44), etc.

15. Ibid., membrana VI^{xx}VII, lines 52–61.

16. Georges Doutrepont, *La Littérature française à la cour des ducs de Bourgogne: Philippe le Hardi, Jean sans Peur, Philippe le Bon, Charles le Téméraire* (Paris: Champion, 1909), 277.

17. Cognasso, "L'influenza francese," 11.

18. AST, Sezione riunite, Museo storico, ms. without call number, ff. 253v–254r.

19. Sheila Edmunds, "The Medieval Library of Savoy, II: Documents," *Scriptorium* 25 (1971): 268, par. 96, m.

20. Ibid., 279. F. E. Bollati di Saint-Pierre, "Documenti inediti sulla casa Savoia," in *Miscellanea di storia italiana* (Turin: Bocca, 1884), 22:354, 356, 357.

21. Christine de Pizan, *Les Sept Psaumes allegorisés*, ed. Ruth Ringland Rains (Washington, D.C.: Catholic University of America, 1965).

22. *Le lettere e le arti alla corte di Savoia nel secolo XV: Inventari dei castelli di Ciamberi, di Torino e di Ponte d'Ain 1497–1498*, ed. P. Vayra (Turin: G. Paravia, 1883), 28, 43, 47, 51, 69. Also reprinted in the *Miscellanea di storia italiana*, 22:11–248. The MS described in this work under no. 254 does not seem identical to MS J. b. II. 15 of the Turin archives, to be described later in this study. Cf. Sheila Edmunds, "The Medieval Library of Savoy, III: Documents," *Scriptorium* 26 (1972): 284.

23. A. Bayot, "Les manuscrits de provenance savoisienne dans la Bibliothèque de Bourgogne," *Mémoires et documents publiés par la Société savoisienne d'histoire et d'archéologie* 47 (1909): 305–410. C. Gaspar and F. Lyna, *La Bibliothèque de Marguerite d'Autriche* Catalog of exhibit, Brussels, May–July 1940 (Brussels: Bibliothèque royale, 1940), 21–25.

24. *Correspondance de l'empereur Maximilien 1er et de Marguerite d'Autriche, sa fille, gouvernante des Pays-Bas, de 1507 à 1519*, ed. E. Le Glay, 2 vols. (Paris: Renouard, 1839), 2:474, 476.

25. Gaspar and Lyna, *La Bibliothèque de Marguerite d'Autriche*, 33, n. 42. Marguerite of Austria also possessed another copy, in paper, of this work (46, n. 92).

26. For a history of the various library collections of the House of Savoy, including their current locations, see Stelio Bassi, "Introduzione ai manoscritti della Biblioteca nazionale universitaria di Torino," in C. Segre Montel, *I manoscritti miniati della Biblioteca nazionale di Torino*, vol. 1, *I manoscritti latini dal VII alla metà del XIII secolo*, ed. A. Bertini and S. Bassi (Turin: G. Molfese, 1980), xvii–xxxiii.

27. A. Manno, "Il tesoretto di un bibliofilo piemontese," *Curiosità e ricerche di storia subalpina* 2 (1876): 500.

28. Angus J. Kennedy, *Christine de Pizan: A Bibliographical Guide*, Research Bibliographies and Checklists, no. 42 (London: Grant and Cutler, 1984), 108, nos. 450–51.

29. A. Manno, "Alcuni cataloghi di antiche librerie piemontesi," *Miscellanea di storia italiana* 19 (1880): 382–91.

30. AST, Sezione prima *Corte. Casa Reale. Gioie e Mobili*, packet (*mazzo*) 5 d'addizione, n. 30: *Recognitione, osia inventaro*, MS in paper, 93 pp.

31. Ibid., p. 54, col. a, lines 3–2 from bottom: "Vegece de l'art militaire, copie 2—Le mesme art de chevallerie"; col. b, line 20: "Vegece de Chevalerie"; line 40: "Vegece de chevalerie"; line 43: "L'art de chevallerie de Vegece"; p. 55, col. a, line 2: "Vegece de l'art militaire"; line 12: "Vegece de l'art militaire"; line 17: "Vegece de l'art militaire."

32. Concerning the fire and its consequences, see Bassi, *Introduzione ai manoscritti*, xxiv, and also A. Giaccaria, "I fondi medievali della Biblioteca nazionale universitaria di Torino," *Pluteus* 2 (1984): 175–94.

33. Bassi, *Introduzione ai manoscritti*, xxiv.

34. This inventory is preserved in the Biblioteca nazionale of Turin under the call number R. I. 5. *Index alphabétique des livres qui se trouvent en la Bibliothèque royale de Turin en celle année 1713*, MS of 777 + 2 pp.

35. Ibid., 272, lines 4–6: "Vegece de l'Art militaire, nos. 41, 42, 48, 50, 51.— Vegece Art de Chevalerie MS. 333, 334"; 262, line 1 from bottom: "Frontin Art Militaire MS. no. 335."

36. *Gesamtkatalog der Wiegendrucke*, 2d ed., 9 vols. (Stuttgart: A. Hiersmann; New York: H. P. Kraus, 1968), vol. 6, cols. 465–66, n. 6647.

37. Cf. n. 47 above.

38. Giaccaria, *Fondi medievali*, 181, 186.

39. Jean de Meun, *Li Abregemens noble honme Vegesce Flave René des Establissemenz apartenanz a chevalerie*, ed. Leena Löfstedt, Annales Academiae Scientiarum Fennicae, Ser. B, no. 200 (Helsinki: Suomalainen Tiedeakatemia, 1977), 14, n. 20: "Les Archives [de Turin] ne possèdent qu'un ms. de la traduction de Jean de Meun."

40. Robert Bossuat, "Jean de Rovroy traducteur des *Stratagèmes* de Frontin," *Bibliothèque d'Humanisme et de la Renaissance* 22 (1960): 273–86, 469–89.

41. Pietro Vayra, "Il Museo storico della Casa di Savoia," *Curiosità e ricerche di storia subalpina* 4 (1880): 53–56.

42. On the history of these holdings, cf. Giuseppe Dondi's note in the *Annuario delle biblioteche italiane* (Rome: Palombi, 1969–81), 5:38–43.

43. These two copies are described by Giselda Russo, "Gli incunaboli della Biblioteca reale e della Biblioteca civica di Torino" (Ph.D. dissertation, University of Turin, 1972–73), 30–31. The catalogue numbers of the two copies are 54 and 55.

44. On the second flyleaf of MS III. 23 is written: "Bought by Triphort for Mr. W. T. at the White Knights sale 1819, for £18.0.0"; "April 1823 Watson Taylor sale . . . £13.10.6."

45. This passage is attested by the ex-libris: "Libri di Cesare Saluzzo," "Biblioteca di S. A. R. il Duca di Genova," "Biblioteca di S. A. R. il Principe Tommaso di Savoia Duca di Genova. Museo." The second flyleaf bears the handwritten notes by Cesare Saluzzo and A. Ripa di Meana. The latter would specify, in his handwritten note dated 1864, that the author of the work contained in this incunabulum was Christine de Pizan. Four loose leaves preserve the "Cose e luoghi notati dal Cav. Omedei nel libro 'L'art de la Chevalerie selon V[é]gèce.' "

46. J. Guigard, *Nouvel armorial du bibliophile: Guide de l'amateur des livres armoriés*, 2 vols. (Paris: E. Rondeau, 1890), 2:360.

47. "I know of one edition of it in quarto {marginal note: "In folio according to Brunet, entry: 'Vegetius' "] printed in gothic letters by Antoine Vérard in 1488, it is in two columns with signatures, but without numbers or catchwords. There are, after the seventeenth and last chapter of the fourth part, two leaves containing some verses divided by stanzas on the twelve virtues that a nobleman must possess: nobility, faith, loyalty, honor, rectitude, prowess, love, courtesy, diligence, forthrightness, generosity, sobriety; yet one does not find the fragments which form pages 239 verso and the following in this manuscript: the twelve leaves of headings in red at the top (marginal note: "with table of chapters, according to Brunet"); or the introduction; or the dedication, whose beginning is missing from the manuscript, the work beginning in this edition in quarto with the body of the work: "*Ci apres s'ensuit*, etc."

48. *Mémoires de Nicolas Goulas, gentilhomme ordinaire de la chambre de duc d'Orléans,*

ed. Charles Constant, 3 vols. (Paris: Renouard, 1879–82), 2:154. *Mémoires de François de Paule de Clermont, marquis de Montglat*, in *Nouvelle collection des mémoires relatifs à l'histoire de France, depuis le XIIe siècle jusqu'à la fin du XVIIe siècle*, ed. Joseph François Michaud and Jean-Joseph-François Poujoulat (Paris: Féchoz and Letouzey, 1881), 29:167.

49. Cf. J. Camus, "Notice d'une traduction française de *Vegece* faite en 1380," *Romania* 25 (1896): 393–400; Paul Meyer, "Les anciens traducteurs français de Végèce et en particulier Jean de Vignay," *Romania* 25 (1896): 401–23, esp. 402–5.

PART THREE

Christine

BETWEEN THE CHURCH FATHERS AND HUMANISTS

The Preface to the *Avision-Christine* in ex-Phillipps 128

CHRISTINE RENO

A manuscript of Christine de Pizan's *Avision-Christine* that was sold from Sir Thomas Phillipp's collection to another owner brought to light not only a slightly later revised version, but also the unique copy of a preface explaining the allegories of the *Avision*'s early chapters.[1] While the reappearance of any text by an important author is a singular event, the resurfacing of the *Avision* preface is all the more noteworthy for two reasons. First, a medieval key to interpreting a literary work is even rarer than the recovery of a forgotten text. Second, the Phillipps preface permits a fuller understanding of the shaping sources of allegory, a form, with its "subtle covers and beautiful material hidden under pleasant and moral fictions," which Christine equated with the notion of literature itself.[2]

We shall perhaps never know for whom the preface was intended— the manuscript is a presentation copy of unknown provenance—and as the opening suggests, the impetus for writing it may have come from the author herself. Christine addresses the reader who might want to appreciate the work's mulitiple meanings. For this reader, Christine will "open the way" to the work.

The Phillipps preface recalls briefer explanatory comments in certain manuscripts of the *Epistre d'Othéa a Hector*, B. N. fr. 606 and Harley 4431. Both contain comments on fourteen of the early miniatures that accompany each chapter. The comments, written as purplish rubrics, serve to identify the subject matter of the miniatures or to explain their main features. As scholars have noted, the rubrics guide the reader: "in order that those who are not poets themselves might have a brief understanding of the meaning of the stories in this book."[3]

The Phillipps preface, here published for the first time, is written on a quire of six folia. It is transcribed in full; rejected readings are in the footnotes, and two additions to the text, which insert words left out, are marked off by slant lines.[4] The transcription is followed by a discussion of the figurative levels and the idea of allegory the preface presents, as well as probable influences on each.

The Preface to the *Avision-Christine*

{1a} Glose sur la premiere partie de ce present volume

Pour ouvrir la voie a declairier les choses soubz figures dictes en la premiere partie de ce livre, laquelle appert aucunement obscure, se aucun le temps a venir au gloser plus estanduement vouloit entendre, est asavoir selon la maniere de parler des pouetes, que souventesfois soubz figure de methaphore, c'est a dire de parole couverte, sont muciees maintes secretes sciences et pures veritéz. Et en telle parolle dicte par poisie puet avoir mains entendemens, et lors est la poisie belle et subtille quant elle puet servir a plusieurs ententes et que on la puet prendre a divers propos.

Et pour toucher en brief de toutes, sans declairier chascune chose particulierement, comment se[5] peuent prendre les figures baillees en ceste dicte partie, par quoi on pourra par les | {1b} plus obscures choses declairier entendre les plus legiers et la sentence du dictié, est asavoir que songe puet estre pris pour pensee, pelerinage pour vie humaine. Le grant ymage dont a son commencement ce dit livre parle pour tout le monde puet estre pris, c'est asavoir ciel, terre et abeisme. Son nom qu'escript en son front portoit, c'est assavoir «Chaoz», puet estre entendu que a son commencement les pouetes anciens nommerent la masse que Dieu fourma, dont il trey ciel et terre et toutes choses, «chaoz», qui est a dire confusion, qui encore assez est au monde. Les ·ij· conduis qu'il avoit, par ou peuz estoit et purgiéz, se puet entendre la naissance de toutes corporelles choses et aussi la mort de toute creature vive. La chere adoullee qu'il faisoit est assez par soi meismes exposé.

| {1c} Item, ce dit ymage puet estre pris pour une chascune creature humaine a par soi, selon le parler des philosophes qui nommerent homme ymage de petit monde. Il est grant en creacion, car de Dieu fourmé. Il a la teste ou ciel, c'est son esperit qui en vint et la doit tendre. Les estoilles dont son chief est aourné, ce sont les vertus de l'ame, si comme entendement, congnoissance, memoire et les autres. Son ventre, ce sont les operacions foraines pour son vivre. Ses piéz qui marchoient les abeismes, c'est enfer ou il cherra s'il ne s'en garde. Il a ·ij· conduis, ce sont ·ij· natures, terrestre et celestre, c'est assavoir le corps et l'ame. Par fois il fait chere doulereuse, ce sont les tribulacions que souvent sent. Et ainsi plus au long se puet exposer.

Item, par le corps de cest ymage se puet pren | {1d} dre le royaume de France, lequel est grant et n'est que ung corps. Sa teste qui est ou ciel, c'est foi catholique, laquelle d'ancienneté a esté plus augmentee, acreue et honnouree en ce royaume que nulle autre part. Les estoilles d'environ son chief peut segnifier les nobles princes et baronnie. Il a ·ij· conduis, c'est le temporel et l'esperituel. Il marche les abismes, c'est l'abisme des escriptures et de sciens, qui y sont es estudes, sur quoy son bel gouvernement fu fondé.

[1a] Gloss on the First Part of This Volume

To open the way toward declaring those things said by means of figures in the first part of this work, which appears somewhat obscure, in the event someone might in the future want to understand the glosses of the work more fully, that is to say according to the style of the poets, by which often, under the figure of metaphor or veiled speech, are hidden much secret knowledge and many pure truths. What is put in poetic language can have several meanings, and poetry becomes beautiful and subtle when it can be understood in different ways.

And to touch briefly upon all the figures of the first part of this work, without entering into every particularity, so that the | [1b] most obscure things may be understood most easily, as well as the sense of this work, the dream can be taken as thought, and the pilgrimage for human life. The great image depicted at the beginning of this book can be understood as the entire world, that is to say, the sky, the earth, and the abyss. The name that was inscribed on its forehead, that is, "Chaos," can be interpreted that at its beginning the ancient poets named the mass that God created and from which he formed heaven and earth and all things "chaos," which is to say confusion, which still reigns in the world. The two conduits by which his food was taken in and eliminated can be understood as the birth of all corporeal beings, and also the death of each living creature. The meaning of his sorrowful countenance is self-evident.

[1c] Likewise, this image can be interpreted as the individual human being, according to the language of the philosophers who called man the image of the microcosm. He is great with regard to creation, for he was formed by God. His head reaches the sky, for his spirit comes from there and must strive to return there. The stars that adorn his head are the virtues of the soul, such as understanding, knowledge, memory, and the others. His belly represents the exterior operations which are necessary for his survival. His feet, which tread the abyss, signify hell, where he will fall if he is not careful. The two conduits signify his two natures, earthly and heavenly, that is to say, body and soul. The woeful countenance that he sometimes makes is the tribulations that he experiences frequently. And the explanation could continue in this fashion.

In like manner, the body of this figure can be understood [1d] as representing the kingdom of France, which is great and forms a whole. His head, which reaches the sky, can be understood as the Catholic faith, which from the early days has grown and been honored more in this land than in any other. The stars about his head can signify the princes and the nobles. The two conduits are the temporal and spiritual. That he treads the abyss signifies the abyss of scriptures and the sciences that are studied in the schools, and on which his beautiful government was formed.

Le livre ou ·ij·ᵉ chappitre dit que une grant ombre couronnee estoit esta-
blie pour admenistrer au grant ymage sa nourriture et tout l'environnoit,
laquelle dicte ombre se puet prendre pour Nature, que nous pouons appeller ombre. Car combien que nous l'apelions «Nature» et que nous lui
ayons donné \ce nom/, toutefois | [2a] ne la voions nous mie en corps ma-
teriel. Elle puet estre dicte couronnee par digneté de son auctorité. Elle
paist le monde que elle comprent, tout ce pouons nous veoir par les genera-
cions qui naturellement se font, dont le monde c'est asavoir espece humaine
et les autres especes vives sont maintenues. Les ·iiij· choses diverses dont
elle fait sa destrampe se peuent apliquier aux ·iiij· elemens dont toutes
choses sont composees. Les outilz ou elle met ladicte destrampe sont les
corps d'estranges fourmes ou elle oeuvre en generacion, comme de gens,
de bestes, et aussi mesmement les arbres et plantes. La naissance de toutes
choses vives est a bon entendement assez declairié par le texte.

Item, ceste ombre se puet atribuer a vie humaine, laquelle passe comme
ombre. Et toutefois elle paist ung chascun homme | [2b] tant qu'il est vif
au monde. Mais de quoi le paist elle? D'amertume, comme fiel; de folle
plaisance, comme miel; de pesanteur, comme plomb; de legiereté, comme
plume. La gueule ou elle met ceste destrampe, c'est sa pensee ou a divers
outilz, c'est assavoir diverses differences de cogitacions. Elle les laisse cuire
par espace de temps et puis les tire hors, non mie toutes ensemble, ce sont
ses operacions qui saillent de lui diversement et cheent sus la terre par diverses oeuvres qu'il fait.

Item, au propos que pour le royaume de France puis[t] estre pris ladicte
ombre, puet de rechief segnefier foi catholique qui a esté d'ancienneté nourriture de cestui royaume. Et n'est mie doubte que pieça fust decheue France,
se Dieu ne l'eust gardee pour sa catholique foy. Car je ne cuide mie qu'en
Crestienté autre part soit l'Eglise mieulx | [2c] servie, Dieux mercis, que
elle est en ce royaume. Et ce puet savoir qui va par les autres terres. Foi
coagule et met ensemble ·iiij· matieres moult diverses que elle met cuire en
la gueule dudit ymage de France pour sa nourriture, c'est assavoir fiel, miel,
plomb et plume. La gueule de l'image, c'est l'Eglise; fiel, c'est remors de
conscience; miel, c'est esperance de la misericorde divine; plomb, crainte
d'enfer; plume, vie tost passee. Les divers outilz sont gens de diverses pro-
phecions, de quoi foi catholique qui les a mis ou ventre de l'Eglise fait
naistre saintes operacions en maintes guises.

Par ce que Cristine dit ou ·iij·ᵉ chappitre que son esperit estoit par les
mains de l'ombre gecté en la gueule de l'image et puis en espace de temps
trait hors en ung petit corps qui chiet ou ventre dudit ymage, et puis fu
nourri par la chamberiere | [2d] de ladicte ombre tant qu'il pouoit se souste-
nir et aler, se puet clerement entendre la naissance et premiere nourriture et
de elle et semblablement de toute creature humaine.

In the second chapter the book states that a large, crowned shadowy figure was set over the first large figure to nourish it, and this other figure can be understood as Nature, which we can call a shadow. For although we have given it the name "Nature," [2a] nonetheless we do not see it as a material body. Nature can be said to be crowned by the dignity of her authority. That she nourishes the world which she envelops can be understood as the generations which succeed one another naturally, by which the world, which is to say the human as well as the other living species, are sustained. The four different ingredients that she puts into her mixture can be understood as the four elements of which all things are composed. The tools in which she puts the said mixture are bodies of various forms which she generates, such as people, animals, and even trees and plants. The birth of all living creatures is rather evident from a proper understanding of the text.

Moreover, this shade can be interpreted as human life, which passes like a shadow. And yet it nourishes each man [2b] as long as he is alive in the world. But with what does she nourish him? With bitterness, like gall; foolish pleasure, like honey; heaviness, like lead; and lightness, like feathers. The gullet in which she places this mixture is that of thought, which has diverse tools or ways of thinking. She lets them cook a certain length of time and then pulls them out, but not at the same time: that signifies man's diverse operations, which enter the world by the different works he performs.

Likewise, with regard to the kingdom of France, the shadow can also signify the Catholic faith which has nourished this kingdom from the early days. And there is no doubt that France would have fallen had God not protected her because of her faith. I do not believe that in all of Christianity is the Church better [2c] served, thanks be to God, than she is in this kingdom. Whoever ventures into other lands can discover that for himself. Faith forms and puts together four very different sorts of matter that she lets cook in France's belly for her food: gall, honey, lead, and feathers. The figure's belly is the Church; gall is the remorse of conscience; honey, hope in divine mercy; lead, fear of hell; feather, life that is soon over. The different tools are men of different stations, by whom the Catholic faith which put them in the belly of the Church gives birth to good works of many sorts.

By what Christine says in the third chapter with regard to her spirit, which was thrust into the belly of the figure by the shade and a while later taken out in a small body which fell into the belly of the said figure, and then was nourished by the servant [2d] of the said shade until it was able to sustain itself and move about on its own, can be clearly understood her birth and early nourishment, and likewise that of every living creature.

Likewise, this can be understood morally with regard to each man: the

Item, que ce puisse servir au propos d'un chascun homme a entendre moralement: le grant ymage que nous entendons pour homme, par son aspiracion, c'est asavoir par ses desirs, attrait acoustumance, laquelle chet es mains de l'ombre que nous prenons pour vie humaine. Celle vie prent telle acoustumance et la laisse cuire en perseverence, dont naissent petis corps; ce sont diverses oeuvres. Aprés vient la chamberiere de l'ombre qui nourrist ces[6] corps: c'est sansualité qui nourrist et endurcist delectacion en perseverence tant que l'omme est endurci en coustume.

Item, que estre puist dit pour le royaume de France, ce puet ainsi exposer | [3a] l'ombre que nous prenons pour foi: prist France et la mist en la gueule de l'Eglise et tant la laissa quiere que elle fu enfantee ou ventre de la terre, c'est ou cuer de la terre, si comme est assis ce noble royaume ou millieu de vraie foi. Et ce puet segnefier comment la foi fu portee en France et puis nourrie par la chamberiere de foi, c'est Sainte Theologie qui la nourry France tant que elle fu fort pour passer et marcher sur toutes heresies.

Nous avons ja dit comment la fiction de cestui livre se puet alegorisier triblement, c'est assavoir assimiller au monde general, qui est la terre, aussi a homme singulier et puis au royaume de France. Aussi comme se chascun en soi parlast en contant son estre, si pouons prendre ce que Cristine dit ou ·iiij·[e] chappitre, comment | [3b] par le cri de Fama elle estant enfant fu transportee avec ses parens ou païs d'une noble dame couronnee, peut dire la terre, que ou temps de son enfance, c'est asavoir de son innorance—qui segnefie le temps ouquel loi n'estoit au monde encore donnee—elle fu transportee par le cri de Fama, qui est a entendre par le cri des sains prophettes, a la loi de Dieu en laquelle sont toutes biautés comprises; mais de grans ruines y vid, ce puet estre dit pour plusieurs heresies qui ont esté. Aussi ce puet segnefier le peuple d'Israel mené en la terre de promission.

Item, puet segnefier l'omme pecheur quant il se tire de l'ingnorence de pechié a penitence par la vois des Saintes Escriptures ou par saintes predicacions, et puis vient vie de perfection ou il treuve toutes beautéz par devotes meditacions. | [3c] Et les ruines de quoy il parle peut estre pris pour les assaulx de temptacion qui sont en vie juste.

Item, cellui meismes ·iiij·[e] chappitre puet segnefier comment Cristine, ou temps de son enfance, fu avec ses parens transportee en France du païs de Lombardie dont elle estoit nee, si comme elle declaire plus a plain cy aprés en la ·iij·[e] partie, ouquel dit païs elle vid les beautéz que elle devise a la letre, et aussi des ruines qui par les guerres estoient venues.

Par le ·v·[e] chappitre puet estre entendu ce que le monde ou la terre pouoit dire aprés ce que la loi ot duré ung temps en perseverence; lequel monde ou terre se pouoit resjoir en telle maniere comme de dire qu'il fust acointé de sainte sapience divine qui ja l'eust faicte antigraffe de ses aventures, c'est assavoir qui l'eust faicte registre de ses commandemens, si comme | [3d] nous veons les commandemens de Dieu establis sur la terre.

figure that we understand to be man, by his aspiration, which is to say, his desires, attracts habit, which falls into the hands of the shade, which we take to be human life. This life takes said habit and lets it cook in perseverance, thus forming little bodies: these are various works. Afterwards, the handmaid of the shade comes and nourishes these bodies; that is sensuality, which nourishes and strengthens delight in perseverance until man is affirmed in habit.

Likewise, with regard to the kingdom of France, [3a] the shade which we interpret as faith can be explained thus: it took France and put her into the belly of the Church, and left her to cook until she was born in the belly of the earth, that is, the heart of the earth, as this noble kingdom is established upon true faith. And this can signify how the faith was carried into France and then nourished by faith's handmaid, Holy Theology, which nourished France until she was strong enough to trample all heresies.

We have already stated that the fiction of this book can be allegorized in triple fashion, that is to say, applied to the world as a whole, which is the earth, and also to the individual man, and then to the kingdom of France. And imagining how each being could recount his life, we can interpret what Christine says in the fourth chapter, how [3b] by Fama's cry she was transported as a child along with her parents to the land of a noble crowned lady, that is, to the land where in her youth, which is to say her ignorance—which signifies the time before the law had been given to the world—she was transported by the cry of Fama, which is to say by the cry of the holy prophets, to the law of God in which all beautiful things are contained. But she saw great ruins there; this can signify the many heresies which have been in the world, and also the people of Israel, who were led into the land of promise.

Likewise, it can signify sinful man when he is drawn from the ignorance of sin to penitence by the voice of the Holy Scriptures and by holy preaching, and afterwards comes the life of perfection where he finds every beauty through devout meditations. [3c] And the ruins spoken about can be understood as the assaults of temptation that are made upon the just life.

Moreover, this same fourth chapter can signify how Christine was transported with her parents as a child into France from the land of Lombardy, where she was born, as she explains more fully hereafter in the third part, the beauties of which land she saw and speaks about in literal fashion, as well as the ruins which followed upon the wars.

By the fifth chapter can be understood what the world or the earth could say after the law had been established for a time, which said world or earth could rejoice by saying that it was close to blessed divine knowledge, which appointed it recorder of its adventures, which is to say the depository of its commandments, as [3d] we see the commandments of God established on earth.

Item, ce puet segnefier l'omme ja entré en perseverence de vertu qui ja sent la douceur de contemplacion.

Item, puet segnefier comment Cristine estoit ja parcreue quant elle apperçut les coustumes de France, par quoy elle en pouoit devisier.

Es ·vi·ᵉ chappitre, ouquel commence la complainte de la dame couronnee, doit estre entendu que ainsi se puet complaindre la terre a Dame Droiture. Et commence la terre sa complainte a ses premieres gestes, c'est asavoir depuis l'aage qui s'appella l'age doré, ouquel les gens vivoient franchement et sans convoitise; et puis comment ce temps failli lors que les gens devindrent convoiteux et si tost que Rapine vint au monde, qui puet estre | [4a] entendu par les fremis qui de leur nature sont convoiteux d'amasser. Toutefois ne fu mie vertu si destruite par les convoiteux que partie n'en demourast au monde en divers lieux, tellement que de plus vertueux hommes vindrent aprés que n'avoient esté les premerains. Et en ceste fiction de cestes plantes d'or qui furent transportees peuent estre comprises maintes histoires du temps du second aage et gens particuliers qui vindrent des bon filz de Adam, comme les patriarches, les prophetes, et plusieurs autres sains preudesommes.

Item, puet segnefier l'ame raisonnable qui se complaint a Raison et dit comment Dieu l'avoit creé innocent et bonne, et puis comment par divers inconveniens les vertus lui ont esté ravies, et non si ravies qu'il n'y ait encore de bons gitons, comme entendement et autres | [4b] biens.

Item, puet segnefier une telle ymaginacion que Cristine prent que France parle a elle et lui die sa complainte. Et premierement lui dist comment ses gestes vindrent premierement des nobles Troiens, que Cristine appelle l'arbre d'or pour leur richece et noblece. Les hoirs des fremis qui l'arbre aracherent sont les Greigois qui destruirent les Troiens. Pourquoy les nomme elle fremis? Pour ce qu'ilz furent grant quantité, et aussi les anciens Persiens dient que les Grieux vindrent premierement de fremis. Les gitons de l'arbre d'or qui furent plantéz en plusieurs pars se puet entendre plusieurs des parens du roy Priant de Troie qui se transporterent en divers païs, dont sont venues plusieurs nobles generacions comme les Rommains et autres; et meismement en France vindrent yceulx Troiens, | [4c] dont sont descendus les princes françois d'un des nepveus du roy Priant de Troie, si comme on puet savoir par les croniques qui de ce font mencion.

Le ·vij·ᵉ chappitre se continue a cellui de devant. Et semblablement puet faire l'exposicion ce que le texte dit qu'en ceste contree fu transportee une vergete yssue de la cosme du sus dit arbre d'or qui tant crut. Et ce puet segnefier le lignaige Nostre Dame et premierement Abraham et les autres descendues, dont la terre se pot esjoir de si noble semence qui tant crut que elle surmonta toutes autres plantes, ce fu Jhesucrist qui surmonta toute chose. La terre en prist son nom et fu «Libera» appellee. Voirement fut terre franchie par celle noble plante, c'est Jhesucrist qui franchi homme \de/

Likewise, this can signify man who, having entered into the state of perseverance in virtue, already smells the sweetness of contemplation.

Likewise, it can signify how Christine was already grown when she became aware of the customs of France, and was able to speak of them.

The sixth chapter, wherein begins the complaint of the crowned lady, must be interpreted as the earth's being able to lament to Lady Righteousness. And the earth begins its plaint at its first events, which is to say with the time called the golden age, when men lived openly and without covetousness; and then how this time disappeared when people became covetous, and Rapine entered the world, which can be [4a] understood as ants who are eager for riches. Nonetheless, virtue was never so entirely destroyed by the greedy that some of it did not remain in various places, so that afterwards men even more virtuous than the first were born. And in the fiction of the golden plant that was transported can be understood several stories from the second age, and individuals who descended from Adam's good sons, such as patriarchs, prophets, and several other holy and noble men.

Likewise, this can signify the rational soul, which complains to Reason and tells how God created it innocent and good, but then how through diverse mishaps the virtues have been taken from it, but not so entirely that some favorable growth does not remain, such as understanding and other [4b] goods.

Likewise, it can signify Christine's imagining that France speaks to her in lamentation. And first she recounts how her deeds issued originally from the noble Trojans, whom Christine calls the golden tree because of their richness and nobility. The hordes of ants who uprooted the tree are the Greeks who destroyed the Trojans. Why does she call them ants? Because they came in great numbers, and also because the ancient Persians said that the Greeks were descended from ants. The branches of the golden tree that were planted in various places can be understood as several relatives of King Priam of Troy, who traveled to various countries, giving birth to several noble generations, such as the Romans and others; and these Trojans even traveled to France; [4c] and the princes of France are descended from one of the nephews of King Priam of Troy, as one can learn from the chronicles that speak of this.

The seventh chapter continues the preceding one. And in like manner the exposition can be made of what the text says concerning a tiny sprout issued from the said golden tree that grew so large. And this can signify the lineage of Our Lady, first Abraham and the other descendants; the earth can rejoice in such noble seed, which grew so much that it surpassed all other plants: this was Jesus Christ, who surpassed all things. The earth took its name from it and was called "Libera." Truly the earth was liberated by this noble plant, Jesus Christ, who liberated man from the enemy. They

l'ennemi. Ils couronnerent le ·iij·ᵉ giton, ce fu la | [4d] tierce personne de la Trinité, c'est Jhesucrist, Roy de ciel et de terre; cestui porta fruit de grant dignité. Et le surplus du chappitre se[7] peut assez entendre a ce propos par lui meismes.

Item, tout ce puet estre deduit et ramené a l'ame et vie humaine selon perfection de vertu.

Item, et ce puet segnefier comme dit est la premiere venue des roys de France, desquelz elle prist son nom, si comme aucuns dient que ce fu d'un d'iceux dis princes qui fu appellé Francio. Les autres dient qu'ilz lui donnerent cellui nom France pour la grant liberté qu'ilz y establirent. Ilz couronnerent le ·iij·ᵉ giton de leur venue, ce fu le ·iij·ᵉ prince qui vint d'eulx par succession, lequel avoit nom Pharamon. Et fu le premier roy de France, comme il est dit es croniques.

Par ce qui est dit en le | [5a] ·viij·ᵉ chappitre se[8] puet entendre ce que la terre pouoit dire au commencement de Crestienté en parlant des sains pappes et des autres sains prescheurs et cultiveurs de la sainte loy. Et la peuent estre comprises plusieurs histoires de payens et mescreans convertie a la foy crestienne et la conversion Vaspasien le noble empereur qui moult honnora la foi de Dieu et acrut.

Item, ce puet estre ramené a meditacions de l'ame devote.

Item, ce puet estre France qui parle de soi meismes, et puet estre la compris le temps qui couru jusques au bon roy Clovis qui fu le premier roy crestien, qui fu prince de grant valeur. Et par ce que le texte dit de l'eaue vive que le bon prince atray, se[9] puet entendre la conversion d'icellui Clovis et la bonté et valeur de lui.

Ce qui est contenu ou | [5b] ·ix·ᵉ chappitre puet segnefier le temps qui vint aprés ouquel plusieurs princes crestiens furent remplis de luxures et de tres grans vices, et meismes des papes et des plus grans de l'Eglise, esquelz ot de tres grans hersies, qui semerent de fausses sectes et introducions perverses; et la peuent estre comprises maintes histoires des temps de lors.

Item, puet segnefier les tribulacions qui sont en corps humain, et mesmement en esperit.

Item, puet segnefier la perversité qui fu en plusieurs roys de France, comme le roy Childerich qui fu chacié pour sa luxure, puis enmena la femme du roy qui l'avoit recueilli, comme dient les croniques; aussi les autres roys qui furent perceux et sans vertu, et leurs successeurs tres crueulx mariéz a femmes de grant cruauté.

| [5c] Le ·x·ᵉ chappitre, qui dit que d'un pepin du fruit du sus dit arbre sailli une noble plante qui tant crut, etc., ce puet segnefier les filz de vertu, comme les bons sains papes et autres sains docteurs, qui tant crurent qu'ilz destruisirent les heresies et augmenterent la foi catholique. Et puet aussi estre entendu de saint Pol l'apostre ou de saint Augustin ou d'autre grant augmenteur de l'Eglise et de foi catholique. Et ce qui est dit aprés que la

crowned the third offspring, this was the [4d] third person of the Trinity, Jesus Christ, king of heaven and earth; he bore fruit of great worth. And the rest of the chapter can evidently be interpreted in this fashion.

Likewise, all of this can be applied to the soul and human life in the perspective of the perfection of virtue.

Likewise, it can signify the arrival of the kings of France, whence she took her name, as some say that it came from one of these princes named Francio. Others say that the name France came from the great freedom that was established there. They crowned the third offshoot, the third prince to issue from that line, who was named Pharamond. And he was the first king of France, as the chronicles relate.

By what is said in the [5a] eighth chapter can be understood what the earth could have said in the early days of Christianity in speaking of the holy popes and other preachers and holy men who cultivated the sacred law. And in that can be incorporated many stories of pagans and unbelievers converted to the Christian faith, and the conversion of the noble emperor Vespasian, who honored and spread the faith of God.

It can moreover be applied to the meditations of the holy soul.

Likewise, it can be understood as France speaking of herself, and in that can be encompassed the period up to good King Clovis, who was the first Christian king, a prince of great worth. And by what the text says concerning the living water that the good king drew unto himself, can be understood Clovis's conversion as well as his goodness and worth.

That which is contained in the [5b] ninth chapter can signify the time which came after, in which several Christian princes were filled with covetousness and other grave vices, and even popes and high men of the Church, whence sprang great heresies that spread false sects and perverse beliefs; and in that can be included many stories from those times.

Likewise can be understood the tribulations that the human body suffers, and also the spirit.

Likewise, it can signify the perversity which was in several French kings, such as Childerich, who was banished for his lustful ways and who carried off the wife of the king who had given him hospitality, as the chronicles relate; and also the other kings who were lazy and lacking in virtue, and their cruel successors married to women of great cruelty.

[5c] The tenth chapter, which tells how a noble plant sprang from a seed of the fruit of the said tree, and so forth, can signify the sons of virtue, such as the holy popes and other holy doctors, who flourished so that they destroyed heresies and increased the Catholic faith. And this can also be understood to mean Saint Paul the apostle or Saint Augustine or other great men who helped the Church and the Catholic faith grow. And what is said afterwards concerning the decrease in virtue, and so forth, can be in-

vertu ala en descroissant etc., puet estre pris pour aucuns barateurs qui
aprés vindrent, qui se ficherent es dignetéz, et ou pappe et es prelacions de
Sainte Eglise, et aussi es seigneuries temporelles par tirannie, et par plusieurs successions ont possedé ycelles. Et ce qui est dit aprés puet segnefier les meschiefs qui ont esté sur terre par maintes fois diversement par
estranges | [5d] angoisses.

Item, tout ce se puet ramener a homme simgulierement.

Item, au propos de France ce puet segnefier Charlemaine, roy de France,
qui glorieusement augmenta la Crestienté et duquel le renom de France est
encore auctorisié, et puis le roy Hue Capet qui de France s'atribua la couronne, lequel Hue Capet estoit venus d'estrange lignee; et puis comment la
couronne revint au pere saint Louys qui estoit descendu de la lignee Charlemaine, et tout depuis ce temps la, les rebellions et maulx qui sont venus en
France en maintes guises.

Ce qui est contenu en le ·xi·ᵉ chappitre puet segnefier le bon pappe
Urbain qui moult repara l'Eglise et remist a son droit et en paix.

Item, puet segnefier la bonne conscience adrecee a Dieu.

| [6a] Item, au propos de France, puet segnefier le bon sage roy Charles
quint d'icelui nom, par qui France fu remise en estat des ruines qui devant
avoit eues.

Le ·xij·ᵉ chappitre qui parle des ·ij· oysiaux de proie qui sourdirent des
entrailles du devant dit peut notter les ·ij· aucuppas le pappe qui ont con-
tinué environ l'espace de ·xxviij· ans. La louenge qui semble estre dicte
d'aucun d'ieux se peut entendre selon une reigle de gramaire que on dit par
antifrasis, c'est a dire au contraire de ce qui est dit. Ce qui est dit de Fortune
qui par son vent trebuscha le noble faucon se puet entendre de la ruine de
l'Eglise, laquelle Eglise est si noble que elle fait sa roe par tout le monde,
c'est a dire que tout le monde doit comprendre.

Item, ce puet segnefier l'ame et le corps ensemble.

Item, au propos de France, ce puet segnefier le roy | [6b] Charles ·VI·ᵉ
d'icellui nom qui a present regne, le bien qui est en ses nobles condicions,
et la pitié de sa maladie et le temps qu'elle lui prist; et avec lui monseigneur
le duc d'Orlians son frere.

Par le ·xiii·ᵉ chappitre et par ce qui est dit aprés ensuivant es autres
chapitres puet estre notté ce que les prophecies anciennes de Merlin, des
Sibilles, de Joachin et de Jehan dient des pestillences a avenir au monde,
tant au royaume de France comme autre part, par les pechéz qui y cueurent,
c'est asavoir par l'orgueil des riches et puissans, et par la luxure, fraude,
convoitise et faulte de foy qui est au monde.

Et tout ce qui est contenu es dis chappitres ensuivant, se a droit sont re-
gardéz, sont concurrans et acordans aux dis des prophettes sur les temps
a venir avec lesquelz s'acorde la Sainte Escripture; et qui a droit les lira et
entendra, les | [6c] trouvera corespondans et semblables.

terpreted as some usurpers who came later who took over the papacy or other high stations in the Church, and also positions of temporal power by tyranny, and remained in possession thereof through successive generations. And what is said afterward can signify the various misfortunes that have often [5d] plagued the world from various parts.

Likewise, all of this can be applied to the individual.

Likewise, with regard to France, this can be interpreted as Charlemagne, king of France, who spread Christianity in most glorious fashion and from whom France still justly derives renown, and afterwards Hugh Capet, issued from another line, who took the crown, and then how the crown returned to Saint Louis's father, who was a descendant of Charlemagne, and everything since that time, including rebellions and ills that fell upon France in many forms.

What is contained in the eleventh chapter can signify good Pope Urban, who mended the Church and restored it to right and peace.

Likewise, it can signify the good conscience turned to God.

[6a] Likewise, with regard to France, it can signify good King Charles V, by whom France was restored from the state of ruin which had prevailed.

The twelfth chapter, which speaks of the two birds of prey that sprang up from the entrails of the preceding, can signify the two birds of prey sitting on the papal throne for the past twenty-eight years or so. The seeming praise said of one of them can be interpreted by a figure of rhetoric named antiphrasis, by which is understood the opposite of what is said. What is said of Fortune who by her wind brought the noble falcon down, can be understood as the ruin of the Church, which Church is so noble that she makes her nest throughout the world, which is to say that she should encompass the entire world.

Likewise, it can signify the soul and the body taken together.

Likewise, with regard to France, it can signify King [6b] Charles VI our present ruler, the good of his noble circumstances, and the pity of his illness and the time it has taken from him, and with him our noble lord the duke of Orleans, his brother.

By the thirteenth chapter and by what is said afterwards in the other chapters can be understood what the ancient prophecies of Merlin, the Sibyls, Joachim, and John say of the plagues that are to visit the world, both in the kingdom of France and elsewhere, because of the sins that are rampant there, that is to say, because of the pride of the rich and powerful, and also the lasciviousness, dishonesty, covetousness, and lack of faith that prevail.

And everything contained in the following chapters, if understood correctly, is in accordance with the prophecies on the times to come, which prophecies echo Holy Scripture; and whoever reads and understands them [6c] correctly will find them to correspond.

The initial paragraph of the preface states in a nutshell a concept of poetry that equates it with allegory. Christine's notion of poetry involves two main factors: (1) poetic language presents, under the guise of metaphor or "veiled language," hidden truth or knowledge; and (2) the beauty of poetry derives from the multiplicity of meanings it can convey.

In the remainder of the preface, Christine offers, chapter by chapter, a three-tiered interpretation of the first thirteen chapters of the *Avision* as they relate to (1) "the world in general, which is the earth," (2) man alone, and finally (3) the kingdom of France (f. 3a). Thus, for example, the figure of Chaos in the first chapter can be seen as representing the whole world, the individual human being, and the kingdom of France (ff. 1b–d). In similar fashion, the sixth chapter, which begins the complaint of the "dame couronnee" (France), can be taken as (1) the world's lamentation over the fall from the golden age, (2) the individual soul's lament over its fall from grace, and (3) the historical complaint the figure of France delivers to Christine (ff. 3d–4c).

A closer look at the preface soon reveals that the stated allegorical categories are not immediately transparent, and that the first two bear close resemblance to the traditional categories derived from religious exegesis. The first category, "le monde general," presupposes a religious teleology, the history of the world being cast in the shape of the history of salvation. The second, "l'homme simgulier," presents interpretations that are inevitably of a moral or spiritual nature.

The preface, in addition, shows signs of having been hastily composed. The final paragraph encompasses all chapters from the fourteenth to the end of the first part of the work; a pair of et ceteras shorten the expositions of chapter 10 (f. 5c); the second allegorical interpretation for chapter 10, "Likewise all of this can be applied to the individual" (f. 5d), is not explicative at all; and the summary nature of the gloss for chapter 13 (f. 6b), does not distinguish, as do all the preceding ones, different levels of interpretation. The language of the gloss supplies the best justification for this apparent haste. Throughout, the reader is reminded by the constant repetition of introductory terms like "puet prendre," "se puet prendre," "se peuent prendre," and "puet estre pris" ("can be taken or interpreted"), that the explanations that follow are of a tentative nature, offering only some of the possible meanings readers might decipher on their own.

Thus we can add a third characteristic to the idea of allegorical writing outlined in the opening paragraph of the preface: the various levels on which allegory is interpreted—four in traditional exegesis and three in the preface—are not considered by Christine to be exhaustive. Rather, the possibilities for meaning are seen as open-ended. It is not by chance that *Avision* both begins and ends with a kind of invitation to the reader to exercise his interpretative powers. As already noted, the preface begins with the statement that its purpose is to "open the way" for the reader who might want to explore the full richness of the work (f. 1a). The closing metaphor of the *Avision*, the ruby to which Christine compares its third part "which has the property of becoming more pleasing the more one looks at it," seems intended to draw the reader back into the work in a process of reflective analysis.[10]

Comparing the allegorical schema in the *Avision* to that set out by the structure of the *Epistre d'Othéa*—the only other work of Christine's for which a specific reading is proposed[11]—one cannot help but be struck by the shift from the traditional exegetical categories of moral and spiritual interpretation represented by the "glosses" and "allegories" of the *Epistre* to the emphasis on the political meaning of the *Avision*. Sandra Hindman has recently demonstrated how the miniatures of two manuscripts of the *Epistre d'Othéa* produced within a few years of the Phillipps manuscript (1406), B.N. fr. 606, and London, Harley 4431, encourage a political reading of those manuscripts in addition to the moral and spiritual allegories made explicit in the text.[12] The *Avision* provides additional evidence that at the height of her career, which coincided with particularly strife-ridden years on the political scene, Christine was engaged in an attempt to use her writings as a platform to speak to those in power—her patrons—to exhort them to the practice of virtue in the resolution of their disputes and in the conduct of political affairs.

While the schema of allegorical interpretation proposed in the *Avision* does not appear to stem from any one source, still it is clear that the category of political interpretation, which from a reading of the work emerges dominant over the others, owes much to the tradition of political allegory represented by such works as the *Arbre des batailles* and the *Somnium super materia schismatis* of Honoré Bouvet, and the *Songe du vieil pelerin* of Philippe de Mézières.[13] It is tempting, in addition, to speculate on the possible influence of Gerson, Christine's ally in the *Rose* quarrel. In November 1405, shortly before the *Avision* preface was composed, Gerson delivered in French before the assembled court the resounding sermon "Vivat rex" in which he analyzed the office of the king from three perspectives: (1) "corporeal, material, and personal life," (2) "civil, political or universal life," (3) "the life of divine grace, or spiritual life."[14] Although the connection between Gerson and Christine has not yet been studied in any detail, it would appear unlikely that it came to an end with the winding down of the *Rose* controversy, for both were to remain important figures in Paris for more than a dozen years after and would have had numerous opportunities for contact.

If the allegorical framework of the *Avision* preface was influenced by the tradition of political allegory popular during Charles VI's reign, the concept of poetry expressed therein would appear traceable to non-French sources. As was noted above, the concept of allegory outlined in the *Avision* preface includes three aspects: (1) poetic language serves as a "cover" for hidden truth; (2) poetry's beauty is a function of the work's multiple meanings; (3) in theory at least, the different ways poetry can be read are limitless.

The *Avision* preface is not the first work of Christine's where these critical notions were put forth. Numerous passages in the *Epistre d'Othéa a Hector* (ca. 1400) suggest the definition of poetry as "fable" which carries a hidden truth, as for example the following statements from the glosses of chapters 3 and 29: "The poets, who speak under a cover and in the manner of fable," "as the poets who hid truth under the cover of fable" (London, B. L. Harley 4431, ff. 97v, 109v). Moreover, the *Epistre* contains numerous claims for poetry's capacity to carry multiple meanings. The following statement from gloss 56 is typical of these: "This fable can be explained in several different ways" (Harley 4431, f. 121r). Echoing the third characteristic of allegory pointed out for the *Avision* preface, the *Epistre* suggests, finally, that the shape of poetry's meaning is more a function of the reader's ingenuity than anything else: "This fable can be explained in various ways, as can the others. It was for this reason that the poets made them, so that men's minds could be sharpened and refined in looking for various interpretations" (Harley 4431, f. 106v).

In 1403 Christine tried her hand at a very different kind of work, the pastoral, and in the prologue to the *Dit de la Pastoure*, she called for a similar—if less complex—allegorical reading of that work:

> Et m'est avis, que veult drois
> Y visier qu'on puet entendre
> Qu'a aultre chose veult tendre
> Que le texte ne desclot,
> Car aucune fois on clot
> En parabole couverte
> Matiere a tous non ouverte,
> Qui semble estre truffe ou fable,
> Ou sentence gist notable.

> (Those, in my opinion, who wish
> To view this work correctly, will understand
> It aims at a meaning quite other
> Than that which the text reveals.
> For sometimes one enfolds
> In a secret parable

Material not accessible to all;
Within seeming play or fable
Lies meaning of great weight.[15]

Finally, in the *Livre des fais et bonnes meurs du sage roy Charles V*, completed the following year, Christine devoted an entire chapter to poetry (3.58), in which she once again equated it with allegory capable of being interpreted on multiple levels. Poetry is defined here as "narrative that appears to signify one thing" ("tout narracion ou introduction apparaument signifiant un senz") but which "contains one or several hidden meanings" ("occultment en segnefie un aultre ou plusieurs").[16] The author goes on to specify: "It may be said that the end of poetry is truth, and its process, doctrine clothed in poetic ornaments which give delight, as well as fitting figures of rhetoric. These ornaments appear other in relation to the message to be communicated." ("Plus proprement dire celle soit poesie, dont la fin est verité, et le proces doctrine revestue en paroles d'ornemens delictables et par propres couleurs, lesquelz revestments soient d'estranges guises au propos dont on veult.")

Thus, the concept of poetry found in the *Avision* preface had been espoused by Christine as early as the *Epistre d'Othéa a Hector*, and reiterated in intervening works. Moreover, it is this particular notion of poetry that Christine considered best suited to her, as she states in a passage of the *Avision*: "Puis me prist aux livres des pouetes, et comme de plus en plus, alast croiscent le bien de ma congnoiscence. Adonc fus je aise quant j'oz trouvé le stile a moy naturel, me delittant en leurs soubtilles covertures et belles matieres mucees soubz fictions delictables et morales." ("Then I turned to the books of the poets, and my knowledge increased more and more. I was delighted to discover that I had a natural affinity for their style, and took pleasure in their subtle covers and the beauty they hid under delightful and moral fictions.")[17]

A clue to Christine's source for this notion of poetry can be found in the passage quoted immediately above, for among the "books of the poets" that the author studied in her program of self-education must be included Boccaccio's *Genealogia deorum gentilium*. As recent scholarship has indicated, the *Genealogia* was one of the most influential works circulating in Parisian intellectual circles at the time Christine was writing.[18] If Laurent de Premierfait mined it for mythological material in his second and much expanded translation of the *De casibus virorum illustrium* in 1409,[19] others were more interested in the sections of the work dealing with the nature of poetry. Jean de Montreuil, provost of Lille and a principal voice in the *Rose* controversy, referred to the key theoretical chapter of the *Genealogia* (14.7) in the letter "Auffugiente michi," in which he tried to inculcate in an unidentified lawyer friend his own love of poetry.[20] Nicolas de Gonesse adopted in the *Collatio* Boccaccio's arguments for the defense of poetry in the fourteenth and fifteenth books of the *Genealogia*.[21] Finally, the Augustinian humanist Jacques Legrand cited the *Genealogia* in the chapters concerning the nature of poetry in both his *Sophologium* and his *Archiloge Sophie*.[22]

The *Genealogia* contains all three ideas about poetry that have been shown operative in the *Avision* preface. The key image of poetry as a veil or cover is expressed in the prologue of that work, where Boccaccio announces his desire to tear "the hidden significations from their tough sheathing."[23] The image is repeated in several different sections of the *Genealogia*; for example, poetry is a "cover" (1.3); it "veils truth in a fair and fitting garment of fiction" (14.7); the early poets "enclosed the high mysteries of things divine in a covering of words with the intention that the adorable majesty of such things should not become an object of too common knowledge" (14.8).[24]

Christine's second notion, that poetry's aesthetic value is tied to the multiplicity of meanings it can convey, is both explicitly stated in the *Genealogia* and implicit in the method of exposition Boccaccio employs. For in composing his mythological accounts, not only does Boccaccio relate interpretations from multiple sources such as Vergil, Cicero, Theodontius, Lactantius, Eusebius, Jerome, Augustine, Macrobius, Fulgentius, Cassiodorus, Isidore, Hrabanus Maurus, Vincent of Beauvais, and Leontius, but he also points out discrepancies in the various accounts and injects interpretations of his own. Different methods of interpretation are used, principally euhemeristic, naturalistic, and moral.[25] The result is a kaleidoscope of meanings to which the explanations lead: "These fictions do not convey a single meaning, but rather it can be said that they have several meanings ("His fictionibus non esse tantum unicum intellectum, quin imo dici potest potius polisenum, hoc est moltiplicium sensum").[26]

Finally, Christine's third notion of the open-ended quality of allegorical exposition can be seen as echoing Boccaccio's statement in the *Genealogia* 1.4 that the potential commentary for one legend alone—that of Pan—could itself be the subject of an entire book: "Nam si omnia que ad expositionem huius fabule possent induci describere vellem, ipsa sola fere totum excogitatum volumen occuparet."[27] ("For if I should wish to describe everything that could be brought into the exposition of this fable, that [exposition] alone would occupy virtually an entire carefully thought-out volume.")

Thus, the evidence is strong that the *Genealogia* was the work from which Christine derived her chief critical notions on the nature of poetry. As these ideas were already operative in Christine's first full-length work, the *Epistre d'Othéa a Hector*, it can be assumed she read Boccaccio before 1400.[28] Since no French translation of the *Genealogia* was made until the end of the fifteenth century, she had to have read the work in the original Latin.[29]

Charity Cannon Willard has characterized Christine de Pizan as "a child of two worlds," in whom French and Italian influences converged in a unique blend.[30] The *Avision* preface, which echoes both contemporary French political allegories and Boccaccio's ideas on allegory, bears witness to the aptness of that characterization. If Christine embraced French culture wholeheartedly, she never forgot her Italian roots. Her half-taunting recommendation to her opponents in the *Rose* quarrel that they turn to Italy for models superior to Jean de Meun[31] was advice she herself had already followed.

Notes

1. For a description of the manuscript, see Gilbert Ouy and Christine Reno, "Identification des autographes de Christine de Pizan," *Scriptorium* 34 (1980): 221–38. On the subject of Christine's revision of her works, see James C. Laidlaw, "Christine de Pizan: An Author's Progress," *Modern Language Review* 78 (1983): 532–50. The Phillipps manuscript, which is now in a private collection, forms the base of the new edition of the *Avision* I am preparing.

2. Christine de Pisan, *Lavision-Christine*, ed. Mary Louise Towner (Washington, D.C.: Catholic University Press, 1932), 163.

3. B.N. fr. 606, f. 12v°. See Rosemond Tuve, "Notes on the Virtues and Vices," *Journal of the Warburg and Courtauld Institutes* 26 (1963): 289; Mary Ann Ignatius, "Christine de Pizan's *Epistre Othea*: An Experiment in Literary Form," *Medievalia et Humanistica*, n.s. 9 (1979): 14; and Sandra L. Hindman, *Christine de Pizan's "Epistre Othéa": Painting and Politics at the Court of Charles VI*, Texts and Studies, no. 77 (Toronto: Pontifical Institute of Mediaeval Studies, 1986), 75. On this same page and on 78, Hindman makes the further claim that the rubrics served as guides to the illuminator as well. However, both Christine's opening statement in B.N. fr. 606 (quoted above) and the usual practice of writing artists' instructions either in the margin (where they would be trimmed) or under the illumination (which would cover them up) would suggest the narrower interpretation.

4. In the transcription, modern conventions for punctuation and capitalization are followed, and the use of *j, i, u,* and *v* are regularized according to modern usage. The acute accent is used on tonic *e* except for the second person of the verb and the word *assez;* modern use of the cedilla is followed, and the trema is used to avoid confusion between similarly spelled words. Feminine endings are left unaccented.

5. ce

6. ses

7. ce

8. ce

9. ce

10. "Qui a propriete de tant plus plaire comme plus on le regarde," *Lavision-Christine*, 193.

11. See Rosemond Tuve, *Allegorical Imagery: Some Mediaeval Books and Their Posterity* (Princeton, N.J.: Princeton University Press, 1966), 34.

12. Hindman, *Christine de Pizan's "Epistre Othéa,"* 112.

13. The most complete assessment of Christine's debt to these two writers is to be found in Hindman, *Christine de Pizan's "Epistre Othéa,"* 143–69. The interpretation of the *Songe du vieil pelerin* as proposing a trilevel allegorical reading similar to the *Avision*'s is, however, open to debate. Philippe de Mézières does not propose a formal interpretative schema, and when he does intervene in the text to suggest how it should be read, he mentions only a second, "moral" reading of the allegory. See Hindman, *Christine de Pizan's "Epistre Othéa,"* 32, and Philippe de Mézières, *Le Songe du vieil pelerin*, ed. G. W. Coopland (Cambridge: Cambridge University Press, 1969), 1:91, 92, 93, 96, 97.

14. Joannes Gerson, *Harengue faicte au nom de l'Université de Paris, devant le roy Charles Sixiesme et tout le conseil en 1405* (Paris: Debeausseaux, 1824), 8. The gloss for the twelfth chapter of the *Avision* (ex-Phillipps, f. 6a), which places the composition of the preface twenty-eight years into the Schism, permits us to assign it the date 1406.

15. Christine de Pizan, *Oeuvres poétiques de Christine de Pisan*, ed. Maurice Roy, 3 vols. (Paris: Firmin Didot, 1886–96), 2:224.

16. Christine de Pizan, *Le Livre des fais et bonnes meurs du sage roy Charles V*, 2 vols., ed. Suzanne Solente (Paris: Champion, 1936–40), 2:176.

17. *Lavision-Christine*, 163.

18. Giuseppe di Stefano, "Il Trecento," in *Il Boccaccio nella cultura francese: Atti del Convegno di studi "L'opera del Boccaccio nella cultura francese" (Certaldo 2–6 settembre 1968)* (Florence: Olschki, 1971), 11.

19. Carla Bozzolo, "L'Humaniste Gontier Col et Boccace," in *Boccaccio in Europe: Proceedings of the Boccaccio Conference, Louvain, December, 1975*, ed. G. Tournoy (Louvain: Presses universitaires de Louvain, 1977), 21.

20. Ezio Ornato, "Per la fortuna del Boccaccio in Francia: Una lettera inedita di Jean de Montreuil," *Studi Francesi* 11 (1970): 260–62.

21. Di Stefano, "Il Trecento," 12–21.

22. Bozzolo, "L'Humaniste," 21; and Jacques Legrand, *L'Archiloge Sophie et le Livre des bonnes meurs*, ed. E. Beltran (Paris: Champion, 1986), 150.

23. Giovanni Boccaccio, *Genealogia deorum gentilium*, ed. Vincenzo Romano (Bari: Laterza, 1951), 1.8. *Boccaccio on Poetry: Being the Preface and the Fourteenth and Fifteenth Books of Boccaccio's "Genealogia deorum gentilium,"* trans. Charles G. Osgood (New York: Liberal Arts Press, 1956), 11.

24. *Genealogia deorum gentilium* 1.19; *Boccaccio on Poetry*, 39, 44. See also *Genealogia deorum gentilium* 14.9, 10, 12, 13, 17, 18, 22. As Osgood points out (*Boccaccio on Poetry*, 8), the idea of allegory as a veil did not originate with Boccaccio but can be found also, for example, in Petrarch, Dante, Vincent of Beauvais, Isidore, Macrobius, Augustine, and Lactantius.

25. See Osgood, *Boccaccio on Poetry*, xxiii; and Ernest Hatch Wilkins, *The University of Chicago Manuscript of the "Genealogia deorum gentilium" of Boccaccio* (Chicago: University of Chicago Press, 1927), 3.

26. *Genealogia deorum gentilium* 1.19.

27. Ibid., 24.

28. Campbell had hypothesized that Christine might have used the *Genealogia* as a source for certain mythological details of the *Othéa*, cf. P.-G.-C. Campbell, *L'"Epître d'Othea": Etude sur les sources de Christine de Pisan* (Paris: Champion, 1924), 49, 123–24, 132, 142. Had he included within his purview the idea of poetry expressed in that work, his findings would doubtless have been less tentatively put. As for manuscripts of the *Genealogia* available in early fifteenth-century France, see Gianni Mombello, "I manoscritti delle opere di Dante, Petrarca, e Boccaccio nelle principali librerie francesi del secolo XV," in *Il Boccaccio nella cultura francese*, ed. Carlo Pellegrini (Florence: Olschki, 1971), 81–209, esp. 99, 148; and Bozzolo, "L'Humaniste," 21. See also Pier Giorgio Ricci, "Contributi per un'edizione critica della *Genealogia deorum gentilium*," *Rinascimento* 2 (1951): 99–144, 195–208.

29. The first French edition of the *Genealogia* was published by Vérard in 1498; in 1531 Jehan Petit and Philippe Le Noir published succeeding editions. Curiously enough, all three omitted the final two theoretical books (14 and 15). A partial translation of chapters 2 and 3 of book 14 had been done by Jean Miélot in 1471. See Carla Bozzolo, *Manuscrits des traductions de Boccace* (Padua: Editrice Antenae, 1973), 36–37.

30. Charity Cannon Willard, *Christine de Pizan: Her Life and Works* (New York: Persea Books, 1984), 15–31. On the subject of Italian influences on Christine's writings, see, for example, Arturo Farinelli, "Dante nell'opera di Christine de Pisan," *Aus romanischen Sprachen und Literaturen: Festschrift Heinrich Morf* (Halle: Niemeyer, 1905), 117–52; Marie-Josèphe Pinet, *Christine de Pisan, 1364–1430: Etude biographique et littéraire* (Paris: Champion, 1927), 395–401; Alfred Jeanroy, "Boccace et Christine de Pisan: Le *De claris mulieribus* principale source du *Livre de la Cité des Dames*," *Romania* 48 (1922): 93–105; Carla Bozzolo, "Il *Decameron* come fonte del *Livre de la cité des dames* de Christine de Pisan," in *Miscellanea di studi e ricerche sul Quattrocento francese*, ed. Franco Simone (Turin: Giappichelli, 1967), 3–24; Liliane Dulac, "Inspiration mystique et savoir politique: Les conseils aux veuves chez Francesco da Barberino et chez Christine de Pizan," in *Mélanges à la mémoire de Franco Simone: France et Italie dans la culture européenne*, vol. 1, *Moyen âge et renaissance* (Geneva: Slatkine, 1980), 113–41; and Earl Jeffrey Richards, "Christine de Pizan and Dante: A Reexamination," *Archiv für das Studium der neueren Sprachen und Literaturen* 137 (1985): 100–111. In the light of these studies, it is surprising to see a statement dismissing the Italian influence on Christine's work in Sandra Hindman's recent review of Willard's *Christine de Pizan*, in *Speculum* 62 (1987): 223.

31. Eric Hicks, ed., *Le Débat sur le "Roman de la Rose"* (Paris: Champion, 1977), 142.

Compilation and Legitimation in the Fifteenth Century: *Le Livre de la Cité des Dames*

JOËL BLANCHARD

TRANSLATED BY EARL JEFFREY RICHARDS

A misunderstanding hangs over the work of Christine de Pizan. She has mistakenly been credited with a distinction that has been all the more readily accepted as it flatters a certain inclination of the modern mind. The influence exerted by the *Livre de la Cité des Dames*, a work that some have welcomed as a feminist manifesto, undoubtedly lies at the origin of this misunderstanding. The very idea of secession, of forclusion, brought about by the representation of the *cité parfaite* that shelters celebrated women, has been considered as the sign of a change in the area of social representation during the late Middle Ages and as a prime document for women's history and for Western thought in general. Many have taken a feminist utopia, suggested by assembling these famous women in an impregnable fortress, to be the subject of a book that in fact is animated by quite a different ambition. This feminist bias has only seen the surface of things. A reading of Christine in such an univocal and reductive fashion represents a somewhat naïve belief in the letter of the fiction. In the final analysis, interpreters from Gustave Lanson to recent English-language critics [1] have more or less openly taken this perspective as their point of departure. Despite the precautions sometimes taken to differentiate the eternal themes (Christine and women, Christine and politics, and so on), critics have remained the captives of surface appearances and have disregarded Christine's essential literary intentions. In light of this misapprehension, one must try to grasp the unity and amplitude of a literary process that is Christine's own and that finds its consummate expression in *Le Livre de la Cité des Dames*: the construction of the book itself, and more specifically the work of compilation, its necessities, and its order, which are what is at stake in the work, the ante in this new writing game.

One might observe that compilation was not the exclusive prerogative of Christine during the Middle Ages, and indeed, the practice of integrating *auctoritates* into a text for the purpose of enlightenment and commentary is documented starting in the thirteenth century. Compilation had experienced considerable development long before the fifteenth century, especially in religious writings, thanks to the impetus given it by Vincent de Beauvais.[2] But such works are compilations in the narrow sense and serve to highlight or recommend select passages. This textual practice supports and contextualizes but does not truly enter into the literary undertaking. The organic use that Christine makes of texts that she selects from other works is a different matter. Through the means of compilation, the transfer of one text into another corresponds to an architectural gesture. The book arises and continues through a constant flow of correspondences. The development of a book is maintained, extended, and organized, setting up its own reflecting mirrors. Compilation in Christine is a matter of temperament and a game of the imagination.

This vocation is abundantly clear in the illustrations found in Christine's manuscripts: the image of a school girl, *une fille d'escole,* sitting in her *recet,* surrounded by books. This representation itself of the privileged female reader has contributed to establishing its permanence in her work. The act of reading for her is a veritable labor of humanist investment, an illumination of the universe, a manner of refining both her research and her mind (*s'asoutiler*).[3] This kind of commitment to reading constitutes without doubt the one aspect through which it is possible to grasp more concretely the nature of Christine's literary activity. She does not conceive of this enterprise as the result of a constant interplay between reading and writing. From such encounters arises the habit of pillaging (*pilloter*)[4] according to the demands of the moment, to accomplish through compilation the transfer from one book to another. It is in the *Livre de la Cité des Dames* that this long appropriative commerce with books can be subjected to the most precise inspection.[5]

The *Livre de la Cité des Dames* has been known first for the celebrated miniatures that decorate the autograph manuscripts whose production Christine personally oversaw.[6] These miniatures are closely tied to the meaning of the text that they illustrate. The association of book and city, held iconographically in tandem in the first double miniature in which both book and city occupy the same place in their respective panels, underscores the meaning of the literary emblematic practice here: the city for which Christine is invited to dig the foundation and to raise the walls is the book to come, the one book. The very architecture of this city presupposes, as is the case for Italian cities of the fifteenth century for which maps were drawn up, a structure with dimensions and proportions in which a strategy of writing is easily discerned, which is that of a compiler used to taking the measure of the texts selected. Christine, in effect, armed with the "truelle de sa plume" (f. 25 v), begins an extended construction project. Compilation, like the architecture from which Christine borrows her images, presupposes lines of force, points of juncture, and distributions—in short, everything that haunts geometricians. But this construction project uses literary texts as its building materials. From reading one book to writing another there is a movement controlled by the logic and coherence of an attitude that considers reading as the touchstone for all writing. The walls of the *cité parfaite* have been trimmed with stones that the compiler has gathered in the "champ des écritures" (f. 11r, 1.8.1): they are the tales of celebrated women that Christine had read in widely diverse authors.

The kind of activity that the miniature valorizes comes to be identified with Christine's own destiny, with that of the *fille d'escole* so haunted by "la frequentacion d'estude" (f. 3r, 1.1.1). But to speak of the book, a narrative pretext still had to be found, and it was entirely contained in the literary context then in fashion. The first years of the fifteenth century were agitated by a literary quarrel whose echo Christine amplified. What did the Quarrel of the *Roman de la Rose* consist of? In a redirection of interest.[7] The admiration for Jean de Meun felt by a circle of scholars and writers was changed into indignation. Of course Christine unleashed the scandal and converted their perspective into something different whose impact was more striking: antifeminism. She was the one who sent letters and drew up a dossier which she addressed to the queen, Isabeau de Bavière. Henceforth the notion that a corpus of antifeminist writings existed was accredited. This artifice must constantly be kept in mind in order to gauge Christine's good faith. A literary theme—antifeminism—which, to be precise, lacked any real historical or sociological reference, served as her alibi to speak more freely of something else: the book as such. We need to begin with an analysis of this *mise en scène,* of this production of effects.

I. The Mask of the Indignant Female Reader

The miniature illustrating the first folio of the *Cité des Dames* shows the author surrounded by books, reading one, with her hand resting on the folio. In front of her stand the three allegorical virtues, Reason, Rectitude, and Justice, each carrying a typical attribute. This iconographic model, apparently conceived by the Master of the *Cité des Dames* whom Christine had supervised and guided, is characteristic since it inspired the illustration of other manuscripts of the *Cité des Dames.* By depicting the author in the midst of so many books, the miniature supplies, in any event, the significance of the fiction with which the work opens. The *Cité des Dames* begins in effect with the representation of an act of reading whose stages and vicissitudes are recounted in a familiar tone: Christine, *travaillé de requillir la pesenteur des sentences,* decides to stop reading serious works and take up something light. She happens upon a *livret* "and [sees] from its title page that it [is] by Matheolus" ("l'auteur se clamoit Matheolus," f. 3v, 1.i.1), and she opens it, but does not have the time to read as her mother calls her to supper. However, the next day, recalling her intention from the previous evening, she decides to resume reading. After quickly glancing through the book, "browsing here and there and reading the end" ("visitant un pou ça et la et veue la fin," f. 3v), she realizes that the book in question is "not very pleasant for people who do not enjoy lies, and of no use in developing virtue or manners" ("moult deplaisant . . . ne de nul proufit," f. 3v). She resolves to stop reading, but not before the book provokes a whole new train of thought.

What the narrative here so keenly recounts is the story of a woman reader faced with choosing from among the books available to her. The book, first shut and then open (the miniature faithfully reproduces this play between relinquishment and resumption), illustrates the destiny of the female reader and of the book, the encounter with books and the uncertain effort of appropriation that attaches the book to its reader: the cessation of difficult reading, the conjecture of joyful but interrupted reading, the resumption of reading and the disappointed expectations (Matheolus's book is not written to glorify but to denigrate women) are the vicissitudes of an adventure through which one attempts to isolate the figure of the privileged female reader.

Christine supplies all the details in the stages of this game with the book: first the choice of the book on which her glance falls, next the recognition of the category to which it belongs (a book "of no authority," *de nulle autorité*), the discovery of an inspiration that she does not recognize as her own ("ne me semblast moult plaisant a gent qui ne se delitent en mesdit," f. 3v), but which gives rise in her mind to meditation ("ot engendré en moy nouvelle pensée"). All of these steps clearly belong to a virtually cinematic kind of production that illustrates the drama of reading.

This book which speaks against women reawakens the remembrance of other similar books that come rushing back into the reader's memory "like a gushing fountain" ("comme une fontaine ressourdant," f. 4v). The effect thus created by the abundance and the authority of so many books plunges Christine into a profound moral langour, *en [l']etargie.* Her plight illustrates the omnipotence of the book and the final effect of a logical process that is an integral part of the narrative from the outset. Christine as reader, comparing her natural state to what the authors claim, falls into a melancholy that leads her to belittle herself, to present herself as a "monstre en nature" (f. 4v), and to regret the fact that she was not born a man.

Christine's indignation as reader moves her to appeal directly to God.

In her plea she relies heavily on a series of exaggerated rhetorical gestures, such as false syllogisms along the line of "you were not good to me, therefore I have neglected your service." Her intention here is to lend credence to the notion that men have played a dirty trick on women. Christine plays the game with perfect bad faith because the authors who speak against women are at the same time the very ones who will inspire her in the course of her compilation, as we will see. This game with appearances is kept up all throughout the *Cité des Dames* with such skill that even the most sensitive readers fall into the trap. The game is sustained by the questions raised by Christine the indignant reader—whose own moral authority is enhanced by the visit of the three allegorical virtues, Reason, Rectitude, and Justice— because it foregrounds the injuries wrought by a real or supposed antifeminist literature (*aucuns auteurs, les clers mesdisant, Matheolus et tous les autres jangleurs*).[8]

Christine's entire practice really sets a trap. One can actually imagine that these books are bad because they are antifeminist, when in reality they are bad because they are different and the implicit intent is to lend credence to the coming of the one book that is worth creating, precisely the one Christine is writing. Here again the technique of masking pays off. Christine as author claims for herself the work of writing not as a woman but as the creator of a unique literary form. A significant difference emerges between the commonly recognized medieval practice, seen in the work of Marie de France and the *contes bretons*, of seeking refuge in the writings of distinguished predecessors, and the problems arising from establishing compilation as a system of writing. The compiler openly assumes responsibility for a consummate technique for which he claims novelty or *nouveleté*.

II. The Emblematic Status of the Book

Christine advances behind a mask unfolding a scenario that prepares her reader for the idea of the book to come. The assumed role of a *faux-semblant* underscores the double intent of the *Cité des Dames*: an apparent defense of women, which however masks Christine's ante, around which the destiny of the poet, the book, and its elaboration are constructed. Of course, the reality of the stakes here is based first on the identification of the city and the book; and the idea behind the book, as we shall see, is negotiated at length.

The appearance of the three allegorical virtues, Reason, Rectitude, and Justice, constitutes an important stage in the scenario. It follows the scandal of the misogynist writings that plunged Christine *en [l]etargie*. Their appearance signifies the election of Christine as a reader chosen among others to receive the proper teachings, which will allow her to surmount her depression. This choice consecrates those qualities and gifts that predispose Christine as reader to "investigating the truth through long and continual study" ("l'inquisition des choses vrayes par lonc et continuel estude," f. 7v, 1.3.2). Christine as a reader, "solitary and separated from the world" ("solitaire et soustraite du monde," f. 7v), is thus singled out in her function as the privileged interlocutor of the three Virtues, but is also designated to construct the city which is not yet called a book. The genesis of this idea occasions a long discourse. This city is connected with mythical cities whose fame is echoed in books: Thebes, Troy, the Amazon Kingdom (f. 8v, 1.4.2), so that the distinction fades between the event and its written memory, its taking of literary form. The idea of the book is in coming. The effect of this metonymic relationship between book and city becomes more specific when it becomes evident that the city will serve to secure women in advance from the erroneous principle in which the reader Christine had stumbled ("to vanquish from the world the same error into which you had fallen," "pour forclorre du monde la semblable esreur où tu estoies encheute," f. 8r, 1.3.2). The book, in effect, becomes an instrument against ignorance. Finally, Reason conducts Christine to the field of writings, the *champ des escritures,* in order to dig the foundations with her pick of understanding, her "pioche d'Inquisicion" (f. 12r, 1.8.1). Henceforth, the relationship between city and book is forged.

One sees to what extent the mask which Christine wears occupies an essential place in the *Cité des Dames,* and quite naturally, the problem arises of the possible interpretation of the functions of the three allegorical figures associated with the construction project. It seems to me that one can see in them, consistent with the logic of masking, the three functions of the book. From the perspective of a specific interest in the book as such, the traditional moral values designated by these allegories are necessarily convertible into aesthetic categories. This situation applies in particular to Rectitude, whose attribute, the yardstick, lays down balanced proportions. The list of activities presided over by Rectitude ("frequenter entre les justes personnes, rendre à chascun ce qui est sien, dire et soustenir verité," and so on, f. 9v) is the epitome of the idea of proportion which supports the equation City equals Book. Rectitude incarnates a function going back to a central authorial preoccupation: distributing in a balanced way topics, sentences, and literary components—in short, everything that sustains and justifies the proportions between the elements of a specific book, proportions that arise from the technique of compilation. This same principle holds true for Justice, whose function cannot be superimposed over that of Rectitude. Her office is to "judge, distribute, and proportion according to the correct merits of everyone, to hold all things in balance" ("jugier, departir et faire la paie selons la droite desserte d'un chascun, de soustenir toutes choses en estat"). If Rectitude is the architect of the order, Justice renders the object fixed, not subject to imbalance. She inspires a body of lasting, harmonious relationships. Rectitude and Justice are the order and value that guarantee a literary yield. As for Reason, she carries a mirror that transmits the work's effect back to her, a principle of truth and unity. Christine does not gloss but expects the reader to do so. She lets the game play itself out. Behind the homiletic front a fabric of subtle and specific interrelationships is woven for each of the allegorical virtues. An approximative relationship exists between book and city. What was shown above establishes a foundation for the specific procedure that alone secures the book's interest as compilation. The dimension complies with the quality of proportion and unity that the three allegorical virtues guarantee. Their action is associated with that of Nature, who depicts astrologically ("pourtraict par les signes d'astrologie," f. 25v) the stones that Christine has built into the walls with her pen's trowel (*la truelle de sa plume*). This effect specifically reinforces the nature of the artefact, of the diagram traced in this way thanks to the exact and balanced measures of the book.

If it were a matter of taking measurements and determining proportions, this action could only be accomplished with reference to specific landmarks. At this point the essential alterity of this book begins to appear. It is a matter of measuring one thing against entirely different objects. The relationship to other objects implies therefore a constant relationship with books, an unwavering glance, and the attention paid to other books is never for a moment broken off anywhere in the *Cité des Dames*. But even before the compilation as such begins, one notices on Christine's part the compiler's tropism toward what fascinates her. What is important is less the content of the books cited than the gesture of turning toward the model, whatever it is, and pointing toward it. Within the *Cité des Dames* there is a body of literary attitudes and habits that announce the rise of a future system in the book, the compilation as such. The idea of books, of their abundance, of their diversity, is imprinted almost obsessively in the work. The opening miniature illustrates this attitude dramatically: books are everywhere, some open, some closed. The miniaturist has sought to create a climate. The point is to illustrate a veritable fetishism of the compiler and to signal in advance the vocation of writing founded upon reading. This vocation is apparent in any event in the body of the *Cité des Dames*, where the multiple references (authors' names, titles, citations) pile up as though these allusions prefigured a literary system. It is clear that before undertaking the great task of the book in the compilation, Christine mobilizes her attention to gather materials everywhere, announcing this attitude by indicating that books will be present.

III. First Signs

This taste for written objects is a precocious form of the spirit of compilation. Before treating the model that will be compiled, there is an approach and a waiting. The brief encounter with Petrarch, Boccaccio, or the others to whom Christine makes rapid allusion is a manner of creating a special condition, a form of incantation in the mouths of the allegorical Virtues who actually speak. In an excursus on the ingratitude of children toward their parents, Reason supports her arguments with Petrarch's *De remediis utriusque Fortunae* even before she draws on Boccaccio's *De claris mulieribus* for examples of filial piety which she will treat more extensively later (f. 72r). Signals are given even before the actual task of confrontation with the model begins. One cannot yet speak of the task of compilation but rather of a simple exercise of memory operating with a certain leeway. No rewriting has yet occurred, no reshaping of the text cited, but only a rapid allusion to an episode that runs through the argumentation.

But let us proceed further, for a more general problem arises regarding Christine's commitment as compiler. No compilation begins abruptly. For this reason, Christine has a reader raise questions to which the allegorical figures respond at length. It is no longer a question of fleeting allusions to authors, with short quotations woven into the body of the text, but of teasing out the question raised. One can focus here on the use of rhetorical shifts or of expatiations in the course of an exchange. Take an example: the question raised by Christine the reader in conformance with the system adopted at the outset brings to the foreground some alleged charge by antifeminists: women do not plead in courts of law or hand down judgments ("ne tiennent plaidoirie en court de justice . . . ne font jugemens," f. 21r, 1.11.1). Rectitude responds initially to the question raised by referring to an inequality founded in nature between men and women that justifies men's role in the legal system. But, continues Rectitude, if some claim that women lack sufficient understanding to learn the laws, the contrary has been manifestly demonstrated by the experience of many women (f. 21v). An important shift has taken place: Rectitude has displaced the problem from considering the notion of justice to addressing the idea of government. The more one continues, the more the first concept has been transcended. The shift is symptomatic of Christine's uncomfortable position as compiler. The allegorical virtues never respond directly but frequently reformulate the question in different and more general terms. Rather than a concerted effort to make the texts compiled enter into the logic of question and response, one must see these hesitations, these transferrals, in short, these shifts, as reflecting difficulties of the moment when the compiler has a text to be compiled in view.

The hesitations, the delays that arise from the literary undertaking should be examined in light of the *aporias* or unresolved doubts and questions that Christine as compiler puts to herself as she wonders how to begin her enterprise, which no preexisting order legitimates since its newness— "nouveleté" (f. 11v)—consists precisely in looking elsewhere for its materials. Christine's text necessarily raises a problem of identity. To the extent to which compilation is not an autonomous literary activity, Christine as compiler must search for her markings and underline them. Every gesticulation on her part signals that a compilation is about to be undertaken: parasitic arguments in an extended discourse, which attempt, by coiling back on themselves, to avoid or to deflect the question raised or to pick it up in a different form, as one saw above. Her techniques include dilations, suspense, rhetorical questions, an indignant pose (*antiphrasis,* irony), taking sides by the speaker, allusions to the most diverse facts with only an attenuated relationship to the question, sometimes even turning completely around the question that Christine as reader asks.

Opening such a more or less important space before beginning the compilation and revealing Christine's displacements and efforts as compiler to put herself in the right position is symptomatic of what is disturbing in the nature of compilation itself. One does not don borrowed garments improperly. Here lies the weakness of the compiler's position amply demonstrated in the techniques of shifting, gesticulation, and grimacing. The position of weakness is compensated for by an entire range of legitimizing activities that follow precisely the act of compilation proper.

IV. Recentering and Legitimacy

When the compiler is finished with the compilatory act itself, the work is far from complete. The work must still be legitimized to the extent that the compilation occasions a feeling of incompletion. This concern for legitimacy, a constant given of compilation, can take different forms. It can be accomplished by recalling the question raised and by making Christine as reader testify to the excellent choice of the compiled text (the women whose exemplary conduct has been cited weaken the arguments found in books). Recalling the question raised is the occasion for the compiler to return to the initial fiction, that of the assaults made on women in general ("generaument," f. 4r). It is a means of securing the book's organization at every moment: "Si me di, je t'en pri, où fu oncques homme qui ce faist? Et tu, comme folle, te tenoies nagaires mal content d'estre du sexe de telz creatures" (f. 67v). The course of the book is meant to recall its beginnings, what we have termed the posture of the indignant female reader.

By stressing the perennial feature of the scenario upon which the book is built, Christine finds a way to affirm the verisimilitude that she as compiler requires to support her undertaking.

In this process of evocation, Christine as compiler has her glance constantly fixed on her own activity. The compiler must always remember the initial point of departure, not forgetting to legitimize the entire operation. This manner of recentering is a definitional feature of compilation. For example, the compiler can stop to mark stages, to announce the coming of the book. The new kingdom of Femininity ("le nouvel royaume de Femmenie," f. 75r), whose coming Reason prophesies to Christine, constitutes the horizon of expectations in the book to come, that mass of stories that she will yet compile. In this way Christine takes the matter in hand again and makes a necessary point. She keeps a running account of her activity, sets up an inventory, maintains what has been acquired. Reason's prophecy of the Book in the very course of the fiction is a way of affirming an insecure position. Fear of losing her markings, of not finding materials to support her argument, constantly forces her to maintain a sharp focus. The reader must feel that there are phases and movements, that the work has been laid out according to measurements and a compass. The compiler needs to illuminate this perpetually threatened movement. This vigilance, this attention to the outlines of a course whose path must incessantly be marked out is a means of proclaiming the eminent dignity of a minor genre.

Recentering is a unique and fruitful notion for the compiler, because it permits legitimizing the work, of securing a coherence in the act of translating from one text to another. One of the examples will be supplied by the compiler's glancing at the series of texts created. Boccaccio, as is well known, had one celebrated woman follow another, without any intention of regrouping them, whereas Christine for her part organizes them in series. These series, this organization, which we will address below, need to be secured and gone over with a critical eye. Here lies one of the first effects of what one can call recentering. The story of Lilia provides a good example, introduced by the following sentence: "Et combien que la noble dame Lilie ne fut en propre personne en la bataille, ne fait elle bien a louer comme tres preux de ce qu'elle fist en admonestant Tierris son fils de retourner en la bataille?" (f. 37v, 1.22.1; "Although the noble lady Lilia was not personally present at the battle, should she not be greatly praised for her bravery in admonishing Theodoric her son, the valiant knight, to return to battle?") The story of Lilia, taken from the *Grandes Chroniques de France*, exemplifies a mother's feelings for her son. A distortion appears immediately. The overriding theme is that of female warriors. The example put forth exalts a mother's attitude toward her son's fleeing the battlefield. Christine can neither renounce the particular form of the story being compiled, the celebrated dignity of a mother confronted with a dishonorable son, nor undo the straight line that she has imposed as the rule in this particular series. But she finds a way by glossing her own compilation and thereby legitimizing the apparent difference. Thus she remarks, "Si me semble que l'onneur de ceste victoire doit plus estre atribuee a la mere que au fils" (f. 38v). She preserves the initial scenario, the mother's words which provoke her son's return to battle, and she maintains at the same time the alignment of examples chosen: the exaltation of female warriors. This manner of preserving her markings, of fine tuning her narrative, clarifies her concern for legitimizing her work, and it reflects, not the slavishness of compilation, but an optimistic way of measuring, of setting her yardstick. A further example can illustrate this recentering. After having compiled a relatively large number of stories inspired by Boccaccio's *De claris mulieribus*, all of which demonstrate how women have brought about decisive progress in civilization, Christine as compiler takes up and summarizes several stories already compiled—those of Ceres. Isis, and Minerva—to bring out the unity of the movement, the idea of progress not found in Boccaccio (ff. 51–52, 1.38.5).

This problem of recentering ceases to arise as soon as the question of regrouping the compiled *exempla* is no longer at stake. This situation arises in part 3 when Justice leads the Virgin and a procession of female saints into the finished city. Christine produces a litany—"letanie" (f. 139r)—of the lives of female saints drawn from Vincent de Beauvais's *Speculum historiale* or the *Golden Legend*. This litany presupposes that the interest in the book has been exhausted and that any measure to transform or control the content is useless. No vigilance is required.

V. Expropriating and Relinquishing Models

We have spoken of constitutive series. It is time to ascertain more precisely the particular form assumed by the process of compilation that supplies these series. The stories are to be put in direct relationship with the meaning of the questions raised by Christine as reader. These series are constituted around the subject matter evoked by the answers to the various questions. "Are women capable of judging?" and the examples pour in to answer, like an echo to the allegorical virtue's affirmative response. Certain questions are more fruitful than others (Are women brave, faithful, enterprising?) and attract texts as a magnet draws iron filings. Those subjects are cultivated rather than others that promise fainter echoes. In collections like Boccaccio's *De claris mulieribus*, examples are treated at random. In Boccaccio the stories of various women follow each other without thematic regrouping, somewhat by chance. He fails to discriminate among the component texts. Christine's first invention was to establish an order. Following the nature of the questions asked by Christine as reader, Christine as compiler establishes a sequence of celebrated women who have exercised political power, of learned women (poets, philosophers, sorcerers), of female founding figures, of female inventors (in agriculture, gardening, letters, arms, weaving), of past women who were masters in applied arts (painting, eloquence), and finally, women who offer edification by incarnating an exemplary moral position (constancy in love, filial piety, chastity). Christine as compiler organizes her stories according to the order of questions, as was evident. This regrouping constitutes a major instance of compilation as such, since it also commands the totality of operations by which the model assumes the status of compiled text. This translation constitutes the second aspect of our study of compilation as such.

This aspect of compilation has been the most studied, but practice here has been limited to drawing up the most exhaustive list possible of compiled models: Boccaccio essentially (*De claris mulieribus*, *Decameron*), the Bible, *Ovide moralisé*, the *Grandes Chroniques de France*, Vincent de Beauvais's *Speculum historiale*, the *Histoire romaine jusqu'à César*, among others. But the detailed work of measurement and adaptation must be observed more closely. All of these procedures are remarkably well staged in one story of the *Cité des Dames* that might be termed the *mise en abysme* of the compiler's activity. Christine as compiler thus lets us view an illustration of her own technique in the story of a woman writer, an example that Christine had borrowed from Boccaccio and reworks in conformance with her habits. Proba had frequented (*henter*) Vergil's work so much that she conceived the plan to rewrite the Old and New Testaments in grammatically correct Vergilian verse. The details of this operation are described: "[Elle] couroit, c'est a dire visetoit et lisoit . . . par merveilleux artifice et soubtiveté a son propos ordenneement vers entiers faisoit et les petites parties ensemble mettoit, et coupploit et lioit en gardant la loy, l'art et les mesures des piez et conjonctions des vers." (ff. 42v–43v, 1.29.1; "She would run through the *Eclogues*, then the *Georgics*, and the *Aeneid* of Vergil—that is, she would skim as she read . . . and through marvelous craftsmanship and conceptual subtlety, she was able to construct entire lines of orderly verse. She would put small pieces together, coupling and joining them, all the while respecting the metrical rules, art, and measure in the individual feet as well as in the conjoining of verses.") Her harvesting of Vergilian fragments was so skillful, so apt, that any reader would have thought Vergil had written it and was a prophet. There is a series of explanations spread throughout the story that cast light on the compiler's activity. To compile is a game playing off the same with the other. It means simultaneously remaining faithful to a text and reworking it by making it serve a different purpose than originally intended. The technical operations of the compiler are depicted in detail, and the description here carries a definitional value. It entails first the memorization of the text to be compiled (*henter, viseter*), then a selection of those parts which can be reused and grafted onto another text (*prendre, toucher*) and a new assemblage of these fragments selected in this way (*mettre, coupler, lier*), with the whole of this operation responding to a concern for order and unity (*ordenoit tant magistraument*).

The translation of one text into another, the body of operations that permit this alchemy (the selection and assembling of disparate elements) can serve as a definition of the specific work entailed in compilation. There is, it seems to me, a difference between a commonly recognized medieval practice that limits itself to only a few sources of inspiration, to taking up a theme or image or proper name, and a systematic procedure that elevates borrowing to a genre. The position Christine takes is revealed by the place assigned to the story of Proba within the *Cité des Dames*, a story that illuminates the entire work from the inside. This position confers on the detailed story of Proba a quasi-programmatic value and casts sudden light on the compiler's activity conceived as a signal of the model under treatment, as the body of manipulations effected on the model that the compiler simultaneously appropriates and betrays. We need to turn our attention now to several of these operations.

First, the compiler's work on the reference text is a reduction. Boccaccio, who insists in *De claris mulieribus* on the historical origin of the celebrated figures subsequently transformed into gods, attempts to establish a comparative chronology of the facts he relates. Christine has no use for his suppositions nor for his euhemerism. Generally, she eliminates certain historical and descriptive circumstances and selects one feature that seems to her to play a deciding role, a feature upon which she bases her narrative. In this regard the story of Semiramis is exemplary of a form of reduction (ff. 25–27r, 1.15). Boccaccio constructs his narrative in two balanced parts illustrating various aspects of the heroine's personality, at once martial and sexually perverted. Christine as compiler brushes aside the circumstances surrounding the incest without passing judgment on the act itself.[9] And to erase more effectively the unpleasant aspect of this character, which is inappropriate to her design, Christine as compiler invents a kind of mythic sociology that diminishes the horror of incest: Semiramis lived during the historical epoch of natural law. The reduction here is accompanied by a remodeling so as to suppress any notion of conflict in the central figure, which is a way of reducing the central figure to its essential aspect, fitness for rule.

Reworking the reference text is accomplished through reduction. The tendency to reduction whose multiple manifestations have often been uncovered has as its immediate consequence a certain tension of the new narrative into which passes only what is essential. Christine is rigorously concerned with demonstrating, a guideline for making use of texts that forces her to go straight to her goal. She keeps a close watch on herself because she is moved precisely by a concern for the unity of point of view that governs the compilation. She does not permit herself to diverge in the slightest from this strict discipline, even when she passes from one model to another, from the *De claris mulieribus* to the *Decameron*.

On four occasions Christine borrows the subject matter for her tales from the *Decameron*.[10] The recourse to a model, a direct borrowing (she read the *Decameron* in the original and used a translation for the *De claris mulieribus*) can be explained by the attraction that the model exerts over a compiler sensitive to the "sweetness of poetic language" (*doulceur du pouétique langaige*), but especially by the very nature of the model. The *Decameron*'s aesthetics are profoundly different from those of the often very brief tales in *De claris mulieribus*. With the stories recounted in the *Decameron*, one goes from founding myths to a narrative endowed with abrupt dramatizations and with tragic surprises whose backdrop is close to everyday life. In the stories of the *Decameron* the entry of the woman into a world filled with allurements, traps, and ambushes lends an even greater exemplary quality to the trials that she undergoes. Christine immediately availed herself of the profit that she could derive from these situations for her argument. But such taking into account of the qualities of the model does not prevent her from intervening once more and exercising the same violence toward the *Decameron* that she had shown toward the *De claris mulieribus*. In the ninth tale of the tenth day, Boccaccio tells of Griselda, whose long-suffering—patience—is tested by her husband. In the narrative Boccaccio is interested in the social origins of the woman whose fate he narrates. The moral lesson drawn from Griselda's renewed trials is that treasure can be born anywhere. Heaven, says Boccaccio toward the end of his story, can ordain that spirits endowed with divine grace be born in the poorest thatched huts; and, moreover, it is better for certain men to herd pigs than to govern other men. In all this, the story of Griselda, a unique model of faithfulness in love, takes on features belonging to social morality: the fact, for example, that Janicola, the poor father of Griselda, is conversing with his lord at the moment when the latter decides to make his marriage proposal. The model itself is not simple: a social perspective on women is combined with an edifying moral tale about them. Christine simplifies a complex story (f. 106r–110v, 2.50). When the character of Griselda is stripped of all its secondary traits in Boccaccio, it becomes an exemplary image of a single virtue, constancy, the compiled version of which requires illustration.

In the course of this analysis we have encountered an activity whose character lies both in the choice of models and in their treatment by Christine as compiler. The ways in which she intervenes are highly varied—one could multiply the examples. They accentuate the traits of women whose impression the compiler takes at the expense of the incidental features more characteristic of the authors of novellas. One of the literally subversive aspects of the compiler is that the compiler never narrates for the sake of narration, even though it is true that the compiler is always dependent on an interest to which as compiler he must respond. The compiler has the guarantee of a textual design, such as the general scenario, but within this scenario the compiler must suddenly remember the focus of the compilation, the question raised that governs the rewordings and necessary adjustments of the text.

VI. Autobiographical Effects

The manner in which the compiler mobilizes various literary techniques in reworking the model is undeniable. Every book possesses a quality that depends on the model and the compiler's reworking of it, on the effects that the compiler seeks to emphasize within a well-defined framework. Christine's architectural design compels her to measure her models exactly and to know what she must preserve and what she must eliminate so that the balance remains intact. This balance rests on the fictional coherence between the question that is raised and the answer that is supplied to it. The focusing of interest requires both an orientation and a submission to the reference text for the sake of argument. This obsession of the compiler is seen in a kind of writing that constantly does violence to its model. The displacement of references, suppression or amplification, contamination or hybridization of models betrays a kind of passion, the literary bias on the part of the compiler who takes liberties with the chosen text. The appearance of the subject through these variations and reversals is the most important aspect because it points to a hitherto unknown definition of compilation that runs counter to its ordinary meaning. Far from disappearing behind the models compiled, the compiler appears aroused to provocation. The practice of compilation demands a total commitment of the agent who improves, cuts, withdraws, or adds. Each intervention is an act of force. Compilation implies a game with "the other," and this discovery of otherness presupposes every time a displacement of the compiler's position, a different face. It can only be a kind of intellectual and affective violence that surveys texts with such a bias. Why do these reference texts give the impression that they are being used and not recopied unless it is because a single person has given the direction and imposed the color, and this person has done so in such a continuous and coherent way that it is no longer a question only of the adventurous domination of a text but of the violence shown by someone who wants to be what he is? Christine confronts the other text in order to be herself more effectively. The book opens with the image of Christine as reader under the command of allegorical entities in order to build the perfect city—*la cité parfaite*. In time the book reveals, through the literary means unleashed, a personality, that of the compiler, that presents itself to us with its needs and its literary bias. We must address this psychology of the compiler, and we must theorize on the personal positions that can be read transparently behind the compiled text.

Compilation presupposes at once an appropriation and a confrontation. Christine is an interventionist. This technique is a matter of a strategy, a will, and not of moods. The compiler indulges in tinkering with the compiled text. As with any patchwork, the compiler uses scraps, fragments, and pieces to construct a work whose design he or she alone is privy to. In responding to a question, the compiler approaches the foreign subject matter, which was not created a priori to serve the purposes of compilation, and selects and sorts out the arguments encountered. A critical review takes place to determine what can be pillaged, and a work is recomposed in differing degrees with selected pieces illustrating the particular subject that has been ordered up. One should not imagine that thinking has been surrendered during this process; instead, a kind of quest is here triumphant, a means of self-affirmation that goes hand in hand with the demands of a unique book.

This compilatory activism presupposes imagination and renewal, resurrection and development. Compilation is not an activity that can be pinpointed. To take account of compilation is not to draw a list of borrowings; literary criticism, by privileging source studies, ignores this movement. Compilation in Christine is a major act that does not take place to fill a void or to overcome ignorance but to amplify a radical passion. Compilation for her is a kind of pride because the book she writes is a novelty—*nouveleté*—whose creation she claims. And *nouveleté* must be understood in this sense, as the unique work of a female reader filled with enthusiasm and not as a book about women. Rather than being evidence for the compiler's scotomizing—for the compiler's blind spots—compilation is a means of flaunting *la fille d'escole*.

Compilation is a practice in itself. The compiler's responsibility is preeminently manifest here. It is seen in the stitching together of the models that are reworked, cut, and patched together. Christine recognized the pettiness and grandeur of this practice during the Quarrel of the *Rose*. Pettiness because, in her own words, "she did not climb the tall trees" ("elle ne va sur les grands arbres"),[11] because she depended on others, because she relied not

Figure 1. Reason, Rectitude, and Justice appear to Christine. Reason helps Christine build the City. Paris, Bibliothèque Nationale, ms. fr. 607, f. 2r°.

on a personal form of discourse but on a game that the compiler plays with models, on a game that never ends, because Christine never stops arranging her mirrors. Grandeur because in compiling she is conscious of responding to a sense of a vocation, the realization of the *cité parfaite* and of the unique book. Compilation for her is not an avatar of writing, but rather a way of finding and being herself. The work of compilation in Christine does not originate solely in the concern for taking refuge in the shelter of an idea that proves itself; it presupposes a passion, a bias whose stakes are precisely the affirmation of self. Her procedure is never disinterested. And the myth of the studious woman arises as the final result of a long process which begins with the mobilization of literary techniques.

The appropriation and relinquishment of reworked models defines the problem at the heart of the *Cité des Dames*. It is the book that should hold our attention, as the miniature opening the *Cité* directs us to do (figure 1). In elaborating this vignette, Christine flaunts a clear desire to emblematize the meaning of the literary work. The third miniature depicts the Virgin leading a procession of haloed women saints (figure 3). She is welcomed at the entrance of the City by Justice and Christine. In her right

Figure 2. Rectitude welcomes Christine and
companions to the City. Paris, Bibliothèque Nationale,
ms. fr. 607, f. 31v°.

hand the Virgin is carrying a closed book while the finished city stands before her. This arrangement of the picture focuses the reader's attention on
the destiny of the book, the event that it constitutes, for the book that the
Virgin, that supreme dedicatee, carries is situated at the center of the book,
over the city. The closed book and the finished city—two architectural designs—are thus superimposed. The book's destiny appears in the double
vision combining the book with the city, and the first miniature shows us
both the layout and the finished achievement. The juxtaposition of the two
designs (book and city) created by the bipartition of the first miniature corresponds in the third one to the superimposition of the two designs that link
book and city in the same destiny.

   The destiny of the book so conceived as the founding act of a city explains
the deeper meaning of the book, which is not the argument it parades, that
is, a defense of women. We have seen what meaning should be assigned to
the portrayal of the indignant female reader in the first pages of the book.
The reader serves as a mask, a persona, whose reactions should not be taken

Figure 3. Justice and Christine welcome the
Virgin and saints. Paris, Bibliothèque
Nationale, ms. fr. 607, f. 67v°.

literally. There is enormous bad faith entailed in this way of citing authors
"in general" (*generaument*), without actually citing them all by name, and
thereby generating the idea of a case brought against women from such
a poorly defined consensus. The polemic *pro et contra mulieribus* to which
Christine's pitch is attached belongs to a universal literary debate which in
fact has neither historical nor sociological referent. When Christine speaks
of books written against women, one must not view in this outburst a sign
of cultural obstruction, or even the designation of new stakes in the field of
social representation. Her claims do not betoken militancy but constitute a
kind of alibi dissimulating a literary need. The issue of Christine's feminism
is a pseudo-problem, even when one takes precautions in practice to avoid
excessive anachronism.

The pseudo-attention Christine pays to the arguments of her opponents
is manifest in the rhetorical effects that such a carefully prepared discourse
aims at: the examination of probabilities, the paraphrasing of such cowardly
reasoning, asides, parasitic arguments, long deliberations of questions. One

recognizes the mask and considers the irony that runs through the entire work.[12] This irony exposes the trap that is laid for every future reader. The idea of an antifeminist literary consensus that Christine attempts to sanction with so much bad faith is the pretext for the elaboration of the unique book. The New Kingdom of Femininity—*le nouvel royaume de Femmenie*—becomes assimilated with the founding of the first cities by the gods. Commanded by intermediary entities that have traced out the design in heaven, Christine herself elaborates the consummate workmanship of her book. The book is a diagram with its lines of force, its junctures, its distribution. The values imposed by the allegories are the values of order, of proportion, of equilibrium, and of harmony.

There can be no compilation without legitimation. The compiler is not an author but the operator of the text on others. This translation of one text into another is not an operation without further ramifications. It presupposes—and this is the meaning of legitimation—that one openly shows how the work is accomplished, in exposing where the pieces are stitched together, in pointing to the movement of approach taken by the compiler toward the model. This mobilization of the compiler, this constant legitimation of the procedure of compilation reveals in Christine's case a position of power, a triumphant commitment. She legitimizes her undertaking because she is sure of its newness, its *nouveleté*. Thus she enters into the circle of intellectuals who, during the first years of the fifteenth century, claim their recognition, their admission into the area of public interest. Henceforth legitimation takes on a different meaning from that of a literary bias. It will lead to claims of a more universal, more captivating nature.[13]

Notes

This paper is a revised version of a lecture given at Yale University, October 14, 1986. It was first published in French under the title "Compilation et legitimation au XVe siècle," *Poétique* 19 (1988): 139–57.

1. For a survey of this long critical tradition, of the excellent bibliography by Angus J. Kennedy, *Christine de Pizan: A Bibliographical Guide*, Research Bibliographies and Checklists, no. 42 (London: Grant and Cutler, 1984). In the enormous body of English-language criticism, we would single out the introduction by Earl Jeffrey Richards to his English translation, *The Book of the City of Ladies* (New York: Persea Books, 1982). It constitutes an interesting advance and a reorientation of literary criticism toward more immediate questions of literary construction and structure.

2. The development of compilation in the strict sense and its effect on the organization of the context of a book (drawing up of tables, index, concordances, etc.) has been studied by M. B. Parkes, "The Influence of the Concepts of Ordination

and Compilation on the Development of the Book," in *Medieval Learning and Literature: Essays Presented to Richard William Hunt*, ed. J. J. Alexander and M. T. Gibson (Oxford: Clarendon Press, 1976), 115–41. Little research has been done on the problem of compilation in Christine. One can, however, refer to several pertinent remarks by Jean-Louis Picherit, "Le *Livre de la Prod'hommie de l'homme* et le *Livre de Prudence* de Christine de Pizan: Chronologie, structure, et composition," *Moyen Age* 91 (1985): 381–413. On Christine's appropriation in *L'Avision* of a Boethian model taken from the *Consolation of Philosophy*, see Joël Blanchard, "Artefact littéraire et problématisation morale au XVe siècle," *Moyen Français* 17 (1985): 1–47. For a number of hints on compilation within the medieval tradition of historiography, see Bernard Guenée, *Histoire et culture historique dans l'Occident médiéval* (Paris: Aubier, 1980), 22–214.

3. Christine de Pizan, *Lavision-Christine*, ed. Mary Louise Towner (Washington, D.C.: Catholic University of America, 1932), 164.

4. Montaigne, *Les Essais*, ed. P. Villey (Paris: Presses universitaires de France, 1965), bk. 1, essay 26.

5. An unpublished edition of the *Livre de la Cité des Dames* exists, the 1975 Vanderbilt dissertation by Maureen Curnow (see *DAI* 36 (1975–76), 4536–37A). References here are to B.N. f.fr. 1178 and to the English translation.

6. Cf. Millard Meiss, *French Painting in the Time of Jean de Berry: The Limbourgs and Their Contemporaries* (New York: Pierpont Morgan Library, 1974), 1:12–15; (the miniatures of the *City of Ladies* Master are reproduced there in 2:33–45); Sandra L. Hindman, "With Ink and Mortar: Christine de Pizan's *Cité des Dames* (An Art Essay)," *Feminist Studies* 10 (1984): 457–84. In light of the argument proposed here concerning compilation, it is significant that Christine, with the aid of two or three trained copyists, sought to spread her own works. Concerning the activity of this small scriptorium, cf. Gilbert Ouy and Christine Reno, "Identification des autographes de Christine de Pizan," *Scriptorium* 34 (1980): 221–38, and Gilbert Ouy, "Une Enigme codicologique: Les Signatures des cahiers dans les manuscrits autographes et originaux de Christine de Pizan," in *Calames et cahiers: Mélanges de codicologie et de paléographie offerts à Léon Gilissen*, ed. J. Lemaire and E. van Balberghe (Brussels: Centre d'étude des manuscrits, 1985), 119–31.

7. Cf. Pierre-Yves Badel, *Le "Roman de la Rose" au XIVe siècle: Etude de la réception de l'oeuvre* (Geneva: Droz, 1980), 411–36.

8. In the fifteenth century this antifeminist literature consisted primarily of a body of clichés—proverbs and *sententiae* that circulated independently of their original context—which lacked a cultural and social resonance and which for the most part, as Badel correctly noted (*Le "Roman" au XIVe siècle*, 178–200), are taken from the *Rose*.

9. Cf. Liliane Dulac, "Un Mythe didactique chez Christine de Pizan: Sémiramis ou la veuve héroïque," in *Mélanges de philologie romane offerts à Charles Camproux* (Montpellier: C.E.O., 1978), 1:19–23.

10. Cf. Carla Bozzolo, "Il *Decamerone* come fonte del *Livre de la Cité des Dames di Christine de Pisan*," in *Miscellanea di studi e ricerche sul Quattrocento francese*, ed. Franco Simone (Turin: Giappichelli, 1966), 19–23.

11. Eric Hicks, ed., *Le Débat sur le "Roman de la Rose"* (Paris: Champion, 1977), 148.

12. The first pages of the *Livre de la Cité des Dames* illustrate this idea of masking. Is it not apparent that Reason raises the problem of speaking *par semblant* when she speaks of the poets' "farfelues, les mençonges trop mal coulourees" (f. 6v) which they commonly use? And Reason continues, "As far as the poets of whom you speak are concerned, do you not know that they spoke on many subjects in a fictional way and that often they mean the contrary of what their words openly say. . . . Thus I advise you to profit from their works and to interpret them in the manner in which they are intended in those passages where they attack women." ("Et des pouetes dont tu parles, ne sces tu pas bien que ilz ont parlé en plusieurs choses en maniere de fable et se veulent aucunes foiz entendre au contraire de ce que leurs diz demonstrent. . . . Si te conseille que tu faces ton prouffit de leurs diz et que tu l'entendes ainsi, quel que fust leur entente, és lieux ou il blasment les femmes," 1.2.2.) Christine has no difficulty, as one can see, in making use of this same strategy of rhetorical effect evoked by Reason.

13. Cf. Joël Blanchard, "L'Entrée du poète dans le champ politique au XVe siècle," *Annales ESC* 41 (1986): 43–61.

Christine de Pizan, the Conventions of Courtly Diction, and Italian Humanism

EARL JEFFREY RICHARDS

Non satis est pulchra esse poemata.
— HORACE, *Ars poetica*

Christine's poetics are closely linked to her political beliefs. Her transformation of lyrical conventions, her rejection of the *Roman de la Rose*, and her indebtedness to Petrarch and Boccaccio can be tied to her celebration of Charles V as the ideal monarch and her portrayal of France as the most "humane" nation. Christine's works creatively combine French and Italian traditions, providing a unique synthesis that also points to the affinities between Christine's lyrical and prose works, frequently considered separately from one another.

This division is based on two unspoken assumptions: first, that her shorter lyrical pieces are, at least formally, less interesting than the productions of her two great fourteenth-century predecessors, Machaut and Deschamps; and second, that Christine's shorter lyrical compositions, coming from the early part of her career, are apprentice pieces. Christine's own remarks in *L'Avision-Christine* (1405) have perhaps misled critics in this regard: "Adonc me pris a forgier choses jolies, a mon commencement plus legieres, et tout ainsi comme l'ouvrier qui de plus en plus son oeuvre s'asoubtille comme plus il la frequente, ainsi tousjours estudiant diverses matieres, mon sens de plus en plus s'imbuoit de choses estranges, amendant mon stile en plus grant soubtilleté et plus haulte matiere." [1] ("Then I began to compose pretty pieces, and when I first began lighter ones, and just like the artisan who makes his work more subtle the more he devotes himself to it, so too my mind, always studying different topics, became more and more imbued with alien matters, modifying my style to be much subtler and loftier.") Christine's remark that she modified her style under the influence of unnamed "choses estranges" ("alien," or "foreign," or "strange matters") provides a key to understanding her attitude toward the courtly conventions current in the late fourteenth century, because Christine, under the influence of Italian humanism, in fact did modify her compositions.

"Choses jolies"—the beautiful for its own sake—would cease to be of interest to her as she moved toward more lofty subjects, "plus haute matiere." For this reason, a prose/verse dichotomy affords little purchase in analyzing Christine's works. She consistently composed verse throughout her long career, so that it is inexact to consider her lyrics separately from her mature prose. What links her lyrics and prose is the move away from inherited formal categories. As Daniel Poirion has noted, the most characteristic feature of Christine's lyricism—and of her entire literary career—is its effort at transcendence or *dépassement,* [2] and this development in turn occurred in the broader context of poets who wrote after 1380, turning away from courtly forms as cultivated by Machaut. Christine clearly tried to go beyond the received conventions of courtly lyric. Prompted by the rehabilitation of Christine's originality as a lyric poet by recent scholarship,[3] I wish to compare the values informing her lyrical poetry and her prose compositions. Christine was acutely aware of the political implications of courtly literature in her time, and her manipulation of lyrical conventions reflects this consciousness.

I. Christine and the Limits of Lyrical Conventions

Daniel Poirion noted that Machaut's lyrical poetry used courtliness to refurbish the French royalty's position under Charles V and that the succeeding age, from 1380 to 1400, saw the composition of lyrical poetry that reflects considerable reserve toward this orientation, evidence for Poirion of a generational conflict.[4] Christine's lyrical works fit well into this second period. They reveal a dissatisfaction with courtly diction and with courtly narrative conventions, a fact that needs to be recalled when considering Christine's remarks during the Quarrel. Charity Cannon Willard suggested that one of the most recurrent features of Christine's lyrics is their persistent criticism of courtly love.[5] Christine's critique of courtly love extends beyond the form and conventions of courtly lyric, aiming directly at its implicit ideology, one that in Christine's time supported a corrupt and morally bankrupt political system.

Christine's lyrics are contemporary to attempts to systematize courtly poetry, as for instance, by Eustache Deschamps in his *Art de dictier et de fere chançons, balades, virelais, et rondeaux,* written in 1393. Christine's declaration in her letter to him, the "Epistre à Eustache Morel (February 10, 1403)", that she was his disciple is often taken as partial proof of the apprentice status of Christine's lyrics. In his reply, however, Deschamps did not hesitate to call attention to Christine's unique erudition,

Tes epistres et livres
Me font certain de la grant habondance
De ton sçavoir qui tousjours mouteplie,
Seule en tes faiz ou royaume de France.   (VI, 251–52)

(Your letters and books . . . make me certain of the enormous bounty
of the ever increasing knowledge which you, alone in your deeds in the
kingdom of France, possess.)

Christine's avowal shows above all her acute consciousness of both the social
status and the formal possibilities of lyric in the society of her time. Her
works are provocative when compared to earlier lyrics. Consider, for example, the prominence of grief and mourning in Christine's lyrics, a subject
quite explicitly barred from courtly lyric by Machaut. While Christine accepted the importance of honor in Machaut, a word strongly emphasized
at the beginning of his *Voir-Dit*, she took her grief as her lyrical point of
departure, departing radically from Machaut's championing of joy in the
prologue to his works.

Christine's partial disaffection with courtly convention may stem from a
belief that courtly lyric, particularly in Machaut's case, had become overly
artificial and virtually an end in itself. Jean de Meun and Machaut were
themselves acutely aware of the artifice of their craft but were content to
thematize rather than to criticize this feature. Christine would have agreed
with Horace that "non satis est pulchra esse poemata" (*Ars poetica* 99; "it
is not enough for poems to be beautiful," which is ironic, considering the
beauty of Horace's works), and as the quotation above from *L'Avision-
Christine* seems to indicate, moved from "composing pretty pieces" to more
lofty subjects. This overreliance on artifice entailed a flight on the part of
lyrical poets from the social upheavals of the fourteenth century. Machaut's
interiorization of the *Roman de la Rose* and its implicit poetic values illustrates this point. Perhaps dream visions are truer than reality; but in the
midst of civil disturbances, the potential vanity of cultivating such dreams
must have struck Christine as particularly galling, though she did herself make use of the dream vision format. Indeed, Jean de Meun's use of
noncourtly language in the *Rose*, far from calling courtly language into
question, celebrates the artificiality of the earlier lyrical tradition: it is no
coincidence that the great midpoint scene of the *Rose* celebrates the continuity of lyric poets who died in the service of love. Christine, as a careful
reader of Dante, must have rejected this view of poetic tradition and held
up to it instead Dante's vision of poetic continuity—the celebrated scene in
Limbo where Dante becomes the "sixth of that company" ("sesto tra cotanto
senno") which includes Homer, Vergil, Ovid, Lucan, and Horace.

By Christine's time the artificiality, narcissism, and endless celebration of convention for its own sake were tired devices. One indication of Christine's disaffection with such artificiality comes in the *Dit de Poissy*, in which Christine takes the stereotypic courtly conventions regarding female beauty and in an innovative move applies them to the male figure, rather than relying on the existing courtly stereotypes of male portraiture.[6] Barbara Altmann has pointed to Christine's description of male beauty in the *Dit de Poissy* (lines 1088–1167), which shocked late nineteenth-century (male) readers. As Altmann demonstrates, Christine's highly erotic portrayal of a man's body—and her description includes chest, buttocks, and thighs, features rarely mentioned in courtly literature—shows that Christine was no prude, the position she is often given for having criticized Jean de Meun's use of the word *coilles*. Her portrayal of male beauty shows she could make a convention function in a radically new context. Christine was aware of the hypocrisy of the *Rose*'s defenders, who themselves declined to use the words they championed.[7]

Courtly literature is itself surprisingly silent on courtly diction. Deschamps, for instance, says nothing about diction in his *Art de dictier*. Courtly literature primarily relied on convention and on rhetorical *topoi,* a feature that explains its subtlety, its delicacy, its insistence on the continuity between classical models and itself—the values of the *translatio* topos—even when such continuity is often forced and anachronistic, and its omnipresent nostalgia, which often entailed a confusion between cultural and political legitimacy. These same features when taken to an extreme explain its artifice, its implicit political conservatism (particularly in the hands of Machaut) and its frequent bloodlessness. The fabliaux poets exploited in particular the apparent conflict between noncourtly diction and the artifice of convention itself in order to underscore the role of conventions in courtly literature. It should also not be surprising that the *Rose* links conventions of courtly diction, the artificiality of poetic conventions, and irrationalism (or antirationalism). In other words, the *Enéas* poet, Chrétien, the fabliaux poets, Guillaume de Lorris, and Jean de Meun all share a fundamental belief in the artificiality of poetic diction which in some sense, at least partially, suspends linguistic referentiality. Dante, in the *De vulgari eloquentia*, wants it both ways, linguistic artifice combined with linguistic realism; he wants to combine *gramatica,* which is explicitly defined as an artificial secondary form of speech (*artificialis locutio secondaria*), with the linguistic realism of the vernacular. A conflict between the courtly paradigm of poetic language and a Dantean model of vernacular eloquence—which influenced Christine—seems virtually preprogrammed. Dante's own critical attitude toward courtly literature is clearly evident in *Inferno* 5's account of Paolo and Francesca's fateful reading of the *Prose Tristan*, whose conversion to adultery, as Robert Hollander has shown, parodies Augustine's conversion to Christianity, and who, as avid readers of courtly literature, acted as though they lived in some autonomous moral sphere. Christine's remarks in the "Epistre à Eustache Morel," written in 1403, only a year after the *Dit de la Rose* (which is generally taken as Christine's last contribution to the polemic), help demonstrate that her rejection of the *Rose* was founded on very profound poetic considerations that go to the heart of courtly literature itself.

Christine's calling herself Deschamps's disciple in this letter is an attempt to align herself with his emphasis on rhetorical clarity and lack of equivocation. In the *Art de dictier* he defines rhetoric in terms that must have appealed to Christine: "Rethorique est science de parler droictement [et] . . . tout bon rethoricien doit parler et dire ce qu'il veult moustrer *saigement, briefment, substancieusement* et *hardiement*" ("Rhetoric is the science of speaking directly [and] . . . every good rhetorician must speak and say what he wants to show *wisely, briefly, substantially* and *boldly*"). If one applies these four criteria to the *Roman de la Rose*, Guillaume de Lorris and particularly Jean de Meun, with his cultivation of digression, would fail, particularly in the areas of brevity and substance (though brevity was hardly Christine's strong suit either). For Christine, the appeal of Eustache Deschamps's definition—not his actual lyric—lies in the fact that it is diametrically opposed to the cultivation of linguistic and referential ambiguity in the *Roman de la Rose*. There, the principle that opposites gloss one another, by suspending the principle of noncontradiction, champions a preeminently irrational, indeed antirational, philosophy of literary discourse. According to this philosophy words are untethered from reality in a manner uncannily reminiscent of the fundamental deconstructionist claim regarding the ultimate ambiguity of linguistic referentiality, calling into question the possibility of difference itself. One needs to recall the pertinent passage in the *Rose* on glossing:

> Ainsinc va des contreres choses
> les unes sunt des autres gloses;
> et qui l'une an veust defenir,
> de l'autre li doit souvenir,
> ou ja, par nule antancion,
> n'i mettra diffinicion;
> car qui des .II. n'a connoissance,
> ja n'i connoistra differance,
> sans quoi ne peut venir en place
> diffinicion que l'an face.   (Lines 21543–52)

(Contraries work this way: the one is the gloss of the other; and whoever wants to define the one must remember the other, otherwise, despite his best intentions, he will never succeed in defining them; for whoever does not have cognizance of both will never understand the difference, without which a definition which one arrives at cannot be applied.)

In the *Rose* this principle of the interrelationship of contraries—the fact that one *significans* can refer to various contradictory *significata*—must recall Abelard's *Sic et non*, and the affinity of this principle to courtly literature is perhaps nowhere better illustrated and exploited than in Gottfried von Strassburg's *Tristan*.[8] In an important sense, the Quarrel over the *Rose* revolves around a dispute about the very nature of literature itself, in which different paradigms of vernacular eloquence collide with one another. The *Rose* champions an essentially formalist paradigm of literary composition. Seen from a Russian formalist point of view, the *Rose* serves as a classic example of "literariness": its use of digressions (not unlike that of Laurence Sterne in *Tristram Shandy*), its slowing down of the plot, its "defamiliarization" or "making strange" of courtly and Chartrian conventions, and its concomitant celebration of the artificiality of these conventions, are standard formalist criteria in determining the literariness of any particular work.[9] But it would be wrong to posit the *Rose* as the only kind of literary discourse possible, and it is specifically from this perspective that Christine's objections to the *Rose* need to be understood.

In examining the reasons behind Christine's rejection of the *Rose*, it is useful to remember that Christine showed herself sensitive to the distinctly literary merits of the work. She was not reacting like a prude or cranky philistine bluestocking, as Gustave Lanson would have us believe. Were her reactions so easily pigeonholed, they would hardly merit consideration. She praised both the diction and the prosody of the work, which nevertheless did not prevent her from rejecting it. As she admitted:

> Bien est vray que mon petit entendement y considère grant joliveté, en aucunes pars, tres sollennellement parler de ce qu'il veult dire—et par moult beaux termes et vers gracieux bien leonimes; ne mieulz ne pourroit estre dit plus soubtilment ne par mesurez trais de ce que il voult traictier. . . . Mon jugement confesse maistre Jean de Meun moult gran clerc soubtil et bien parlant, et trop meilleur oevre plus prouffitable et de sentement plus hault eust sceu mectre sus s'il s'i feust appliquié . . . je ne reppreuve mie *Le Rommant de la Rose* en toutes pars, car il y a de bonnes choses et bien dictes sans faille.[10]

> (It is quite true that my small intellect finds in it great prettiness, in some parts, and that he speaks most solemnly about what he wants to say—with extremely beautiful words and with graceful well-turned leonine verses; nor could what he wanted to treat have been better or more subtly or in measured phrases expressed. . . . My judgment acknowledges that Jean de Meun is a great and subtle clerk, and eloquent, and that he could have made a much better, more profitable work with

> loftier sentiment if he had applied himself at it. . . . I do not reprove the *Roman de la Rose* in all its parts, for there are many good things there, and doubtless well said.)

Christine's rejection of the *Rose*, therefore, had nothing to do with her failure to recognize the work's literary qualities. Indeed, she understood that the *Rose* is a profoundly unsettling work. Its subversiveness lies in its insistence on the artificiality of poetic diction, in its implicit but complicated rejection of linguistic referentiality, in its treatment of Reason, and in its utter self-absorption.

Christine, we must remember, was quick to discount any analogies between Dante and Jean de Meun, because the mixture of heaven and hell in Dante was for her a far cry from the *Rose*'s use of ecclesiastical and worldly elements. Gerson, Christine's ally in the Quarrel, was particularly shocked at this concatenation of sacred and secular elements in the work, and he noted: "Quant il [Jean de Meun] parle des choses saintes et divines et espirituelles, il mesle tantost paroles tres dissolues et esmouvans a toute ordure; et toutevois ordure ja n'entrera en paradis tel comme il descript" ("When he speaks of holy and divine matters, he sometimes mixes in extremely dissolute and filthy words; but filth will never enter into paradise as he describes it").[11] Gerson's aversion to the *Rose* stems from his abhorrence that a poet would describe holy subjects with words otherwise used to refer to filth. A poet's ability to compose such mixed verse is central to the *Rose* and to a large body of courtly literature, implying that *verba, significata,* and *res* are not indissolubly linked (for example, Chrétien often uses religious imagery or language to describe sex; and the fabliaux poets developed the convention even further in order to stress the artificiality of poetic diction).[12] Christine's objection is not to the conventionality or artificiality of poetic composition, but rather to poets' using these qualities as ends in themselves. (Perhaps the "radical ambiguity of Machaut's poetry"[13] is tied to his conservative political values.) Christine is working within the system of courtly conventions, to be sure, but she radically redefines those conventions, in an attempt to shift attention away from the overemphasis on the purely formal and contrived. Christine's attitude toward courtly conventions anticipates closely her redefinition of received political categories.

II. Humanism as an Alternative to Courtly Conventions

It is clear that Christine's relationship to her lyrical predecessors is considerably more complicated than a question of *lexis* and prosody. On ideological grounds, there seem to be curious parallels between Christine's critique of courtly conventions and later Renaissance humanist criticisms of medieval courtly romance, so much so that Christine's attitude toward courtly literature, far from being indicative of her opposition to humanism, as Coville long ago argued, can be directly tied to her humanist orientation and to her assimilation of Italian humanist thought.

Examining the later humanist critique of medieval romance as found in the writings of More, Erasmus, Coles, and Vives, Robert P. Adams listed four topics on which a clear courtly/humanist opposition is present, all four of which are directly anticipated and reflected in Christine's writings: (1) tyrants versus just kings; (2) a war-ridden and disintegrating late-medieval society versus a concept of a desired Renaissance social order of peace and Christian justice; (3) a conflict between two opposed codes of value (ethical, aesthetic, political, economic, and so on) involving radically different ideas of "honor," "glory," and human "greatness"; (4) opposed ideas of woman's nature and potential role in society.[14] Christine's treatment of Charles V as a just king in her biography falls under the first heading; her *Livre du corps de policie* and *Livre de la Paix* both fall under the second; her adaptation of courtly convention under the third; and her writings on women under the fourth. From the perspective of the history of Christine's reception it is perhaps significant that later French humanists such as Martin LeFranc and Clément Marot clearly esteemed Christine's works, and her *Cité des Dames* was frequently cited during both the Renaissance *querelle des femmes* and in eighteenth-century discussions of feminism.[15]

Christine's most immediate connections to humanism is evinced in the presence of Dante, Boccaccio, and Petrarch in her writings. While her indebtedness to Dante and Boccaccio has long been a subject of critical scrutiny, her relationship to Petrarch has been less so,[16] and it must be evaluated in the context of her relationship to Dante and Boccaccio. For example, Christine's use of Petrarch's version of the Griselda story in the *Cité des Dames*, 2.48, in order to refute Boccaccio might indicate that Petrarch's importance for Christine has been underestimated and requires reconsideration. The influence of Boccaccio on Christine has been clearly documented, and is generally taken to be more prevalent than that of Petrarch. An examination of Petrarch's influence on Christine, however, will demonstrate that, although Boccaccio is quantitatively more often her source than Petrarch, she frequently used Petrarch against Boccaccio, and that on a significant number of questions, she took her cue directly from Petrarch.

Christine was at home in both Italian and French literary traditions, "a child of two worlds," to recall Professor Willard's felicitous phrase. Her offer to Pierre Col in 1402 to explain passages from Dante's *Commedia* for his benefit in order to prove the superiority of the Italian work over the *Roman de la Rose* captures her situation. Her intermediary position seems also to be evidenced in the mistaken reception of the *Livre de la Cité des Dames* by its contemporary audience as a translation of Boccaccio's *De claris mulieribus* rather than as an original work, much less an implicit refutation of Boccaccio.

Where can one sketch out in very general terms the affinities between Christine and Petrarch? Christine may have taken her ideal of contemplative solitude from Petrarch. Her *Sept psaulmes allegorisés*, which treat the penitential psalms, may have been inspired in part by Petrarch's *Seven Penitential Psalms*, a copy of which was in the library of the duke of Berry.[17] Jean Gerson, Christine's ally in the Quarrel and an avid reader of Petrarch, also wrote an *Expositio super septem psalmos poenitentiales*. I would also add that Petrarch's appeal for Christine may have derived from his reputation as a moralist and as an allegorical author. Nicholas Mann has shown that the specific reception of Petrarch as a moralist is apparent in the works of Jean Gerson and Jean de Montreuil, Christine's adversary in the same dispute.[18]

Petrarch's reconciliation of classical and Christian literary culture must have also been attractive to Christine as an answer to Boccaccio's clear division between pagan and Christian history in *De claris mulieribus*.[19] At the same time, in general literary historical terms, Petrarch, inspired by Boethius, had developed for prose works (in a departure from the mixture of prose and verse in Boethius) the dialogue between himself as protagonist and allegorical personifications to its highest form in the fourteenth century.[20] Precisely this kind of treatment of allegorical personifications by Petrarch furnished an alternative model to the *Roman de la Rose* for writers like Christine who were disenchanted with the dubious moral quality of the French poem. Petrarch as author of *De remediis utriusque fortunae* could not have failed to interest Christine in her *Livre de la mutacion de Fortune*.

After looking at these general affinities between Christine and Petrarch, it is helpful to focus our analysis more sharply. I would suggest that Christine used Petrarch in the *Cité des Dames* in part as an authority against Boccaccio in two highly prominent ways: first, from the "Proemium" to Petrarch's *De viris illustribus* (1342/43; 1352/58) she took her ideal of compilation,[21] which she deliberately used as part of her opposition to the *Rose*, a work to which she refers at least twice during the Quarrel as a compilation ("compilacion du *Rommant de la Rose*");[22] and second, she used Petrarch's treatment of the Griselda story, contained in his *De oboedientia ac fide uxoria mythologia* (1373) to answer Boccaccio's version. Joël Blanchard has demonstrated how important Christine's textual strategy in the *Cité des Dames* depended on a skillful use of compilation and suggests that the model of compilation in general was Vincent de Beauvais.

One can be even more specific in determining a model in Christine's case.

Petrarch's remarks in the "Proemium" to *De viris illustribus*—a compilation
that differs from Boccaccio's *De claris mulieribus* in that it treats only positive
examples whereas Boccaccio had treated both positive and negative ones—
formulate a clear philosophy of compilation that is entirely compatible with
Christine's treatment of her sources, as Blanchard and others have shown,
and shows a certain creative variation on Christine's part. Compilation in
Christine is intended to create a new kind of book and entails a series of
shifts and displacements of source materials. Petrarch explained his compilatory practice in the following terms:

> Illustres itaque viros, quos excellenti quadam gloria floruisse doctissi-
> morum hominum ingenia memorie tradiderunt, eorumque laudes, quas
> in diversis libris tanquam sparsas ac disseminatas inveni, colligere locum
> in unum et quasi quodammodo constipare arbitratus sum. . . . Quoniam
> vero sicut in philosophicis aut poeticis rebus nova cudere gloriosum
> sic in historiis referendis vetitum, neque michi fabulam fingere sed
> historiam renarrare propositum est, et ideo oportet scriptorum clarissi-
> morum vestigiis insistere nec tamen verba transcribere sed res ipsas, non
> me fugit quantus labor in continenda sermonis dignitate suscipiendus
> sit. Nam, si nec eisdem verbis uti licet et clarioribus non datur, quid sit
> tertium patet. Ordinem quisque et dispersorum congeriem advertat et
> quod fideliter effeci grato animo suscipiat. . . . Nam ea que scripturus
> sum, quamvis apud alios auctores sint, non tamen ita penes eos collocata
> reperiuntur.[23]

> (I have therefore resolved to bring together in one place, and crowd
> together, after a fashion, the famous men who, as the talents of
> learned men report, flourished with singular renown, together with
> their praises, which I found scattered and disseminated in different
> books. . . . Since in fact just as in philosophic and poetic endeavors it is
> glorious to fashion new things, so by the same token it is forbidden in
> recounting history, nor is it my intention to invent a fable but instead
> to retell history. Therefore it is necessary to follow in the footsteps of
> the most famous writers, not to transcribe their words but the deeds
> themselves, nor does it escape me how much effort must be made to
> preserve the dignity of their discourse. For since it is not permitted
> to use the same words, and since better words are not available, it is
> obvious what alternative remains. Let the reader consequently turn his
> attention to the order and collection of the dispersed writings . . . and
> take up with a grateful mind what I have done faithfully . . . for what
> I have undertaken to write, although present in other authors, is not
> found brought together in this way.)

For Christine, Petrarch was the pioneer of compilation as a literary form
in itself. Christine translates Petrarch's achievement focusing on illustrious
men into a compilation about illustrious women.

Her debt to Petrarch's *Secretum* is even more apparent. The opening of the *Cité des Dames* seems modeled directly on the opening of Petrarch's *Secretum*, and the psychological situation of both autobiographical protagonists is remarkably similar; both are in a state of spiritual despair, or better put, *acedia*.[24] Recall that Petrarch tells how in the midst of one of his frequent meditations, while he was awake and not overcome by sleep, he sees a lady of indescribable age and radiance whose beauty transcends human intellection. Truth has appeared to him in order to free him from his errors. Of course Petrarch himself structured this opening scene following Boethius, and Boethius could have been, and was indeed, available to Christine as a model independent of any Petrarchan intermediary.

While commentators on the opening passages of Christine's *Cité des Dames* have detected very diffuse Boethian echoes, an examination of parallels between Petrarch and Christine will show a very distinct Petrarchan presence. Petrarch and Christine are both in the midst of studying when they receive allegorical visitors. Petrarch's self-depiction as "mihi quidem et sepissime cogitanti" ("to me, so typically sunk in thought") seems echoed in Christine's memorable self-portrayal in her study, surrounded by books "en la frequentation d'estude de lettres." The Boethian given of both works could not be more conventional: a protagonist requires the intervention of an allegorical entity in order to free himself from some moral error—in Petrarch's case, his less than satisfactory renunciation of the life of this world; in Christine's case, her failure to understand the true historical position of women and her resulting despair. Significantly, the exchanges in both works occur while both protagonists are wide awake. Petrarch notes, "Contingit nuper ut non, sicut egros animos solet, somnus opprimeret, sed anxium atque pervigilem" ("It happened recently, not while sleep oppressed me as is wont to befall ailing souls, but while I was anxious and watchful"). Christine says of herself, "Tressailly adoncques si comme se je feusse resveillee de somme" ("I shuddered then, as if wakened from sleep"). Christine's waking state alludes both to the last lines of the *Rose*—her watchfulness contrasts with the dream of the *Rose*—and it also recalls Petrarch's anxious watchfulness in the *Secretum*. For Christine, resolute critic of the *Rose*, the only protagonist to be taken seriously must be an alert and awake one, and she found in Petrarch's *Secretum* the literary sanction for exactly such a protagonist. Petrarch in the *Secretum* and *De remediis* furnished a model of allegory that fit Christine's purpose. Admittedly, Christine's lengthy description of her devotion to study and to letters expands drastically on Petrarch's laconic "mihi quidem et sepissime cogitanti," but even this kind of rhetorical amplification can be expected in the shift from Latin to vernacular. Latin poetry was ipso facto learned; vernacular not necessarily so.

Christine, as Maureen Curnow demonstrated on the basis of clear verbal parallels, utilized Philippe de Mézières's translation of Petrarch's *De oboedentia ac fide uxoria mythologia* (1373) in recounting the Griselda story in the *Cité des Dames*, 2.50. Only two chapters later she returns to Boccaccio as her source to recount the story of the wife of Bernabo, originally found in the *Decameron*, Second Day, Ninth Tale. Significantly, in redoing the story of Bernabo's wife, Christine shortens the original and places considerably more emphasis than Boccaccio on the moral implications of wifely constancy. By the same token, Petrarch's version of Griselda is also more "moral" and didactic than Boccaccio's tale, and Petrarch stressed this aspect in his dedicatory epistle, addressed to Boccaccio himself: "Hanc historiam stilo nunc alio retexere visum fuit, non tam ideo, ut matronas nostri temporis ad imitandum huius uxoris patientiam, quae mihi vix imitabilis videtur, quam ut legentes ad imitandam saltem foeminae constantiam excitarem." ("It seemed appropriate to reclothe this story now in a different style, not so much so that I wanted to urge married women of our time to imitate the suffering of this wife, which strikes me as hardly imitable, as to inspire readers at least to imitate this woman's constancy.") The question arises why Christine switched from her usual source, Boccaccio, to Petrarch. With both Griselda and the wife of Bernabo, Christine shortens her originals and lays much more emphasis on the moral implications of wifely constancy. Christine was motivated to use Petrarch's version in order to sharpen the moral edge of her account. Petrarch himself had retold the Griselda story, it seems, in order to correct Boccaccio, and Christine had understood this intention on Petrarch's part.

In addition to these textual presences of Petrarch in Christine's work, the two writers both shared a hostile attitude toward the *Roman de la Rose*. Petrarch's aversion to the *Rose* is well known to students of Franco-Italian literature.[25] In his letter to Guido Gonzaga from 1340, Petrarch claimed that the obvious shortcomings of the *Rose* were proof of the superiority of Italian eloquence. This same argument forms the basis of Christine's critique some sixty years later concerning the *Commedia*'s superiority over the *Rose*. In the history of the reception of the *Rose*, Petrarch's and Christine's remarks, which shared an openly expressed hostility to the French romance, are, to the best of my knowledge, perhaps the only examples for this early period of a less than enthusiastic response to the poem. Perhaps Christine took her cue from Petrarch, but in all events her critique of the *Rose* continues Petrarch's. Both disliked the *Rose* as a model of vernacular eloquence. The affinities between Petrarch and Christine must be more than coincidental.

The likelihood that Christine was moved to criticize the *Rose* on the moral authority of Petrarch seems substantial. Scholars of the Quarrel have hitherto had difficulties in ascertaining Christine's motives for criticizing the *Rose* and have generally supposed that protofeminist reasons played an important role. But Christine's opposition to the *Rose* does not only revolve around the slander of women there. The Quarrel over the *Rose* thus arose in part from the collision of different paradigms of literary creation and of vernacular eloquence: that implicit in the *Roman de la Rose* and the courtly lyrical tradition of a Machaut, that of Dante, and that of Petrarch. One must above all recall that there was no single or monolithic medieval paradigm of vernacular eloquence, that many vernacular writers had radically conflicting notions of their relationship to Latinity.

Let me illustrate briefly what the competition between these various paradigms meant in early fifteenth-century terms. It is clear on the basis of evidence that I have already published that Christine extrapolated from her knowledge of the *Commedia* certain notions regarding vernacular eloquence.[26] She did not know, and for codicological reasons could not have known, Dante's *De vulgari eloquentia*. But the selectivity exhibited in her use of Dante shows that she understood clearly the ideals of erudition and linguistic realism which are the touchstones of Dante's theory of poetic language and that she tried in her own works to imitate in French terms Dante's pioneering lexical innovations. In textual terms, Dante's influence on Christine translates into an appreciation of the learnedness of Latin but a turning away from Latin as the language of poetic composition. While Christine shared Petrarch's aversion to the *Rose*, she was far more positively disposed toward Dante, stressing in her letter to Pierre Col, dated October 2, 1402, that the *Commedia* was "a hundred times better written" (*cent fois mieux composé*) than the *Rose*. Since she strongly disapproved of Jean de Meun's use of the word *coilles*, "testicles," Dante's gently referring to them by silence, "è più bello/tacer che dire" (*Purgatorio* 25.43–4, "passing over in silence is more fair than speaking," a phrase also used in Limbo to characterize Dante's conversations with the great poets of antiquity) must have been immensely appealing to her. Christine, as an intermediary of Italian literary culture in France, felt free to combine and to recast her Italian sources. Petrarch represents a revalorization of Latin as a poetic language and a deemphasis of the vernacular, whereas the *Rose* and Dante both stress, albeit with decidedly different orientation, the ideal of literary continuity between classical and vernacular poets, of the values associated with the topos of *translatio studii*. But for Christine the French poem suffered from superficiality, antirationality, and immorality, with its allegory in no way approaching that of Dante's in complexity, density, or dignity, and it was therefore a defective paradigm of vernacular eloquence.

III. The Revolutionary Nature of Christine's Work

What emerges from Christine's work is a consistent, generally implicit but nevertheless clear-cut critique of courtly values that reworks and transforms inherited and highly rigid hierarchical categories. Christine's writings are essentially humanist with a courtly veneer. This conclusion might seem at first surprising, since Christine's work reflects particularly on its surface all of the rituals of courtly hierarchy, etiquette, and ceremony. Christine's mastery of these courtly forms and categories—both social and literary—is essential to her own implicit ideological program and should not be construed as Christine's automatic or obligatory identification with them. As Norbert Elias showed in his study *Die höfische Gesellschaft, Untersuchungen zur Soziologie des Königtums und der höfischen Aristokratie*,[27] ceremonies and rituals have a far greater significance in courtly societies than in bourgeois ones and are indicative of the division and structure of power.

These observations are obvious, of course, but bear repeating before one tries to evaluate the ideological import of Christine's use of courtly categories. Christine's *Livre du corps de policie* (1404–7) is perhaps her most overtly political work. It sets out to expound on the political and social duties of each estate in society and comes out clearly against the participation of the third estate—students, clergy, merchants, artisans, and workers —in government, though she states that it is a sin to be ungrateful for the services which they perform ("Si est pechie d'estre ingrat de tant des services comme ilz nous font," 199). Christine was attached to the royal court, was the biographer of Charles V, and, taking her cue from the civil unrest in many Italian cities during the fourteenth century, was against popular rule. Yet the essence of her political position was to force men in ruling positions to live up to their own standards.[28] Her own *Livre du corps de policie* begins with Christine claiming the right to speak out politically as a woman and overcome the ignorance and silence men impose on the female sex, and this demand is followed quickly by an appeal to virtue:

> Ainsi que pluseurs hommes au sexe feminin imposent non-sçavoir taire ne tenir soubz silence l'abondance des leurs corages, or viengne donc hors hardiement et se demonstre par plusiers ruisseaux la sourse et fontaine intarissable de mon corage qui ne peut estanchier de getter hors les desirs de vertu. O vertu chose digne et deifice, comment m'ose je vanter de parler de toy quant je cognoys que mon entendement ne te sçauroit pas bien au vif comprendre ne exprimer.[29]

> (Since many men force the female sex to ignore, to silence, or to censure the abundance of their hearts, now let the source and inexhaustible

fountain of my heart—which cannot be stopped from pouring forth
its desire for virtue—bravely come forward and show itself in so many
rivers! O worthy and divine virtue, how can I dare boast to speak of you
when I know that my intellect cannot grasp or express you vividly?)

While some of the content of Christine's political writings is monarchical
and antidemocratic, the fact remains that Christine is first and foremost
claiming women's right to speak politically. The male hierarchy is not overturned, but Christine exposes its hypocrisy and double standard nevertheless. Christine's earlier use of hierarchy in the *Cité des Dames* is easily comparable: women from all estates are admitted to the City of Ladies, and
the social category of inherited nobility is borrowed to designate quite a
different kind of nobility. In evaluating Christine's political message it is
also important to consider what Christine either only implies or deliberately omits. Christine, for example, does not openly denounce the corruption of the Church in her own time but simply relies on implicit comparisons and on ellipsis to get her message across: "Et pareillement je te dis
des pappes et des gens de sainte Eglise, qui plus que autre gent doivent
estre parfais et esleuz. Mais quoyque au commancement de la christienté
fussent sains, depuis que Constantin ot douee l'eglise de grans revenues et
de richesces la saintité qui y est . . . ne fault que lire en leurs gestes et
croniques."[30] ("Let me also tell you about the popes and churchmen, who
must be more perfect and more elect than other people. But whereas in the
early Church they were holy, ever since Constantine endowed the Church
with large revenues and riches, the remaining holiness . . . well, you only
have to read through their histories and chronicles.") This example—one of
the few where Christine deliberately broke off a thought in mid-sentence—
is telling of Christine's skill in making a political statement without appearing to do so, and she ends the section from which the quotation above is
taken by saying, "Si me tairay a tant de ce" ("The point is clear, I won't say
more"). Maureen Curnow in a note on the passage speculates, "This seems
to be a willful ellipsis; perhaps Christine did not dare to write further criticisms of the Church."[31] In the context of her writings, the critique is clear
enough, albeit more implicit than explicit.

Recently, Sheila Delany has launched a major political criticism of Christine, calling into question the alleged "revolutionary" nature of Christine's
writings: "I have been charmed by some of her lyrics, impressed by her
determination to educate herself and above all by her will to write. Yet I
have also been terminally bored by the tedious, mind-numbing, bureau-
cratic prose of the *Cité des Dames*, imitated from the style of royal notaries
and civil servants. I have been angered by Christine's self-righteousness,
her prudery, and the intensely self-serving narrowness of her views."[32] It
is wrong to characterize Christine as revolutionary, we are told, because
Christine was "in the rearguard of the social thought of the period," and,

like King Canute trying to beat back the tide with a broom, "Christine tries to beat back the tide of social change, of protest and nascent democracy, with her little broom of pious anecdotes and exhortations gathered from the Bible and other ancient authorities. In a time when even courtiers and clerics wanted change, Christine continues in her quiet neo-Platonic hierarchies and her feudal nostalgia."[33]

Delany has interpreted Christine out of context. She takes the term *revolutionary* as used earlier by this writer as synonymous with her own understanding of contemporary radical politics and anachronistically projects this contemporary frame of reference onto the early fifteenth century. With her loyalty to the French monarchy Christine, we are told, was "the Rosemary Woods of her day" (Richard Nixon's secretary, who claimed during the Watergate affair that she had accidentally erased the infamous Oval Office tapes). Since Christine sided with Gerson in opposing the "dirty talk" in the *Rose*, she was "a Phyllis Schlafly of the Middle Ages," though it is doubtful that Phyllis Schlafly would have written anything like the description of the male physique in the *Dit de Poissy*. Delany alleges that Christine opened up the Quarrel of the *Rose* in order to enhance her position at the French court, a clear-cut example of blatant political opportunism. She did not have to write, after all, observes Delany; she could have gone into the book trade, but no, Christine consciously chose to support the oppressors of the urban working classes. Nowhere in the entire *Cité des Dames* do we have a single woman from the working class named, irrefutable evidence of Christine's aversion to the urban proletariat. Since Christine was against popular democracy, and since her age was one of enormous political and social upheaval, obviously Christine was on the side of the oppressors. Thus concludes what Delany herself calls her "short dossier."

Delany has read Christine too quickly. For example, in the *Livre de la Paix* (3.11), Christine condemns "celle diabolique assemblee" but she does not condemn "political meetings" per se, as Delany claims, but rather such assemblies when they turn into ravaging mobs. Moreover, although tensions among classes or estates were pronounced in late medieval society, the important matter is that in the midst of these tensions Christine spoke out as a woman and claimed her right to speak out as a woman. As Rodney Hilton points out in his article "Ideology and Social Order in Late Medieval England," the emphasis on social harmony in writings from the beginning of the fifteenth century was a typical reaction to social upheaval: "Particularly up to the middle of the [fifteenth] century, there was evidently a sharp perception by the writers and their patrons that peasants and artisans were making significant advances in the social and economic sphere and might well be mobilised politically. To answer this it was important to justify the existing order in terms of celestially sanctioned harmony."[34]

Christine's use of social hierarchy to sanction harmony could simply be taken at face value in an uncareful reading, and not as the veiled admonition it is. Christine, however, consistently thematized her right as a woman to speak out, and, as Hilton is also quick to point out, the arguments circulating in the early fifteenth century on behalf of social hierarchy categorically prescribed women's nonparticipation in political discussions. He quotes both Hoccleve's early fifteenth-century remark, "Some women eke thogh her wit be thynne, / wole argumentes make in holy writ" ("Even some women, though their intelligence is slight, will argue about the holy scriptures"), and a sermon writer of the same period who advised women, "It is enough to thee to believe as Holy Church teacheth thee, and let the clerks alone with the argument." The "exclusion of women and plebeians from discussions about doctrine" is precisely what Christine answers when she celebrates Joan of Arc, the most prominent woman in the early fifteenth century to defy the strictures of male ecclesiastics. Her endorsement of social hierarchy forms part of her overall claim that men have subverted the ideal hierarchy in order to oppress women, and that, by implication, if the hierarchy could only be "restored," (Christine does not use the word herself), then justice could be achieved, though surely Christine had no illusions about the status of women in the past.

Christine's conciliatory position between king and people is clear in the ballade "Trop hardement et grant presumpcion."[35] In this *ballade* she condemns those who write against the princess, calling it a sin, but at the same time she pointedly ends the poem by saying that a ruler should not raise a sword against the people or against those who write against the princes, using the same refrain to call such action a sin as well:

> Pour ceulx le di, qui, par destraccion,
> Osent blasmer princes, pour enflamer
> Peupple contre eulx par grief commossion,
> Et les osent, ours, lyons, loups nommer
> . . . .
> Je dis que c'est pechié a qui le fait.
>
> Sy ne faites, bons François, mencion,
> Que vous ayés tirans fiers plains d'amer;
> Laissiez parler a autre nacion;
> Car ne sçavés qu'est tirant, et semer
> Souffrez a tort telz dis
>   . . . c'est chose ville
> De soustenir contre eulx si grant tort fait.
> Et de ditter balades de tel stille.
> Je dis que c'est pechié a qui le fait.
>
> Princes poissans, criminelle ou civille
> Vengenance pour telz diz en voz cuers n'ait;

Car qui glaive contre son puepple affille,
Je dis que c'est pechié a qui le fait.   (Lines 11–14, 20–25, 27–34)

(I say it for those who by distraction dare to blame princes in order to
incite the people against them by stirring up grievances and dare to call
them bears, lions and wolves . . . I say to whoever does it that it is a sin;
therefore, good French, do not claim that you have proud tyrants filled
with gall; let another nation talk like that; for you do not know what a
tyrant is; and you wrongly allow such writings to be disseminated . . .
It is a vile thing to compose ballades in such a style. I say to whoever
does it that it is a sin. Mighty princes, let there be no criminal or civil
vengeance in your hearts because of these writings, for whoever raises
his sword against his people, I say to whoever does it that it is a sin.)

The refrain is used skillfully to convey a political message to all parties concerned. The poem above should not be seen as a reactionary denunciation of
antimonarchical works (it would be easy to do so) but as a reminder to the
princes to govern humanely.

Christine was a monarchist, it is true, but her conception of the role of
the monarchy within the French nation was itself innovative within the context of her time. Franz Walter Müller analyzed Christine's attitude toward
France as part of a much larger study.[36] Since Delany has taken pains to characterize her own analysis of Christine as Marxian, one cannot fail to notice
that the analysis brought forth by Müller—whose own Marxian creden-
tials are solid and widely recognized, at least within the German-speaking
world—is conspicuously absent from Delany's dossier against Christine.
Müller found that the *ballade* quoted above was particularly critical because
it views the French nation as one body of subjects under the king rather
than an entity divided along estate lines, and because it invoked a new
ideal of humanity that anticipated later developments in humanist political
thought. By comparison, for example, Müller demonstrated with extensive
documentation that Machaut's works, by cultivating the delicate but petrified conventions of courtly lyric, serve as a mirror for the ruling feudal
estates and implicitly favor a kind of class separatism. According to Müller,
the historical challenge for political thought in the early fifteenth century,
after all the social upheaval of the mid- and late fourteenth century, was
to develop a unifying nationalist ideology that transcended estate divisions.
Courtly literature in the form in which it existed and was cultivated during
most of the fourteenth century was unsuited for this challenge.

Remarkably, it was Christine who pioneered a breakthrough in her concept of the French nation, and for Christine, France holds the first place
among nations, primarily because of its humanity rather than because of
its exemplary Christianity, a shift which for Müller marks the transition
from feudalism to a Renaissance princely ideal. Consider the remarks that
Christine makes that serve as the basis for Müller's observations:

>Mais Dieu mercy en France n'avons mie princes crueulx ne plains de sang contre leur peuple. Car de toutes les nacions du monde je l'ose dire sans flaterie, car il est vray, n'a tant benignes princes ne tant humains qu'il y a en France; et de tant leur doit estre plus doulcement obey. En quoy que aucunesfoys il semble par aventure au peuple qu'il soit grevé et chargié, ne cuident point que autre part, c'est assçavoir es aultres royaumes ou pays le peuple soit moins grevé que celui de France.[37]

>(But thank God in France we do not have cruel or bloodthirsty princes turned against the people. For of all the nations of the world—and I dare say it without flattery, for it is true—there are not so many kind or humane princes as in France, and these must, by the same token, be all the more readily obeyed. And although sometimes it perhaps seems to the people that they are oppressed and burdened, they should not think that anywhere else, that is, in other kingdoms or countries, that the people is less oppressed than in France.)

Christine's rhetorical strategy should be apparent: she raises the questions of princely humanity and social oppression and couches her remarks in a highly idealistic pose. By the same token, her biography of Charles V is not an exercise in political nostalgia but, like later humanist mirrors for princes, an indirect means of positing a princely ideal for an age rampant in political abuses. As Thelma Fenster noted to this writer, Christine almost always works with indirection or irony. She applies new categories to discuss political realities, moving away from the Christianity used by the thirteenth-century *Grandes chroniques de France* to justify royal power to a new secular ideal of humanity in which comparisons regarding social oppression can openly be drawn. Beneath Christine's conciliatory language is a clear, albeit implicit, political message that is closely tied to the emergence of humanism. Unlike Delany, Müller is categoric in assigning Christine a decisive role in the emergence of a new consciousness of French national unity that transcends earlier estate conflicts and that is based on the new ideal of humanity.[37]

What emerges from this examination of the connections among Christine's lyrical works, her position during the Quarrel of the *Rose*, the influence of humanist thought in her works, and her championing of an ideal of humanity is a more balanced view of the profound coherence underlying Christine's work, a fuller understanding of the poetological values that stand behind her works and that led to a penetrating transformation of courtly conventions, and an appreciation of the consistently provocative, innovative, and, within the context of her time, revolutionary nature of her writings. The better we understand the late fourteenth- and early fifteenth-century literary historical and social context of Christine's works, the more clearly we will perceive the impressive unity of her thought.

Notes

1. *Lavision-Christine*, ed. Mary Louise Towner (Washington, D.C.: Catholic University of America, 1932), 164.

2. Daniel Poirion, *Le Poète et le prince: L'Évolution du lyrisme courtois de Guillaume de Machaut à Charles d'Orléans* (Paris: Presses universitaires de France, 1965), 254.

3. In addition to Suzanne Bagoly, "Christine de Pizan et l'art de 'dictier' ballades," *Moyen Age* 92 (1986): 41–67, the essays by Barbara Altmann, Nadia Margolis, Patricia Stäblein-Harris and Lori Walters in this volume facilitate a new understanding of the creative nature of Christine's lyrics.

4. Poirion, *Le Poète et le prince*, 616.

5. In *Court and Poet: Selected Proceedings of the Third Congress of the International Courtly Literature Society (Liverpool, 1980)*, ed. Glyn S. Burgess (Liverpool: F. Cairns, 1981), 357–64.

6. Cf. Alice M. Colby[-Hall], *The Portrait in Twelfth-Century French Literature: An Example of the Stylistic Originality of Chrétien de Troyes* (Geneva: Droz, 1965), 60–62. Courtly literature contains, as Colby-Hall demonstrates, relatively few descriptions of male beauty, and none of the examples she gives seem quite as extensive or as detailed as Christine's.

7. See Thelma Fenster's essay in this volume for details on this point.

8. Cf. Hans Fromm, "Gottfried von Strassburg und Abaelard," in *Festschrift für Ingeborg Schröbler zum 65. Geburtstag*, ed. Dietrich Schmidtke and Helga Schüppert (Tübingen: Niemeyer, 1973), 196–216.

9. Cf. Victor Erlich, *Russian Formalism, History—Doctrine* (The Hague: Mouton, 1955), 145–63.

10. Eric Hicks, ed., *Le Débat sur le "Roman de la Rose"* (Paris: Champion, 1977), 13, 10–21.

11. Ibid., 62.

12. Arno Borst in *Der Turm von Babel* documents the disagreement among early Christian thinkers regarding the connections between words and objects. Augustine, it will be remembered, noted that objects are not Hebrew, Greek, Latin, or barbarian, whereas Isidore of Seville viewed etymology as a means of connecting words to their objects. For the use of religious language to describe sex, see my article "Le Problème du langage poétique dans les fabliaux et dans le *Roman de la Rose*," in *Actes du Quatrième colloque international "Épopée animal, fable, fabliau" (Évreux, 1981)*, Publications de l'Université de Rouen (Paris: Presses universitaires de France, 1985), 469–80.

13. Jacqueline Cerquiglini, *"Un engin si soutil": Guillaume de Machaut et l'écriture au XIVe siècle* (Geneva: Slatkine, 1985), 245.

14. Robert P. Adams, "Bold Bawdry and Open Manslaughter: The English New Humanist Attack on Medieval Romance," *Huntington Library Quarterly* 23 (1959–60): 33–48; the quotation here is from pp. 34–35.

15. See my article "The Medieval *Femme Auteur* as a Provocation to Literary History: Eighteenth-Century Readers of Christine de Pizan," in *Visitors to the City: Readers of Christine de Pizan*, ed. Glenda McLeod, Michigan Medieval Monographs.

16. Patricia A. Phillippy, "Establishing Authority: Boccaccio's *De claris mulieri-*

bus and Christine de Pizan's *Le Livre de la Cité des Dames*," *Romanic Review* 57 (1986): 167–94.

17. This possibility was first raised by Charity Cannon Willard in her review of Rains's edition of the *Sept psaulmes allegorisés* in *Romance Philology* 21 (1967/68): 132–33.

18. Nicholas Mann, "La Fortune de Pétrarque en France: Recherches sur le 'De remediis,' " *Studi Francesi* 13 (1969): 3–13; "Petrarch's Role as Moralist in Fifteenth-Century France," in *Humanism in France at the End of the Middle Ages and in the Early Renaissance*, ed. A. H. T. Levi (Manchester, England: Manchester University Press, 1970), 6–28; "La prima fortuna del Petrarca in Inghilterra," in *Il Petrarca ad Arquà*, ed. Giuseppe Billanovich and Giuseppe Frasso (Padua: Antenore, 1975), 279–89.

19. Cf. Giulio Augusto Levi, "Pensiero classico e pensiero cristiano nel *Secretum* e nelle *Familiari* del Petrarca," *Atene e Roma* 35 (1933): 63–82.

20. Cf. Victoria Kahn, "The Figure of the Reader in Petrarch's *Secretum*," *PMLA* 100 (1985): 154–66.

21. See Joël Blanchard's contribution in this volume, first published in *Annales SEC* 41 (1986).

22. Hicks, *Débat*, 12, 49.

23. Francesco Petrarca, *Prose*, ed. G. Maretellotti et al. (Milan: Riccardi, 1955), 218, 220.

24. Cf. Siegfried Wenzel, *The Sin of Sloth: Acedia in Medieval Thought and Literature* (Chapel Hill: University of North Carolina Press, 1967), 155–63.

25. See my study *Dante and the "Roman de la Rose": An Investigation into the Vernacular Narrative Context of the "Commedia,"* Beihefte zur Zeitschrift für romanische Philologie, no. 184 (Tübingen: Niemeyer, 1981), 62–64, 71–73.

26. "Christine de Pizan and Dante: A Reexamination," *Archiv für das Studium der neueren Sprachen und Literaturen* 222, no. 137 (1985): 100–111.

27. Norbert Elias, *Die höfische Gesellschaft, Untersuchungen zur Soziologie des Königtums und der höfischen Aristokratie* (Neuwied: Luchterhand, 1969).

28. F. Douglas Kelly, "Reflections on the Role of Christine de Pisan as a Feminist Writer," *Sub-Stance* 2 (1972): 63–71.

29. Christine de Pizan, *Le livre du corps de policie*, ed. Robert H. Lucas (Geneva: Droz, 1967), 1–2.

30. Maureen Curnow, "The *Livre de la Cité des Dames*: A Critical Edition," 2 vols. (Ph.D. dissertation, Vanderbilt University, 1975), 898.

31. Ibid, p. 1103.

32. Sheila Delany, " 'Mothers to Think Back Through': Who Are They? The Ambiguous Example of Christine de Pizan," in *Medieval Texts and Contemporary Readers*, ed. Laurie A. Finke and Martin B. Schichtman (Ithaca, N.Y.: Cornell University Press, 1987), 182; Delany's "Rewriting Women Good: Gender and Anxiety of Influence in Two Late-Medieval Texts," in *Chaucer in the Eighties*, ed. Julian Wassermann and Robert J. Blanch (Syracuse, N.Y.: Syracuse University Press, 1986), 75–92, takes a different position toward Christine.

33. Delany, "Mothers," 188.

34. Rodney Hilton, "Ideology and Social Order in Late Medieval England," in *Class Conflict and the Crisis of Feudalism: Essays in Medieval Social History* (Lon-

don: Hambleton Press, 1985), 252. This essay was originally published in French in 1978.

35. *Autres ballades*, no. 49, in *Oeuvres poétiques de Christine de Pizan*, ed. Maurice Roy, 3 vols. (Paris: Firmin Didot, 1886–96), 1:263–64.

36. Franz Walter Müller, "Zur Geschichte des Wortes und Begriffes *'nation'* im französischen Schrifttum des Mittelalters bis zur Mitte des 15. Jahrhunderts," *Romanische Forschungen* 58/59 (1947): 247–321, esp. 312–14. See Karlheinz Barck, Eine unveröffentliche Korrespondenz, Erich Auerbach/Werner Krauss," *Beiträge zur Romanischen Philologie* 27 (1987): 301–26, esp. 316, n. 6.

37. *Le Livre du corps de policie*, ed. Lucas, 188.

38. Müller, "Zur Geschichte des Wortes und Begriffes *'nation,'*" 294.

Orléans, the Epic Tradition, and the Sacred Texts of Christine de Pizan

PATRICIA STÄBLEIN-HARRIS

Since this volume pays scholarly and friendly tribute to Charity Cannon Willard, I would like to acknowledge her work on Christine and the Court of Orléans by focusing on *Le Dit de la Rose*. Christine's representation of the court in this poem may be linked to the history of Orleans itself as a place marked for divine interventions. One might object that *Le Dit de la Rose* concerns portentous events in the Paris *hôtel* of the duc d'Orléans, but it is predicated on the extraordinary being of both group and associated writer. Christine extenuates the sacred reflections of her text by using allegorical figures, but the enigmatic preaching of divine truths remains an important structural force. The divine revelations and the tightly enclosed initiates are thus located by common lexical and design elements between what Christine had argued was the blasphemous secularity of the *Roman de la Rose* and the sacred text of the New Testament, particularly that of Pentecost.

Although that sense of cognitive and existential privilege stems immediately from contemporary sources best elucidated in Charity Cannon Willard's biography, *Christine de Pizan: Her Life and Works*,[1] another recent book, Stephen G. Nichols, Jr.'s *Romanesque Signs*,[2] shows the older vision of Orléans as a locus for divine and human contact in a discussion of the eleventh-century *Historiae* by Rodolphus Glaber of Cluny. To set up his key concept of *theosis* as the "manifestation of God in the creature,"[3] Nichols analyzes how Glaber uses symbolic acts to express first the polluted evil and then the Christological transfiguration of the cathedral and city of Orléans. Nichols' argument is important here not only for its focus on the inscription of Orléans's space into that of Jerusalem but also for its emphasis that such a narrative sacralizes its own space and that of its author. Christine's bonding of the Court of Orleans in the other space of Paris to a divine mission restores the court to the sacred space of Orléans and enacts her own bond to that space. The truth of her spatial reading and writing would be mystically realized at Orléans itself in her lifetime with the appearance of Jeanne d'Arc and witnessed in Christine's last known work, *Le Ditié de Jeanne d'Arc*. Like

Glaber, Christine wrote in the medieval narrative traditions of symbolism and inversion, which also were those of her reference texts and often her antitexts (compare the *Roman de la Rose*).

The critical divisions of late fourteenth- and early fifteenth-century France tended to move Christine's symbolic and mirrored diction back from the self-referential style preferred then to the signing forth of sacred truth that narrative (prose and poetry) performed in Rodolphus's vision of history and Eriugena's philosophy to argue the mystical structure of early twelfth-century epic, especially the Oxford *Roland*. The same features are widely present in the fourteenth-century epics such as *Lion de Bourges*, so the passage from Glaber cited and translated by Nichols is also important to our understanding of the city as sacred space.

> Contigit igitur quadam die, dum caementarii, fundamenta basilicae locaturi soliditatem perscrutarentur ipsius telluris, ut reperirent copiosa auri pondera, quae scilicet ad totius, quamvis magnae, basilicae fabricam reformandam certissime crederentur sufficere. Suscipientes ergo qui fortuito casu invenerant aurum, ex integro episcopo detulerunt. Ipse vero, omnipotenti Deo pro collato sibi munere gratias agens, ac suscipiens illud, custodibus operis tradidit, totumque fideliter in opus ejusdem ecclesiae expendi jussit. Fertur namque quod etiam illud aurum solertia beati Evurtii, antiqui ejusdem sedis praesulis, ibidem hujus restaurationis gratia fuisset reconditum. Idcirco permaxime, quoniam, dum isdem vir sanctus quondam, potiorem quam fuerat primitus, eamdem informaret ecclesiam, contigit illi huic simile munus divinitus sibi reservatum inibi reperire.
>
> Sicque praeterea factum est ut et domus ecclesiae videlicet sedis pontificalis, priore elegantior reformaretur. Ipsoque suadente pontifice, caeterarum, quae in eadem civitate deperierant, basilicarum sanctorum quorumcunque meritis dicatarum aedes anterioribus potiores constituerentur, atque divinorum operum cultus in eisdem excellentior haberetur prae omnibus. Ipsaque urbs paulo post referta domorum aedificiis, plebs tandem illius mitigata a flagitiis Domini pietate subventa, tantoque citius convaluit, quanto sagacius propriam calamitatem excepit ob correptionis ultionem. Fuit namque praedicta civitas antiquitus, ut est impraesentiarum, regum Francorum principalis sedes regia, scilicet pro sui pulchritudine ac populari frequentia, nec non et telluris ubertate, perspecuique irrigatione fluminis.

> (For it came to pass one day, when the masons were testing the solidity of the ground to situate the foundation of the basilica, they discovered a great quantity of gold. They believed it to be sufficient to pay for all of the reconstruction of the basilica, however great the expense. They took this gold discovered by chance and brought it intact to the bishop. He gave thanks to Almighty God for the gift He had given

him, took it and gave it to the construction foremen and ordered that
it be faithfully expended in the building of this church. It was said that
the gold was hidden thanks to the shrewdness of Saint Evurtius, the
first prelate of the same see, who buried it for this very reconstruction.
The idea came to this holy man because, when he was renovating the
church for the first time, he too discovered a divine gift placed there for
that purpose.

In this way, the edifice of the church, that is the Cathedral, was rebuilt more splendidly. And also, on the recommendation of the pontiff,
the buildings of the other churches, dedicated to various saints, were
rebuilt more beautifully than the former buildings, and the worship
of God's works was better in that city than in any other. The city itself
was rebuilt soon after with dwellings, and the people, purified of their
corruption with the aid of divine forgiveness, recovered all the more
quickly because of their wisdom in accepting the calamity as an exemplary punishment. This city was in ancient times, as it presently is, the
principal seat for the court of the kings of France because of its beauty,
of its large population, the fertility of its soil, and the purity of the river
that nourishes it.)[4]

For Nichols, this narrative is an example of *theosis,* and he declares that
"Rodolphus's work is the textual mimesis of the dialectic of divine descent
and human ascent it records."[5] These same statements could be made about
Christine and *Le Dit de la Rose,* with allowances for their courtly reformu-
lations. Furthermore, the authority structures in the passage from Glaber
and in the *Dit* resemble each other. In the *Dit,* truths and treasures are discovered to the small and elite group of the duc d'Orléans's household and
then personally to Christine. These marks of divine favor are to be used ultimately to rebuild society in good love and honor just as Christine builds
Le Dit de la Rose from the contaminated disorder of the *Roman de la Rose.*
Models of wicked behavior and its punishment are also part of the design
just as they are elsewhere in Rodolphus on Orléans. Above all, it is the act
of writing in both cases that fully realizes the manifestations of the sacred
truths.

Much has been said about Christine's attempt to better her economic
lot through poems seeking patronage from the licentious duc d'Orléans,[6]
but the realization of this paradox within the poems themselves has been
little studied. In the *Dit,* the inverted relationship of the real to the ideal
preached a warning that was realized in the duke's own disordered life[7]
and that of France. The epic nature of Christine's advocacy of the ideal
is attested in the lengthy (about twenty-two thousand lines) *Mutacion de
Fortune* (1401–3) which she was composing at the time she wrote the *Dit*
(1402). Further confirmation of the breadth of Christine's concept of social
metamorphosis is in her confrontation of the encyclopedic *Roman de la Rose*

and her exploitation of epic texts relative to her own life, that of France, and the history of the world in the *Mutacion*. As Nichols argues well for Rodolphus's day, the ultimate ground of the epic and the heroic is the vision that Christine also had of the material connection between the divine and the human.

Christine's assertion of unity between the ideal human world and its validating abstractions is evident in the opening lines of *Le Dit de la Rose*.[8] She rejects the problematization of dreams, appearances and truth which begins the *Roman de la Rose*[9] to start her text by addressing and thus positing the existence of distinguished knights and ladies who love honorably. Her opening not only sets her *Rose* text apart from the *Roman* but also attacks that work by using words present elsewhere in the *Roman* to express meanings and structures opposed to their *Roman* context and by joining these inverted reflections of the *Roman* to the few other words that do not appear in the late twelfth-century fragment by the courtly Guillaume de Lorris (lines 1–4028), later completed in the mid- to late thirteenth century by the scholastic Jean de Meun (lines 4029–21751).

Words in Christine's text that I consider especially important to her enactment of this convergence are italicized if they are present in Joseph Danos's *Concordance to the "Roman de la Rose" of Guillaume de Lorris*[10] and are printed in small capitals if present only in the *Dit*. My evaluation of their importance is based on my knowledge of the entire *Roman* just as Christine's choices were based on her own knowledge of this whole. For the sake of concision, and given the continuity of Guillaume de Lorris's shapes and semantics in Jean de Meun's poetic architecture and Christine's placing of her own poem in the courtly mode of Guillaume de Lorris, my references will stress Guillaume's section. Even under these limitations, the textual references to the *Roman* are so constant and complex that I can only briefly discuss a few of them. One might argue that semantic intimacy might be advocated for the *Dit* and numerous other contemporary and past courtly texts. Because the courtly vocabulary was so limited, perhaps even great coherences could be discovered with texts that Christine never saw. Nonetheless, I maintain that the title of this poem and Christine's participation in the *Querelle de la Rose*[11] testify to her determination to rewrite the *Roman* here.

At any rate, initially there is no *songe* or *mençonge* (cf. *Roman de la Rose*, lines 1–20) but a poet addressing an elite group that is of wide provenance (lines 7–8) in the echoing words, syllables and vowels that here point beyond poetic style to textual echoes of the *Roman*.

> A tous les Princes *amoureux*
> Et aux *nobles chevalereux,*
> Que *vaillantise* fait *armer,*
> Et a ceulz qui seulent *amer*

Toute *bonté* pour avoir pris,
Et a tous amans bien *apris*
De ce Royaume et autre part,
Partout ou *vaillance* s'espart:
A toutes dames renommées
Et aux *damoiselles amées,*
A toutes femmes HONNORABLES,
Saiges, courtoises, agreables:
Humble RECOMMANDACION
De loyal vraye entencion.
Si fais *savoir* a tous *vaillans,*
Qui pour HONNEUR sont *travaillans,*
Unes nouvelles merveilleuses,
GRACIEUSES, non perilleuses,
Qui avenues de nouvel
Sont en *beau lieu* plain de revel;
Aussi est *droiz* que ceulz le *sachent*
Qui *mauvaistié* devers eulz *sachent,*
A fin qu'ilz *amendent* leurs *fais*
Pour estre avec les bons PARFAIS.   (Lines 1–24)

If knighthood, arming, *vaillantise* (valor, value), *pris (prendre,* prize) and *apris (aprendre)* are key concepts in the male-female conflict that is the dynamic of the *Roman,* here the warriors of love are linked to the distinguished and honorable ladies in words that are not applied to women in Guillaume's section and infrequently if at all in Jean's part. (Indeed, in the famous Complaint of Nature, human *noblesse* is attacked as a false value, lines 28557ff.) The men are thus expressed in language common to the *Roman* and other courtly texts but the typical *damoiselles amees* of courtly expression are famed—even walled off—by the untypical and sober *dames renommees* and *femmes honnorables* placed on either side of them. Christine thus changes her audience's expectation from courtly play to morality by alternating the dense formulaic presence of the courtly and the *Roman* with semantic aporias that shift it into an ideal realm. Such a region exists within the courtly imagination, but that space is highly charged with conflict in the *Roman.*

The ideal takes on a theological tinge in lines 15–25, where Christine emphasizes her intention to make known "unes nouvelles merveilleuses." Although the site of this revelation—"en beau lieu plain de revel" (*revel* does not occur in Guillaume)—the "maison close" (line 32) of the duc d'Orléans at Paris is courtly, the emphasis on closure, exclusion (lines 50–53, 66–67) and the paradisiacal effects of the luminous descent of Dame Loyalty (sent by Love, lines 83–107) link the Gospel resonance of her marvelous news to Pentecost (Acts 2). In this way, Christine places the divine world and the courtly in contact without transforming the one into the other. Hers becomes then a secretive text because it is constantly invoking meanings and forms that it does not intend to realize fully. The enigmatic lines 21–24 convoke *Roman* passages where rightness (lines 190, 1903, 2084, 2293, 2472, 3340, 3499) and good conduct in love are at issue and also where the improvement of the *Roman* itself is announced (line 2025). The referential vagueness of "ceulz le sachent / . . . eulz sachent" is increased by their phonetic resemblance while the following "faiz," "amendment," and "les bon parfais" add mystical resonances to the vagueness. On the courtly level, the most probable explanation of the convoluted signals is a cleverly turned compliment to a maligned court whose reputation is to be righted ("ils amendent") by its passage through Christine's poetic design. The well-known libertinism of the Court of Orléans indicates, however, that an occulted compliment is more likely to be an oblique warning. In addition, the referential distance built into the poem's structure here expresses the boundaries of secrecy essential to a text that recounts initiation into an order and then initiates the reader. Furthermore, this convocation of homogeneity and diversity hints at kinship with sacred texts where hidden recesses and privileged knowing are similarly indicated—particularly those of the Gospel parables.[12]

This manipulation of levels of meaning and knowing continues through the arrival of Dame Loyalty with her *nymphes* and *pucelletes* (line 99), her singing of three *ballades* (lines 129–224) and the accomplishment of the group initiation into the Order of the Rose (lines 225–68). There is no explanation of how Christine can know this marvelous news and the words of the *ballades* so the poet and read occupy the same indeterminate space outside and inside the secret phenomena until Christine is afterward declared a witness to these events (lines 304–9) prefatory to her own private initiation: a scene that suggests a cult baptism in its setting of a white bedroom, nude Christine sleeping, then awakened, initiated, sleeping, and awakening to the real truth of her mission. *There* the *order* is in prose but here the *ballade* form is considered appropriate to *court* ritual. These *ballades* feature many references to the *Roman* (a highly referential text itself)[13] as do the narrative verses of the *Dit* because Christine's object is to reform the *Roman* message from the God of Love in its own words. Dame Loyalty ends the first *ballade*, for example, by declaring against *mauvaises fauvelles*, which are apparently also pejorative in the *Roman* (see lines 183ff. and 7447ff.) but the sheer mass of deception in the *Roman* makes their condemnation ambiguous:

> Ains, pour tousjours loyauté soustenir
> Et pour oster les mauvaises fauvelles
> Et les mauvais desloyaux escharnir,
> Venue suis vous apporter nouvelles.

(Lines 149–52)

The earlier obliquity is present in these verses only in their referential shift to the *Roman*: the moral position of Dame Loyalty is clear. Still, when this passage is taken together with those earlier verses, there is enough interpretative room to see this initiation as more of a conversion or purification than the confirmation of an already pure state—just as the *Roman* itself is purified in this recasting of its language and form. Though the description of the preceding dinner (*revel* is not in Guillaume) certainly shows a worthy company, the recurring suggestion of contrary narratives points to another dimension of the poet's knowledge—one shared perhaps with her contemporary readers and also with the historically aware audience of today.

In the second *ballade* where Dame Loyalty declares her mission from the *dieu d'Amours* to present the roses gathered (*cueillies*)—presumably—from his *vergiers,* the setting, dynamics (*cueillir*), and language of both parts of the *Roman* are reformed by the being redirected to a single meaning: the honor of women (the noun does *not* appear in Guillaume). The text thus performs the supporting action it commands from its initiates. Christine's *Dit* is the material accomplishment of the reshaping of the cognitive design of the *Roman*. In its appropriation of sacred space Christine's poem emphasizes and formalizes silences about evil. Since that sacrality implies performance, Christine's poem disseminates the ideal to counter not only the wicked knowledge about women disseminated by the *Roman* but also its advocacy and enstructuring of boundless dissemination. On the social level, the fictive nature of her reshaping is evident in her occasional obliquity and, by a contrast that is paradoxically homogeneous, in her stacking of textual references.

For example, the third *ballade* is introduced by a passage featuring numerous inverted references to the *Roman*. This referentiality is further actualized by making this piece the rolled-up *ballade* that accompanied the roses distributed by Dame Loyalty. While the writing down of the other two *ballades* was a copying effort, the composition of this *ballade* is the direct writing that "recorde / Qu'Amours veult" (lines 185–86). Such a problematization of writing engages the textual structure of the *Roman*. More important, Christine has progressively sealed the truthfulness of her text by setting the other two *ballades* in vague circumstances of transmission. This third *ballade* is located within the "beaux rolez" (line 184) that Dame Loyalty flings among the plucked roses and the cups she has placed on the table (an allusion to the Eucharist?). Writing that is the same yet multiple fills the space among the diverse but similar (*roses blances, vermeilles*) objects. Reflecting the rose's own closure in its rolled form and ultimately the female anatomy that is the emblem of the *Roman*, the written vow closes the action in which the closed flower is taken. Again the complex manipulation of sealed forms suggests a sacred design that is confirmed by the parallelism of such a vow with the marriage ceremony and by the *ballade*'s semantic invocation of passages involving Narcissus's death in the *Roman:* thus a vow until "death do us part." Here are the lines from this crucial area of the text:

> Et celle qui j'ay ma dame nommée
> Souveraine, *loyaute* CONFERMÉE
> Je luy tendray jusques a la *parclose*
> Et de ce ay *voulenté* AFFERMÉE:
> Et pour ce *prens* je l'*Ordre* de la *Rose.*
>
> Et si merci Amours et son *humblesse*
> Qui nous a cy tel *semence semée*
> Dont j'ay espoire que serons en l'adresse
> De mieux valoir; c'est bien chose INFORMÉE
> Que de lui vint HONNEUR trés renommee.
> Si *defendray,* s'aucun est qui dire ose,
> Chose par quoy dame estre puist *blasmée:*
> Et pour ce prens je l'*Ordre* de la *Rose.*
>
> Princes haultains, ou *valeur* est *fermée*
> Faites le VEU, *bonte* y est *enclose,*
> L'*enseigne* en vueille porter en mainte armée:
> Et pour ce prens je l'*Ordre* de la *Rose.*
>
> Adonc furent en audiance
> Levez et, senz *contrariance*
> Firent tous le *beau* VEU *louable*
> Qui est *gentil* et HONORRABLE
> Quant nullui ne vit *contradire*
> La deesse adonc *prist* a dire
> Ce rondelet, prenant *congié*
> Si n'y a pensé ne songié.   (Lines 208–31)

The entire company accomplishes the ritual proposed by Dame Loyalty, who then leaves to tell her good news to the God of Love in the extra-repetitive form of the rondelet (lines 233–39) as the whole poem apparently rolls in upon itself to closure.

After the goddess's departure (lines 241–42), Christine begins her text again with the melody begun by the attendant nymphs ("commencierent tel mellodie") which referentially reinvokes the *Roman* (compare lines 667, 707) and even the *Roman*'s beginning with her use now of *mençonge, sembloit,* and doubt constructions.

> Aucunes gens dient qu'en songes
> n'a se fables non et mençonges;
> mes l'en puet tex songes songier
> qui ne sont mie mençongier

ainz sont aprés bien aparant,
si en puis bien traire a garant
un auctor qui ot non Macrobes,
qui ne tint pas songes a lobes,
ainçois escrit l'avision
qui avint au roi Scypion.
Qui c'onques cuit ne qui que die
qu'il est folor et musardie
de croire que songes aviegne,
qui se voudra, por fol m'en tiegne,
quar endroit moi ai ge fiance
que songes est senefiance
des bien as genz et des anuiz,
que li plusor songent de nuiz
maintes choses covertement
que l'en voit puis apertement.[14]

Christine has reopened and widened her poem, incorporating the most dangerous elements of artifice from the *Roman* to reform them into an even tighter closure. The sealed company is refined down to Christine nude and alone in a white chamber whose preparation by the goddess Diana makes even clearer the intent to specify sacred events in sacred spaces in the *Dit*. Both closeness to the *Roman* and secular distance are maintained by the use of gods and goddesses to establish the divine context, but such a structuring position is no less located in the sacred. Again the appearance of the goddess is replicated but the context is also far more closed: the elegant social trappings have been abolished.

The implications that this poem presents an even purer and more truthful text—*nuda veritas,* indeed—are confirmed in the goddess's discourse where she uncovers her preceding disguise as Dame Loyalty:

Tu scez comment en ta presence
Je vins presenter par plaisance
Naguere les roses jolies.   (Lines 304–6)

She is again the messenger of Love, but now the covered criticisms of the earlier text are uncovered in the denunciations of human villainy under chivalric appearances and in the endorsements of true, over false, nobility. The language now invokes that of the military allegorization of sexual relationships in the *Roman* (both parts) and the *Roman*'s ambiguous moral harangues. Because the less terrible parts of the *Roman* have already been purified by the reformulation in the preceding verses, licentious and vicious meanings can be directly confronted here. They are at issue in the sacred mission that is being conferred upon the poetess by the Goddess of Chastity, who is associated with birth (Diana/Lucina; baptism/rebirth) here and in the *Roman* (lines 10463–650). Even at this point Christine works primarily through another, an opposed text, to form her own: the textualization is never really direct. Indeed, this procedure could also be considered a reconstruction of the earlier, more courtly, and, as such, more contaminated verses. Such an architectural position is emphasized as Diana's speech closes by stating the contrary mechanism of its teaching—just as does the *Roman* ("Ainsinc va des contreres choses, / les unes sont des autres gloses," lines 21543–44):

> Sens orgueil qui maint homme affolle
> Si ait hault cuer et haulte emprise,
> Ce n'est pas l'orgueil qu'on desprise
> Que d'avoir si haultain courage
> Qu'on ne daingnast faire viltage
> Et que l'en aime les hautaines
> Choses contraires aux vilaines.   (Lines 387–93)

The entire structure of Christine's text is based on substituting her "haultaines choses contraires aux vilains" belonging to the *Roman* in a hostile Midrash where the Father text is broken and a woman text substituted.[15] In taking this structural position, she has created an antistructure in the same way the original was created, since the *Roman* itself was Midrash. Both the Midrash and *theosis* traditions privilege interpretation to the point of mystical revelation.

Nancy Regalado Horowitz's recent and very brilliant article on "des contreres choses" in the *Roman*[16] focuses on the passage immediately preceding the lover's final victorious assault on the Rose as a statement of the *Roman*'s basic formal dynamics:

> Ainsinc va des contreres choses,
> Les unes sunt des autres gloses.   (Lines 21543–44)

This reading can be verified in Christine's rewriting of the *Rose*. The *contreres choses* of the *Roman*, according to Christine, can only be righted by the reproduction of the *choses contreres*. Ideas and isotopies of turning, inversion and contrariness (lines 404, 405, 412, 416–26, 430–33, 444–53, and so forth) continue throughout Diana's speech, which itself works through the turning and returning of the *Roman*. It is this movement that has compelled Love's request to give the news of the new order—because it is an order of words and speaking (lines 480–503) that controls deeds. The sacred order brought by Diana to Christine is indeed a literary gift but that it also erases the *songe* and *mençonge* of the *Roman* is proved by the beautiful and material presence of the lettered order after the disappearance of the goddess from the sealed room (lines 552–95).

Christine's task, like that of the *Roman* lover whose language she uses, is one of dissemination, but she remains a textual reformer even in relation to the beautiful letters of her sacred text.[17] The order she receives from Diana seems unearthly and is in *belle* prose: that contrary form is what Christine reflects into terrestrial poetry (lines 590–606). Indeed, she even closes the *Dit* in the contrary by stating that this text of eternal fidelity is written on Saint Valentine's Day, when a lover is chosen for the year.[18] A final set of verses restates the reading model for the poem by revealing the truth of the author's name in an enigma.[19] It is not difficult but demands the reading of the message by erasing certain letters and words so that the correct or true ones remain standing or visible. In the *Dit de la Rose* Christine has performed precisely this kind of transformation of the *Roman de la Rose*, and in interpreting the *Dit* the reader must reproduce this transformation in order to see how the two texts are related. Why was this reading guide not placed at the beginning? In one sense, of course, it was. The use of the *sachent* rhyme scheme and the paradoxical image of the household of the duc d'Orléans both point to it. The initial positing of a semiveiled model of reading is frequent in medieval works.[20] Christine, however, preferred to put the reader first in the position of a wondering initiate rather than to invoke and simultaneously to provoke a deconstructive reading that forces the reader to supply whole gaps in the poet's writing.[21]

At the same time Christine was engaged on this restructuring mission of epic dimensions, she was recasting her life and times through the epic texts that echo in her multireferential *Mutacion de Fortune*. Her experiences with the Court of Orléans provided much fuel for both of these endeavors. Perhaps also Orléans itself stimulated her with some shred of its divinely organized past or with the aura of sacred events yet to bind them both.[22]

Notes

1. Charity Cannon Willard, *Christine de Pizan: Her Life and Works* (New York: Persea Books, 1984). Cf. also Enid McLeod, *The Order of the Rose: The Life and Times of Christine de Pisan* (London: Chatto and Windus, 1976).

2. Stephen G. Nichols, Jr., *Romanesque Signs* (New Haven, Conn.: Yale University Press, 1983), awarded the prestigious Lowell Prize by the Modern Language Association.

3. Defined by Nichols according to his reading of Eriugena, *Romanesque Signs*, 19–20; cf. also 15–65.

4. Translated by Nichols, *Romanesque Signs*, 18, from Glaber, *Historiae* 1.5, *PL* 142, col. 635.

5. Nichols, *Romanesque Signs*, 19.

6. Willard, *Christine de Pizan*, 51–71; McLeod, *The Order of the Rose*, 33–44; Diane Bornstein, *Ideals for Women in the Works of Christine de Pisan*, Medieval and

Renaissance Monograph Series, no. 1 (Detroit: Michigan Consortium for Medieval and Early Modern Studies, 1981), esp. Charity Cannon Willard, "Christine de Pizan and the Order of the Rose," 51–61.

7. He was assassinated at Paris near a residence of the queen, who was rumored to be his mistress; see Willard, *Christine de Pizan*, 150, 182; and McLeod, *The Order of the Rose*, 139–41.

8. *Oeuvres poétiques de Christine de Pisan*, ed. Maurice Roy, 3 vols. (Paris: Firmin Didot, 1886–96). I have been in correspondence with Thelma Fenster (Fordham University) regarding her forthcoming edition, translation, and commentary for the *Dit* but have not seen her texts. She has, however, seen the final draft of this essay.

9. Jean de Meun, *Le Roman de la Rose*, ed. Félix Lecoy (Paris: Champion, 1970–73).

10. Joseph Danos, *Concordance to the "Roman de la Rose" of Guillaume de Lorris* (Chapel Hill: University of North Carolina, Department of Romance Languages, 1975). Cf. Roger Bertrand, *Guillaume de Lorris, "Le Roman de la Rose": Concordancier complet des formes graphiques occurentes* (Paris: Champion, 1976).

11. Eric Hicks, ed., *Le Débat sur le "Roman de la Rose"* (Paris: Champion, 1977).

12. Frank Kermode, *The Genesis of Secrecy: On the Interpretation of Narrative* (Cambridge, Mass.: Harvard University Press, 1979), esp. 49–73. See also Georgette Kamenetz, "La Promenade d'Amant comme expérience mystique," in *Études sur le "Roman de la rose" de Guillaume de Lorris*, ed. Jean Dufournet (Geneva: Slatkine, 1984), 83–104.

13. For fine discussions of such phenomena, see especially the following, among many others: D. W. Robertson, Jr., *A Preface to Chaucer* (Princeton, N.J.: Princeton University Press, 1962); Alan M. F. Gunn, *The Mirror of Love: A Reinterpretation of the "Roman de la Rose"* (Lubbock: Texas Tech Press, 1952); Daniel Poirion, *Le Roman de la Rose* (Paris: Hatier, 1973); John V. Fleming, *The "Roman de la Rose": A Study in Allegory and Iconography* (Princeton, N.J.: Princeton University Press, 1968); David F. Hult, *Self-Fulfilling Prophecies: Readership and Authority in the First "Roman de la Rose"* (Cambridge: Cambridge University Press, 1986); Kevin Brownlee, "Reflection in the *Miroër aux Amoreus*: The Inscribed Reader in Jean de Meun's *Roman de la Rose*," in *Mimesis: From Mirror to Method, Augustine to Descartes*, ed. John D. Lyons and Stephen G. Nichols, Jr. (Hanover, N.H.: University Presses of New England, 1982), 60–70; Kenneth J. Knoespel, *Narcissus and the Invention of Personal History* (New York: Garland, 1985); and Patricia Harris Stäblein, "La Femme-*Pharmakon*: L'Amour et le mariage dans les transgressions structurales du *Roman de la Rose*," in *Amour, mariage, et transgressions au moyen âge*, ed. Danielle Buschinger and André Crepin (Göppingen: Kümmerle, 1984), 349–58.

14. *Le Roman de la Rose*, ed. Lecoy, lines 1–20.

15. Harold Bloom, *The Anxiety of Influence: The Theory of Poetry* (New York: Oxford University Press, 1973); *A Map of Misreading* (New York: Oxford University Press, 1975), esp. 3–105.

16. Nancy Regalado Horowitz, " 'Des Contreres Choses': La Fonction poétique de la citation et des *exempla* dans le *Roman de la Rose* de Jean de Meun," *Littérature* 41 (1981): 62–81.

17. Cf. Stephen G. Nichols, Jr., *Romanesque Signs*, 66–147 and also his "Romanesque Imitation or Imitating the Romans," in *Mimesis*, ed. Brownlee, 36–59.

18. Cf. Willard, "Order of the Rose," and her discussion of the importance of the feast of Saint Valentine to the Court of Orléans presided over by a duchess of Orléans named Valentine Visconti.

19. Nancy Freemann Regalado Horowitz, "La Fonction poétique des noms propres dans *Le Testament* de François Villon," *Cahiers de l'Association Internationale des Etudes Françaises* 32 (1980): 51ff.

20. Chrétien de Troyes, *Cligès*, ed. Alexandre Micha (Paris: Champion, 1978), lines 1–47; *Le Roman de Perceval*, ed. William Roach (Geneva and Paris: Droz/Minard, 1959), lines 1–68; Nigel de Longchamps, *Speculum stultorum*, ed. John A. Mozley and Robert R. Raymo (Berkeley and Los Angeles: University of California Press, 1960), lines 1–80, esp. 9–30; and *Ecbasis cuiusdam captivi per tropologiam*, ed. E. H. Zeydel (Chapel Hill: University of North Carolina, Department of Romance Languages, 1964), lines 1–68.

21. There are many discussions of the operation of *béance* in Jacques Lacan, *Ecrits* (Paris: Seuil, 1966), and in his *Séminaires*, 20 vols. (Paris: Seuil, 1973–75), esp. vol. 20, *Encore* (1975). For a good compact analysis, cf. Anthony Wilden's fine essay, "Lacan and the Discourse of the Other," 159–311, which is an appendix to his translation of *Jacques Lacan: Speech and Language in Psychoanalysis* (Baltimore: Johns Hopkins University Press, 1981). Cf. also *Feminine Sexuality: Jacques Lacan and the Ecole freudienne*, ed. Juliet Mitchell and Jacqueline Rose (London: Macmillan, 1982), esp. 123–61; Ellie Ragland-Sullivan, *Jacques Lacan and the Philosophy of Psychoanalysis* (Urbana: University of Illinois Press, 1986), esp. 130–95; and Jane Gallop, *Reading Lacan* (Ithaca, N.Y.: Cornell University Press, 1975), esp. 74–92.

22. Cf. Christine de Pizan, *Le Ditié de Jeanne d'Arc* (Oxford: Society of the Study of Medieval Languages and Literatures, 1977), dated 1429.

A Selective Bibliography of Christine de Pizan Scholarship, circa 1980–1987

ANGUS J. KENNEDY

The selective bibliography of Christine de Pizan scholarship that follows, covering the period circa 1980–87, is designed to supplement my bibliographical guide published by Grant and Cutler in 1984, which lists material up to approximately November 1981. As a tribute to Charity Cannon Willard, a bibliography of this kind may be seen to be doubly appropriate: it provides, first, an *état présent* of a research area that Professor Willard has made distinctively her own; and second, many of the items it contains furnish eloquent testimony to the encouragement which she has so generously given over the years, to colleagues old and new, and in particular to younger scholars coming to the texts and the period for the first time.

The bibliography is divided into five main sections: (1) Bibliographies; (2) Manuscripts; (3) Editions, Translations, Anthologies; (4) Critical Studies; (5) Language and Language-related Studies. Section 2 contains only those manuscripts that have come to my attention or been sold since 1981. Section 3 lists editions of, and relating to, Christine de Pizan. Section 4, the main section, lists literary and historical studies 1980–87 but includes also some pre-1980 items not covered in the Grant and Cutler volume. Only a few reviews are included, usually those which widen out to become general articles on Christine de Pizan. Section 5 lists books only— the bibliographies they contain will serve to guide the reader to material in article form. It should be noted also that some of the language studies contain material on texts that do not overlap chronologically with those of Christine de Pizan. As reference works on language are still, relatively speaking, few in number for the Middle French period, it was thought useful to list all those available. References to Kennedy, followed by a number, should be understood as references to the appropriate item in Angus J. Kennedy, *Christine de Pizan: A Bibliographical Guide*, Research Bibliographies and Checklists, no. 42 (London: Grant and Cutler, 1984). In the period between submission of the present manuscript (June 1987) and publication of this book, a number of items (20, 22, 24, 39, 40, 60, 61, 110, 125, and 139) were kindly added by the editor.

Among the most welcome trends that one can detect underlying the flow of publications are three that deserve special mention. First, work on editions has continued steadily, with the result that it is now possible to read almost all of Christine's works, in either published or dissertation form. The only exceptions are the *Livre de la prod'hommie de l'homme / Livre de prudence* and the *Heures de contemplation de la Passion*, both of which are being prepared for publication. Second, a large number of the works listed are devoted almost entirely to the study of the manuscripts themselves, a trend that must be particularly pleasing to Professor Willard, whose own achievements in this field have been so influential. Third, one must take stock of the sheer volume of production, particularly in the last decade. This material presents a bibliographical challenge not just to Christine de Pizan scholars but also to all those whose interests lie in the fourteenth and fifteenth centuries, once regarded as an autumnal period of decay and decline and now more properly seen as a fascinating era combining both tradition and innovation and worthy of study in its own right. Perhaps the time has come to organize an annual bibliography of fourteenth- and fifteenth-century studies, based on the excellent principles of the annual Arthurian bibliography.

I. Bibliographies

1. Burgoyne, Lynda, and Renée Gélinas. "Christine de Pizan, Alain Chartier, Charles d'Orléans: Cinq ans d'études (1976–1980)." *Le Moyen Français* 8/9 (1981): 291–308.

2. Frey, Linda, Marsha Frey, and Joanne Schneider. *Women in Western European History: A Select Chronological, Geographical, and Topical Bibliography from Antiquity to the French Revolution.* Brighton: Harvester Press, 1982. lv + 760 pp.

3. Kennedy, Angus J. *Christine de Pizan: A Bibliographical Guide.* Research Bibliographies and Checklists, no. 42. London: Grant and Cutler, 1984. 131 pp.

4. Krueger, R. L., and E. Jane Burns. "A Selective Bibliography of Criticism: Women in Medieval French Literature." *Romance Notes* 25 (1985): 375–90.

5. Yenal, Edith. *Christine de Pisan: A Bibliography of Writings by Her and About Her.* Scarecrow Author Bibliographies, no. 63. Metuchen, N.J.: Scarecrow Press, 1982. x + 175 pp.

II. Manuscripts

6. *Heures de contemplation de la Passion.* The Hague, Koninklijke Bibliotheek 73 j 55, ff. 51–92v.

7. *Livre de la mutacion de Fortune.*
The Bérès manuscript referred to in Kennedy, no. 401, was sold at Sotheby's, London, July 13, 1977. Cf. *Catalogue of Western Manuscripts and Miniatures*, Sotheby's, July 13, 1977 (London: Sotheby's, 1977), 37–39.

8. *Livre des fais d'armes et de chevalerie.* Turin, Biblioteca reale, Raccolta Saluzzo, 317 ff.

9. *Livre du chemin de long estude.* Cracow, Jagiellonian Library, Gall. fol. 133.
This codex is the Berlin manuscript, assumed lost, listed in Kennedy, *Christine de Pizan: A Bibliographical Guide*, no. 460.

III. Editions, Translations, Anthologies

10. Bergner, Heinz, et al. *Lyrik des Mittelalters: Probleme und Interpretationen.* Reclam, 7896–7. Stuttgart: Reclam, 1983. 2 vols., 579 pp., 446 pp.

11. Bozzolo, Carla, and Hélène Loyau. *La Cour Amoureuse dite de Charles VI.* Vol. 1, *Étude et édition critique des sources manuscrites (Armoiries et notices biographiques, 1–300).* Paris: Le léopard d'or, 1982). 185 pp.

12. Cerquiglini, Jacqueline, ed. *Cent ballades d'Amant et de Dame*, by Christine de Pizan. (Paris: Union générale d'éditions, 1982. 160 pp. (10:18, 1529).

13. Fox, Denton, and William A. Ringler. *The Bannatyne Manuscript, National Library of Scotland Advocates MS 1.1.6.* London: Scolar Press in association with the National Library of Scotland, 1980. xlvi + 60 pp. + 734 pp.
Contains Hoccleve's translation of the *Épistre au dieu d'amours*.

14. Haselbach, Hans. *Seneque des IIII. vertus, La "Formula honestae vitae" de Martin de Braga (pseudo-Sénèque), traduite et glosée par Jean Courtecuisse (1403): Etude et édition critique.* Publications universitaires européennes, series 13, Langue et littérature françaises. Bern: Lange, 1975. 505 pp.

15. Kennedy, Angus J., ed. *Epistre de la prison de vie humaine*, by Christine de Pizan. Glasgow: University of Glasgow, French Department, 1984. 83 pp.

16. Lalande, Denis, ed. *Le Livre des fais du bon messire Jehan le Maingre dit Bouciquaut.* Textes littéraires français, no. 331. Geneva: Droz, 1985. lxxiv + 549 pp.
Argues that text should not be attributed to Christine.

17. Lawson, Sarah, trans. *The Treasure of the City of Ladies*, by Christine de Pizan. Harmondsworth, U.K.: Penguin Books, 1985. 180 pp. Modern English translation.

18. Moreau, Thérèse, and Eric Hicks, trans. *La Cité des Dames*, by Christine de Pizan. Paris: Stock, 1986. 291 pp. Modern French translation.

19. Paquette, Jean-Marcel. *Poèmes de la mort de Turold à Villon*. Paris: Union Générale d'Editions, 1979. 272 pp. (10:18, 1340).

20. Ponfoort, Tine, trans. *Het Boek van de Stad der Vrouwen*, by Christine de Pizan. Amsterdam: Feministische Uitgeverij Sara, 1984. 262 pp. Dutch translation.

21. Richards, Earl Jeffrey, trans. *The Book of the City of Ladies*, by Christine de Pizan. New York: Persea Books, 1982; London: Picador, 1983. li + 281 pp. Modern English translation.

22. Stummer, Maria, trans. *Der Sendbrief vom Liebesgott (L'Epistre au dieu d'Amours)*, by Christine de Pizan. Graz: Verlag Leykamm, 1987. 46 pp. + 27 pp. Modern German translation.

23. Wisman, Josette A., ed. and trans. *"The Epistle of the Prison of Human Life" with "An Epistle to the Queen of France" and "Lament on the Evils of Civil War,"* by Christine de Pizan. Garland Library of Medieval Literature, series A, no. 21. New York: Garland, 1984. 99 pp. Edition and modern English translation.

24. Zimmerman, Margarete, trans. *Das Buch der Stadt der Frauen*, by Christine de Pizan. Berlin: Orlanda-Frauenverlag, 1986. 312 pp. Modern German translation.

IV. Critical Studies

25. Altman, Leslie. "Christine de Pisan: Professional Woman of Letters (French, 1364–1430?)." In *Female Scholars: A Tradition of Learned Women Before 1800*, edited by J. R. Brink, 7–23. Montreal: Eden Women's Publications, 1980.

26. Altmann, Barbara K. "Les Poèmes de veuvage de Christine de Pisan." *Scintilla* (University of Toronto) 1 (1984): 24–47.

27. Bagoly, Suzanne. "Christine de Pizan et l'art de 'dictier' ballades." *Moyen Age* 92 (1986): 41–67.

28. Baird, Joseph L. "Pierre Col and the Querelle de la Rose." *Philological Quarterly* 60 (1981): 273–86.

29. Batany, Jean. "Allégories et typologie: Le tiers état dans quelques sotties et moralités." In *The Theatre in the Middle Ages*, edited by Herman Braet, Johan Nowé and Gilbert Tournoy, 220–37. Mediaevalia Lovaniensia, series 1, studia 13. Louvain: Presses universitaires de Louvain, 1985.

30. Bath, Michael. "The Image of the Stag in Literary and Iconographic Traditions in the Middle Ages." Ph.D. dissertation, University of Strathclyde, 1981. 244 pp. + 72 plates.

31. Beck, Jonathan, and Gianni Mombello, eds. *Seconda miscellanea di studi e ricerche sul Quattrocento francese*. Chambéry and Turin: Centre d'études franco-italien, 1981. xix + 231 pp.

32. Bell, Susan Groag. "Medieval Women Book Owners: Arbiters of Lay Piety and Ambassadors of Culture." *Signs* 7 (1981–82): 742–68.

33. Beltran, Evancio. "Christine de Pizan, Jacques Legrand, et le *Communiloquium* de Jean de Galles." *Romania* 104 (1983): 208–28.

34. Beltran, Evancio. "Le 'Sophilogium' de Jacques Legrand et ses adaptations françaises, l'"Archiloge Sophie' et le 'Livre des bonnes meurs': Recherches sur la vie intellectuelle et morale aux origines de l'humanisme francais." Thesis, University of Bordeaux, 1984.

35. Berriot-Salvador, Evelyne. "Les Femmes et les pratiques de l'écriture de Christine de Pisan à Marie de Gournay." *Réforme, Humanisme, Renaissance* 9, no. 16 (January 1983): 52–69.

36. Blanchard, Joël. "Pastorale et courtoisie: *Regnault et Jehanneton*: Le Discours et ses limites." In *La Littérature angevine médiévale: Actes du colloque du samedi, 22 mars 1980, Université d'Angers*, 199–209. Centre de recherche de littérature et de linguistique d'Anjou et des Bocages: Hérault Imprimerie, 1981.

37. Blanchard, Joël. *La Pastorale en France aux XIVe et XVe siècles: Recherches sur les structures de l'imaginaire médiéval*. Bibliothèque du XVe siècle, no. 45. Paris: Champion, 1983. 375 pp.

38. Blanchard, Joël. "L'Entrée du poète dans le champ politique au XVe siècle." *Annales SEC* 41 (1986): 43–61.

39. Blanchard, Joël. "Christine de Pizan: Les Raisons de l'histoire," *Moyen Age* 92 (1986): 417–36.

40. Blanchard, Joël. "Compilation et legitimation au XVe siècle." *Poétique* 19 (1988): 139–57.

41. Bodenham, C. H. L. "The Nature of the Dream in Late Mediaeval French Literature." *Medium Aevum* 54 (1984): 74–86.

42. Bornstein, Diane. "Women's Public and Private Space in Some Medieval Courtesy Books." *Centerpoint* 3 (1981): 68–74.

43. Bornstein, Diane. "An Analogue to Chaucer's Clerk's Tale." *Chaucer Review* 15 (1981): 322–31.

44. Bornstein, Diane. *The Lady in the Tower: Medieval Courtesy Literature for Women*. Hamden, Conn.: Archon Books, 1983. 152 pp.

45. Boutet, Dominique, and Armand Strubel. *Littérature, politique, et société dans la France du moyen âge*. Littératures modernes, no. 18. Paris: Presses universitaires de France, 1979. 248 pp.

46. Bozzolo, Carla, and Ezio Ornato. *Pour une histoire du livre manuscrit au moyen âge: Trois essais de codicologie quantitative*. Paris: CNRS, 1980. 361 pp. and *Supplément* (1983). Total pagination, 408 pp.

47. Bozzolo, Carla, and Ezio Ornato. "Les Fluctuations de la production manuscrite à la lumière de l'histoire à la fin du moyen âge français." In *Bulletin philologique et historique (jusqu'à 1610) du Comité des travaux historiques et scientifiques, année 1979*, 51–75. Paris: Bibliothèque nationale, 1981.

48. Braden, Gordon. "Beyond Frustration: Petrarchan Laurels in the Seventeenth Century." *Studies in English Literature, 1500–1900* 26 (1986): 5–23.

49. Briesemeister, Dietrich. "Christine de Pisan." In *Lexikon des Mittelalters*, edited by Gloria Avella-Widhalm, Liselotte Lutz, Roswitha Mattejiet, and Ulrich Mattejiet, vol. 2, cols. 1918–19. Munich: Artemis, 1983.

50. Bumgardner, George H. "Christine de Pizan and the Atelier of the Master of the Coronation." In *Seconda miscellanea di studi e ricerche sul Quattrocento francese*, edited by Jonathan Beck and Gianni Mombello, 32–52. Chambéry and Turin: Centre d'études franco-italien, 1981.

51. Burnley, J. D. "Christine de Pizan and the So-called 'Style Clergial.'" *Modern Language Review* 81 (1986): 1–6.

52. Bush, Douglas. "Podloze Mitologii Klasycznej W XVI Stuleciu." *Pamietnik Literacki* 73 (1982): 381–404.
Polish translation of Douglas Bush, *Mythology and the Renaissance Tradition in English Poetry* (New York: Pageant Books, 1957), part 2, "The Background of Classical Mythology in the Sixteenth Century," 25–47.

53. Calvez, Daniel. "La Structure du rondeau: Mise au point." *French Review* 55 (1982): 461–70.

54. Cerquiglini, Jacqueline. "Le Lyrisme en mouvement." *Perspectives Médiévales* 6 (1980): 75–86.

55. Châtelet-Lange, Liliane. "Galiot de Genouillac entre Fortune et Prudence." *Revue de l'Art* 64 (1986): 7–22.

56. Collet, A. *L'Expression du réalisme dans le "Livre de la mutacion de Fortune" de Christine de Pisan*. Grenoble: Maîtrise de lettres modernes, Université de Grenoble, 1977–78.

57. Combettes, Bernard. "Une Notion stylistique et ses rapports avec la syntaxe: Narration et description chez Christine de Pisan." In *Le Génie de*

la forme: Mélanges de langue et de littérature offerts à Jean Mourot, 51–58. Nancy: Presses universitaires de Nancy, 1982.

58. Cropp, Glynnis M. "Boèce et Christine de Pizan." *Moyen Age* 87 (1981): 387–417.

59. Dahmus, Joseph. *Dictionary of Medieval Civilisation*. London: Collier Macmillan, 1984. viii + 700 pp.

60. Delany, Sheila. "Rewriting Women Good: Gender and Anxiety of Influence in Two Late-Medieval Texts." In *Chaucer in the Eighties*, edited by Julian Wassermann and Robert J. Blanch, pp. 75–92. Syracuse, N.Y.: Syracuse University Press, 1986.

61. Delany, Sheila. " 'Mothers to Think Back Through': Who Are They? The Ambiguous Example of Christine de Pizan." In *Medieval Texts and Contemporary Readers*, edited by Laurie A. Finke and Martin B. Schichtman, 177–97. Ithaca, N.Y.: Cornell University Press, 1987.

62. Demougin, Jacques. *Dictionnaire historique, thématique, et technique des littératures: Littératures française et étrangères anciennes et modernes*, vol. 1, p. 326, cols. b–c. Paris: Larousse, 1985.

63. Engel, Monique. "Le *Miroir de mariage* d'Eustache Deschamps: Sources et tradition." In *Seconda miscellanea di studi e ricerche sul Quattrocento francese*, edited by Jonathan Beck and Gianni Mombello, 143–67. Chambéry and Turin: Centre d'études franco-italien, 1981.

64. Favier, Marguerite. *Christine de Pizan, muse des cours souveraines*. Lausanne: Editions Rencontre, 1967. Reprint. Geneva: Edito-service, 1984. 213 pp.

65. Fraioli, Deborah A. "The Image of Joan of Arc in Fifteenth-Century French Literature." Ph.D. dissertation, Syracuse University, 1981.

66. Fraioli, Deborah. "The Literary Image of Joan of Arc: Prior Influences." *Speculum* 56 (1981): 811–30.

67. Fraioli, Deborah A. "L'Image de Jeanne d'Arc: Que doit-elle au milieu littéraire et religieux de son temps?" In *Jeanne d'Arc: Une époque, un rayonnement*, 191–96. Colloque d'histoire médiévale, Orléans, octobre 1979. Paris: CNRS, 1982.

68. Françon, Marcel. "Notes sur les rondeaux." In *Seconda miscellanea di studi e ricerche sul Quattrocento francese*, edited by Jonathan Beck and Gianni Mombello, 53–70. Chambéry and Turin: Centre d'études franco-italien, 1981.

69. Garey, Howard B. "The Variable Structure of the Fifteenth-Century Rondeau." In *The Sixth Lacus Forum, 1979*, edited by William C. McCormack and J. Herbert Izzo, 494–501. Columbia, S.C.: Hornbeam, 1980.

70. Garey, Howard B. "The Fifteenth-Century Rondeau as Aleatory Polytext." *Le Moyen Français* 5 (1980): 193–236.

71. Gauvard, Claude. "Féministe ou bas-bleu? Le Cas Christine de Pizan." *L'Histoire* 62 (1983): 94–96.

72. Gilbert, Sandra M., and Susan Gubar. "Ceremonies of the Alphabet: Grandmatologies and the Female Authorgraph." *New York Literary Forum* 12 (1984): 23–52.

73. Gottlieb, Beatrice. "The Problem of Feminism in the Fifteenth Century." In *Women of the Medieval World: Essays in Honor of John H. Mundy*, edited by Julius Kirshner and Susanne F. Wemple, 337–64. Oxford: Blackwell, 1985.

74. Green, Richard F. "The *Familia regis* and the *Familia Cupidinis*." In *English Court Culture in the Later Middle Ages*, edited by V. J. Scattergood and J. W. Sherborne, 87–108. London: Duckworth, 1983.

75. Gripari, Pierre. "Christine de Pisan ou la Cité des Dames." *Le Spectacle du Monde* 249 (1982): 108–9.

76. Guillot, R. P. "Will the Battle of the Sexes Take Place?" *Historia* 470 (1986): 67–76.

77. Gumbrecht, Hans Ulrich. *Literatur in der Gesellschaft des Spätmittelalters*. Grundriss der romanischen Literaturen des Mittelalters, Begleitreihe zum GRLMA, vol. 1. Heidelberg: Winter, 1980. 346 pp.

78. Heitmann, Klaus. "Französische Lyrik von Guillaume de Machaut bis Jean Marot." In *Neues Handbuch der Literaturwissenschaft*, edited by Klaus von See, vol. 8, *Europäisches Spätmittelalter*, edited by Willi Erzgräber, 355–72. Wiesbaden: Athenaion, 1978.

79. Hicks, Eric. "La Tradition manuscrite des *Epîtres sur la Rose*." In *Seconda miscellanea di studi e ricerche sul Quattrocento francese*, edited by Jonathan Beck and Gianni Mombello, pp. 93–124. Chambéry and Turin: Centre d'études franco-italien, 1981.

80. Hindman, Sandra. *Pen to Press: Illustrated Manuscripts and Printed Books in the First Century of Printing*. College Park: University of Maryland, Art Department, and Baltimore: Johns Hopkins University, Department of History of Art, 1977. viii + 234 pp.

81. Hindman, Sandra. "The Composition of the Manuscript of Christine de Pizan's Collected Works in the British Library: A Reassessment." *British Library Journal* 9 (1983): 93–123.

82. Hindman, Sandra. "The Iconography of Queen Isabeau de Bavière (1410–15): An Essay in Method." *Gazette des beaux arts* 102, no. 1,377 (1983): 102–10.

83. Hindman, Sandra. "With Ink and Mortar: Christine de Pizan's *Cité des Dames*: An Art Essay." *Feminist Studies* 10 (1984): 457–84.

84. Hindman, Sandra. *Christine de Pizan's "Epistre Othéa": Painting and*

Politics at the Court of Charles VI. Texts and Studies, no. 77. Toronto: Pontifical Institute of Mediaeval Studies, 1986. 220 pp.

85. Hogetoorn, C. "Christine de Pisan, auteur à la mode." *Rapports* 53 (1983): 141–53.

86. Hook, David. *"Fons curarum, fons lachrymarum*: Three Variations upon a Petrarchan Theme: Christine de Pisan, Fernando de Royas, Fray Luis de Granada." *Celestinesca* 6 (1982): 1–7.

87. Huchet, Jean-Charles. "Le *Sorplus*: Des femmes écrivent au moyen âge." *L'Ane* 10 (1983): 23.

88. Huot, Sylvia J. "Lyric Poetics and the Art of Compilatio in the Fourteenth Century." Ph.D. dissertation, Princeton University, 1982.

89. Huot, Sylvia J. "Christine de Pizan." In *Dictionary of the Middle Ages*, edited by Joseph R. Strayer, 3:315–17. New York: Scribner's, 1982.

90. Huot, Sylvia J. "Seduction and Sublimation: Christine de Pizan, Jean de Meun, and Dante." *Romance Notes* 25 (1985): 361–73.

91. Kehler, Robert. "Historical Sketch of the Rondeau: The Widening Gap Between Music and Poetry." *Proceedings of the Annual Meeting of the Western Society for French History* 10 (1984): 41–51.

92. Kelly, Joan. "Early Feminist Theory and the *Querelle des femmes*, 1400–1789." *Signs* 8 (1982): 4–28.

93. Kelly, Joan. *Women, History, and Theory: The Essays of Joan Kelly.* Chicago: University of Chicago Press, 1984. xxvi + 163 pp.

94. Kemp, Walter. *"Dueil angoisseus* and Dulongesux." *Early Music* 7 (1979): 520–21.

95. Kennedy, Angus J. "Christine de Pizan and Maximianus." *Medium Aevum* 54 (1985): 282–83.

96. Kooijman, Jacques. "Une Etrange Duplicité: La Double Ballade au bas moyen âge." In *Le Génie de la forme: Mélanges de langue et littérature offerts à Jean Mourot*, 41–49. Nancy: Presses universitaires de Nancy, 1982.

97. Krynen, Jacques. *Idéal du prince et pouvoir royal en France à la fin du moyen âge (1380–1440): Étude de la littérature politique du temps.* Paris: Picard, 1981. 341 pp.

98. Laidlaw, James C. "Christine de Pizan: An Author's Progress." *Modern Language Review* 78 (1983): 532–50.

99. Laidlaw, James C. "Christine de Pizan: A Publisher's Progress." *Modern Language Review* 82 (1987): 35–75.

100. Lecoy, Félix, "Notes sur quelques ballades de Christine de Pisan." *Le Moyen Français* 12 (1983): 43–49. Reprint of Kennedy, 258.

101. Lemaire, Jacques. "Le Thème de la vie curiale en France sous les premiers Valois (1328–1498)." Thesis, Université libre de Bruxelles, 1980–81.

102. Liebertz-Grün, Ursula. "Marie de France, Christine de Pisan, und

die deutschsprachige Autorin im Mittelalter." *Euphorion* 78 (1984): 219–36.

103. Liebertz-Grün, Ursula. "Autorinnen im Umkreis der Höfe (Marie de France, Christine de Pisan)." In *Frauen, Literatur, Geschichte, Schreibende Frauen vom Mittelalter bis zur Gegenwart*, edited by Hiltrud Gnüg and Renate Möhrmann, 16–34. Stuttgart: Metzler, 1985.

104. Lowinsky, Edward E. "Jan van Eyck's *Tymotheos:* Sculptor or Musician? With an Investigation of the Autographic Strain in French Poetry from Rutebeuf to Villon." *Studi musicali* 13 (1984): 34–105.

105. Luria, Maxwell. *A Reader's Guide to the "Roman de la Rose."* Hamden, Conn.: Archon Books, 1982. xii + 282 pp.

106. McMillan, Ann Hunter. " 'Evere an hundred goode ageyn oon badde': Catalogues of Good Women in Medieval Literature." Ph.D. dissertation, Indiana University, 1979.

107. Margolis, Nadia. "Christine de Pizan: Poetess as Historian." *Journal of the History of Ideas* 47 (1986): 361–75.

108. Moody, Helen F. "The Debate of the Rose: The Querelle des femmes as Court Poetry." Ph.D. dissertation, University of California, Berkeley, 1981.

109. Müller, Franz Walter. "Zur Geschichte des Wortes und Begriffes 'nation' im französischen Schrifttum des Mittelalters bis zur Mitte des 15. Jahrhunderts." *Romanische Forschungen* 58/59 (1947): 247–321. Section on Christine, 312–14.

110. Muhlethaler, Jean-Claude. "Le Poète et le prophète: Littérature et politique au XVe siècle." *Le Moyen Français* 13 (1983): 37–57.

111. Ott, Karl August. *Der Rosenroman.* Erträge der Forschung, no. 145. Darmstadt: Wissenschaftliche Buchgesellschaft, 1980. 222 pp.

112. Ouy, Gilbert. "Autographes d'auteurs français des XIVe et XVe siècles: Leur utilité pour l'histoire intellectuelle." *Studia Zrodloznawcze Commentationes* 28 (1983): 69–103.

113. Ouy, Gilbert. "Une Énigme codicologique: Les Signatures des cahiers dans les manuscrits autographes et originaux de Christine de Pizan." In *Calames et cahiers: Mélanges de codicologie et de paléographie offerts à Léon Gilissen*, edited by J. Lemaire and E. van Balberghe, 119–31. Brussels: Centre d'Étude des Manuscrits, 1985.

114. Pernoud, Régine. *Christine de Pisan.* Paris: Calmann-Lévy, 1982. 222 pp. Issued also by Livre de Poche, 6011, in 1985.

115. Phillippy, Patricia A. "Establishing Authority: Boccaccio's *De claris mulieribus* and Christine de Pizan's *Le Livre de la Cité des Dames*." *Romanic Review* 77 (1986): 167–93.

116. Picherit, Jean-Louis. "De Philippe de Mézières à Christine de Pizan." *Le Moyen Français* 13 (1983): 20–36.

117. Picherit, Jean-Louis. "Christine de Pisan et le *Livre des faicts du bon messire Jean le Maingre, dit Boucicaut, mareschal de France et gouverneur de Gennes.*" *Romania* 103 (1982): 299–331.

118. Picherit, Jean-Louis. "Le *Livre de la prod'hommie de l'homme* et le *Livre de prudence* de Christine de Pisan: Chronologie, structure, et composition." *Moyen Age* 91 (1985): 381–413.

119. Poirion, Daniel. *Précis de littérature française au moyen âge.* Paris: Presses universitaires de France, 1983. 405 pp.

120. Quillet, Jeannine. *Charles V, le roi lettré: Essai sur la pensée politique d'un règne.* Paris: Librairie académique Perrin, 1984.

121. Reno, Christine. "Christine de Pizan: Feminism and Irony." In *Seconda miscellanea di studi e ricerche sul Quattrocento francese,* edited by Jonathan Beck and Gianni Mombello, 125–33. Chambéry and Turin: Centre d'études franco-italien, 1981.

122. Richards, Earl Jeffrey. *Dante and the "Roman de la Rose": An Investigation into the Vernacular Narrative Context of the "Commedia."* Beihefte zur Zeitschrift für romanische Philologie, no. 184. Tübingen: Niemeyer, 1981. vii + 116 pp.

123. Richards, Earl Jeffrey. "Christine de Pizan and the Question of Feminist Rhetoric." *Teaching Language Through Literature* 22 (1983): 15–24.

124. Richards, Earl Jeffrey. "Christine de Pizan and Dante: A Reexamination." *Archiv für das Studium der neueren Sprachen und Literaturen* 222 (1985): 100–111.

125. Richards, Earl Jeffrey. "Finding the 'Authentic' Text: Editing and Translating Medieval and Modern Works as Comparable Interpretive Exercises (Chrétien's *Charrette,* Christine de Pizan's *Cité des Dames* and Diderot's *Neveu de Rameau.*" *L'Esprit Créateur* 27 (1987, *The Poetics of Textual Criticism, The Old French Example,* ed. Karl D. Uitti), 111–21.

126. Robin, Françoise. "Louis d'Anjou et le rayonnement de l'art parisien (1360–80)." *Journal of Medieval History* 12 (1986): 55–80.

127. Rouse, Richard H., and Mary A. Rouse. *Preachers, Florilegia, and Sermons: Studies on the "Manipulus florum" of Thomas of Ireland.* Toronto: Pontifical Institute of Mediaeval Studies, 1979. xi + 476 pp.

128. Shamar, Shulamith. *The Fourth Estate: A History of Women in the Middle Ages.* London: Methuen, 1983. 351 pp.

129. Schibanoff, Susan. "Comment on Joan Kelly's 'Early Feminist Theory and the *Querelle des femmes,* 1400–1789.'" *Signs* 9 (1983): 320–26.

130. Strubel, Armand. *Le Roman de la Rose.* Paris: Presses universitaires de France, 1984. 127 pp.

131. Tuttle, Lisa. *Encyclopedia of Feminism.* London: Arrow Books, 1987. 248–49.

132. Wareham, T. E. "Christine de Pisan's *Livre des fais d'armes et de chevalerie* and Its Fate in the Sixteenth Century." In *Seconda miscellanea di studi e ricerche sul Quattrocento francese*, edited by Jonathan B--k and Gianni Mombello, 135–42. Chambéry and Turin: Centre d'études franco-italien, 1981.

133. Wilkins, Nigel. "Music and Poetry at Court: England and France in the Late Middle Ages." In *English Court Culture in the Later Middle Ages*, edited by V. J. Scattergood and J. W. Sherbourne, 183–204. London: Duckworth, 1983.

134. Wilkins, Nigel. "A Pattern of Patronage: Machaut, Froissart, and the Houses of Luxembourg and Bohemia in the Fourteenth Century." *French Studies* 37 (1983): 257–84.

135. Willard, Charity Cannon. "A New Look at Christine de Pizan's *Epistre au dieu d'Amours.*" In *Seconda miscellanea di studi e ricerche sul Quattrocento francese*, edited by Jonathan Beck and Gianni Mombello, 71–92. Chambéry and Turin: Centre d'études franco-italien, 1981.

136. Willard, Charity Cannon. "The Franco-Italian Professional Writer: Christine de Pizan." In *Medieval Women Writers*, edited by Katharina M. Wilson, 333–63. Athens: University of Georgia Press, 1984.

137. Willard, Charity Cannon. *Christine de Pizan: Her Life and Works*. New York: Persea Books, 1984. 266 pp.

138. Willard, Charity Cannon. "Concepts of Love According to Guillaume de Machaut, Christine de Pizan, and Pietro Bembo." In *The Spirit of the Court: Selected Proceedings of the Fourth Congress of the International Courtly Literature Society (Toronto, 1983)*, edited by Glyn S. Burgess and Robert A. Taylor, 386–92. Cambridge, U.K.: D. S. Brewer, 1985.

139. Willard, Charity Cannon. "Punishment and Reward in Christine de Pizan's Lyric Poetry." In *Rewards and Punishments in the Arthurian Romances and Lyric Poetry of Medieval France: Essays Presented to Kenneth Varty on the Occasion of His Sixtieth Birthday*, edited by P. V. Davies and A. J. Kennedy, 165–74. Woodbridge, England: D. S. Brewer, 1987.

140. Williamson, Joan B. "La première traduction française de l'*Histoire de Griseldis* de Pétrarque: Pour qui et pourquoi fut-elle faite?" In *Amour, mariage, et transgression au moyen âge*, edited by Danielle Buschinger and André Crépin. Göppinger Arbeiten zur Germanistik, no. 420, 447–56. Göppingen: Kümmerle, 1984.

141. Williamson, Joan B. "Philippe de Mézières' Book for Married Ladies: A Book from the Entourage of the Court of Charles VI." In *The Spirit of the Court: Selected Proceedings of the Fourth Congress of the International Courtly Literature Society (Toronto, 1983)*, edited by Glyn S. Burgess and Robert A. Taylor 393–408. Cambridge, England: D. S. Brewer, 1985.

142. Williamson, Joan B. "Philippe de Mézières et l'influence du cycle de la croisade au 14e siècle." In *Les Épopées et la croisade: Premier colloque international (Trèves, 6–11 août, 1984)*, edited by Karl Heinz Bender. Beihefte zur Zeitschrift für französische Sprache und Literatur, N.F., vol. 11: 163–69. Stuttgart: Steiner, 1987.

143. Winter, Patrick M. de. "Copistes, éditeurs, et enlumineurs de la fin du XIVe siècle: La Production à Paris de manuscrits à miniatures." In *Actes du 100e Congrès national des sociétés savantes (1975)*, 173–98. Paris: Bibliothèque nationale, 1978.

144. Winter, Patrick M. de. "The *Grandes heures* of Philip the Bold, Duke of Burgundy: The Copyist Jean l'Avenant and His Patrons at the French Court." *Speculum* 57 (1982): 786–842.

145. Winter, Patrick M. de. "Christine de Pizan: Ses enlumineurs et ses rapports avec le milieu bourguignon." In *Actes du 104e Congrès national des sociétés savantes (Bordeaux, 1979), Archéologie*, 335–76. Paris: Bibliothèque nationale, 1982.

146. Winter, Patrick M. de. *La Bibliothèque de Philippe le Hardi duc de Bourgogne (1364–1404): Etude sur les manuscrits à peintures d'une collection princière à l'époque du style gothique international*. Paris: CNRS, 1985. xiii + 462 pp.

147. Wisman, Josette A. "L'*Epitoma rei militaris* de Végèce et sa fortune au moyen âge." *Moyen Age* 85 (1979): 13–31.

148. Wolfzettel, Friedrich. "Zur Poetik der Subjektivität bei Christine de Pisan." In *Lyrik des ausgehenden 14. und des 15. Jahrhunderts*, edited by Franz V. Spechtler, 379–97. Amsterdam: Rodopi, 1984.

149. Zink, Michel. "Le Lyrisme en rond: Esthétique et séduction des poèmes à forme fixe au moyen âge." *Cahiers de l'Association internationale des études françaises* 32 (1980): 71–90.

V. Language and Language-Related Studies

150. *Actes du Ve colloque international sur le moyen français (Milan, 6–8 mai 1985)*. Scienze filologiche e letteratura, no. 31, 3 vols. Milan: Vita e pensiero, Pubblicazioni della Università cattolica del Sacro Cuore, 1985–86. Vol. 1, *Les Grands Rhétoriqueurs*, 177 pp. Vol. 2, *Le Moyen français*, 238 pp. Vol. 3, *Etudes littéraires sur le XVe siècle*, 240 pp.

151. Brademann, Karl. *Die Bezeichnung für den Begriff des "Erinnerns" im Alt- und Mittelfranzösischen: Eine synchronische-diachronische Untersuchung*. Beihefte zur Zeitschrift für Romanische Philologie, no. 176. Tübingen: Niemeyer, 1979. 369 pp.

152. Dees, Anthonij, ed. *Actes du IVe colloque international sur le moyen français*. Amsterdam: Rodopi, 1985. 470 pp.

153. Hassell, James Woodrow. *Middle French Proverbs, Sentences, and Proverbial Phrases*. Subsidia mediaevalia, no. 12. Toronto: Pontifical Institute of Medieval Studies, 1982. x + 274 pp.

154. Jokinen, Ulla. *Les Relatifs en moyen français: Formes et fonctions*. Annales Academiae scientiarum Fennicae, Dissertationes humanarum litterarum, no. 14. Helsinki: Suomalainen Tiedeakatemia, 1978. 428 pp.

155. Kaiser, E. *Strukturen der Frage im Französischen: Synchronische und diachronische Untersuchungen zur direkten Frage im Französischen des 15. Jahrhunderts (1450–1500)*. Tübingen: Narr, 1980. 156 pp.

156. Marchello-Nizia, Christiane. *Histoire de la langue française aux XIVe et XVe siècles*. Paris: Bordas, 1979. 378 pp.

157. Martin, Robert. *Etudes de syntaxe du moyen française*. Recherches linguistiques: Etudes publiées par le Centre d'analyse syntaxique de l'Université de Metz, no. 4. Paris: Klincksieck, 1978. 193 pp.

158. Martin, Robert, and Marc Wilmet. *Manuel du français du moyen âge*. Vol. 2, *Syntaxe du moyen français*. Bordeaux: Sobodi, 1980. 316 pp.

159. Stefano, Giuseppe di. *Essais sur le moyen français*. Ydioma Tripharium, no. 4. Padua: Liviana, 1977. 139 pp.

160. Wilmet, Marc, ed. *Sémantique lexicale et sémantique grammaticale en moyen français: Colloque organisé par le Centre d'études linguistiques et littéraires de la Vrije Universiteit Brussel (28–29 sept. 1979)*. Brussels: VUB, Centrum voor Taal- en Literatuurwetenschap, 1979. 338 pp.

161. Wunderli, Peter, ed. *Du mot au texte: Actes du IIIe colloque international sur le moyen français (Düsseldorf, 17–19 septembre 1980)*. Tübinger Beiträge zur Linguistik, no. 175. Tübingen: Günter Narr, 1982. 315 pp.

Contributors

BARBARA K. ALTMANN is an assistant professor of French and Medieval Studies at the University of Oregon. She completed her doctorate on Christine de Pizan's *Dit de Poissy* in 1989 and is preparing a critical edition of Christine's three love debates.

JEANETTE M. A. BEER is a professor of French at Purdue University. She is the author of several books, including *Villehardouin, Epic Historian* (1968), *A Medieval Caesar* (1976), *Medieval Fables* (1980) and *Narrative Conventions of Truth in the Middle Ages* (1981). She has recently edited a collection of essays on *Medieval Translators and Their Craft* (1989).

JOËL BLANCHARD is a professor of Medieval French at the University of Maine in France. In addition to his many scholarly articles on French literature, he is also the author of *Le Roman de Tristan en prose: les deux captivités de Tristan* (1976); *La Pastorale en France au XIVe et XVe siècles, recherches sur les structures de l'imaginaire médiévale* (1983) and *Le pastourelet* (1983). He translated the Old French epic *Ami et Amile* (1985) and edited *La Moralité à cincq personnes* (1988).

MAUREEN CHENEY CURNOW is a professor of French at the University of Montana. In addition to a number of articles on Christine de Pizan, her 1975 Vanderbilt Ph.D. dissertation was a critical edition of the *Livre de la Cité des Dames*.

LILIANE DULAC is Maître de Conférences in the department of French at the University of Montpellier. Besides being the author of numerous articles on Christine de Pizan, in 1988 she edited a special number of *Revue des Langues Romanes* dedicated to Charity Cannon Willard.

THELMA FENSTER is associate professor of French at Fordham University and director of the Medieval Center there. She coedited *Lion de Bourges, poème épique du XIVe siècle* (1980), and published, with Mary Carpenter Erler, *Poems of Cupid, God of Love: Christine de Pizan's «Epistre au dieu d'Amours» and «Dit de la Rose»*, *Thomas Hoccleve's «The Letter of Cupid»*, *Editions and Translations with George Sewell's The Proclamation of Ovid* (1990).

ERIC HICKS holds the Chair for Medieval French Literature at the University of Lausanne. Apart from numerous articles on Christine de Pizan and other medieval topics, he published *Le Débat sur le «Roman de la Rose»* (1977). He edited, with Charity Cannon Willard, *Le Livre des Trois Vertus* (1989) and has just published an edition of the letters of Abelard and Heloise in Latin and medieval French translation.

ALLISON KELLY is an assistant professor of French at Princeton University, where she completed her dissertation in 1987 on *Le Petit Jehan de Saintré*.

ANGUS J. KENNEDY is the chaired professor of French at the University of Glasgow. In addition to publishing the now standard reference work, *Christine de Pizan, A Bibliographic Guide* (1984), he prepared critical editions of Christine de Pizan's *Ditie de Jehanne d'Arc* (1977) and *Epistre de la prison de vie humaine* (1984) and edited *Rewards and Punishments in the Arthurian Romances and Lyric Poetry of Mediaeval France* (Festschrift Kenneth Varty).

GLENDA MCLEOD teaches at Gainesville College in Georgia. She has recently edited a collection of essays on the historical fortunes of Christine de Pizan entitled *Visitors to the City* (1991).

NADIA MARGOLIS is an independent scholar living in Amherst, Massachusetts. In addition to several articles on Christine de Pizan, she has recently published *Joan of Arc in History, Literature and Film* (1990).

GIANNI MOMBELLO is a professor of French at the University of Turin and the editor of *Studi francesi*. Among several other books, in the medieval field he has published *La tradizione manoscritta dell'«Epistre Othea» di Christine de Pizan, prolegomeni all'edizione del testo* (1967) and *Les avatars de talentum, recherches sur l'origine et les variations des acceptions romanes et non romanes de ce terme* (1976); *Le raccolte francesi di favole esopiane del 1480 alla fine del secolo XVI* (1981).

CHRISTINE RENO is an associate professor of French at Vassar College. Besides having published numerous articles on Christine de Pizan, she has prepared a forthcoming critical edition of *L'Avision-Christine*.

EARL JEFFREY RICHARDS is an associate professor in the department of French and Italian at Tulane University. He has published *Dante and the «Roman de la Rose», An Investigation into the Vernacular Narrative Context of the «Commedia»* (1981), *Medievalism, Modernism and Humanism, A Research Bibliography on the Reception of Ernst Robert Curtius* (1983), and a translation of Christine de Pizan's *Book of the City of Ladies* (1982). He is the author of the forthcoming *European Literature and the Labyrinth of National Images*.

PATRICIA STÄBLEIN-HARRIS is a scholar-in-residence at the Folger Library in Washington, D.C. In addition to being the author of several articles on medieval topics, she published *Poems of the Troubadour Bertram de Born* with the University of California Press in 1986.

ELENI STECOPOULOS recently completed her studies in comparative literature at Princeton University. She is a poet and now resides in Salt Lake City.

KARL D. UITTI is the John N. Woodhull Professor of Modern Languages at Princeton. He is the author of *The Concept of Self in the Symbolist Novel* (1961), *La passion littéraire de Rémy de Gourmont* (1962), *Linguistics and Literary Theory* (1969), and *Story, Myth and Celebration in Old French Poetry, 1050–1200* (1973). He published, with Alfred Foulet, the Classiques Garnier edition and modern French translation of Chrétien de Troyes's *Le Chevalier de la Charrette* (1989).

LORI WALTERS is an associate professor of French at Florida State University at Tallahassee. Besides being the author of numerous articles on medieval romance, she is coediting the two-volume *The Manuscripts of Chrétien de Troyes*.

Index

Note: this index does not refer to the items listed in Angus J. Kennedy's bibliography (see pages 285–98). Individual works by an author are listed under the author's name.